D1639538

THE FINAL YEARS OF
MARILYN MONROE

THE FINAL YEARS OF

MARILYN MONROE

THE SHOCKING TRUE STORY

KEITH BADMAN

JR
BOOKS

First published in Great Britain in 2010 by
JR Books, 10 Greenland Street, London NW1 0ND
www.jrbooks.com

A catalogue record for this book is available from the British Library.

Photo credits (T = top, B = bottom)

p. 1, p. 2(B), p. 3(T, B), p. 5, p. 7, p. 10(T), p. 13, p. 14(B), p. 15(T, B): Bettmann/Corbis
p. 2(T), p. 4, p. 6(T): Getty Images
p. 6(B): United Archives GmbH/Alamy
p. 8(T): Underwood & Underwood/Corbis
p. 8(B): 20th Century Fox/The Kobal Collection
p. 11(T): Time & Life Pictures/Getty Images
p. 11(B): Rex Features
p. 16(T): SNAP/Rex Features
p. 16(B): TopFoto

ISBN 978-1-906779-27-6

1 3 5 7 9 10 8 6 4 2

Printed in Great Britain by Clays Ltd, St Ives plc

Contents

Acknowledgments

During the course of my research, I travelled thousand of miles, sat in a hundred different libraries, resided in numerous dissimilar hotel rooms and, naturally, spent countless hours typing on my laptop. Do I regret it? Absolutely not; it was an utter joy. Along the way, I was ably assisted by many different people. In no specific order, they were . . .

(In the States) Douglas Kirkland, Miranda Bracket, Clive David, Vince Palamara, Mitch Ison, John William Tuohy, Philip J. Weiss, Rob Hudson, Mark Hitchens, Su Kim Chung, Nick Scire, Joyce Duffy, Judy Simms, Donald R. Burleson and (in the UK) Juan Carty. I am indebted to you all.

Plus Ray and Helen Boyer, Peter Ciraolo, Carrie Salafia, Jeff Dalton, John McEwen, Erik Taros, Stephen Plotkin, the guy at the New York Public Library who 'loves Rita Hayworth', Lauren Daley (of the newspaper *South Coast Today*), and the many others who assisted me with my research and made me so very, very welcome during my stay in the USA. Special thanks must also go to the great Bob Boyer (of Sunset Records) who was a superb host/guide/assistant/friend, you name it, during the visit. Thank you all big time.

Gratitude also goes out to the wonderful individuals at the following libraries, archives, auction houses and sites: The Colindale Newspaper Library (in particular Jane Walsh and Victor Bristoll), the truly marvellous medical department at the British Library, the Westminster Reference Library, the BBC Written Archives Centre, the British Film Institute, Slough Public Library, The Kennedy Library in Hyannis Port, The JFK Library in Boston, The Nevada State Library, The Newspaper Archives, 20th Century Fox, NBC Television, the Internet Movie Database, the

UCLA Film and Television Archive Collection in California, eBay, The Carnegie Hall Archives, Scott at the truly superb www.MarilynMonroe Collection.com, Monroe collector Syd Stanwell, Greg Schreiner at his excellent www.themarilynmonroesite, Heritage, Sotheby's, Christie's, Philips and Margaret Barrett at Bonhams.

The same goes to the following who were there either to help or lend support in my project: my webmistress, Anne-Marie Trace (at www.keithbadman.com), Alan G. Parker (for help in putting the wheels of this book in motion), Mark Saunders (for his invaluable insight into air travel and political history), Richard Higgins and John Nolan (at ITN Source), Fred Rivers (in Hyannis Port), Mike Dalton, Wayne Allen (at Odeon Entertainment), Macundray Shukna, Dave Carter, Terry Rawlings, Fiona Early, Maxine Forrest, Lucinda MacGregor, Greg Schmidt, Spencer Leigh, Spencer Peet, Mick O'Toole, Ross Landau, Brian Luck, Stephen Rouse, Mick O'Shea and Tasha, Danny Wall, Michael Murtagh, Laurence Moore, Richard W. Irwin (at Reel Radio.com), Pete and Fenella Walkling, Tony and Sunny Dogra, and so many, many others, including the late, great Tom Keylock. I cannot list you all but you sure know who you are.

I am also indebted to the following.

Newspapers, magazines and columns: *The New York Daily News, The New York Post, The New York Herald Tribune, The New York Times, Life, The Los Angeles Times, The Washington Post, The Washington Times-Herald, The Philadelphia Daily News, The Times, Daily Mirror, The Globe, The Oneonta Star, Hollywood Today, The Los Angeles Herald Examiner, Variety, Hedda Hopper's Hollywood, Independent Press-Telegram, The Post-Tribune, Winnipeg Free Press, The Evening News, Corpus Christi Caller Times, Fresno Bee, The Gleaner, Gazette-Mail, Ogden Standard Examiner, Lowell Sunday Sun, Journal-American, Ames Daily Tribune, Good Housekeeping, Vogue, Confidential, Woman's Day, Ladies Home Journal, Observer, Middlesboro Daily News, Redbook, Films and Filming, National Geographic, Oui, L'Osservatore Romano, Gentle* and *Vanity Fair* (October 2008 issue).

Reporters who covered Marilyn back in her day: Walter Winchell, Dorothy Kilgallen, Louella O. Parsons, Sheilah Graham, Hedda Hopper, Maurice Zolotow, Aline Mosby, Ezra Goodman, Mike Connolly, Fenton Bresler, George Carpozi Jr, Donald Zec, William Woodfield, Joe Hyams, Florabel Muir, Allan Levy, Erskine Johnson, James Bacon, Martin Buckley, Ben Hecht, Dorothy Manners, James Gray-Gold, Earl Wilson, Bob Thomas, Scott Carson, Marie Torre, Patricia Clary.

The authors of the following books: *The Mysterious Death Of Marilyn Monroe* (James A. Hudson), *My Sister Marilyn* (Berniece Baker Miracle and Mona Rae Miracle), *Marilyn: The Last Months* (Eunice Murray and Rose Shade), *My Story* (Marilyn Monroe and Ben Hecht), *Mr S.: My Life With Frank Sinatra* (George Jacobs), *Goddess* (Anthony Summers), *Marilyn Monroe: The Biography* (Donald Spoto), *Marilyn Monroe* (Barbara Leaming), *Assassination Of Marilyn Monroe* (Donald H. Wolfe), *Marilyn: The Ultimate Look at the Legend* (James Haspiel), *Marilyn's Addresses* (Michelle Finn), *Marilyn: The Tragic Venus* (Edwin P. Hoyt), *Marilyn: An Untold Story* (Norman Rosten), *Norma Jean: The Life of Marilyn Monroe* (Fred Lawrence Guiles), *The Last Sitting* (Bert Stern), *The DD Group: An Online Investigation Into the Death of Marilyn Monroe* (David Marshall), *Marilyn* (Norman Mailer), *Cursum Perficio: Marilyn Monroe's Brentwood Hacienda* (Gary Vitacco-Robles), *The Strange Death of Marilyn Monroe* (Frank A. Capell), *Marilyn Monroe: A Composite View* (Edward Wagenknecht), *Marilyn and Me* (Susan Strasberg), *Marilyn: The Last Take* (Peter Harry Brown and Patte Barham), *Cal-Neva Revealed* (Philip J. Weiss), *The Show Business Nobody Knows* (Earl Wilson), *Show Business Laid Bare* (Earl Wilson), *Bitch!* (Lady May Lawford), *Chief: My Life in the LAPD* (Daryl F. Gates), *Answered Prayers* (Truman Capote), *Memories Are Made of This* (Deanna Martin), *The Dark Side of Camelot* (Seymour H. Hersh), *Marilyn Monroe Confidential* (Lena Pepitone), *The Men Who Murdered Marilyn* (Matthew Smith), *The Marilyn Conspiracy* (Milo Speriglio), *The Marilyn Scandal* (Sandra Shevey), *Crypt 33: The Saga of Marilyn Monroe – The Final Word* (Adela Gregory and Milo Speriglio), *The Many Lives of Marilyn Monroe* (Sarah Bartlett Churchwell), *Coroner* (Thomas T. Noguchi), *The Unabridged Marilyn* (Randall Riese and Neal Hitchens), *Violations of the Child: Marilyn Monroe* (by her psychiatrist friend), *The Fifty Year Decline and Fall of Hollywood* (Ezra Goodman), *Peter Lawford: The Man Who Kept the Secrets* (James Spada), *The Peter Lawford Story* (Patricia Seaton Lawford), *Grace And Power: The Private World of the Kennedy White House* (Sally Smith), *Timebends: A Life* (Arthur Miller), *Confessions of a Hollywood Columnist* (Sheilah Graham), *Nothing But Regrets* (Arnold Schulman), *My Life With Cleopatra* (Walter Wanger & Joe Hyams), the itineraries, diaries and personal notes of both John and Bobby Kennedy and the files of the CIA, FBI and the Los Angeles Police Department.

The producers of the following film and television programmes/reports: *Marilyn Monroe: The Final Days* (20th Century-Fox), *Something's Got To Give* (20th Century-Fox), *Marilyn Monroe: Mortal Goddess* (20th Century-Fox), *Say Goodbye to the President* (BBC), *The Body of Marilyn Monroe* (BBC), *48 Hours Mystery* (CBS), *CBS 60 Minutes*, *Larry King Live* (CNN), *Eyewitness News* (ABC), *Inside Edition* (ABC), *Marilyn: The Last Interview*

(HBO), *Legend of Marilyn Monroe* (Wolper Productions), *Marilyn in Manhattan* (Parco International), *Who Killed Marilyn Monroe?* (Channel 5), *Dead Men Talking* (Biography Channel), *The Marilyn Files* (KVC Entertainment), *Marilyn: The Last Word* (Paramount), *Marilyn Monroe: Beyond the Legend* (Wombat Productions), *Marilyn: The Last Sessions* (Les Films/Patrick Jeudy), *Sinatra: Good Guy, Bad Guy* (Meridian), *Conspiracy Theories* (Discovery Channel).

This book would not have been possible without two very important individuals. The first is Jeremy Robson of JR Books, who saw instantly what I had in mind and knew instinctively why it was so very different to the rest. The other is my diligent agent, Robert Kirby at United Agents. He was instrumental in shaping the project towards the version you have now. I thank you both.

Last but by no means least, immense thanks must also go to my wonderful Dell laptop, my family, Sheila, Pauline, Michael, mother Kathleen (a true rock and a superb proof-reader), dear friend Marion, and Charlotte Knee at United Agents. I thank you all . . .

Introduction

Marilyn Monroe is surely the most written about, talked about movie star of all time. Every moment of her short, tempestuous life has been the subject of countless books, magazine articles and television programmes. Not surprisingly, even the most non-fanatical fans of the actress feel that they can recite the key moments of that life without even trying. 'Born 1926, died 1962. Probable suicide. Starred in movies such as Bus Stop, The Misfits and Some Like It Hot. Married (and divorced from) Jim Dougherty, playwright Arthur Miller and baseball star Joe DiMaggio. John F. Kennedy and his brother, Bobby, were among those who supposedly shared her bed.' And so it goes on . . .

These, as well as many other supposed facts, are now etched deep in her folklore; details that are as much a part of her story as the famous dress-blowing sequence in her smash-hit film, *The Seven Year Itch*. Why then do we need yet another book on the actress? The simple truth is that, due to the ineptitude of many researchers, the lies told by people she never encountered, the errors of scandal-hungry gossip columnists and the inaccuracies of various money-hungry acquaintances, who were forced to embellish their mundane or fabricated stories in order to secure a lucrative five-figure publishing deal, much of what we now believe about Marilyn is sheer and utter nonsense.

Her history is sadly awash with these deceptions; especially between 1960 and her death in 1962, a time when she was rubbing shoulders with the likes of Frank Sinatra, the Kennedys and the Rat Pack, and a period when she was mixing with nasty, mean, rotten little people and nasty, mean, rotten *big* people too. Mistakes regarding her naturally circulated while she was alive. When she was confronted about them in 1962, she replied simply, 'Consider the source.'

So, with this in mind, in the middle of 2005, with the aid of numerous original, highly reliable notes, interviews, photographs, cuttings, files, receipts, invoices and eyewitness accounts – maay of them long thought lost – and a mountain of genuine, diehard facts, I forensically set about my task of separating the fact from the fiction, the myths from the reality and the veracity from the bullshit about this phase of her life. My intention was simple: to deliver, in book form, the most honest and accurate account of this period ever published.

Well, five years later, here it is. The result? A wealth of stories and facts that, I hope, even some of the most ardent fans of the actress will be unaware of. Among many other tales, you'll learn the unequivocal truth about her finances, her incredible spending habits, her abandoned television play, *Rain*, her final movie, *Something's Got To Give*, her jealousy of film legend Elizabeth Taylor, her romance with Sinatra, her infamous July 1962 trip to his Cal-Neva lodge, her father (I will personally name him and end forever the conjecture about it), how appallingly she was treated by her so-called best friends (in both life and death), Joe DiMaggio's love for her and their apparent plan to remarry, the night she sang for the President (and how much exactly she paid for that renowned dress), her rumoured, tell-all August 1962 press conference, her legendary farewell message, 'Say goodbye to the President,' the dithering by her associates on the night she passed away and the Hollywood-style cover-up that ensued.

Of course, no book on the actress will be complete without a mention (or two) of both John and Bobby Kennedy and her untimely death. This publication is no different. With regard to the former, using private, previously unpublished itineraries, I will reveal in precise detail just how deeply involved she was with them and end for ever the speculation about it. Pertaining to the latter, hypothesis upon hypothesis has been piled up in the history surrounding the actress's demise. Did she commit suicide, we wondered. Was it an accident? Was she murdered by her housekeeper? Her doctor? The CIA? The FBI? Or the Kennedys, perchance?

The debates rage to this day. However, in the way I have clarified it, as you will see, this is the *only* conceivable way she could have died. How did I reach this conclusion? Besides the assistance of some of the world's greatest medics, in the wise words of Sherlock Holmes, 'When you've eliminated the impossible, whatever remains, however improbable, *must* be the truth.'

Strange as it may seem, we've now had almost 700 books on Marilyn Monroe, yet, with regard to her final months, not one has been truly definitive. I believe this one is. I sincerely hope you enjoy it.

As an act of kindness, I also hope, for Marilyn's sake, it goes a long way towards setting her most cherished memory straight.

Keith Badman
London, England

Chapter One

Prelude – Childhood/Adulthood

Birth to June 1961

t 9.30 on the morning of Tuesday 1 June 1926, in the fortress-like confines of the charity ward of the Los Angeles General Hospital, Dr Herman M. Beerman unwittingly delivered his most famous baby. Originally called Norma Jeane Mortenson, the illegitimate child would later become known as Marilyn Monroe, the world's most celebrated movie star.

Her mother was a 24-year-old motion-picture negative film cutter, Gladys Pearl Monroe Mortenson. Described by her work colleagues as a 'talkative, short, cute blonde' and 'a lot of fun when she wanted to be', at the time of the birth, Gladys was so broke that, to help pay her hospital costs, colleagues at the Consolidated Film Industries, where she worked, were obliged to share her medical expenses. The problems did not end there. According to those who would treat her, Gladys soon developed schizophrenia.

Her family had a history of mental instability. Both of her parents, Otis Elmer Monroe and Della Monroe Grainger, lived out their twilight years in mental institutions, and her brother, Marion, had suffered from a problem best described at the time as paranoid schizophrenia. Though Gladys herself was most likely a manic-depressive, it was not uncommon during the 1930s and 1940s for those suffering from manic depression to be diagnosed as paranoid schizophrenics. Whatever the exact nature of her mother's disorder, Marilyn Monroe naturally came to possess a morbid fear of genetic insanity.

Marilyn's paternity remains a subject of debate to this day. Although the name of Norwegian immigrant Edward Mortenson, Gladys's second husband (her first being a man named Jasper Baker) was listed as the father on the certificates pertaining to Norma Jeane's birth and Marilyn's marriages to Joe DiMaggio and Arthur Miller, it was never the case. Other men have been suggested as candidates. As Donald Spoto pointed out in his 1993 book, *Marilyn Monroe: The Biography*, these included 'Harry Rooney, a co-worker who was besotted with her; the adoring Clayton MacNamara or, perhaps most likely of all, Raymond Guthrie, a film developer who ardently courted her [Gladys] for months . . . ' Marilyn, however, perhaps wistfully, believed Mortenson to be her father, having been shown a picture of the man as a child and primed '*this* is your father'. In fact, however, he was Charles Stanley Gifford, born on Sunday 18 September 1898 in Newport County, Rhode Island.

In her posthumously published 1974 memoir, *My Story*, Marilyn recalled of the man in the picture that 'There was a lively smile in his eyes and he had a thin moustache like Clark Gable', while her mother told her he had been 'killed in an auto accident in New York'. As surviving images prove, however, the man in the picture was evidently not Edward Mortenson, but Gifford, who did bear a strong resemblance to Gable. And her mother was wrong that the man had been killed in a motor accident. Gifford was *not* killed in a motor accident,

Mortenson, however, was. The fateful collision occurred on Tuesday 18 June 1929, at approximately 5pm, and in Ohio rather than New York; Mortenson was riding his motorcycle along the road from Youngstown to Akron and when he tried to overtake a car in front of him, he smashed into a sedan, breaking both of his legs. He fell to the ground unconscious and paralysed. Mortenson passed away just as the ambulance he was travelling in reached the nearby hospital. (To add to the confusion, a second man bearing the name, Martin Edward Mortenson, also entered the scene claiming to be Marilyn's true biological father. When he died of a heart attack on Tuesday 10 February 1981, aged 83, in Riverside, California, a copy of Norma Jeane's birth certificate was found among his possessions.)

The actress's mother had become besotted with the stout, dark-haired Gifford during his stint in charge of the day shift at Consolidated Film Industries in early 1925. Gifford's employment with the motion picture plant Thomas H. Ince Studios in Culver City had recently been terminated and his wife, Lillian Priester, was suing him for divorce. Her claims against him (he associated himself with low-life women, was addicted to narcotic drugs and had beaten her on numerous occasions) made it abundantly clear what kind of man he was. In an attempt to rebuild his life and earn some useful dollars, Gifford took a post at Consolidated as a hypo-shooter and developer and, within months, had worked his way up to the position of superintendent of the night crew. By the spring, the pair were having an affair and on Wednesday 6 May, his divorce became final. Twenty days later, on Tuesday 26 May, Gladys walked out on her husband, Mortensen. Her intention was clear to everyone; she had set her sights on becoming the next Mrs Gifford. However, he saw Gladys as just another fling and, by Christmas Eve 1925, had tired of it and promptly fled. But there was a catch: Gladys was now three months pregnant. Norma Jeane would become that child.

The idea of placing Norma Jeane with neighbours Albert and Ida Bolender on Sunday 13 June 1926, just 12 days after the baby's birth, came from Gladys's mother, Della. She had asked the couple, who lived across the road at 215 Rhode Island Avenue in Inglewood, Los Angeles County, to watch over her granddaughter while she travelled to South America to reconcile with her husband.

Contrary to the long-held belief that Gladys totally abandoned her daughter, she actually resided with Norma Jeane at the property and dutifully paid Albert and Ida $25 a month rent. Della knew Gladys and Norma Jeane would be in good hands and that a visit to them would always be just a short distance away. 'Mrs Baker [i.e. Gladys] *was* with me,' Ida confirmed in 1956. 'She stayed in Hollywood when working nights as a negative cutter, and stayed with me while working days . . . She [Norma Jeane] was never neglected and always dressed nicely. Her mother supported her all the time and bought all her clothes.'

Incontestable proof that both Gladys and her daughter lived under the Bolenders' roof can be found in an official census of Inglewood Township, Los Angeles County (enumeration district no. 19). Details of that Rhode Island Avenue house, as registered on Tuesday 1 April 1930, revealed that, besides Gladys and Norma Jeane, the other occupiers of the building were Albert, aged 46, Ida, 42 and their son Lester, 3. (Albert made a mistake when he filled out the form, noting Gladys as being 27 years of age and Norma Jeane as 63.)

In spite of his carefree, unconcerned exterior, Gifford did not (despite what we have been told before) wash his hands of the child. When Norma Jeane was just one or two years old, after learning of the child's placement with the Bolenders, the concerned father actually came forward and tried to adopt her. However, Gladys now despised the man; still smarting at how he had absconded during her pregnancy, she was having none of it and his request was denied.

With the Bolenders ably watching over her child, Gladys returned to work at the Consolidated Film Industries. Each Saturday she would take her child on an outing, usually a walking tour to the streets outside the movie stars' homes in the Hollywood hills. Another of Gladys's favourite journeys was to the recently opened Grauman's Chinese Theater on Hollywood Boulevard, famous for its red-carpet movie premieres. Norma Jeane and her mother would stare down adoringly at the world-famous foot and hand prints captured in cement outside the building. Norma Jeane would intently place her small hands and feet over the imprints.

Despite her mother's warmest intentions to display love and affection to her daughter, however, Norma Jeane would forlornly recall Gladys only as 'the woman with red hair' or 'the pretty woman who never smiled'. She did not regard her as her real mother. In her primary years, she looked upon Ida and Albert as her true parents and would call them 'Mama' and 'Daddy'.

It is intriguing to see how often Monroe's childhood has been portrayed in despondent, dull, quite depressing tones, insisting that she was, for the better part of her young life, unloved, unpopular and poor. The truth is that, from birth until she was eight years old, Norma Jeane lived in only one place, the cosy yet austere, old-fashioned six-room home in the middle-class city of Inglewood belonging to the devoutly Catholic Albert and Ida Bolender. Even as far back as 1952, Hollywood spokespeople were dramatising Marilyn's upbringing at the Bolenders' by saying that she was pounded with religious precepts that dictated damnation for her slightest transgression, brainwashed into thinking that 'drinking, smoking and dancing was the works of the devil', made to promise she'd never drink or swear, ordered to scrub and polish the house's floors and forced to attend church several times a week. True, the young girl *did* attend church with the Bolenders, but quite happily.

However, some truly disturbing incidents did happen to her in that time. First, in July 1927, her grandmother Della attempted to smother her with a pillow. For no perceptible reason, she walked over to the Bolenders' home in a state of complete undress, smashed her way in through the glass in the front door and made an unprovoked attack on the young child. The ramifications from the incident were immense. A few weeks later, on Thursday 4 August, she was committed to Norwalk's Metropolitan State Hospital where, just 19 days afterwards, she died of a heart attack. She was found to be suffering from manic-depressive psychosis.

The second incident came when Gladys attempted to murder her. 'Her mother tried to kill her three times,' Marilyn's third husband, playwright Arthur Miller, shockingly revealed in an April 1968 interview for the BBC. 'Her mother was quite mad.' Throughout most of her life, Marilyn often remarked how she could still vividly recall these horrific encounters.

Due to the highly dependable statements of both Miller and the Bolenders, I believe these events *did* happen; most of the other accusations about Norma Jeane's time with the family were, however, untrue. 'People like to make things sensational,' Nancy, the youngest Bolender sibling and by then the only surviving family member, admitted in 1996. 'Because she [Norma Jeane] was moved around later, they want to make it sound like it was *all* awful, but it wasn't. She was happy in our home.' Over the ensuing years, Nancy naturally became resentful and angry about the way Monroe's time in Inglewood was inaccurately portrayed. In a 1966 interview for the *Daily Breeze* newspaper, Ida Bolender added, 'When my mother was alive, she was very upset about it. We treated her [Marilyn] like our own child because we loved her.'

Quite possibly, the only accusation one could hurl at the Bolenders was that Norma Jeane was inadvertently made to feel like an outsider in their home. For instance, during the regular, once-a-week bath time, the children would all share the same water and, according to her, she would always bathe last. Another example came on Christmas Day morning 1926, when she happily made her way over to her first gift-laden festive tree. Aware that she was going to receive a present from Albert and Ida, she waited patiently for her turn while the other children unwrapped their expensive gifts of huge toys and bicycles. However, when her present was brought out, it was nothing more than a cheap trinket purchased from the five and ten cent (nickel and dime) store. Frantically, she tried to hide her dejection. She knew then that she was regarded as an outcast in the family. (Marilyn often remarked how extremely vivid her memories as a young child were. 'I can remember when I was just six months old,' she once admitted. 'I know you're not supposed to, but I *do*.')

Norma Jeane was, in general, lovingly doted on by Ida and her husband, Albert, a postman by trade. In time, she went on to enjoy a warm relationship with the dwelling's five other siblings, Lester, Mumsey, Alvina, Noel and Nancy. She grew particularly close to Lester. Norma Jeane also relished normal schoolgirl activities, such as playing hopscotch, learning the piano and (from December 1933, at 7.30 each Friday evening) listening to her favourite radio show, *The Lone Ranger*, starring Earle W. Graser. (It has long since entered Marilyn folklore that she also used to enjoy tuning in to *The Green Hornet* during this time, but that is incorrect. The show did not reach American radio until January 1936, by which time she was living away from the Bolenders' home.)

Other pleasurable pursuits for the young child were her frequent visits to the cinema and her play-acting the role of a detective, prowling up and down the nearby streets, intently jotting down the numbers of the local motor car licence plates. Gambolling with her small black and white dog, Tippy, was another favourite pastime. However, their time together was cut short when the pet was tragically sliced in two by Raymond J. Ernest, her hoe-wielding next-door neighbour, who became enraged over the dog's incessant barking. 'I loved that dog,' Marilyn sorrowfully announced, 'and he loved me. He was the only one who did love me in all those years. I told him everything.'

Deprivation was an occasional occurrence for Norma Jeane. Once, when she requested from her mother a white pair of shoes, she was given a black pair instead, because they were cheaper. Yet in her posthumously published, ghost-written, highly embellished 1974 book, *My Story*, on the subject of her childhood, Marilyn paradoxically wrote, 'When I look back on those days, I remember, in fact, that they were full of all sorts of fun and excitement. I played games in the sun and ran races.'

In 1962, she reminisced to American show business columnist Bob Thomas, 'When I was five, I think that's when I started wanting to be an actress. I loved to play. I didn't like the world around me because it was kind of grim.' Two years later, at the age of seven, Norma Jeane became fascinated by screen actress Jean Harlow. 'I had white hair,' she recalled. 'I was a real towhead and she was the first grown-up lady I had ever seen who had white hair like mine.'

In July 1934, Norma Jeane and her mother moved out of the Bolenders' home. Using money saved from her job as a negative film cutter, and an advance from the California Mortgage Company at Long Beach, Gladys managed to put down a payment on a three-bedroom, six-room bungalow situated at 6812 Arbol Drive, a short distance away from the world-famous concert venue, the Hollywood Bowl. 'It was a pretty little house,' Marilyn recalled in 1961, 'with quite a few rooms. But there was no furniture in it, except for two cots that we slept on, a small kitchen table and two kitchen chairs. The living room was entirely empty, but I didn't mind. It was a very pretty room.'

The house's most prized fixture was an early 20th century white baby grand piano, a belated eighth birthday present from Gladys to her daughter. Previously owned by eminent Tinseltown actor Fredric March, it had been secretly secured by Gladys at an auction of his household effects (although others say she actually purchased it on credit, along with the other furniture in the home). 'After several weeks,' Marilyn continued, 'my mother came home from work in a truck. I watched two men carry in the first furniture she had bought for our house. It was a wonderful-looking white piano. It was put in the living room. There wasn't any piano bench. It just stood there by itself. Neither my mother nor I could play it. But it looked very beautiful to me . . . I always remembered the white piano. I saw it in my mind every night as I grew up.'

Procuring hospitalisation and life insurance and even paying regular deposits of money into her bank account for emergencies, Gladys seized every means possible to ensure her daughter's new-found home life would be permanent. Marilyn excitedly recalled how, during this period, she and her mother would attend all the openings at the Coconut Grove in the Ambassador Hotel, positioning themselves outside to watch the glamorous stars arrive. Sometimes they would wait for several hours until the movie ended just to see a very special favourite of theirs walk by. Unfortunately, it was at this point that another truly harrowing incident in the young child's life occurred.

In the second half of November 1934, to safeguard further the life she had envisioned for her daughter, Gladys decided to raise extra money by renting out three rooms of her house to a married English couple; people who were employed in the Hollywood film industry. The woman was working on the fringe, earning a wage as a movie extra. It has often been stated that her husband was Mr Kimmel, the stand-in for the Academy Award-winning 20th Century-Fox actor, George Arliss. In fact he was 45-year-old, London-born Murray Kinnell, who had been instrumental in acquiring actress Bette Davis's first big break in the movies. By the time he and his wife moved in, Kinnell's main claim to fame was as a co-star to Arliss on five of his productions, namely *Old English* (1930), *A Successful Calamity* and *The Man Who Played God* (both 1932), *Voltaire* (1933) and *The House of Rothschild* (in 1934). A suggestion by Marilyn biographer Donald Spoto that actor George Atkinson was the boarder was inaccurate; he and Arliss worked together only once, in 1929 on the film *Disraeli*, some five years prior to the time Gladys and her daughter moved into the property.

However, Norma Jeane would not see the Kinnells as stars of the silver screen. Instead, she would view them as nothing but unpleasant, foul-mouthed alcoholics. The problems began soon after the couple moved in. Her already frail self-confidence was shattered further when the uncouth thespians asked if she would perform a dance for them. Suggestions of the Spanish fandango, the hula-hula and the sailor's hornpipe were offered. She agreed. But instead of applause, they laughed. Further attempts to appease Kinnell and his wife were greeted with similar callous rebuffs, and in turn, Norma Jeane would come to expect identical putdowns from each new set of adults she would confront. And one afternoon in January 1935, just six months after moving into the delightful new home, eight-year-old Norma Jeane horrifyingly, in her own, rather embellished words, 'found out about sex without asking any questions'.

She recounted the shocking, life-changing tale as follows: 'I was passing his room when his door opened and he came out. I literally collided with him . . . I tried to see beyond him, but there was nothing to look at but this monstrous man standing in the doorway . . . He said quietly, "Please come in here, Norma."' As Marilyn remembered, Kinnell closed and locked the door behind the cowering young girl, who stood motionless and stared back at the man.

> When he put his arms around me, I kicked and fought as hard as I could but I didn't make any sound. He was stronger than I was and wouldn't let me go. He kept whispering to me to be a good girl. 'I'll be just a moment washing my hands,' he said, as if my being there was an everyday matter. He came towards me, his hands outstretched, palms upward, as if pleading with me that, whatever he might have in mind to do to me, his hands *were* clean . . . .He then picked me up bodily, carried me to the sofa beyond the chair, sat down on it and dropped me into his lap. 'Just take it easy and keep your mouth shut, kid and I won't have to get rough with you.' I tried to console myself by remembering scenes in which little girls I knew were placed in this special place by fond fathers. I myself had missed such a demonstration of fatherly affection, so was it possibly coming to me now? A moment later one of those enormous hands was travelling the way of the Ashman, only it was a hand much firmer and more determined in its course . . . I cried out lustily with my pain, but it appeared to make that relentless hand more determined.

Thankfully for the child, the torment soon ended. 'When he unlocked the door and let me out, I ran to tell my aunt [i.e. her mother] to tell what Mr. Kinnell had done,' she recalled. But when she came face-to-face with Gladys, she was unable to fully explain what had happened. Her traumatic experience had precipitated a stammer. 'I want to tell you something, about Mr. Kinnell. He . . . he . . . '

However, her mother was uninterested and moved swiftly to interrupt her troubled daughter. She smacked her across her mouth. 'Take this for lying about a friend of mine. Don't you dare say anything against Mr. Kinnell,' Gladys screamed. 'He's a fine man. He's my star boarder.' The actor walked out of his room, handed Norma Jeane a nickel and told her to go and buy herself an ice cream. She picked up the coin, threw it back at his face and ran out of the house. Marilyn later revealed that that night, when recalling the horrendous incident, she cried herself to sleep and 'wanted to die'.

'A week later, the family, including Mr Kinnell, went to a religious revival meeting in a tent,' Marilyn recalled to the London *Observer* in 1958. 'My aunt [i.e. mother] insisted I come along. The tent was jammed. Everybody was listening to the evangelist. Suddenly he called on all the sinners in the tent to come up and repent. I rushed up ahead of everyone else and started to tell him about my sin. I fell on my knees and began to tell about Mr Kinnell and how he had molested me in his room. But other sinners started wailing about their sins and drowned me out. I looked back and saw Mr Kinnell standing among the non-sinners praying loudly and devoutly for God to forgive the sins of others.' She was innocent, yet had been abused and discarded like a piece of soiled linen.

It's worth noting that – regardless of what we have been led to believe in the past, thanks mainly to the actress's somewhat inflated recollections – Marilyn was *not* raped during the incident. Her first husband, James Dougherty, was among those who would verify the fact, saying he knew it was a lie on their wedding night. 'She was a virgin, as I soon found out,' he recalled in 1976. Eight years earlier, in a conversation with American reporter Darwin Porter, he had gone one step further by explicitly confirming that 'her delicate threshold had never been crossed before'. In fact, Norma Jeane went into her marriage to 21-year-old Dougherty in 1942 so ignorant of sex that her aunt Ana had to purchase for her a guide book of 'useful tips' for the bride-to-be.

And there were doubts about the tale's legitimacy. 'Over the years, she told me three different versions of the same story, forgetting what she had said previously,' Marilyn's close friend, room-mate and fellow actress Shelley Winters once admitted. 'In time, I think Marilyn could no longer distinguish between what was real and what wasn't . . . Don't get me wrong, I loved the girl dearly, but the biographers of Marilyn's early life each bought into her fantasy.'

Whatever the precise details, the story goes that, immediately after this traumatic event, Norma Jeane began suffering from insomnia and night terrors. Along with her other childhood frights, the occurrence would return to haunt her in twisted shapes during her briefest snatches of slumber. Later in life, Marilyn compensated for her inability or disinclination to rest by reading or talking to friends or colleagues, usually by way of late-night phone calls. Also, before she attempted any kind of slumber she would place her pillows over her telephones. She did this for two reasons: first, pillows served as a frightening reminder of the suffocation attempt; and second, in order to avoid the risk of having her sleep disturbed she would sometimes (but not always) place her head rests in that position to deaden the noise of any possible telephone rings.

Naturally, Gladys was also distressed by the assault. On Tuesday 15 January 1935, her brave new attempts at motherhood came to a shuddering halt when she suffered a nervous breakdown, precipitated no doubt by her continuing failure as a mother and the molestation of her child, and was forced to move out of their new home. But there was *another* reason why she had to do so. A fact that has been somewhat lost over the ensuing years is that, in the opening weeks of 1935, shortly after the incident with the young child, actor George Arliss left Hollywood to travel to Paris to shoot the movie *Cardinal Richelieu* with Maureen O'Sullivan. Naturally his co-star and close friend, Kinnell, travelled too. The loss of Kinnell's rent money was so significant that Gladys had no option but to relinquish the premises and move into other, more squalid accommodation.

In a 1956 interview, Marilyn revealed she could remember the precise moment when her mother's fragile mind finally snapped. 'I will never forget how my mother stabbed a friend in front of me as I sat crying,' she recalled.

The incident she was recalling occurred when, late one evening, Gladys sat talking with her good friend, divorcee Grace Atchison McKee. The pair were working together at Columbia Pictures: McKee as film librarian, Gladys as a film cutter. Their encounter became heated when Gladys accused Grace of trying to poison her. She lunged at her with a kitchen knife and stabbed her. The police were called and Gladys was immediately escorted to California's Norwalk State Asylum, where she was diagnosed with paranoid schizophrenia. Gladys spent much of the next 35 years in various institutions; despite making monthly provisions for her care in 1953 when, after months of allowing the press to believe that both of her parents were dead, the true details of Marilyn's parentage became known, the actress rarely contacted or visited her mother. On Monday 26 October, however, Marilyn created a trust fund for Gladys, to which she transferred 100 shares of preferred stocks of 'Marilyn Monroe Productions, Inc.'

With Gladys now institutionalised, Norma Jeane had once again lost her mother. 'No one will ever quite understand the warmth and sweetness between my mother and me until the day the police broke into our house and plucked her out of my life,' Marilyn would later recall. Unsurprisingly, Grace was installed as both guardian of the child and custodian of Gladys's estate. Her home and the furniture within were promptly sold off, except for the white baby grand piano, which was held for Norma Jeane by Grace's aunt Ana.

Naturally, the child moved in with McKee. However, their time together was short: just seven months. In 1962 Marilyn recalled, 'Grace was my legal guardian . . . But when she remarried all of a sudden the house became too small and someone had to go and you can guess who that someone was. On Monday 9 September 1935, she packed my clothes and took me to her car. We drove and drove without her ever saying a word.

'When we came to a red brick building she stopped the car and we walked up the stairs to the entrance of the building. At the entrance there was this big black sign with bright gold lettering . . . emptiness came over me. My feet absolutely couldn't move on the sidewalk. The sign read "Orphan Asylum – The Los Angeles Children's Home Society". I began to cry, "Please, please don't make me go inside. I'm not an orphan. My mother's not dead. I'm not an orphan. My mother's just sick and can't take care of me."'

The building has often been depicted as a shabby, run-down wreck. In fact it was a fine, well-kept 18th-century style mansion. At the front of the privately endowed, 24-year-old building, in the middle of a large playing field, there was a flag pole on which the Stars and Stripes proudly flew. At the rear, there were five acres of land, on which the children could run and play. Visitors, keen to see where the young Marilyn lived and expecting to discover a dingy, dirty, depressing-looking place, were shocked to find the orphanage was sparklingly clean and extremely well-equipped.

Norma Jeane became child number 3463. The young girl later learnt that Grace McKee cried all day afterwards. 'When a little girl feels lost and lonely and thinks nobody wants her, it's something she doesn't forget as long as she lives,' Marilyn remarked in 1958. 'I think I wanted more than anything in the world to be loved. Love to me then and now means being wanted and when my aunt Grace put me in that place, the whole world around me crumbled. It seemed nobody wanted me, not even my mother's best friend.'

Unsurprisingly, no doubt borne out of the horrifying suffocation attempt, the molestation and the deep-rooted realisation that no one wanted her, Norma Jeane's stammer continued to blight her. 'The day they brought me there [the orphanage], after they pulled me in, crying and screaming, suddenly there I was in the large dining room with a hundred kids sitting there eating, and they were all staring at me. So I stopped crying right away [and] I stuttered.' Her speech impediment became so bad that she could not even finish her sentences. In a 1955 discussion with the American columnist Maurice Zolotow, Marilyn recalled, 'I guess you might say I gave up talking for a long while. I used to be so embarrassed in school. I thought I'd die whenever a teacher called upon me. I always had the feeling of not wanting to open my mouth, that anything I said would be wrong or stupid.' One day, the young girl managed to escape from the orphanage. However, her attempt to flee was thwarted by a policeman who immediately escorted her back.

Each day at the institute began at 6am and before the 60 other children went off to school, they would have to do their chores. 'We each had a bed, a chair, and a locker,' Marilyn remembered (although officials for the orphanage would dispute her account of daily life there). 'Everything had to be very clean and perfect because of inspection. And I worked in the kitchen, washing dishes. There were a hundred of us, so I washed a hundred plates and all those spoons and forks. I did these three times a day, seven days a week. But it wasn't so bad. It was worse to scrub out the toilets.'

Dressed in a blue dress and white shirt-waist, Norma Jeane earned five cents a month for cleaning those dishes, one penny of which went into a Sunday church collection plate. The remaining cent allowed the young girl a little childish luxury: a ribbon for her hair. Despite her solitary attempt at fleeing, Norma Jeane's conduct in the orphanage was best described as 'prim and proper'. An early report on her time at the institution read, 'Norma Jeane's behaviour is normal and she is bright and sunshiny.' Grace McKee visited the child every week and regularly handed over clothes and gifts. Thanks to her constant support, many close to Marilyn would see McKee as an unsung hero in the woman's life. (Later, she would even pay for the girl's singing and dancing lessons.)

Norma Jeane slept at nights in a room crammed with 27 beds, and as a prize for good behaviour the children could work their way up to the 'honour bed'. But her own time in the room's most comfortable berth was short-lived. 'One morning,' the actress recalled, 'I was late and was putting on my shoes when the matron said, "Come downstairs!" I tried to tell her I was tying my shoes, but she said, "Back to the 27th bed."'

The festive season was always a poignant time for the young child. In 1951, Marilyn remembered, 'When Christmas came there was a big tree and all the kids in the house got presents but me. One of the kids gave me an orange. I can remember that Christmas day, eating that orange all by myself . . . and I could look up and see the RKO [film studios] water tower. I cried because I knew my mother had worked there. I think that was when I decided that some day, I would be an actress and maybe I would get inside that studio.'

Norma Jeane's veneer of self-confidence naturally became increasingly vulnerable and seemingly began to crack apart at the slightest repulse. For instance, during her second Christmas at the orphanage, she was given a part in a school play, but lost it when her current teacher, fearing she would forget her lines and embarrass the class, asked the person in charge of the production to give the part to someone else. Another knock-back to her confidence came one Easter when she was on a stage for the first time, at the Hollywood Bowl as one of 50 black-robed youngsters forming a cross.

'We all had on white tunics under the black robes,' Marilyn recalled in

1951, 'and at a given signal we were supposed to throw off the robes, changing the cross from black to white. But I got so interested in the people, the orchestra and the hills that I forgot to watch the conductor for the signal and there I was; the only black mark on a white cross.' As she grew older, Norma Jeane became tall and gawky with short, straw-like hair. Her manner was still described as hesitant, shy and scared, and she still suffered from her stammer.

On Saturday 26 June 1937, Norma Jeane left the orphanage and briefly moved back in with Grace McKee, who at this time was living with her husband, amateur inventor Erwin 'Doc' Silliman Goddard, in a small town near Los Angeles. Despite being most welcoming, they had their faults. With little prospect of being properly fed, due to Grace's new and quite unexpected penny-pinching ways, the young child would while away the hours in the local food stores, picking up whatever items she could and consuming them when no one, in particular the proprietor, was watching. She favoured stores selling fruit, particularly small peaches, cherries and plums. Acquisitions not eaten on the spot, such as the extremely large Wolf River apples, were discreetly hidden in her apron and transported home for consumption later. As Marilyn horrifyingly recalled, 'he [Erwin] was terribly strict. He brought me up harshly, and corrected me in a way I think they never should have; with a leather strap.' (It's worth pointing out that, despite the account of a previous Monroe biographer, at no point during his time with the young child did Goddard ever sexually molest the young child.)

Legend has it that, when news of what happened leaked out, Norma Jeane was palmed off to another foster home and thus found herself, during a three-month period, embarking on a nightmarish roller-coaster ride of 11 different foster homes and successive real-life horror stories such as being scalded for merely flushing the toilet at night. But that was completely untrue. 'After the orphans' home,' child carer Ida Bolender revealed in 1956, 'Norma Jeane stayed with Aunt Ana and Grace McKee Goddard until she got married . . . I don't know where those stories came from about her staying in 12 foster homes.'

So, just where did this tale start and, most importantly, why? To answer these questions we must go forward to Tuesday 1 January 1952, when a new year was dawning and a pristine men's calendar was being pinned to the walls of garages, warehouses and barbershops across America. Represented on each was the colour photograph of a beautiful young lady, lying nude across a red velvet drape. The female in question was Hollywood's hottest new movie star, Marilyn Monroe.

When news of it reached 20th Century-Fox, the studio to which she was contracted, and RKO Pictures, the producers of her latest movie, the drama *Clash By Night*, a crisis of epic proportions was almost reached. Studio heads attempted at first to dismiss it, but that was not easy to do. America in the early 1950s was a country rife with strait-laced public morals. As panic began to intensify, RKO even contemplated delaying the release of their new film because of it. A strategy was urgently needed.

Following a hastily called meeting between one of the movie's producers, Jerry Wald, studio executives and the actress herself, an exercise in damage limitation was decided upon and 39-year-old, Montana-born UPI Hollywood film columnist Aline Mosby was drafted in to help. Between them, in an attempt to gain public sympathy, a story about how Marilyn did the nude shoot simply because 'she was broke and needed the money badly following a sorrowful upbringing in a string of foster homes' was hastily concocted. They figured that nobody on earth could be angry or disgusted by the sad tale of a young girl who had been forced to exploit her body just to survive.

The story confirming that Marilyn was in fact the nude on the calendar was released to the American press on Tuesday 11 March 1952. It appeared one day later. As Mosby wrote:

> A photograph of a beautiful nude blonde on a 1952 calendar is hanging in garages and barbershops all over the nation today. Marilyn Monroe admitted today that the beauty is she. 'Oh, the calendar's hanging in garages all over town,' said Marilyn. 'Why deny it? You can get one any place. Besides, I'm not ashamed of it. I've done nothing wrong.' . . . In 1949, she was just another scared young blonde, struggling to find fame in the magic city, and all alone. As a child she lived in a Hollywood orphanage. She was pushed around among twelve sets of foster parents before she turned an insecure sixteen.

This first part of the narrative was quite true. The session, in a cramped Los Angeles studio belonging to photographer Tom Kelley, had taken place on Friday 27 May 1949. Twelve years later, Monroe recalled truthfully, 'I was hungry. I needed the $50 . . . I'd do it again if I had to.' Since she was too embarrassed to pose during the day, the pictures had to be taken at night.

'Modelling jobs were few and far between then,' she remarked in another March 1952 interview. 'I had some modelling jobs but not enough to pay the bills. There was this photographer [Kelley] I had worked for and he kept telling me he would pay me $50 if I posed in the nude as a calendar girl. I kept telling him, "No, thanks." Not that there was anything wrong in posing for a calendar, but it just wasn't something I would do. But when I had no work and no money, out of desperation, I called him up and said, "Kelley, I need that $50 but promise you won't tell anyone." He promised no one would know except for his wife, who was also his assistant.'

Her reasons for doing the shoot had escalated by the time she met the Hollywood columnist Louella Parsons one month later. 'The truth is, I was not only one month behind in my rent but four months,' Marilyn announced. 'I expected to be thrown out in the street. I didn't have enough money even to eat, and when Tom Kelley asked me to pose, I was glad to accept.'

'The session took three hours,' Kelley admitted to the *American Weekly* in 1955. 'I must have stood about ten feet above her. She was lying on the floor.' When it came to signing the model release form, due to her nervousness, embarrassment and attempts at anonymity, she signed her name as 'Mona Monroe'. 'I sold all my rights in it [the pictures] for a lousy $500,' the photographer solemnly announced. 'A guy out in Chicago, John Baumgarth, he made a fortune on it. Sold close to 8,000,000 calendars!' (In fact two different Marilyn Monroe nude calendars were released: one entitled *Golden Dream*, the other *A New Wrinkle*. The former was the bigger seller.)

Four and a half years on, in December 1953, a new men's magazine appeared on the American news-stands. It was called *Playboy*. Its creator was Hugh Hefner. The first issue sold over 54,000 copies, an amazing tally for a new journal with no advance publicity. The startling sales of that first copy can be attributed to Hefner's good fortune of finding an exceptional double-page, centrepiece 'Sweetheart Of The Month' photo to lure America's hot-blooded males to the news-stand. Inside that maiden edition was Kelley's photo of the nude 22-year-old Monroe lying outstretched across a red velvet sheet.

However, the second half of Mosby's March 1952 report, the part about 'twelve sets of foster parents', was far from the truth. This had actually been unveiled to the American public in the *Cedar Rapids Gazette* newspaper, among others, nine weeks earlier on Sunday 7 January 1952, just six days after the calendar first appeared. In the article, Mosby wrote, 'Marilyn had eleven sets of foster parents before she was 16. She was shunted from one set to the next, unloved and unwanted.' Hastily prepared comments by the actress accompanied the piece. 'They'd keep me for six months, or a year,' she declared, 'then they'd say, 'You make me nervous,' and the county would find me another home. The families I lived with were all poor.'

The true catalyst of Marilyn's foster-home stories was in fact her adopted sister, Beebe Goddard, a girl who truly did encounter an unhappy childhood and a string of different guardians. (Marilyn's last encounter with Goddard took place in June 1953, when the actress celebrated her 27th birthday.) During their occasional encounters, Goddard held Monroe captive with her mournful tales. The actress would later use these as the nucleus for the grand deception perpetrated by herself, Fox and RKO.

Indeed, aside from the revisionist work of Marilyn's overzealous Hollywood publicists, a great part of this misinterpretation of the truth – as we know – regrettably came from Monroe herself, who enjoyed perpetuating the myth of what a poor, sad, orphaned girl from a deprived background could achieve. In June 1952, with the Hollywood news wires awash with the news that the actress was an orphan, Marilyn came clean – possibly out of guilt – and exclusively revealed to the Hollywood columnist Erskine Johnson that Gladys was still alive and that, after urging from Fox, she was actually helping to support her. Her confession just happened to coincide with *Redbook* magazine's current article on the actress, entitled 'Orphan's Life', in which they naturally focused on the sad loss of Marilyn's parents. However, the actress was unrepentant about the misleading information she had contributed and drafted a note to the publication's editor, Wade Nichols, telling him so. In part, it read, 'I frankly did not feel wrong in withholding from you the fact that my mother is still alive ... Since we have never known each other intimately and have never enjoyed the normal relationship of mother.'

In 1955, *Life* magazine's Hollywood correspondent Ezra Goodman was another writer to face a brick wall when attempting to decipher the conflicting stories about Marilyn's formative years. Due to the conspiracy of silence still surrounding it, he encountered first-hand the many people who were determined to either hinder his research or complicate matters. As he wrote in his finished article, 'much of what she and her publicists have said about her past simply do not ring true'. 'The truth is,' as her future publicist, Arthur P. Jacobs, would recall, 'she loved to create gossip. She didn't need *Confidential* magazine; she touted her own dirty linen.'

'She made up those stories to win the public sympathy,' her first husband, James Dougherty, corroborated in 1968. 'When she was revealed as the model who had posed for that nude calendar hanging in every men's toilet, in every garage in America, she got the sympathy vote.' The deceit worked. Public sympathy was achieved, a new legion of fans gained and, with all the extra publicity, crowds flocked to see *Clash By Night* when it was released in June 1952. To this day, fans, historians, documentary makers and movie columnists repeat how Marilyn grew up as an orphan in a succession of foster homes. On both counts, that was totally incorrect.

In fact, in September 1937, at the age of 11, Norma Jeane was moved to West Los Angeles to live with Grace McKee's childless 62-year-old aunt, Ana Lower. It was there that she finally found the warmth and maternal affection she had so badly been deprived of.

'This woman was the greatest influence on my whole life,' Marilyn recalled in a 1962 interview with photographer George Barris. 'I called her aunt Ana. The love I have today for beautiful and simple things is because of her. She was the only person I ever really loved with such a deep love you can give only to someone so kind, so good and so full of love for me. One of the reasons why I loved her was because of her understanding of what really mattered in life . . . She was quite a person . . . She didn't believe in sickness or disease or death. She didn't believe in a person being a failure either. She believed the mind could achieve anything. She changed my whole life.'

Inside Lower's home was an item she had retained for Norma Jeane, the one symbol of life with her mother: her white baby grand piano. Lessons for the instrument began anew. Aunt Ana taught the young Monroe how to play the one-fingered piano waltz 'Chopsticks'.

Marilyn's reunion with the instrument was brief and, as her career began to blossom, she once more found herself estranged from it. But not for long. In 1962 she recalled, 'I got my first good part, in *The Asphalt Jungle* (1950), and I had enough money to do what I'd always dreamed of doing. I started looking for that white piano. I went to all the warehouses and old auction rooms in Los Angeles and after a month I found it. It was just as white and beautiful as ever, I knew it was the same piano because Fredric March's name was engraved on it. I bought it for $100 and took it home. It stood in my room for several years without a piano bench, just a white piano I couldn't play.' The instrument would nevertheless stay by the actress's side, coast to coast, house to house, marriage to marriage, for the remainder of her short life. To her, it symbolised the permanency of a home and the family security she never had.

In September 1938, the miracle of Norma's young physique ripening into womanhood arrived, and with it came a change in her fortunes. A survival instinct instilled in her made her aware that her frame, while wearing a borrowed tight white sweater, was attracting an unusual amount of attention: envious glances from other girls and desire in boys. The change in the attitude of the latter was startling; their previous gibes of 'Norma Jeane, string bean' had changed into appreciative wolf-whistles.

'The boys knew better than to get fresh with me,' Marilyn recollected in 1953. 'The most they ever got was a good-night kiss.' In her posthumously published 1974 book, *My Story*, she wrote, 'I wasn't aware of anything sexual in their new liking for me . . . I didn't think of my body as having anything to do with sex. It was more like a friend who had mysteriously appeared in my life, a sort of new friend.' She was now attracting the attention she had so desperately wished for.

In 1941, at the age of 15, because of aunt Ana's advancing years and ill-health, Norma Jeane was forced to move again – back to the home of Grace McKee and Erwin Goddard, who by this time were living in a rambling bungalow on Odessa Street in Van Nuys, California. During her stay there she met Goddard's 11-year-old daughter, Nona Jeannette, who later became famous as the Columbia Pictures movie star Jody Lawrance. 'I remember she was a shy, introverted little girl,' Lawrance recalled to reporter Ezra Goodman in 1955. 'We made a tree house with boards in a pepper tree in our front yard. We used to crawl up there when we thought we'd get in trouble. We knew my father and stepmother could not climb up there. That tree house was our escape.' Local boys on bicycles would happily drop by and watch while Norma Jeane hung upside-down from the tree. 'I used to look like a monkey,' she remembered in 1952. 'I guess I was a little shy about coming down but I did get down to the curb . . . I would ask the boys, 'Can I ride your bike now?' And they'd say, 'Sure,' and I'd go zooming, laughing in the wind, riding down the block. They'd all stand around and wait till I came back.'

In 1942, due to Erwin's job transfer, the Goddards were forced to move to West Virginia and they were unable (or unwilling) to take Norma Jeane with them. So she was faced with a dilemma. 'I'd had enough of the orphanage,' she remarked, 'more than enough. What could I do? So I got married.' Grace's matrimonial eye soon chanced upon their 21-year-old neighbour, James Dougherty, an employee at Lockheed Aircraft. Their marriage, at 8.30pm on Friday 19 June 1942, was held at the home of the Goddards' close friends, Mr and Mrs Chester Howell, because of its winding staircase, similar to those which appear in the movies. Grace made the arrangements for the wedding just prior to her departure for West Virginia. Ana Lower gave the bride away. She was the only representative of Norma Jeane's family present. It was, in truth, a marriage of convenience.

It was shortly after Marilyn's divorce from Dougherty in 1946, and when she was taking her first tentative steps in Hollywood, that she was intro-duced to tranquillisers. During her early teens, along with the miracle of new-found happiness and burgeoning womanhood, had come the agony of menstruation. For several unaided years, Marilyn endured violent cramps and excruciating stomach tortures until one day, to help ease her discomfort and to aid with her sleep, she was handed some barbiturates.

Initially she consumed Seconal. Other, more fashionable tranquillisers such as Miltown, Equanil and Librium followed. However, Nembutal soon became her drug of choice.

Marilyn first took the pills in October 1947, when she was at 20th Century-Fox shooting her brief walk-on part in the Jeanne Crane/Dan Dailey romantic musical *You Were Meant For Me*. (The role would end up on the cutting-room floor.) Although it was the actress's third for the studio, no one really expected her to linger in the industry. As Fox photographer Leon Shamroy, who shot her first screen test, once disparagingly remarked, 'When you analyse Marilyn, she is not good looking, had a bad nose, bad posture and her figure is too obvious. She has a bad profile. Hers is a phoney sex.' Even her first acting agent, Harry Lipton, was heard to comment, 'She was thought of as a joke by many people and that hurt her badly.'

'I was fired from Fox at 22, and fired from Columbia at 23,' Monroe recalled in 1953. 'They told me I should go home.' Along with her intermittent physical pains, the horrifying thought that her chosen profession might well be a fleeting one was enough to direct the actress towards pills. She needed help to alleviate her anxieties. Slowly and imperceptibly her life began to be centred on these drugs; nobody outside her immediate circle of friends was aware of just how many pills she was beginning to pop, not only during the day but also at night. Subsequently, they began to transform both her emotions and thinking processes.

As with all barbiturate addicts, alterations in Marilyn's personality began to take place, sometimes manifesting themselves in violent outbursts aimed towards either her family, friends or colleagues, while at other times she seemed crazy, eccentric and peculiar. By the 1950s, if you were a star of her calibre, you could get away with such behaviour. But she also had good days when she was sparkling and radiant and seemed absolutely fine to those around her. Such dramatic personality changes are typical of those living under the influence of Nembutal.

The lure of alcohol had already beckoned for Marilyn. Her consumption of spirits had increased in 1942 during her marriage to Dougherty. Aged just 16, she grew to love vodka, wine, occasionally sherry and especially champagne. But as her success in the movie business increased, so too did her intake. Monroe found in alcohol, as well as chemistry, a solution to all kinds of discomfort, not only physical pain but the pains of daily life; a solvent for her internal tensions and demons.

With a difficult childhood and a drug-fuelled adulthood, and with so much insanity running through her family, it would have been amazing had Marilyn turned out completely normal. Lack of emotional bonding in her very formative years, due to a sick and disturbed mother, generated an immense black hole of emotional insecurities that could never be filled. In truth, Marilyn was always ten years of age in some place in her heart, frequently being dragged to the Los Angeles Orphan Home.

She had grown up as a sad-faced little girl, devoid of any firm structure and, aside from her time at the Bolenders', of any consistent experience of living within a good, honest, loving family she could call her own. Unsurprisingly, since her efforts to gain affection and acceptance were sometimes rejected, she became an isolated, frustrated individual who never grew up. The cumulative result of her drug dependencies, childhood terrors and uneasy confrontations with the prejudices and peculiarities of different families was a grave sense of insecurity, low self-esteem and loneliness.

Conversely, despite her poor self-esteem, she became a survivor, motivated to succeed, and a seeker for love wherever she could find it. As Marilyn confided to her friend, leading Hollywood gossip columnist Louella Oettinger Parsons, the so-called 'First Lady of Hollywood', she had a fierce desire to be loved. Having known or experienced so little affection, she was anxious to have visible signs that someone cared for her. In effect, Monroe's entire life was plagued by fear, anxiety and self-doubt, and this emotional dependency often alienated those who were attracted to her. Such was the case with the men in her life. She divorced Dougherty in 1946, and her subsequent marriages, to baseball legend Joe DiMaggio (in 1954) and the aforementioned Arthur Miller (in 1956), went the same way.

Despite its shaky start, her movie career eventually became decidedly more upbeat. With films such as *Niagara*, *Gentlemen Prefer Blondes* and *How to Marry a Millionaire* (all in 1953), Marilyn was launched as both a movie superstar and an international sex symbol. Immensely successful movies such as *The Seven Year Itch* (1955), *Bus Stop* (1956) and *Some Like It Hot* (1959) soon followed.

Even then, she had gained a growing reputation for unreliability on the film set. As Joshua Logan, the director of Marilyn's 1956 movie *Bus Stop*, recalled. 'She'd run in apologising, take a look in the mirror and then go through an agonising process of getting herself in the mood.' On a typical day's shooting of her most recent film, *The Misfits*, co-star Clark Gable would be on the set between 7.30 and 8am with lines memorised and ready to go. Monroe would not usually arrive until noon. A similar scenario had been played out during the production of her preceding movie, *Let's Make Love*. Actor Tony Randall recalled how he reported for work for three days running but, due to the actress's continual absence, did not perform once. On another day, when Marilyn did succeed in coming to the set, he ended up shooting his first scene of the day at 3pm, just two hours before filming was due to wrap.

And more recently, box-office success was not assured. The produced-in-England movie, *The Prince and the Showgirl* (1957), the comedy *Let's Make Love* (1960) alongside co-star Yves Montand and *The Misfits* (1961), written by Arthur Miller, were all far from fruitful at the box office.

Amid fears that her fame was in decline, in the middle of 1961 she was back in Los Angeles, where matters concerning her final movie for 20th Century-Fox were hijacking her life. But on a happier note, she had just celebrated her latest birthday. This is where our astonishing tale of Marilyn Monroe's final years – as it was, as it happened – begins . . .

Chapter Two

June 1961–
Monday 8 January 1962

Her complexion pinkish-white in the radiance of late-afternoon sunlight, Marilyn smiled, wetted her lips and announced, 'I'm very happy I've reached thirty-five. A midway mark perhaps? I don't know. But I do know that I'm growing up. It was wonderful being a girl, but it's more wonderful being a woman.'

It was June 1961, and as the actress had remarked to an American reporter, she had just reached her 35th birthday. Thankfully, there were no signs of the inner conflicts which had troubled her just a few months earlier during a short, turbulent stay at New York's Payne-Whitney Psychiatric Clinic. At this mid-point in the year, Monroe was in fine fettle. In another interview that month, this time with Hollywood columnist Jonah Ruddy, she majestically revealed, 'I feel marvellous. I'm on this high-protein diet and I weigh 123 pounds, which is about right for me. Yes, I feel absolutely wonderful.'

Considering she was receiving 10 per cent of *Some Like It Hot*'s gross box-office takings, she was just about surviving financially too. Two years after the smash-hit comedy's release, the movie was still playing to packed houses across the country. However, by comparison, her next film project was beginning to look decidedly less auspicious.

Unproductive discussions about it had been going on between Marilyn's New York attorney, Aaron R. Frosch, of law firm Weissberger & Frosch, and executives at 20th Century-Fox since Friday 1 July 1960, when the studio approached her with the idea of starring with the

Maverick television star, James Garner, in George Axelrod's comedy *Where's Charlie?*, later retitled *Goodbye Charlie*. However, the gender-swap fantasy, which saw the leading male character, heartless lothario Charlie Sorel (to be played by Monroe), get shot by a jealous husband, fall out of a ship's porthole, become lost at sea and return as a shapely blonde woman, did not impress the actress at all.

'The studio people want me to do *Goodbye Charlie*,' Marilyn raged at the time. 'But I'm *not* going to do it. I don't like the idea of playing a man in a woman's body, you know? It just doesn't seem feminine.' Her tirade against the movie continued for months. 'I used to watch Clark Gable on the set of *The Misfits*, in case I had to play a man,' she announced in October. 'But when I told him this, he laughed and said, "You don't have *that* kind of equipment."'

Matters intensified in mid-January 1961, when, just two weeks before the release of her latest offering, the ultimately unsuccessful *The Misfits*, the studio, this time more forcefully, made it clear to the actress that they were desperate to get another 'Marilyn Monroe' vehicle under way and into the theatres. Despite her recent failings, she was still the studio's biggest commodity and most bankable star. Her 20 movies for the studio had grossed over $200 million at the box office and importantly, as part of a four-film deal dating from December 1955, she owed them one more.

On Monday 30 January, Garner announced to the papers that he was still up for the part in it, but regrettably, Marilyn was not. However, the studio knew that, as long as they engaged one of the directors on her favoured wish-list, she would have no legal way out of shooting the movie. Among her inventory of 16, submitted to the studio late the previous year, were the Hollywood luminaries Joshua Logan (whom Marilyn had worked with on her 1956 movie *Bus Stop*), William Wyler (best remembered for *The Big Country* and *Ben-Hur* in 1958 and 1959 respectively), Carol Reed (fondly known for Orson Welles' landmark 1949 film, *The Third Man*) and John Ford (of John Wayne westerns' fame).

The studio approached everyone on her file, but they all declined the opportunity to direct the actress. In spite of her reservations about the role, Marilyn especially wanted 61-year-old, New York-born director George Cukor to be engaged in the production. However, due to his brief tenure on the Metro-Goldwyn-Mayer period drama *Lady L*, he was unattainable. Her attorney, Frosch, corroborated this in a note to the studio on Friday 14 April, which read, 'Although Miss Monroe had indicated that she would not do the film, Marilyn Monroe's failure to perform in *Goodbye Charlie* stems entirely from George Cukor's unavailability to perform as director . . . ' Six days later, on Thursday 20 April, Fox's chief counsel, Frank Ferguson, responded in writing by saying that every conceivable attempt had been made to secure the services of Cukor and at least one of the individuals she had named, and, since no one was available, they wished to discuss with her a suitable substitute. The claim enraged the actress. She was well aware that her New York-based drama coach and mentor, Lee Strasberg, had not been contacted, and realised that, by not doing so, Fox had failed to honour their original agreement.

On Thursday 4 May, in an attempt to appease their clearly agitated star, Ferguson announced, by way of another memo, that Strasberg was now being considered for the director's role on *Goodbye Charlie*. Time was now running out fast. Friday 12 May, the date on which Fox were legally bound to find work for Marilyn or else risk losing her services for good, was now just eight days away.

After being fired by Fox in 1947, Strasberg, who by now was making a name for himself in New York City with his highly revered Actors Studio, was naturally reluctant to return. But after realising that, by taking the post, he would be helping Marilyn, he soon warmed to the idea. (Assertions by some previous Monroe biographers that he had no previous movie directorial experience are not entirely accurate. In 1945, he was at the helm of the First World War documentary *Story with Two Endings*.) Negotiations commenced immediately when the studio offered him a flat fee of $22,500 to direct the actress, but by now greed had set in. He wanted more, a sum consistent with other contemporary directors. Desperate to get the new Monroe movie into production, the studio caved in to his demand and immediately upped their offer, more than doubling it to a most generous $50,000. However, Strasberg still wasn't happy. Desiring an even higher fee, he promptly dismissed it. But, this time, Fox weren't listening and plans to engage Strasberg were swiftly shelved.

Possibly as a way of killing even more time, he then reappeared on the scene, insisting he would not allow the actress to shoot the movie anyway, asserting that the pressures of this on top of the ongoing problems with her NBC TV drama play, *Rain*, were coming too soon after her traumatic stay at the Payne-Whitney clinic. Fox retaliated by insisting that, as long as she was capable of working and they had engaged (or attempted to engage) one of her favoured directors on the movie, she could not lawfully decline the part. Marilyn meanwhile was adamant. With neither Cukor nor Strasberg at the helm, she would *not* make the picture. Even the announced intention of Fox studio president and true Monroe supporter Spyros P. Skouras to drag her through the courts over the matter failed to change her mind.

So, in May 1961, after almost 11 months of futile deliberations, and two full months after shooting was due to commence, *Goodbye Charlie* was finally put on hold (albeit until Hollywood actress Debbie Reynolds rescued the role in 1964) and another suitable screenplay for Monroe was sought. After concurring with her attorney that she *did* still owe them one more movie, Skouras agreed not to sue the actress. He also gave his blessing to her appearing in *Rain*, but only on the proviso that it was completed by Monday 30 October – a date when, Fox hoped, she would finally be ready to commence work on her next (and final) film for them.

In unison with the movie's abandonment, following the realisation that Hollywood was the only place to be if she wished to prolong her profession, Marilyn packed her bags and, once more, returned to Los Angeles. She was reluctant to do so. As she had announced to the American press on Monday 27 February 1956, 'My real home now is New York.' In her mind, her return showed that her attempts at success as an actress away from Tinseltown had been a failure, and it hurt.

She had worked tirelessly to drag herself out of the industry's gutter, had married America's most admired sports hero and the country's most revered playwright and had toiled endlessly at the Actors Studio just to gain respect as an actress. 'When she came to New York [in December 1954],' Lee Strasberg recalled, 'she began to perceive the possibilities of really accomplishing her dreams of becoming a great actress.'

Marilyn loved being there. The city's people, theatres, night-life and genuine sense of optimism agreed with her immensely. She mixed with intellectuals, socialised in creative circles and had even become friends with top-rated writers Truman Capote and Carson McCullers. She wholeheartedly identified with the place. Yet, just over six years later, she found herself back in Hollywood, back where she started, in a city she hated, filled with people she barely trusted and with whom she had precious little in common. 'Even though I was born there,' she once remarked to her writer friend, Truman Capote, 'I still can't think of one good thing to say about it. If I close my eyes and picture LA, all I see is one big varicose vein.'

'This was the last act for her. She'd come back defeated,' her close, New York-based friend Norman Rosten recalled. 'She was going back to her roots,' screenwriter Arthur Schulman observed, 'back to the way she'd be treated when she was giving blow-jobs in the afternoon . . . She was a queen, but *not* to those people. They patronised her, saying, "You're not really one of us."' Worryingly, Marilyn also knew that she was fast approaching 35, the age when many of Hollywood's most famous female players were known to have been cast aside.

Thanks in part to her few friends, however, Monroe soon warmed a little to the idea of being back in Tinseltown. While the singer was in Hollywood performing a children's charity concert, her initial weeks were spent as a guest of Frank Sinatra at his bachelor pad in Coldwater Canyon.

In an attempt to cheer her up, a present from him, a small white poodle, was waiting for her upon her arrival. Of Scottish descent, it had been acquired from actress Natalie Wood's mother Maria, a renowned breeder. On account of Frank's well-publicised connections to the Mafia (though Sinatra wasn't keen on the moniker), Marilyn affectionately baptised the pet 'Maf'.

On Sunday 11 June, Marilyn had been among a host of Hollywood celebrities at St Cyril's Roman Catholic Church in suburban Encino for the christening of Clark Gable's 10-week-old son, John Clark Gable, who was born just 124 days after his father's death. Wishing to be discreet, the actress slipped quietly through the star-studded crowd in a veil and a subdued black dress. She looked like a widow. After the service, she joined the others at a champagne reception at the Gables' nearby home. She and Gable's widow, Kay, had evidently forgiven each other following Kay's suggestion that Monroe's persistent delays on the set of The Misfits had contributed to her husband's death. In fact, they had become friends. Two months earlier, on Tuesday 11 April, she had drafted a letter to the actress which read, in part, 'I miss Clark each day more. I'll never get over this great loss. But God has blessed me with three great children and precious memories.' Kay even sent Marilyn a copy of the child's first-ever photograph.

With the actress still residing at his home, questions about her alleged affair with Frank Sinatra dominated her early spell back in Hollywood. When columnist Louella Parsons confronted her about this, she made light of the tittle-tattle by replying, 'I couldn't be more surprised . . . He has always been very kind to me,' adding, 'I want to go to his and Dean Martin's birthday party at the Sands Hotel in Las Vegas.' Which she did. At midnight on the night of Wednesday 14 June, at Martin's surprise belated 44th birthday celebration, she was seen seated at the very edge of the Sands' stage, champagne glass in hand, gently swaying along to the music, enthusiastically applauding each number and gazing up adoringly at Sinatra as he performed. Rumours of their affair were ignited further when the two were spotted having an intimate tête-à-tête in the lounge immediately after the show. But despite the gossip, Monroe toddled off to bed alone, while Frank remained behind, chatting with his show business pals way into the early hours. (For the record, by the middle of June 1961 Monroe had dated Frank just twice and not five or more times, as many previous Monroe scholars have led us to believe. Their relationship would, in fact, not intensify for another three months.)

Marilyn's time in Las Vegas was brief. Later that day, accompanied by her press agent, Pat Newcomb, she flew out of the city en route to Los Angeles International Airport. After an exceedingly brief stopover in Coldwater Canyon, Marilyn was escorted back to the airport where, amid great excitement, she caught her flight back to New York's Idlewild Airport, arriving there during the evening of Thursday 15 June. Amid tidal waves of wolf-whistles and flash bulbs, she remarked 'No comment' to reporters who had enquired why she had suddenly returned. In fact, she was there for two reasons. First, business. Thanks to the amount of time she had spent there, most of her ongoing promotional and occupational matters were still being handled in the city. For instance, within an hour of her homecoming, she was holding court in her Manhattan home with Louella Parsons and *The New York Herald Tribune*'s 'Television Today' columnist, Marie Torre. Then, with matters concerning her television play *Rain* deepening, Marilyn held a late-night meeting with the show's scriptwriter, Rod Serling.

Second, she was there to prepare for an operation to remove her gall bladder, a procedure which had to be brought forward when, during the evening of Wednesday 28 June, she began suffering from severe intestinal pains. An ambulance was summoned to her apartment and, with Joe DiMaggio by her side, she was taken to the local Polyclinic Hospital. X-rays confirmed that an impacted gallstone was causing the inflammation and discomfort, and emergency surgery was scheduled. The successful operation (classed as an emergency because it took place outside the normal morning operating hours) took place the following evening, Thursday 29 June.

On Tuesday 11 July, after two weeks of recuperation in her private room, the actress was deemed fit enough to leave hospital. Before doing so, her obligatory New York hair stylist (and that of the First Lady, Jacqueline Kennedy), the eminent Kenneth Battelle, known professionally as plain 'Kenneth', was urgently summoned to fix the actress's tresses. 'I had flown in from Europe that day,' he recalled in 1961. 'I flew to New York for three hours just to do Marilyn's hair' (he received a cool $1,000 for doing so). Since many of her stomach muscles had not yet stretched back to normal and were not fully functioning, she was unable to walk properly, so she was forced to exit the building in a wheelchair. A crowd of approximately 500, comprised of journalists, photographers, well-wishers and the curious, were waiting to witness her departure. 'I feel wonderful,' she shouted before she gingerly stood on her feet and climbed aboard her waiting car, which was ready to escort her back to her Manhattan apartment. One of her other New York press agents, Howard Haines, was ready there to help her inside, where waiting to greet her was her half-sister, Berniece Miracle.

There is no truth in the story that, shortly after Marilyn's exit from the hospital, she and Miracle were driven to Connecticut by the actress's close friend and masseur, Ralph Roberts, for a vacation. At this point, the actress was still barely able to move. Medical reports dated Monday 24 July reveal that, two weeks after she left the clinic, the actress was still recuperating at her New York home and was now just about able to leave her bed, but only for 'several hours a day'. Further evidence that she remained holed up in her apartment for many weeks after her operation came from the manager of Westhampton House on Westhampton Beach, who revealed that, one week after the actress was discharged from the hospital, the ever-thoughtful Joe DiMaggio booked, as a surprise for the actress, two rooms at the Long Island resort. When quizzed about the reservations, an astounded Monroe was quoted as saying, 'I have *no* plans to go anywhere at all.' Nor did she. Closely abiding to a restrictive two-month diet which had been set by her doctors, she did not venture out of her apartment again until Tuesday 8 August.

During her New York internment, however, she did record a voice-over for a new American television special. Entitled *USO – Wherever They Go*, the show was a tribute to the United Service Organization (USO) on its 20th anniversary and to the entertainers who had performed for the American armed forces at bases at home and abroad, in peace and war. Naturally, footage of Marilyn's performance with the Anything Goes Band before the troops in Korea in February 1954 was to be one of the show's high spots. 'She had just been released from the hospital when we called,' the programme's producer, Jesse Zousmer, recalled in 1961. 'So we went to her apartment with a projector, sound equipment and the necessary technicians to show her what we were doing. She got such a kick out of the film and she eagerly agreed to write her own narration.' The finished programme became NBC TV's all-star 'DuPont Show Of The Week' when it aired on Sunday 8 October.

On Tuesday 8 August, following several weeks of convalescence, and after realising that, for professional reasons, she simply *had* to return there, Marilyn clandestinely flew back to Los Angeles. Travelling in a hat, head-scarf and dark glasses, and in the guise of her East Coast secretary, 'Miss Reis', she had managed to keep everyone in the dark about her arrival, even her press agent, Arthur P. Jacobs. However, one person who was not was her former husband, Joe DiMaggio, who was there to meet her at the city's International Airport. A scrum of reporters who had caught sight of the couple, and noticed in particular the actress's new, svelte figure, immediately descended upon them and began asking if they were planning to remarry. Shortly after checking into her hotel, where she would reside for the next month, she was seen at the celebrity hang-out, Chasen's in Beverly Hills. The sycophantic, but highly worshipped columnist Louella Parsons met her there and afterwards wrote gushingly: 'I thought I hadn't seen her look as well since the first time I knew her years ago. She's taken off so much weight that all those bulging curves are gone.'

During the month, Marilyn's warm-heartedness shone through again when she fulfilled the wishes of 14-year-old Barbara Heinz, who was dying of incurable bone cancer in Wisconsin's Appleton Memorial Hospital. With just a month to live, the young girl, a keen collector of toy dogs, penned a letter to the actress requesting a picture of her with Maf. Marilyn duly obliged. The photograph, taken on Friday 11 August, arrived at the girl's bedside on Wednesday 23 August, inscribed with the words, 'From Marilyn Monroe to Barbara Heinz. With love.'

A brief trip to San Francisco with DiMaggio, staying with his widowed sister, Marie, in the family home on Beach Street, and a middle-of-the-month excursion with him to Lake Tahoe, in the Sierra Nevada mountains, peppered the actress's ensuing weeks. Sadly, that period would otherwise prove to be a desperately dreary one. Finding herself back in Los Angeles, a city she despised, Marilyn was desperately lonely. Even the pollution, which seemed to cast a pink veil over the city, was beginning to infuriate her.

The actress's isolation intensified in the first week of September when she moved out of her bungalow at the Beverly Hills Hotel and returned to the small, rented apartment of 925 square feet, situated at 882 North Doheny Drive, West Hollywood, where she had previously lived during the period 1953–4. Built in 1952, it boasted just one bedroom. Since Frank Sinatra, as well as his personal valet George Jacobs, secretary Gloria Lovell and occasional bed-mate Jeanne Carmen also had homes in the building, it would become affectionately known as 'The Sinatra Arms'.

With DiMaggio now back in New York, and with few friends to hand, Marilyn would spend most evenings alone, frittering away the hours by reading, watching television or listening to the wireless. Her favourite station was the radio broadcaster, KDAY. Hosted by Tom Clay, her show of choice was *Words and Music*. With its highly evocative, cohesive mix of news-bites and spoken words, the programme, broadcast daily from 4 to 8pm, soon became a highlight. Marilyn became hooked on the show, which developed into a form of company, and around Friday 8 September even began ringing the station.

Touched by Clay's unique way of telling stories and his superbly executed discussions about childhood and marriage, and knowing full well that he answered every call to his show personally, her contact with the station intensified. To begin with, she preferred to remain anonymous but, after several more discussions, Clay felt courageous enough to ask for her name. 'I'm Marilyn Monroe,' she replied hesitantly. 'Yes, sure, and I'm Frank Sinatra,' he curtly retorted. Incensed by his response, she terminated the call. However, she soon rang back. After sensing desperation in her voice, he agreed to meet her.

One day later, at approximately 9.30 on the morning of Monday 11 September, he knocked on the door of the North Doheny Drive address she had offered. It opened, and he was shocked to discover that the shadowy caller to his show was indeed the world-famous actress. Clay recalled she was wearing a bathrobe, sipping champagne, and was looking depressed and confused. The disc jockey listened compassionately to the actress's problems. During the exchange, she revealed how lonesome she had become. 'How can anyone as famous as you be so lonely?' he asked. 'Have you ever been in a room and felt loneliness?' she enquired. 'Well, multiply that by 40 rooms, then you'll have some idea about how lonely I am.'

However, when Frank Sinatra re-entered her life, she had no further use for Clay. Marilyn began dating the Rat Pack star again immediately. On Wednesday 13 September, they were spotted in the Crown Room at Romanoff's restaurant in Hollywood at a cocktail party given by film producer Harold Mirisch for the director of *Some Like It Hot*, Billy Wilder. With Sinatra by her side, Marilyn enjoyed the night immensely. On the dance floor, she and Sinatra were inseparable. As Dorothy Kilgallen, the so-called 'Voice of Broadway', wrote in one of her columns, 'Marilyn Monroe looked as if she could have danced all night with Frank Sinatra.' Marilyn and Frank would be joined at the hip for the next two weeks.

However, their relationship hit the buffers on Tuesday 26 September. Just hours after the couple had flown into New York from Hyannis Port, and while Marilyn sat alone in her apartment, planning their future, Sinatra went out on a date with his former wife, screen actress Ava Gardner. Following dinner at the Colony restaurant on Madison Avenue, they attended a show by his close friend, jazz pianist Stan Kenton, and his orchestra at the trendy Basin Street East club. Despite their bravest attempts to keep their visit a secret, by the time they reached their table, in one of the far corners of the room, word had got around who had just walked through the door and, unsurprisingly, the press were informed. Marilyn flew into a rage and terminated her brief, two-week relationship with Sinatra with immediate effect.

Sinatra was unconcerned by the rejection. Just two weeks later, he began seeing the South African entertainer Juliet Prowse, who had caught his eye during rehearsals in Las Vegas for the musical *Irma La Douce*. Resentment between Monroe and Sinatra simmered for months. When *Redbook* magazine's Alan Levy dared to ask him, a few months later, how well he knew the actress, he flippantly asked, 'Who?' When told this, Marilyn retaliated by saying, 'Tell him to look in *Who's Who*.' Sinatra counteracted by declaring, 'Miss Monroe reminds me of a saintly young girl I went to High School with who later became a nun.'

Unsurprisingly, with her sanctioned five-month respite from the studio about to expire, Fox were back in touch with Marilyn that month. Following an immense amount of cajoling by their despairing stockholders, the corporation's executives set about drafting a series of letters to the actress's company, Marilyn Monroe Productions (MMP), each one politely reminding her of the fact that she legally owed them another movie and suggesting she star in a new picture they had in mind: a production bearing the title of *Something's Got To Give*.

Largely thanks to their insistence that the film would be made entirely under their terms and that any requests from the actress would be completely ignored, their first two letters to Marilyn's company went unanswered. The third was far more intimidating. Its message was quite clear: make this picture or we'll 'drag you through the courts'. Matters intensified when Spyros Skouras declared that he would, once more, seek an injunction preventing her from working at another studio if she didn't fulfil her four-film deal with Fox. As the final straw, the prearranged deadline for her decision, the end of October 1961, was reimposed.

In truth, since she was still handcuffed to her $100,000-a-movie 'slave' contract with Fox, Marilyn wasn't fervent about making another film for the studio. She knew far greater sums (and more appealing projects) awaited her elsewhere. For instance, she had enthusiastically discussed with French director Henri-Georges Clouzot shooting a movie with him in France and had talked about making *The Naked Truth* with Harold Mirisch in Hollywood. With regard to the latter, she defiantly remarked to Louella Parsons, 'If he gets a director, I'll make it. Mirisch is my favourite producer. He *cares* what happens.'

But Marilyn knew that, for the immediate future anyway, it was academic to make plans away from Fox. The actress had even started to avoid reading the new screenplays she would receive from rival film studios. Instead, she would hurl them on to the heap which had begun to form (and subsequently collapse) in both the bedroom and on the table in the living room of her new apartment. And so, on Tuesday 26 September, a month before the imposed deadline, MMP finally replied to Fox's proposal. Three weeks later, on Monday 16 October, following more discussions with the studio, Marilyn irrevocably agreed in principle to the project and a contract was signed. A starting date of Wednesday 15 November was soon approved.

In another attempt to pacify their clearly despondent star, Fox even arranged a meeting for her that day with Owen McClean, the studio's head of talent. The get-together, set to take place at 3.30pm in office 147 at the studio's West Pico Boulevard locale, was to provide the actress with the opportunity to unburden herself of any worries she had concerning the film. However, industry insiders were already beginning to doubt she would fulfil that appointment. On Friday 6 October, the *Ogden Standard Examiner* sensationally claimed that Marilyn was now 'too thin and run down' to report to the studio that day and even prophetically insisted she should abstain from movie-making until 1962.

Marilyn's spiritless endorsement of *Something's Got To Give* was shadowed by her and her attorney's decision to fight Fox one last time. Their latest, quite unexpected attempt to gain advantage over the studio came in the shape of a considerable list of demands, which included the replacing of David Brown as the movie's producer (he would be excised from the film in December 1961), the rewriting of the script to make it 'more sexy' (even though she had no rights to make such a demand), a promise of a substantial bonus when she completed the film, the rights to approve all publicity stills before they were released to the press, approval of leading man, supporting cast (including the substituting of comic Don Knotts with Monroe's newly acquired friend, Wally Cox of NBC's *Mr. Peepers* fame), the engagement of Franz (also known as Frank) Planer and Billy Daniels as cameramen, the employment of Jean Louis as clothes designer, the hiring of Sydney Guilaroff as hairdresser and chiefly, her obligatory election of director. Remarkably, the studio assented to each and every one of her requests.

Forty-nine-year-old, New Jersey-born Frank Tashlin, a man best known for writing and supervising comedies featuring the likes of Jerry Lewis, Bob Hope and Jayne Mansfield, had been Fox's first choice of director. His fine-tuning of comedy-writer Edmund L. Hartmann's recently completed script was an integral part of his posting. However, no doubt due to his connections to her great platinum-blonde rival at 20th Century-Fox, Jayne Mansfield and to the fact that Tashlin had prepared the screenplay without Marilyn in mind (amazingly, Monroe had accepted the role in the first place completely oblivious to the fact that it had begun life two years earlier as a vehicle intended for Mansfield), she made it clear she didn't want him involved. So the plan was immediately vetoed and Fox had to turn their gazes once more to the obligatory Monroe-approved list of directors, which had been submitted to the studio on Tuesday 26 September.

Among those featured on this inventory of 16 were Billy Wilder (with whom Monroe had worked on *Some Like It Hot*), David Lean (director of the 1957 movie *The Bridge On the River Kwai*) and John Huston (whom Marilyn had befriended during the shooting of *The Misfits*). The *Psycho* director and master of the macabre, Alfred Hitchcock, was the most astonishing name to be listed. The choice became even more astounding when Fox announced that *Something's Got To Give* was, in fact, a reworking of RKO's light-hearted 1940 screwball bedroom comedy, *My Favorite Wife*.

Marilyn was cast in the role of Ellen Wagstaff Arden, a photographer believed killed during a trans-Pacific yacht race, but who turns up very much alive, having spent the previous five years on a desert island, on the day that a judge pronounces her dead and her husband is about to remarry. Rewritten to replicate the style of the highly popular bedroom comedies of the late 1950s and early 1960s starring Doris Day (which featured opulent people in desirable locations experiencing amorous difficulties), the first version of the script of *Something's Got To Give* was packed with frothy, inoffensive humour and lightly contrived pathos.

The part also marked a prominent change of direction for Monroe. After years of portraying either cabaret singers, hookers or short-sighted gold-diggers, she was set to play the role of a normal, San Francisco-based, upper-class suburban housewife and mother. Believing that the movie could possibly make her more popular than ever, the acting challenge slowly began to excite her and she waited anxiously for news of who would be directing her.

For the first time ever in her profession, Marilyn began preparing for the movie devoid of any agency representation. At the start of September, following a suggestion from both her publicist, Arthur P. Jacobs, and her Los Angeles attorney, Milton 'Mickey' Rudin, of the Sunset Boulevard law firm Gang, Tyre, Rudin & Brown, she had severed her ties with Music Corporation of America (MCA). The largest and most successful booking agency in the world and a company which handled the affairs of over 500 of America's biggest and best film and television stars, MCA's domination of the industry was immense. By late 1961, it was estimated that, if any client obtained a post on a film or television show, almost everyone else involved in the production would be an MCA client too. However, the agency had recently fallen foul of Robert Francis Kennedy – better known as Bobby – the Attorney General of the United States, whose Department of Justice had recently decreed that its dual role of agent and producer violated anti-trust laws.

Apprehensive about starting a new project without any kind of management, Monroe immediately sought new representation. A request was made to actress Polly Bergen's husband, former MCA vice-chairman Freddie Fields, and his partner David Begelman, who were in the process of starting their new talent agency, Creative Management Associates (a clever anagram of MCA). To begin with, it operated with just four high-calibre stars: Bergen, entertainer Judy Garland, actor Kirk Douglas and the comedy actor Phil Silvers, best known for starring as the conniving, fast-talking Sergeant Ernie Bilko in the 1950s US Army sitcom, *The Phil Silvers Show*. Publicity-wise, Arthur Jacobs represented them all and Marilyn wanted to be artiste number five on their new roster. However, her request was declined. It seemed her reputation for unreliability had finally caught up with her.

Her decision to fly solo could not have come at a worse time. Severely strapped for cash, on Thursday 14 September she had drafted a typewritten note to the United Artists Corporation, distributors of *Some Like It Hot*, requesting a $25,000 loan, agreeing to pay the money back at the rate of 4 per cent per annum on or before Friday 5 January 1962. Forthcoming royalties from the film were used as a guarantee. (Thankfully for the actress, her application was successful.)

In the third week of October, following a suggestion by Fox's production head, Peter G. Levathes, and consent by Monroe, the studio announced that the director's chair on *Something's Got To Give* was to be handed to George Cukor. With a reputation for being annoyingly belligerent, extremely fussy but intensely stimulating, his track record boasted distinguished Hollywood films such as *Gone with the Wind* (1939), *The Philadelphia Story* (1940) and the Judy Garland version of *A Star Is Born* (1954). Described by many as being 'cranky', Cukor never hid his disgust at an actor (or actress) who arrived late on the set. 'What the hell are you late for?' he was frequently heard to say.

Renowned for his superb handling of the highly tempestuous stars Constance Bennett, Greta Garbo and Katharine Hepburn, in 1960 he had directed Marilyn on the sub-par but quaint comedy *Let's Make Love*. His decision to direct her again took industry insiders by surprise, especially as their time together on the movie had been nothing short of a catastrophe. Her characteristic tardiness had helped make the movie run several weeks and uncounted thousands over budget. In addition, her successful attempts at shattering Cukor's reputation as a great director of women continually disrupted the making of the film. He came to hate her for it and said so in high places around Hollywood.

But surprisingly, in July 1960, at the time of the film's impending release, in an interview for the *Lowell Sunday Sun* newspaper, he waxed lyrical about Monroe and charmingly explained her tardiness away by saying, 'Marilyn's delays are neither irresponsible nor careless. She does not want to do a scene until she is ready for it and can give it her best. We have an agreement that she works only when she is satisfied she is ready to begin.'

Despite his warm and understanding words, Cukor was merely displaying polite professionalism to a colleague in an industry in which they both served. In truth, he despised her. Rather like Marilyn, Cukor had been forced into making *Something's Got To Give*. One of the many unequivocally clandestine homosexuals during Hollywood's golden age, he had signed his two-picture deal with Fox at the time he directed Monroe in *Let's Make Love* and, like the actress, had spent the interim doing his best to shirk his obligation to the floundering studio. Since *Goodbye Charlie* had failed to materialise at the start of the year, Cukor – like Monroe – still owed the studio one more film. When Fox called reminding him of his contractual obligation and offering a rather tempting wage packet, he relented, and on Monday 16 October verbally agreed a 26-week pledge to *Something's Got To Give*.

David Hall was once again appointed as Cukor's assistant. A good-humoured, well-developed man blessed with the curious nickname of 'Buck', he had been Cukor's deputy on *Let's Make Love* and regrettably he too had failed to be captivated by Monroe. 'Next to her,' Hall once cruelly remarked, 'Lucrezia Borgia was a pussycat.'

And so, as the studio saw it, with a leading lady, director, producer and script all now in place, work on Monroe's latest movie had successfully begun. It had not. Realising he was already committed to Warner Brothers and their sex-survey drama *The Chapman Report*, starring Shelley Winters and Jane Fonda (a project once intended for Fox), Cukor, to begin with, refused to sign a contract. (His six-month agreement, for a $300,000 fee and a 10 per cent share of the movie's net profits, would not in fact be signed until Sunday 26 November.)

Despite the fact that there was still no leading man (or director) officially engaged to the production, Fox chose to excitedly rush-release details about the film. 'Everyone can relax now and return to his knitting,' the well-informed Louella Parsons inscribed in her syndicated article on Thursday 19 October, 'Marilyn Monroe is all set for her next movie and it starts Nov 14 (*sic*) at 20th Century-Fox . . . George Cukor has been named by Peter Levathes to direct her . . . David Brown is the producer. *Something's Got To Give* is described as exotic fun and real comedy. Its locale is from snow-capped Connecticut to sun-kissed Hawaii, so I reckon our girl will do a bit of travelling.'

To the outside world, it all appeared decidedly rosy. However, looks were deceiving. On Thursday 9 November, a goodwill meeting between Marilyn, her attorney Milton Rudin and Fox's Peter Levathes was held at the swanky Beverly Hills Hotel. Several hours later, believing the get-together had been constructive, Levathes returned to the studio exultant in the belief that the relationship between the actress and Fox was now a happy one. He was deluded. Unbeknown to him, without a satisfactory screenplay to hand, and with Cukor now curiously absent from all of their meetings, she still wasn't committing herself to the project. Her feeling had not changed by Monday 13 November, just 48 hours before shooting was due to commence. One day later, Rudin instructed the studio that his client would not be reporting for duty until she saw (and approved) the latest version of the script.

In truth, Marilyn had been responsible for many of its delays. Far from happy with the latest adaptations, she had been conveying her thoughts to all concerned about how the screenplay should unfold. Her interference would only manage to produce numerous rewrites from a lengthy succession of disgruntled screenwriters. (In total, between May 1961 – when Edmund L. Hartmann, noted gag writer for Bob Hope, Abbott and Costello, Martin and Lewis and the Three Stooges, dusted down and began work on this newest version of the script – and January 1962, Fox hired and subsequently fired five different writers on the movie, three of which were down to Marilyn's insistence.)

Hollywood screenwriter Arnold Schulman, who had penned A *Hole in the Head* for Sinatra in 1959, was the third from his profession employed on the movie. He quit the film in protest when he discovered the menacing treatment Marilyn had been receiving from certain members of the Fox hierarchy. He had encountered the actress for the first time in 1955 during her first spell in New York and regarded her as a true and trusted friend. However, friendship meant little in the Hollywood movie industry and Marilyn soon made it clear she was unhappy with several parts of Schulman's work. Her loathing of it was manifested in several handwritten notes, scrawled across the screenplay's front page and across several pages inside. 'This is funny?' she asked. 'Not funny', she maintained. 'Not a story for me', she insisted. On another page, she scrawled, 'At one point in the story two women like each other but hate the man – all the fags are going to like it.'

Wednesday 15 November came and went. Marilyn failed to show and Fox unsurprisingly suspended her. Through her attorney, she counteracted by insisting her contract on the film was invalid anyway, since Cukor had failed to sign to the movie by the agreed date. (This was true. He would not officially commit himself to the production for another 11 days.) Immediately, she began pressing ahead with film plans of her own. Believing that she was now free from Fox's stifling control, she hoped that her new scheme would become operational immediately.

Her plot involved her former, albeit transitory lover, the actor Marlon Brando. In a hastily handwritten letter to him on Tuesday 5 December, Marilyn suggested they should set up a film company of their own. In part, it read, 'I need your opinion about a plan for getting out here for more than a temporary basis. Please get back to me as soon as possible as time is of the essence.' (It took him five weeks to reply.)

Marilyn also drafted a note to her acting coach, Lee Strasberg, in which she proposed that he should temporarily leave New York and head back to Los Angeles to assist with her new enterprise. When he appeared unwilling to do so, the actress flew to the Big Apple in the second week of December to talk over the matter with him personally. However, this still failed to sway his mind. Sadly, despite her most valiant attempts, and Brando's initial willingness to discuss Marilyn's plans, the idea never reached the functioning stage.

Her December trip to New York did nevertheless have a high point: she finally got to meet the 83-year-old, American-born Pulitzer Prize-winning writer, editor and poet Carl Sandburg. Their meeting took place at the apartment belonging to his close friend, fashion and beauty photographer Len Steckler. As he recalled on the website, thevisitseries.com, 'Marilyn was three hours late, but [she] had an excuse. She had been at the hairdresser.' The individual in question was her regular East Coast stylist, Kenneth Battelle. During her eleventh-hour visit to his salon, housed in Lilly Daché, Manhattan's most elegant millinery and beauty emporium, located at 70–80 East 56th Street between Park and Madison, she asked him to match her hair colour to Sandburg's: white. 'Hours later I went to open the door,' Steckler recalled for the Reuters news agency, 'and there I was, face-to-face with Marilyn Monroe, and she looked more ravishing than on the screen.'

That afternoon, while Marilyn and Carl spoke and supped Jack Daniels whiskey, Steckler took out his Nikon camera and proceeded to capture a photographic record of the event, throughout which the actress sported her butterfly-shaped shades. She enjoyed Sandburg's company immensely and excitedly counted down the days until they would meet again.

Back in Los Angeles, there were other troubles for Fox to contend with. George Cukor was now unavailable too. Work on his current project, *The Chapman Report*, had fallen way behind schedule and was not set to wrap until Boxing Day. This unforeseen delay meant that the filming of *Something's Got To Give* had to be pushed back by seven weeks. With no other alternative, a new start date of Thursday 4 January was reluctantly pencilled in by both Cukor and the disgruntled Fox executives.

Marilyn had been unconcerned by the suspension or postponement. On Saturday 18 November, consistent with her contract, she knew she was due to be placed back on the Fox payroll. she was set to start earning a weekly wage again, despite the fact that the cameras on the picture had yet to roll. (She had been due to receive payment this way while working on *Let's Make Love* two years earlier; a paltry $7,142.82 – before tax – every seven days.) As it turned out, Marilyn would fail to draw any money whatsoever from her new movie.

Although a request to receive her $100,000 fee for *Something's Got To Give* movie in one lump sum had been flatly rejected by executives, the fact did not greatly trouble her. At this point, thanks to her recently received United Artists loan and her share of the *Some Like It Hot* profits, she was not short of money. A spokesman for the Mirisch Company, the producers of the comedy, spelt out the actress's financial status during an interview in 1963. 'Marilyn had received more than a quarter of a million dollars in the four years since the movie was released,' he declared. Although in essence, for the previous two years, this and the loan had been her only sources of income, on Friday 17 November 1961, her City National Bank of Beverly Hills savings account book boasted a sum of $40,000.

Nevertheless, by following the advice of her lawyers – primarily Rudin – and choosing, for tax reasons, to take a deferment against profits instead of the large salary she could have easily commanded for her movies, the actress was gambling as heavily on her career as any of the motion picture studios. As the Mirisch Company spokesman also explained: 'With *The Misfits*, the company [Seven Arts Productions] called for her to split 15 per cent of the gross with co-star, Clark Gable. He was due to receive $1 million for his role; Monroe just $500,000. But by late 1962, the picture had yet to see a profit.' So concerned did she become about her finances, she resolutely never carried more than $20 with her when she left her home. All of her large purchases were made by cheque.

In the middle of December, Fox executives contacted Marilyn again. They forcibly informed her that her argument (i.e. her claim that Cukor's failure to commit to the movie invalidated her own contract) was not a legitimate one, and persuasively reminded her that, all things considered, she had a legal obligation to the studio. Fearing that the legal ramifications of the actress's decision might result in even further delays, the studio once again, albeit reluctantly, cast their gaze towards Jayne Mansfield to star in the movie. However, Cukor was having none of it. 'I admire Jayne,' he told American show business columnist Mike Connolly, 'not as an actress but as a girl.' Further heated discussions between Fox and Marilyn's attorney soon took place; in the third week of December, shortly after her return from New York, the actress finally relented and agreed in lukewarm fashion to shoot *Something's Got To Give*.

Monroe spent Christmas in her decoratively unfinished Doheny Drive apartment, mulling over yet another mournfully inadequate film script while relaxing in the company of her former husband, Joe DiMaggio. During the day, they were seen out shopping, purchasing Christmas tree ornaments from a Mexican shop in downtown Los Angeles. Marilyn also went out alone, on a buying spree to Beverly Hills. Each of her expeditions was spent in disguise, a thick black wig, although it was now common knowledge in the media that she always travelled this way. On Friday 6 October 1961, the *Times Recorder* newspaper had written, 'Marilyn Monroe is not easy to spot on the street. [She] wears horn-rimmed glasses, peasant skirt and blouse, also chooz gum.' On Christmas Day, they paid a visit to the Santa Monica home of her doctor, Ralph Greenson. She spent New Year's Eve in her apartment with DiMaggio roasting chestnuts in front of her log fire. He broke from his teetotal lifestyle to usher in 1962 with a single glass of Dom Perignon champagne.

December's amicable socialising, optimism and progressive planning quickly diminished as the New Year dawned. On the first day, Marilyn was saddened by the death of her famed defence lawyer, Jerry Giesler, who had suffered a heart attack, aged 75, in his sleep at his Hollywood home. A close confidant of Monroe, he had handled her divorce from DiMaggio in 1954. Further emotional stresses were heaped upon Marilyn when she learnt through the grapevine that Arthur Miller was preparing to remarry. His next wife was to be the photographer Ingeberg Morath, whom Miller had ironically met on the set of *The Misfits*. The actress was also shocked to discover that Morath was pregnant with Miller's child. Overcome with jealousy, knowing she was unlikely to become a mother herself, Monroe was greatly affected by this news and sealed herself away in her bedroom, refusing to see or speak to anyone.

One further traumatic event was still to reach Marilyn. In the second week of January, Hollywood gossip columnists excitedly wrote about the engagement between Frank Sinatra and Juliet Prowse on Monday 8 January. While she proudly showed off her sparkling new 10-carat gold ring, he excitedly declared he was 'very, very much in love'. Even though Marilyn's romance with the Rat Pack star had been dormant for just over three months now, the thought that she was losing him in the marriage stakes severely hurt her. She soon became bitterly jealous of the dancer and began harbouring deep grudges towards her, especially since Prowse was a good decade younger than her and, in Marilyn's own words, 'had better legs'.

Openly dismissive of the heart-wrenching revelations about the former men in her life, Monroe made it clear to the few friends around her that the most significant thing for her at the start of 1962, even more important than her new film, was to move forward with her life, and that buying a home of her own was the key to this. After renting over 35 different homes, flats and hotel rooms (of fluctuating levels of luxury) over the previous 16 years, Marilyn announced she was 'tired of living in apartments'. However, the decision to finally purchase was not entirely her own. It had actually derived from a suggestion made back in May 1961 by celebrated

Californian psychiatrist Dr Ralph Greenson, the latest in a line of psycho-analysts who had managed to practise their dubious methods of counselling on the star.

Born in 1911 in Brooklyn, New York as Romeo Samuel Greenschpoon, Ralph Greenson studied at Columbia University and at Berne University in Switzerland before obtaining a qualified medical degree in 1935, the same year that he married Hildegard Toesch. The couple settled in Los Angeles soon after. The name change occurred concurrently. In 1938, he studied Freudian psychology in Vienna and became close to its creator, Sigmund Freud. During the Second World War, Greenson served in the US military and, following his discharge, returned to Los Angeles where he began to practise the flourishing vocation of psychoanalysis. He would go on to become Clinical Professor of Psychiatry at the University of California, and was soon to be known as Hollywood's 'therapist to the stars' (Vivien Leigh, star of *Gone with the Wind*, was one such).

He and Marilyn had first met in January 1960, in bungalow 21 at the Beverly Hills Hotel, during the filming of *Let's Make Love*, when she was desperately in need of counselling following a heated argument with her acting coach, Paula Strasberg. Counselling sessions between the two of them did not however commence until the following May, shortly before Marilyn began shooting her penultimate movie, the drama-laden *The Misfits*, and it was during that film that he was forced into making his first major decision about the star.

In soaring temperatures of 95 to 110 degrees in the shade, the actress had played out her most demanding role. However, it became too much for her and she had difficulty with her performance. Director John Huston lost his patience and snapped, describing her as both 'useless' and 'hopeless'. To ease her mental anguish she turned to her Nembutal tablets. As Huston recalled, 'She took so many sleeping pills to rest that, in the morning, she had to take stimulants to wake her up and this *ravaged* the girl.'

Time spent on the set with one of the movie's co-stars, Montgomery Clift, no doubt triggered her actions. They shared a lot in common, for instance, a love of New York and a hatred of Los Angeles. He often alluded to it as 'Vomit, California.' He was also a habitual user of narcotics. During a break in filming one day, he demonstrated to the actress how, by pricking the top of a Nembutal capsule and pouring its contents directly into a glass of water or champagne, the drug could be made to take effect much faster. Marilyn would remember this 'trick' and use it to devastating effect.

Production on the movie had been temporarily suspended when, on Monday 29 August 1960, Marilyn was flown out to Los Angeles and, under the name of Mrs Miller, was placed in Westside Hospital, a small private Hollywood-based hospice, where doctors discovered she was a barbiturate addict and had been habitually taking approximately 20 sleeping pills a day, enough to kill a non-user. Amid threats that she was to be sacked, Greenson persuaded the producers of the movie to give Marilyn another try.

Eight months later, in May 1961, she reluctantly returned to Los Angeles and began seeing Greenson again, but this time on a more regular basis. However, he was not her first choice. He was, in truth, a last resort. As a friend of the actress once remarked, 'I felt Ralph had a big ego. Like a lot of doctors he wanted to be God, and of all the analysts in LA she found him.'

In fact, seven other psychiatrists were approached before she decided to contact Greenson again. Due to her previous suicide attempt and the insanity which was known to be prevalent in her family, they had shied away from taking on the actress, fearing she might succeed in a bid to kill herself while under their care. But Greenson had no such qualms and possessed the courage to accept her as one of his patients. There was a dark drawback, though. His form of counselling was experimental, unorthodox and, most worryingly, highly dangerous. With so much time being spent in the doctor's company, Monroe soon became aware that he was an advocate of the copious use of drugs, routinely prescribed barbiturates and tranquillisers. This extreme form of counselling would eventually drive Monroe deep into her own personal hell.

As time rolled on, depending on her emotional state, he would usually end up seeing her, both consistently and intensively, between five and seven times a week. 'He saw her every day, for a fairly prolonged period of time,' Greenson's colleague Dr Hyman Engelberg ominously recalled, 'and I just suspected that there was too much attachment for good, impartial judgement on his part.'

Marilyn's initiation into psychoanalysis had begun in early 1951 when, in the aftermath of an unsuccessful attempt to contact her father, she began seeing Dr A. Gottesman at his clinic in Los Angeles, paying $200 for each session. In February 1955, two months after arriving in New York, and following a suggestion by her business partner, celebrity photographer Milton H. Greene, who sensed that Monroe might have certain mental difficulties, predominantly relating to her troubled childhood, Marilyn began visiting Freudian analyst Dr Margaret Hertz Hohenberg at her office up to five times a week. There she was stripped of her Hollywood glamour, subconsciously taken back to her childhood traumas and reminded of her ongoing depression and anxiety, her schizophrenic mother and her unhappy relationships with men. The therapy clearly did not agree with the actress. In truth, it completely turned her life upside-down. The facts speak for themselves. Before psychoanalysis she appeared in 27 movies in eight years. Afterwards, in the same period of time, she starred in just six.

During the next 24 months, Marilyn's personality was disassembled and reconstructed. Hohenberg also analysed her dreams and partook in free-association games with her, essential elements when searching for clues to the patient's unconscious. To combat the intense emotional pain she was now encountering, and the powerful, all-consuming feelings of hopelessness engulfing her, Marilyn was prescribed larger and larger quantities of barbiturates. In turn, she began to question everything in her life. She told friends she felt as if she was 'going round in circles' and would significantly ask 'not where I was going, but where I had been'.

Her intake of other prescription drugs (stimulants to keep her going during the day and relaxants to help with her insomnia at night) also snowballed. Her dependence on alcohol also grew, all of which was potentially disastrous for someone with so many anxieties and for an individual suspected of being manic-depressive. In 1957, and with no major breakthroughs seemingly accomplished with Hohenberg after two years of consistent consulting, Monroe's then husband, Arthur Miller, recommended that she change to another psychoanalyst. Early that year, he suggested she should start seeing New York psychiatrist Dr Marianne Kris, another practitioner heavily slanted towards the theories of Freud. Monroe would visit Kris at her Central Park West offices five times a week and once again, she was administered barbiturates.

Their four-year doctor/patient relationship came to an abrupt and tragic end on Tuesday 7 February 1961, when the actress entered Manhattan's famed eight-storey Payne-Whitney Psychiatric Clinic of New York Hospital Cornell Medical Center, a hospice also known as 'the rich people's crazy house'. Marilyn had been harbouring guilt about the recent death of actor Clark Gable, and believed wrongly that his fatal heart attack had been precipitated by her perpetual tardiness on the set of *The Misfits*. Her fears apparently intensified when she caught sight of an article in which Gable's widow Kay shockingly announced '*The Misfits* helped kill him . . . It *wasn't* the physical exertion that did it. It *was* the waiting, waiting, waiting.'

Despite what folklore has led us to believe, it is in fact far from certain that Monroe's unreliability contributed in any significant way to Gable's death. For one thing, delays during filming never disturbed him. After working with the alcoholic actor Spencer Tracy, he was actually quite used to them. Tracy's excessive drinking during the shooting of *San*

Francisco in 1936 and *Boom Town* in 1940 had postponed filming for up to a week. In contrast, Marilyn's actions would only defer things for a few hours. Clark was most supportive of her and never once displayed to her or their fellow cast members how impatient he was with her unpunctuality. In an interview carried out just days before his death, on Wednesday 16 November 1960, Gable gave credence to this by remarking, 'She might have arrived late at the studio sometimes but when Marilyn was there, she was *really* there. Other actresses can arrive early and *never ever* be there.' For another, despite being regarded as the fittest man on *The Misfits* set, Clark was in poor health during the making of the movie. His intake of three packs of cigarettes a day, while filming in the scorching, flat Nevada desert, obviously did not help his well-being.

Furthermore, the blame game actually stalked several other paths. American gossip columnist Hedda Hopper, believing the claim that Clark had over-asserted himself in stunts involving wild horses during the filming, placed Gable's death squarely on the shoulders of the film's director, John Huston. (Marilyn herself soon took issue with this, and quickly informed Hopper that Gable only did the things in scenes in which his face was shown and that a stunt man did most of the other heavy work.) Other commentators would announce that they believed the actor's death was actually correlated to overwhelming grief following the death of his good friend, Hollywood actor Ward Bond, just 11 days earlier on Saturday 5 November.

Whatever the truth, Marilyn's attempts to shrug off Kay Gable's remarks failed, and suicide, by throwing herself out of her New York apartment window, was apparently contemplated. In her 1979 book, *Marilyn Monroe Confidential*, the actress's personal maid Lena Pepitone recalled, 'The window was wide open. Marilyn was standing before it with her white robe on . . . The only time she ever came near the window was to wave good night to me. This was more than strange. Both of her hands grasped the outside housing. It looked as if she might jump. I ran over and surprised Marilyn by grabbing her around the waist. She turned round and fell into my arms . . .'

Evidently, details of this recklessness were passed on to Dr Kris and, after one particularly painful counselling session between her and the actress, the psychiatrist suggested Marilyn should book herself into a health centre. The person who gave his blessing to the plan was Joe DiMaggio. Leonard Lyons of *The New York Post* reported. 'Joe DiMaggio apparently has assumed the responsibility for making the decisions about his ex-wife's welfare.' His report continued: 'DiMaggio stepped in quietly, unobtrusively and ably, the way he always moves. He heads the contingent of her advisors who will see to it that Miss Monroe receives the care and rest she needs after her recent, trying experiences both domestic and professional.'

Trusting his instincts and believing it was for a physical examination and rest, Monroe checked herself into the Payne-Whitney Psychiatric Clinic two days later under the alias 'Miss Faye Miller'.

Immediately she was led to a small, white-painted cell completely bereft of any comforts. As the room's heavy door slammed shut behind her, she realised she was not there for a sabbatical. She was being *institutionalised*. Marilyn froze when she heard the ominous snap of a lock closing tightly behind her. Kris had tricked both her and DiMaggio. The actress had been placed in the ward for the most seriously disturbed and depressed. For her, this was the worst fear of her life come true. She had been imprisoned like her mother in a mental asylum.

For four long, excruciatingly distressing days, while most of Broadway and Hollywood thought she was away, studying acting and readying herself for her role in the television drama *Rain*, Marilyn found herself locked away from the world, holed up in two different poky cement block cells completely devoid of lights and buzzers to summon a nurse. She was totally alone. When the sunlight filtered into her first room, the only objects on which Marilyn could gaze were the barred windows, the doorless entrance to her toilet, the scrawling on the walls left by its previous occupants and the door's glass panes, through which the nurses could glance.

Later, when darkness set in, she distracted herself from the mind-numbing blackness and the incessant screams of her fellow inmates by pounding her fists against the cell's rock-hard door until her fists were raw. When Monroe's screams of protest and demands to be released went unheeded, she picked up the chair in her cell and smashed it against the pane of glass in her locked bathroom. 'It was hard to do,' she admitted. 'I had never broken anything in my life.' Marilyn grabbed a small fragment, placed it in the palm of her hand and walked over and sat on her bed waiting for the nurses to arrive, which they did within moments.

The actress was threatened with restraint. 'If you're going to treat me like a nut, I'll act like a nut,' Marilyn shouted and informed them that if they didn't release her, she would harm herself. As she tellingly revealed in a letter of March 1961 to Greenson, 'I'm an actress and would *never* intentionally mark or mar myself. I'm just that vain.'

After the incident, however, the actress was spied on continuously. It has even been erroneously claimed that she stripped off her hospital-style gown and sat naked on the cell's floor so that observers peering through the glass on her small room had something to look at. A Puerto Rican orderly employed on the sixth floor at the hospital remembered, 'Marilyn was afraid of being left alone. On Wednesday night [8 February], she went and stood before a window and took off her clothes (*sic*). Someone thought she might do harm to herself so a nurse was called and Marilyn was taken to a security ward on the ninth (*sic*) floor, where patients have less freedom and are kept under constant guard.' Marilyn recalled the transfer to another floor quite differently, later remarking, 'They asked me to go quietly and I refused to move . . . so they picked me up by all fours, two hefty men and two hefty women and carried me up to the seventh floor in the elevator. I must say, at least they had the decency to carry me face down . . . I just wept quietly all the way there.'

The actress was immediately placed in another small, decidedly poky cell. Almost at once, a rather large, menacing nurse insisted she take a bath. 'I've just had one,' she retorted. 'As soon as you change floors you have to take another bath,' the nurse informed her. But she was unrepentant. No bath. The doctor in charge of the building soon arrived and shockingly informed Marilyn, 'You're a very, very sick girl and have been a very, very sick girl for many years. How could you possibly work when you are depressed? Does it interfere with your work?' The actress was aghast at his line of questioning and angrily fired back, 'Don't you think that perhaps Greta Garbo and Charlie Chaplin and perhaps Ingrid Bergman have been depressed when they worked sometimes? It's like saying a ball-player like [Joe] DiMaggio, could he hit the ball when he was depressed? How *silly*.'

Hours after Marilyn's arrival on 7 February, naturally desperate to escape the hell-hole she found herself in, a concerned nurse at the centre had handed her a notepad and agreed to smuggle out a message to Lee and Paula Strasberg. The couple received this pitiful handwritten note the following day. It read:

Dear Lee and Paula,
    Dr. Kris has put me in the hospital under the care of two <u>idiot</u> doctors. They <u>both should not be my doctors.</u> You haven't heard from me because I'm locked up with these poor nutty people. I'm <u>sure</u> to end up a nut too if I stay in this nightmare. Please help me Lee. This is the <u>last</u> place I should be. Maybe if you called Dr. Kris and assured her of my sensitivity and that I must get back to class so I'll be better prepared for 'Rain'.
    Please help me – if Dr. Kris assures you I am alright – you can assure her <u>I am not</u>. I do not belong here!
I love you both.
Marilyn

P.S. forgive the spelling – and there's nothing to write on here. I'm on the dangerous floor. It's like a cell. Can you imagine – cement blocks. They put me in here because they <u>lied</u> to me about calling my doctor and Joe [DiMaggio] and they had my bathroom door locked and I couldn't get their key to get into it, so I broke the glass. But outside of that I haven't done anything that is uncooperative.

Unfortunately, the Strasbergs, merely being friends of Marilyn, were powerless (or had no desire) to help. One day later, on Thursday 9 February, news of the actress's stay in hospital reached the majority of the national newspapers. The piece in the *Daily News* even went as far as to reveal the alias which the actress had used when she booked herself in. Unsurprisingly, the announcement managed to attract an avalanche of newspaper reporters and photographers to the hospital.

An unidentified close friend of Monroe's seen entering the hospital played down the situation by remarking to a *New York Post* reporter, 'Marilyn's entrance into the hospital means she has retired for a short rest. As for any special significance, this is none. Marilyn is prone into going into hospitals as a way of getting out of environment and escaping any conflict. She would go to a hospital the way another person might visit a doctor.' Another individual making light of the matter was Ann Marlowe, the executive producer of Monroe's planned television drama, *Rain*. Having cut short her Caribbean vacation to see the actress, she was quoted as saying as she entered the hospital, 'The play will be video-taped as scheduled next month . . . Marilyn's simply fatigued, just like she was in California when she was filming her picture, *The Misfits*. She went into the hospital for a rest this time. A hospital is the only place to get a real rest.' On the steps outside, Marlowe added, 'I have been in touch with the star and she will sign the contract for *Rain* as scheduled. All I can say is that she's going to do it. She's very eager to. This may postpone rehearsals a week, but that's all.'

When quizzed about Marilyn's condition, the actress's press agent, John Springer, proceeded to bumble and fluster his way through a sequence of inconclusive, ill-informed answers. At first he confessed his ignorance of his client's admittance to the hospital; then, after checking that she *had* in fact been admitted, decided to deny that the hospital specialised in dealing with psychiatric cases. His third statement was even more absurd, announcing that the actress had been admitted to ease her persistent cough. His fourth was both humorous and honest. 'I have no idea what's wrong with her,' he confessed.

Preposterous stories about Marilyn and the hospital didn't just originate from her unwitting press agent. Other stories broke which said that the actress had been a patient at the hospital since Tuesday 5 December and, far from being confined to her small room, she had been bestowed with the privilege of being allowed to 'periodically leave the building on a pass' and had been seen out about on dates with Joe DiMaggio and *The Misfits'* actor Montgomery Clift.

Journalists gathered in the Payne-Whitney's lobby were now frantic for the truth. However, their endeavours for veracity were continually thwarted by the hospital's tight-lipped officials. 'Is she under restraint?' asked one reporter. 'Is she coherent?' enquired another. But no answer was forthcoming. Nonetheless one shrewd reporter, Chiari Pisani, the American correspondent for the Italian magazine *Gente*, managed to accomplish what no other reporter was able to do. By contacting a staff doctor friend at the hospital and asking him to call one of the psychiatrists at the clinic familiar with Monroe's case, she was able to pierce the hospital's extremely tight barriers around the actress.

While Pisani eavesdropped intently, the friend asked the Payne-Whitney medic, 'Has Marilyn inherited her mother's mental condition, schizophrenia?' Without any hesitation, the doctor clarified there were no symptoms. In her subsequent *Gente* column, Pisani reiterated this – 'Schizophrenia is not a sickness you can inherit like epilepsy' – and neatly summed up Monroe's stay in the hospital by adding, 'Marilyn does not have any mental problems. She is only psychiatrically disconnected in an acute way because she works too hard, two movies in one year and the recent third divorce.'

These revealing disclosures of course meant little to Marilyn, whose heart-rending pleas for assistance to escape her psychological tormentors were finally answered on Friday 10 February, when Joe DiMaggio appeared at the hospital. The actress had used her one permitted phone call to contact her former husband, who was in Fort Lauderdale at his Yankee Clipper Motel. After listening to tales of her torment, and realising that he was the one who had given his blessing to her admission, he assured Marilyn he would fly to New York immediately and do everything he could to release her.

When he reached Payne-Whitney's reception desk early on Friday morning, he was in no mood for small talk. 'I want my wife,' he demanded aggressively. No one had the courage to point out to him that he and Marilyn were no longer legally married and that they had been separated for almost seven years. Instead, they tried telling him that they had no authority to release Miss Monroe to him or to anyone else. But DiMaggio was insistent. 'If you do not release her to me,' he warned, 'I will take this place apart, brick by brick, piece of wood by piece of wood.'

Suddenly, following a hasty telephone discussion with Dr Kris, the

Payne-Whitney staff were informed by the hospital's hierarchy that Monroe was indeed free to leave. It seemed that DiMaggio's influential contacts had yanked the correct strings. (Assertions by Monroe biographer Donald Spoto that, at this point in time, she and the baseball legend 'had not met for almost six years', are completely inaccurate.) Just before she left the building, the actress looked across at the doctors and told them they should get their *own* heads examined.

And so, at five o'clock on Friday evening, when the majority of the waiting press hounds had seemingly gone home for the night, Joe began the daunting process of transferring his former wife from one hospital to another. However, their attempts to flee the building were hampered by two ever-vigilant members of the American paparazzi. *Journal-American* photographer John Dolan hid himself in the hospital's back entrance, while reporter James Clarity held position in the hospital's lobby. His persistent patrolling of the foyer was enough to hinder DiMaggio in his attempt to abscond. When the baseball legend caught sight of the reporter patiently patrolling his patch, he immediately turned on his tracks, returned inside and was forced to flee in a freshly hailed taxi.

Following Joe's tip-off, an emotionally distraught Marilyn was forced to escape from the hospital through a maze of underground tunnels to another exit. This in turn led to a parking lot to where a limousine was waiting, motor running, to whisk her to her next destination, the New York Central Park West home of Lee and Paula Strasberg. Their daughter Susan recalled Monroe's visit that day. 'I saw her face just after she had been released from that New York mental clinic. There was an expression of amazement on her face as she talked. She said, "I was always afraid I was crazy like my mother but when I got in that psycho ward I realised *they* were really insane and I just had a lot of problems."'

Following her brief meeting with the Strasbergs, Marilyn travelled on to the far less intimidating Neurological Institute of New York, at Fort Washington Avenue and West 168th Street. There, for the next 22 days, she rested in a private room to which her maid Lena Pepitone would regularly drop in soup, pasta, chocolate pudding and a fresh nightgown, and which DiMaggio would visit daily and decorate with fresh red roses.

Following her hasty departure from Payne-Whitney, the waiting paparazzi were left completely in the dark as to Monroe's next destination. Innumerable phone calls to all the nearby hospitals and clinics were made by the news-hungry media. However, their attempts to find news of the actress's current whereabouts were thoroughly fruitless. For the first time in many years, Marilyn had, albeit temporarily, successfully managed to evade the nation's reporters. For 19 long hours, the whereabouts of the world's most famous film star were completely shrouded in secrecy.

The ambiguity finally concluded at midday on Saturday 11 February, when a Columbia Medical Center spokesman announced that Marilyn had indeed been admitted there. In an exercise of damage limitation, a now fully clued-up John Springer moved swiftly to announce that 'Miss Monroe was in the hospital for a complete psychical checkup. She is feeling well and is expected that her stay will not be prolonged.' DiMaggio, along with Lee and Paula Strasberg, visited the actress on Sunday 12 February. With a large bunch of flowers resting firmly in his arms, DiMaggio forcibly informed reporters camped outside the building that the 'exaggerated reports' of her illness had 'distressed' her, adding, 'She is suffering from nothing more than exhaustion following completion of two movies.'

Marilyn's time at the hospital was indeed restful but it was also costly. Surviving hospital bills show that, on Thursday 23 February, the costs of a hired television, round-the-clock nurse and telephone calls to California came to a total of $1,113.38. Thanks to DiMaggio's dinner and even more calls to Los Angeles, her bill the following day increased to $1,466.00.

Friends naturally rallied round. On Monday 27 February, the actress received a most uplifting telegram from Marlon Brando. In full it read, 'Dear Marilyn, The best reappraisals are borne in the worst crisis. It has happened to all of us in relative degrees. Be glad for it and don't be afraid of being afraid. It can only help. Relax and enjoy it. I send you my thoughts and my warmest affections. Marlon.'

On Wednesday 1 March, Marilyn handwrote a despondent letter to her doctor, Ralph Greenson. It began, 'Just now when I looked out of the hospital window, where the snow had covered everything, suddenly everything is kind of a muted green. The grass, evergreen bushes – though the trees give me a little hope – the desolate bare branches promising maybe there will be spring and maybe they promise hope.' The letter also displayed her anxieties, announcing that the previous night she was 'awake all night again', adding she sometimes wondered 'what the night time is for. It almost doesn't exist for me – it all seems like one long, long horrible day for me.'

Those observing Joe DiMaggio's rescue of Marilyn from the Payne-Whitney hospital could not help but notice the depth of the love between them. Marilyn could always call, lean and depend on him. As she told a journalist in 1962, 'To know that Joe is there is like having a life guard.'

But all was not well with the actress. Norman Rosten, a close friend of Marilyn's, was another caller to the hospital. He noticed something quite significant. 'During one of our visits,' he recalled, 'my wife and I found her lying pale and distracted on the upraised bed . . . she was ill, not only of the body and mind, but of the soul, the innermost engine of desire. That light was missing from her eyes.'

In truth, the unfortunate events at Payne-Whitney would haunt Monroe for the remainder of her short life. She believed that if Joe had not rescued her from the clinic when he did, she would have perished. Furthermore, Dr Marianne Kris soon realised that the incident was a serious error on her part as a psychoanalyst. Having once thought of her as a close friend, Marilyn now saw Kris as a betrayer and, following a heated confrontation between the pair, fired her soon after her release.

On Sunday 5 March, after 23 relaxing days in Room 719, Marilyn was discharged from the Columbia Presbyterian Center. The ever dependable but discreet DiMaggio was present to help her prepare for her release – although, with anger still running through her blood about what had happened, he was not her original choice. He was only summoned because Arthur Miller had flatly rejected her request to come.

As it transpired, Monroe and DiMaggio's reunion did not end there. He would continue to fill the void left in her existence by Arthur Miller's departure for the remainder of the actress's life.

So was Marilyn's month-long stay in two New York hospitals really precipitated by her inconsolable guilt following Clark Gable's death? Like everyone in the movie industry, she was, of course, upset, but in truth they were hardly close. Furthermore, Marilyn, an emotionally battered woman, weaned on rejection and cruelty in her adolescent years, knew how to ride life's punches. If not Gable's death, what then had troubled Monroe's mind enough to force her doctor's hand into booking her into a psychiatric hospital? Was it her recent divorce from Arthur Miller? That is doubtful. Their marriage was dead many months before their separation became absolute and Marilyn, conjugally hardened by this point, recovered speedily from her latest marital blow.

What then so disturbed the inner peace of Tinseltown's greatest star? My belief is that beauty-obsessed Marilyn had started to wake up to the fact that she was maturing, and the thought that she was no longer a desirable young starlet greatly distressed her. Of course, even by Hollywood standards, at the age of 34 Marilyn was not assumed to be past her prime. She was still young in comparison with many of Tinseltown's finest contemporary stars. But Marilyn Monroe was no ordinary star. Described by millions as 'the girl with the most desirable, childlike beauty in the world' and 'the sex symbol of the age', she knew that, at some point, her time as the globe's leading sex-bomb would pass and her shelf life would expire. However, unlike contemporary blonde sex-sirens such as Jayne Mansfield, Mamie Van Doren and the British star Diana Dors, she was not about to lose her crown and stature without a fight.

In fact, as long ago as Friday 3 October 1952, Marilyn had given an exclusive interview to Lydia Lane for her weekly 'Hollywood Beauty' newspaper column. In a piece entitled 'Marilyn Monroe's Big Secret: She Enjoys Being A Woman', aside from speaking about the movie *Don't Bother To Knock*, her make-up tips and how a woman can make herself more attractive to men, she spoke excitedly about her first publication. At a cost of just 5 cents (and a stamped, self-addressed envelope), it focused on her strenuous yoga and exercise regimes and showed ways in which a woman could streamline her legs and ankles, correct the flabby undersides of her upper arms and firm and uplift her breasts. Available only from the *Oakland Tribune* newspaper, it became the very first star-endorsed keep-fit workout-cum-beauty book. Thirty years before Jane Fonda published her own best-selling celebrity workout, Marilyn was already endorsing keep-fit publications, dabbling in yoga, training at the gym and sprinting through the streets and alleyways of Hollywood before breakfast.

Now, nine years on, the fear that she might be losing her greatest assets, her heavenly body and breathtaking good looks, naturally horrified her. As she once remarked, her beauty was 'something God gave me'. Marilyn's diminishing glamour had first been spotted in January 1960, at the start of the shooting of *Let's Make Love*. Studio technicians noticed that she had piled on a little excess weight, although she remained keen to display for the cameras her generous, God-given curves.

Immensely proud of her public appearance, she was accompanied everywhere she went by a wide range of lotions, potions, skin applicants, paints, powders and hormone creams. Enhancing her beauty was the best way to give meaning to her life. She knew she was a sexpot and rejoiced in the fact, but she knew, deep down, as time moved on, that every glance in the mirror would bring with it an opportunity to spot yet another recently arrived wrinkle and the ghost of another bulge. In Marilyn's paranoiac eyes at the end of 1960, she had started to see her body sag, her beauty and the lines of her young woman's body disappear; in turn, she began to sense that her career was hurriedly heading towards a brick wall. She also began to feel insignificant. Fear and confusion set in and, when the malevolent accusations about Clark Gable's death appeared in the papers, her psychological problems intensified. She believed the only way to escape her emotional turmoil was suicide.

Monroe wasn't the first to consider such madness. While she was saved, others were not. Stars such as Lupe Velez (1944), Carole Landis (1948) and George Reeves (1959) had all managed to do away with themselves simply because they felt their careers had either ended or were in decline. 'I know how Lupe Velez felt. You fight just so long and then you begin to worry about being washed up. You fear there's one way to go and that's down . . . I have no intention of ending my career in a rooming house, with full scrapbooks and an empty stomach,' said Landis just four years before her *own* suicide. Swedish-born Inger Stevens was another casualty. She overdosed on barbiturates in 1970. Curiously, her doctor was one Ralph Greenson.

With regard to the incident at Payne-Whitney, a most invaluable insider to the unfolding events in Monroe's life was Donald Zec, the long-running show business columnist of the *Daily Mirror* and a long-time friend of the actress. In his 1961 piece about Marilyn's admission to the clinic, he wrote:

> In a New York hospital, the best-known and one of the most mixed-up beauties was facing up to a harrowing problem – the problem of being Marilyn Monroe. She is restless, nervous, anxious and ill at ease. So what is driving this highly vulnerable blonde, once called a 'humming-bird made of iron' to a psychiatric couch? My guess, after some years of studying and talking with this tragic beauty, is that she is waking up to the fact that she is thirty-four years old . . .

Chapter Three

Friday 17 November 1961– April (second week) 1962

With the unpleasantness surrounding her operation, and with the problems surrounding *Something's Got To Give* continuing to mount, Marilyn naturally steered clear of any new assignments. However, there was an exception. During the evening of Friday 17 November 1961, with time on her hands following the delay of her latest movie, the actress participated in a photo shoot with 27-year-old, Hollywood-based freelance photographer Douglas Kirkland, who was preparing a special 25th birthday issue of *Look* magazine. He had already photographed contemporary actresses such as Elizabeth Taylor, Judy Garland and Shirley MacLaine, but the one star he really wanted to capture in stills' form was Marilyn Monroe.

The setting for the shoot was the John Engstead Studios on Santa Monica Boulevard, West Hollywood. Accompanied by her publicist, Pat Newcomb, the actress was characteristically late. Set to appear at 6.30pm, she arrived at approximately 9.30. Marilyn soon requested that she and the photographer were left to do the shoot alone. In advance of the session, she had requested two items: chilled bottles of vintage Dom Perignon and a selection of Frank Sinatra's records. 'When she arrived at the studio for the photo session,' Kirkland admitted, 'I felt I'd been hit by a lightning bolt. She didn't walk. She floated in slow motion . . . When I first approached her and met her for the first time, I expected this giant superstar but she wasn't like that. She was quite the contrary.'

Kirkland took some of his pictures from his studio's balcony, on which he draped himself so he could point his camera directly down at a naked Monroe, who was sprawled across a bed with just a pillow and a loosely draped white silk sheet for company. 'Here I was, this young kid from a tiny town called Fort Erie in Ontario, Canada, a town of 7,000 people. That's me. That's who I really am and here I am with this sex-goddess of the world, dropping everything off in front of me.

'At one point,' he recalled, 'she looked up and said, "Why don't you come down here with me?" I got the pictures and I won't claim there was anything between us other than the pictures. But a moment of truth for me, as a photographer, was I going to shoot or go down into the bed with her? I got the picture.'

Kirkland hastily developed the photographs and showed them to Marilyn the following day. She was, in his words, 'dark and depressed and at first unimpressed with the images, until finally she fell in love with them'. The actress shredded the pictures she did not like in front of him. Summing up, Kirkland admitted, 'This was not your average movie star. This was not just your average human being . . . She almost wasn't human.'

In November 1961, following six months of intermittent, in-depth analysis, Ralph Greenson decided that it was the right time to resurrect the idea that it would be psychologically beneficial for Marilyn to live in a home of her own. The suggestion was emblematic of how Greenson, in recent months, had started giving Monroe counselling far beyond the realms of his profession. Advice on the kind of men she should date, the type of movies she should star in and the friends she should keep filled most of his conversational time with the actress. Keeping up with her every thought and word soon became an obsession for him.

Unlawful eavesdropping was his next step. To keep a close eye on Marilyn's day-to-day activities, Greenson appointed a live-in companion for her, a 59-year-old woman by the name of Eunice Murray. Dr Greenson and his fellow psychiatrists had previously employed Murray as a support worker for some of their most prestigious clients. Originally only intending to spend three days a week with the actress, Murray would usually end up devoting five, although she never let on to the actress that she had been employed since 1951 as a psychiatric nurse. Marilyn apparently grew to like her. Pat Newcomb did not, however, and did her utmost to stay out of her way. She did not trust her. Perhaps Marilyn did not either, often decorously referring to Eunice as 'Mrs Murray'. After a few months, however, her initial $60-a-week wage was welcomingly raised to $200. (Between Monday 1 January and Monday 11 June 1962, Marilyn would pay her a total of $3,860.)

To outsiders, Murray's role was that of a friend, confidante and assistant in the actress's everyday life, which included chauffeuring her to her various engagements (most importantly to and from Greenson's nearby home at 902 Franklin Street), seamstress work, receiving visitors, answering the phone, cleaning the house and filling the cupboards and refrigerator with food.

The latter was a task in which she failed miserably. As a close friend of the actress remarked in 1962 to journalist Dorothy Kilgallen, 'Marilyn wasn't being looked after. She was one of the most valuable properties in show business; she had press agents, doctors, hairdressers and a house-keeper. Yet when Marilyn wanted to cook a steak in her *own* house, she found there were *no* steak and *no* food at all! There was champagne, though. Marilyn had liquor and pills, but *nothing* to eat.' Marilyn indeed often remarked to guests visiting her home that she had no food to offer them. For want of a better word, Eunice Murray's primary role in Marilyn's home was that of a spy.

'I didn't like being called Marilyn's housekeeper,' Murray admitted to reporters years after the actress's death. 'I guess there's no word in the dictionary to exactly describe what I was. I was her chauffeur, her cook, her real estate agent, her social secretary.' Privately, Eunice would tell people she was Marilyn's 'friend. She absolutely trusted me.' Greenson believed that Eunice, in whom the nesting and family instincts were strong, would strengthen that side of Marilyn, relieving her of her obsessions and guilts about her failing career and unsuccessful marriages. Murray scrutinised Monroe's every activity and mood and reported the results back to Greenson on a daily basis. He would then use this information during his next consultation with Marilyn and administer suitable advice.

It was his counselling that she should buy a property of her own that excited Marilyn the most, and she was keen to act upon it. Greenson believed the house would fill the void left by a baby or husband. In mid-December, following guidelines set by the actress, who specified that it should be 'little and quiet', 'overlook the ocean' and 'resemble the house occupied by Dr Greenson', Eunice set about searching for Marilyn's dream property. Marilyn soon changed her mind about it overlooking the ocean and swiftly turned down Murray's first suggestions on the grounds that they were not secluded enough.

In the second week of January 1962, after four weeks of frantic rummaging and following a tip-off from a local real estate agent, Eunice viewed another property. Sensing this one had more potential than the others, she made a request for a private tour. When she left it, feeling certain she had just found Marilyn's ideal home, she excitedly rushed to tell the actress, who elatedly demanded to see it at once. Situated among a tangle of avenues, drives and boulevards, it stood just a mile from the Greenson residence.

Built in 1932, the 2,300 square foot (extremely modest by Hollywood standards), L-shaped building with three bedrooms at 12305 Fifth Helena Drive in the fashionable suburb of Brentwood stood at the end of a cul-de-sac in a green forest of similar cul-de-sacs near San Vicente Boulevard and Carmelina Avenue. The single-storey, Mexican-style structure with interior stucco and exterior adobe walls came complete with a red-tiled roof, wrought-iron grilles on the windows, cathedral beam ceilings, tiled fireplaces in both the living room and master bedroom, a garage, lush gardens, a detached guest house and a modest-sized, oval-shaped swimming pool, and was shielded by a high brick wall and a clutch of eucalyptus trees. Unsurprisingly, there were no distinguishing features other than the tiles featuring a coat of arms which sat at the building's entrance; this prophetically read 'Cursum Perficio', a translation from the original Greek of a New Testament verse which, in translation, can mean either 'I complete the course', 'I'm completing my journey' or 'My journey ends here'. Most pleasing for Marilyn, the building was just a ten-minute drive away from the studios at 20th Century-Fox.

Reached only via a winding lane that did not even bear a street sign, the building was almost completely concealed from the outside world. Unsurprisingly, this was what Monroe wanted. For her, the house was love at first sight. On Wednesday 10 January, Marilyn called Joe DiMaggio in San Francisco requesting him to come and view the property. A day later, after a lengthy once-over, he delivered the news she wanted to hear: he liked it too.

Later that evening, back at her North Doheny Drive apartment, Marilyn rang Milton Rudin, told him she wanted to purchase the house and instructed him to set the wheels in motion about obtaining it. On the morning of Friday 12 January, Rudin rang the agent and made a formal offer for the property of $52,500. This initial proposal was declined; however, her second, for $57,500, was not. Later that day, with the sum hastily agreed upon, Rudin drafted a letter to Alfred Hart of the City National Bank of Beverly Hills, on Roxbury and Wilshire Boulevard, requesting a mortgage for the actress through their real estate loan department. As he noted, 'Marilyn is quite anxious to buy this property.'

'I didn't want a house in Beverly Hills,' she remarked later in the year, 'and I didn't want a movie star's palace. I just wanted a small house for me and my friends.' A plan to turn the garage into an apartment, in which her friends could stay, was quickly formulated. But, contrary to what we've been led to believe in the past, she only intended to live in the property while she was working. She regarded her apartment in Manhattan as her real home. In between her Hollywood duties, the actress planned to simply shut the property down and return to New York. 'She bought the house as a place she could close up when she wasn't working,' Ralph Roberts confirmed in 1972. 'She had to work out there [in Los Angeles]. She needed the money.'

Due to some unwise spending and a downturn at the box office, Marilyn was astonished to discover that, once again, she was strapped for cash and had insufficient money available to put down a deposit on the property. (On Wednesday 3 January 1962, her New York Bowery Savings Bank book boasted just $596.77.) 'I don't know where the hell my money goes,' Marilyn once remarked to fellow screen actress Jane Russell. 'I never seem to have anything. The more I make, the less I have . . . I'm coming out worse than when I was modelling.' The simple truth was that, throughout her short life, her income was severely hampered by woeful business advice, the highest tax rates and an unruly assortment of landlords, friends, charities, hairdressers, make-up men, secretaries, housekeepers, decorators, drama coaches, physicians, psychiatrists, attorneys and accountants. Hollywood auditor Jack M. Ostrow, the former treasurer of actor Burt Lancaster's independent production company, Norma Productions, was clearly struggling to keep up with the actress's activities and evidently failing to earn the colossal $2,500-a-year wages she was paying him.

It has regularly been repeated, as printed in *Life* magazine for August 1962, that the house on Fifth Helena cost the actress $77,500, and that, with DiMaggio's help, she had paid a $42,500 deposit. In fact, the property had been put up for sale by Mr and Mrs Pagen for $69,000. Following a discussion with Rudin about the building's leaky roof, the actress came in with her first offer, a rather low $52,500. This was naturally declined by the couple. However, her second offer of $57,500, still $11,500 below the asking price, was not. A deposit of only $5,750 ($5,000 of DiMaggio's money, $750 of Marilyn's) was duly paid on Monday 29 January and the sale was completed by Thursday 8 February, the day she started moving in. The repayments of her 15 year 6 month mortgage, at 6.5 per cent interest, were scheduled to begin on Sunday 1 April. (However, the $320-a-month payment plan soon became a problem for her. In late June, just three months after the mortgage had started, the bank was forced into drawing up a new disbursement schedule for her.)

Before she signed the contract for the property, Marilyn walked into the dressing room of her North Doheny Drive apartment, sat down and burst into tears. She did not know for sure why. 'It was just I could never imagine buying a house alone,' she later theorised. 'But I've always been alone, so why couldn't I imagine it?' In a letter sent to her former father-in-law, Isidore Miller, Marilyn described her new home as 'little . . . with a big swimming pool,' adding, 'the neighbourhood is quiet and yet it is close to shopping areas.' The impressive Brentwood Country Mart, with its shops and stalls arranged around a central courtyard, was just a short drive away.

Even though she had now officially acquired the Brentwood bungalow, she unsurprisingly decided to retain both her apartment in New York and, for the opening few months of 1962 at least, the one in Los Angeles. (Just prior to purchasing the Fifth Helena property Monroe had spent all her spare money – $25,000 – on having her North Doheny Drive apartment redecorated and newly furnished. However, the work was halted when she witnessed the mess that the decorator was creating. The trauma made Marilyn ill and she suspended the project. Citing loss of earnings, the decorator sued her for several thousand dollars, although the case was eventually dropped.) Monroe undertook the lengthy journey between her Los Angeles homes many times during the opening months of 1962.

One such excursion took place during the third week of January, and involved a number of visits to the Beverly Hills Hotel. First, unhappy with the projects Fox were offering her, Marilyn had arranged a lunchtime meet with her publicist, Arthur P. Jacobs. The setting was the hotel's very expensive but comfortable Polo Lounge, a place fabled as 'the only real watering hole in town where deals can make a man or woman a millionaire overnight'.

'She was unhappy with a couple of properties that Fox had offered her,' Jacobs recalled in 1963, 'so she asked me why I didn't find a project and produce it. She even offered to sign a deal splitting the production 50/50 with me.' Nothing was in mind until one of his other clients, entertainer Gene Kelly, handed Jacobs a script he had been working on. Jacobs read it, saw it as a vehicle for Monroe and called Kelly. They immediately began discussing a deal. 'Marilyn flipped over the story and said she wanted to do it,' Jacobs remembered. 'But then Gene got tied up for a year in his [ABC] television series, *Going My Way*.'

The second occasion for her visit to the hotel was to meet *Redbook* columnist Alan Levy. The women's magazine had always been a great favourite of Marilyn's and, ten years after she first appeared in it, she finally assented to a lengthy interview. Sporting a purple dress with matching scarf, an outfit she described as her 'purple people eater wardrobe', she was interviewed one evening in the building's dining room. During the six-hour session, she spoke openly about her marriages, her struggle for self-understanding and her hopes for her future. She also revealingly informed Levy that she stood 5ft 6in in her stockinged feet, weighed less than 120 pounds, wore size 8 slacks, but had lost nothing on top. 'I'm not only proud of my firm bosom,' she philosophically announced, 'but I'm going to be proud of my firm character.' With exhaustion beginning to set in, the interview soon ended. But before they parted, Marilyn agreed to conclude it some time in the not-too-distant future.

Monroe visited the Beverly Hills Hotel for a third time to catch up with her friend Esther 'Eppie' Pauline Friedman Lederer, otherwise known as US advice columnist Ann R. Landers. And she made her fourth visit to meet an old Hollywood hand, Nunnally Johnson, the sixth scriptwriter employed on *Something's Got To Give*. (For a fee of $125,000, his work on the production had commenced on Wednesday 24 January.)

Since May 1961, numerous scripts for the film had been written and systematically rejected, and Johnson had been desperately summoned by Fox to produce what everyone hoped would be the final, Monroe-tailored version. She had worked with Johnson on the hit 1953 film comedy *How to Marry a Millionaire* and trusted his work. In time, they would grow to enjoy each other's company immensely, but their first meetings had been less than gratifying.

'Working with Marilyn Monroe was a disturbing experience,' Johnson recalled in 1961 of that earlier encounter. 'I used to be sympathetic with actresses and their problems. But Marilyn made me lose all sympathy for actresses. She doesn't take the trouble to do her homework. In most of her takes, she was either fluffing her lines or freezing. She didn't bother to learn her lines and if it hadn't been for Natasha Lytess [Monroe's former acting coach] she wouldn't have been able to learn *any* lines. I didn't think she could act her way out of a paper bag. She's got no charm, delicacy or taste. She's just an arrogant little tail-switcher. She's learned to throw sex in your face.'

After a while, however, a firm friendship was formed and in early 1962, the chance to work together again materialised. 'This job came out of the blue,' Johnson recalled at the time. 'I happened to be in New York in January and they [Fox] were getting *desperate*. They asked me to try my hand on a rush job.' He was correct. Since the studio were anxious to get the shooting of *Something's Got To Give* under way at the earliest opportunity, and with each of the five preceding writers employed on the movie failing miserably in their task, it was now of the utmost importance that Johnson should complete a script as soon as possible and – even though she had no legal obligation to do this – obtain approval of it from Marilyn.

Several times during the early part of the year, the actress had circuitously gone public about her dissatisfaction with the standard of screenplays she had received. On Monday 8 January, reporter Sheilah Graham was used as the actress's mouthpiece when, in her column for the *Stars and Stripes* newspaper, she forthrightly declared, 'Marilyn Monroe is right in wanting a good script for *Something's Got To Give*. Until she does,

Marilyn isn't giving her assurance that she will make the film.' A week later, on Monday 15 January, the Associated Press's movie and television writer, Bob Thomas, reiterated Marilyn's displeasure in his column. 'Concerning *Something's Got To Give*,' he wrote, 'it may be Marilyn Monroe who isn't satisfied with the script.'

In an attempt to appease their clearly troubled star, Fox counteracted by releasing a short statement of their own, which read: 'Director George Cukor says Marilyn Monroe doesn't have to wig-wag her derriere in *Something's Got To Give* because the role can be sexy without it.' On Wednesday 24 January, the actress informed Fox she still did not care for the script and would only shoot the movie if her demands for another writer were met.

Three bottles of champagne were consumed by the pair during their latest three-hour seminar, which again took place in the hotel's legendary Polo Lounge. In sharp contrast to the long-held belief that she was always late for her appointments, Johnson announced in amazement, 'I arrived (script in hand) 15 minutes early and surprisingly Marilyn was *already* there. She's just as likely to be too early as too late.'

When discussions about the movie finally got under way, he was equally amazed to discover that the actress was still unconvinced about it, particularly its old-fashioned storyline. She also doubted her own judgement, feeling that she'd made too many dubious mistakes in the past and could no longer reliably trust her instincts. Johnson recalled, 'I outlined the situations in the script to see how she responded. I think she liked it.' Marilyn was especially partial to the sequence where she was set to perform a Hawaiian hula-hula dance. The thought of location work at the Navy Station in San Diego, where her submarine rescue scene was due to be filmed, also appealed to her.

Before their meeting concluded, Johnson handed the actress the latest copy of the screenplay and instructed her to be uninhibited about any changes she wanted to make. As a guide, he told her that whenever she read something that was out of character, she should mark the sequence with a cross and whenever she read a line that wasn't funny enough, she should mark it with a double cross.

Unfortunately, the process of administering these revisions was an extremely arduous one. After Marilyn had read Johnson's latest rendering, she would post her cross-filled copy back to him at his flat in London's Grosvenor Square. Once he received it, he would administer her changes and accommodate them into his own. Afterwards, he would painstakingly send the newly revised script, page by page, back to her in Los Angeles for her approval. Once she had given her endorsement to the latest modifications (usually by way of a late-night transatlantic phone call), the new, bang-up-to-date version of the *Something's Got To Give* script would be read over the phone to Fox executives back in Los Angeles.

With so much to-ing and fro-ing taking place, it was no great surprise when, on Tuesday 16 January 1962, 20th Century-Fox announced that shooting on *Something's Got To Give* had been pushed back two months to Thursday 15 March. Upon hearing this, on Saturday 20 January, Marilyn paid a hastily arranged visit to the movie's new producer, a chain-smoking, podgy young 20th Century-Fox staffer named Henry T. Weinstein, at his home in Beverly Hills. However, there was another reason for her doing so. She knew Carl Sandburg was going to be there too. Just a month after their last encounter, she was eager to see him again.

Instead of outlining fresh plans for the film, those gathered together that night, who also included Weinstein's wife Irena, spent most of their time sipping champagne and Martinis while playing mimic games and dancing the conga. To help with Marilyn's insomnia, Sandburg even demonstrated a series of exercises which involved holding books over their heads. Once exhaustion had set in, physical activity gave way to conversation, not about *Something's Got To Give* but on personal matters. During one such private exchange, the actress took the opportunity once more to pour her heart out to the poet. He replied by curiously informing her, 'You are *not* what is wrong with America.' The actress was truly fond of him. 'He is so pleased to meet you,' she once admitted. 'He wants to know about you and you want to know about him.'

Acclaimed photojournalist and portrait snapper Arnold Newman was also present that evening, and managed to capture a fascinating photographic record of the event. Shortly before his death in June 2006, in an interview with PBS for their *American Masters* television documentary, entitled *Still Life*, he remarked, 'She [Marilyn] had already met Carl Sandburg. They were drinking champagne . . . here they were, the great poet, biographer of Lincoln, and Marilyn, talking together. Two icons talking together and I thought, "This I have got to photograph." When Marilyn spoke with Sandburg, she felt she could really pour her heart out, and she did. She was really troubled. That was a *sad* woman.'

Despite her strongest intentions to do otherwise, Marilyn was still unintentionally disrupting pre-production work on her new movie. *Something's Got To Give* had been officially announced in a blaze of glory on Tuesday 2 January by Peter Levathes. With a cast list still either un-chosen or unsigned, however, the credulous Henry T. Weinstein in the producer's chair and a screenplay Marilyn was far from satisfied with, the movie was nowhere near the starting block.

It was a dire time for Fox. Shooting at the vast lot ground to a complete halt on Friday 26 January, when filming of Jerry Wald's comedy *Mr Hobbs*

Takes a Vacation, starring James Stewart and Maureen O'Hara, concluded. With the cameras still waiting to roll on Monroe's new movie, the next shoot would not take place until Wednesday 14 February, when Irwin Allen shot a few brief, pre-production sequences for *Five Weeks in a Balloon*. The lull at 20th Century-Fox would sadly persist for the next two months.

There were problems elsewhere in Marilyn's career. On Friday 26 January, following a year of sporadic deliberation, word finally seeped out in several newspapers that the actress had turned down NBC's $100,000 offer (at that point the highest in television history) to star as torrid prostitute Sadie Thompson in the 90-minute, colour, video-taped TV adaptation of W. Somerset Maugham's *Rain*. It was actually old news. Following five months of fruitless negotiations between the actress and her representatives, and a deluge of publicity based alternately on both hopelessness and despair, the studio, in particular its president, Robert E. Kintner, had actually washed their hands of it six months earlier on Friday 28 July 1961.

The show's history was a long and expensive one. Featuring stars such as Fredric March and Florence Eldridge, and a specially adapted screenplay by Rod Serling, creator of *The Twilight Zone*, it was originally set to be NBC TV's 'big offering' in the autumn of 1961. The original choice to play Reverend Davidson in the production was Richard Burton, but he declined the role through fear of Marilyn's well-known tardiness. Producers of the play failed in their attempts to assure him he would still able to leave the set each night in time for his 8.30 curtain call at the Majestic Theatre in midtown Manhattan, where he was starring alongside Julie Andrews in the Broadway musical *Camelot*.

Marilyn had been set to sign her contract for *Rain* on Friday 10 February 1961, but was unable to do so because of her admittance to the Payne-Whitney Psychiatric Clinic just three days earlier. Despite this, NBC still worked feverishly on the project and by May had pumped some $100,000 into it: $25,000 each for the TV rights and Serling's reworking of it, and a further $50,000 split between the below-the-line scenery costs and fees for Ann Marlowe as executive producer. With Marilyn still unwell following her bouts in hospital, the studio planned to finally tie up all loose ends in the production during the weekend of 27 and 28 May. They failed. However, work continued into June.

On Thursday 15 June, just hours after flying in from Los Angeles, Marilyn welcomed Serling to her Manhattan home to discuss the project further. (He would later describe her as 'warm, friendly, beautiful but *odd*'.) In an interview carried out that month with television writer Marie Torre, he took the opportunity to air his immense dissatisfaction with the drama. 'I turned in two drafts a while ago,' he remarked, 'then sat back to await reaction. Everyone went silent.' When he contacted NBC again, he was informed Marilyn had become enamoured of the original, 1923 play version, *Rain: A Play in Three Acts* by John Colton and Clemence Randolph, and that she had been rehearsing that adaptation on her own. When he was told this, he flipped. 'If they want the old version of *Rain*, they had better get another boy,' he screamed. 'I accepted the assignment on the understanding that they wanted an updated story, something that would come out fresh. I've seen so much of the old *Rain*, I'm waterlogged. It'd be pointless for me to even bother.'

Nevertheless, production on *Rain* laboured on. On Wednesday 21 June, in preparation for her 3.30 meeting the following afternoon with NBC executives, Marilyn held an emergency, 3.15pm conference at her apartment with both Lee Strasberg and her attorney, Aaron Frosch. However, despite her and the studio's most valiant attempts to prove otherwise, the play hit the buffers on Wednesday 28 June, when the actress was rushed to New York's Polyclinic Hospital for her gall-bladder operation. Scrapping it altogether, shortly afterwards, for a multitude of reasons, then became the most obvious solution.

A fact overlooked by many previous biographers is that, by the time it was shelved, work on *Rain* was so far advanced that sponsorship with the cosmetics giant Revlon had even been arranged. The company had agreed to underwrite the show's estimated $350,000 cost. A locale for the taping of the show had even been reserved not once but twice. For four straight weeks, one of their studios in Brooklyn, New York had been earmarked for the production: the first between March and April, the second, three months later, between Saturday 1 July and Tuesday 1 August.

NBC even went so far as to pencil in when the play would make its TV debut. *Rain's* grand premiere was set to take place as a back-to-back attraction with the new, 60-minute Bob Hope comedy extravaganza, *The World Of Bob Hope* (the first in a series of specials about prominent Americans) during the evening of Sunday 29 October, giving the station an uninterrupted, peak-time, 8.30–11pm television showcase. But, despite shifting the deadlines to suit Marilyn several times (penultimately, the last week of June and finally, the concluding week of July) it came to nothing. As one NBC spokesman desolately remarked, 'It all took a great deal of time and money.'

Although no official reason for the cancellation was given, the industry's rumour mill was already in overdrive, suggesting that the actress's refutation stemmed from her drama coach, Lee Strasberg, or from her either being 'too ill' or 'too tense' to do the show. For once, the rumours were partly true. With regard to the latter, Marilyn was indeed unwell. And with regard to the former, problems had come to a head when Strasberg, in his dual role as production supervisor and 'artistic arranger', began insisting to studio bosses that he should sit in on the shooting and direct Marilyn from the sidelines. Unsurprisingly, *Rain*'s director, George Roy Hill, was against this arrangement and threatened to quit in protest. Although he failed to carry out the threat, it was the last straw.

On the public front, Monroe put on a brave face, showing she was undisturbed by this latest disappointment, but inside she was gravely saddened. In particular, she felt that she had failed *Rain*'s writer, from whom she had received a very flattering and encouraging note. 'I had a letter from Somerset Maugham [it was typed on Tuesday 31 January 1961] saying how happy he was I was going to play the part,' she recalled in an unpublished interview for *Ladies' Home Journal* magazine. 'He even told me something about the real woman on whom he based the character.'

February 1962 started with a second rare photo shoot. Since Marilyn's appearance at the premiere of *The Misfits* one year earlier, and her fleeting visits to hospital, the actress had rarely been seen in public and, aside from November's photo session for Douglas Kirkland, she had not participated in any new projects. So it came as a great shock to everyone when, in late December 1961, she agreed to take part in another photographic assignment, this time with Willy Rizzo, the influential Hollywood correspondent for French magazine *Paris Match*. Due to his already scheduled trip to Tinseltown that month and a friend who knew Marilyn's publicist, Pat Newcomb, Rizzo set his sights on the impossible. He wanted his *own* session with Monroe.

Realising his chances were slim, Rizzo and his friend concocted the angle that a cover story backed by a nice slice of positive publicity might be just what the actress needed. Amazingly it worked. Just days after submitting the request, Rizzo received a call from Newcomb saying Marilyn had agreed to be photographed. A private luxury home belonging to a friend of his in Los Angeles was immediately booked for the assignment. News that Rizzo had managed to secure a session with the semi-reclusive Monroe even reached many American papers on or around Thursday 4 January.

As planned, Rizzo arrived in the city a month later, on Tuesday 6 February. His first discussion about the shoot took place later that day. He informed Newcomb that, to take full advantage of the strong morning sunlight, he should begin the session early. The publicist had reservations about this. She knew her employer was unreliable at that time of the day, so an afternoon starting time was mutually agreed. Agreeing to a date when they could actually carry out the session became the next problem.

A date of Thursday 8 February was soon pencilled in, but after several hours of waiting on that day, Newcomb phoned Rizzo with some bad news. The actress would not be coming. She was tired and feeling unwell. (With the purchase completed and the contracts signed, Marilyn actually began moving into her new home that day.) The publicist went on to promise that she would be fit to attend the following afternoon. But, 24 hours later, the photographer once more found himself at a loose end. At 6pm, however, Monroe finally arrived: not to begin her session, but for a face-to-face apology. Suffering from fatigue after her house move, she gave him her word she would be there the following day and kissed him. His legs turned to jelly. 'For you, I would wait a week,' he affectionately informed her.

True to her word, the following afternoon, a rather tired-looking Marilyn turned up at the rented house in Los Angeles to begin her photo shoot. As Rizzo recalled, she had done her own make-up and made a bit of a 'hash of it'. On that hot afternoon of Saturday 10 February, during a four-hour session, he captured the actress in extreme close-up, perched on a sun-lounger and lying down by the edge of a swimming pool. A mixture of black and white and colour shots were taken, the best of which first saw the light of day in the Saturday 23 June edition of *Paris Match* (no. 689). 'Marilyn was immensely sad at the meeting,' Rizzo later lamented, 'and that sadness was very visible on the pictures.'

In February, beginning the next phase of her life and taking up residence in her new home was the matter of most significance to Marilyn. Although the ten-roomed Brentwood home was extremely cramped and decidedly unglamorous, its purchase was a major accomplishment for her. Eager to leave an immediate mark on the place, just hours after moving in on 8 February, she feverishly began demanding changes. Different fixtures were summoned for the small bathroom and fresh colour schemes were outlined for the walls. With the tiny kitchen decidedly short on cupboard space, cabinets were also ordered. Following a hard sell by a salesman sent from the appliance distributors Kafton Sales Company, at 1518 North Highland Avenue, Hollywood 28, Marilyn felt compelled to spend $545.60 on a modern service space and a whopping $1,393.46 on a new, custom-made kitchen area.

Her outlay at the firm was incessant. For example, on Wednesday 11 April, she paid $624 (approximately $37 more than what she should have been charged) for a large, stainless steel, top-of-the-range upright Hotpoint refrigerator, and, two weeks later, on Wednesday 25 April, she shelled out $272 for a plush stainless steel sink. 'Marilyn was just full of plans and ideas, plans about furnishing and decorating her home. She was just so proud of it,' Eunice Murray recalled. The actress soon discovered that many of the locks within the property were not working. To partly remedy this, on Thursday 15 March, Edward P. Halavati of the well-established A-1 Lock & Safe Company in Santa Monica was called.

Most importantly, in line with Monroe's craving for privacy, another change came with the number printed on one of her telephones. Instead of the real number, GR (Granite Bay) 476-1890, she arranged for digits belonging to the local West Los Angeles Police Department to be attached to the telephone she most commonly used, which was black in colour (and not pink, as is generally believed). With workmen such as electricians and builders about to descend on the property, she was well aware that her phone numbers could easily fall into the wrong hands, especially when news-hungry reporters were ready to offer vast sums of money for them. Just prior to bedtime each night, Marilyn would return this phone to its regular place in the guest cottage and, to avoid being disturbed by any late-night calls, would either cover it with pillows or simply remove the receiver from its cradle.

A white phone was attached to her second line. This, her privately used one, which very few people knew the number of, carried the digits GR 472-4830. Marilyn would keep this telephone beside her bed for her obligatory late-night calls to friends during her regular bouts of insomnia. The cord of each phone was approximately 30 feet long, so she could stroll freely around the house as she spoke.

While Marilyn occupied herself with the joys of moving house and finding ways to avoid the eagle-eyed press, pre-production work on *Something's Got To Give* was continuing frantically over at Fox. Finding a suitable male actor to play opposite Monroe was now the major problem. The eventual male lead in the movie, the Rat Pack star and crooner Dean Martin, was not the first choice. He wasn't the second, or even the fourth. He was in fact the eighth.

As with *Goodbye Charlie* several months earlier, the well-respected character actor James Garner had once again been the original choice to star opposite Marilyn. The official line was that he forced himself out of the film's reckoning by demanding $1 million to play the role. But this was an invention. The truth was that the Mirisch Company, the producers of his next movie, the war epic *The Great Escape*, feared Marilyn's legendary tardiness would prolong production of *Something's Got To Give* and force Garner to miss the start of filming of their movie, which was set to begin shooting in Munich on Wednesday 6 June 1962.

In early December 1961, Fox insiders swept aside the setback by quickly suggesting that 36-year-old Rock Hudson be offered the part. When he proved to be unavailable, the studio shifted their attentions to 37-year-old

TV veteran Steve Forrest, but Monroe was unhappy about this and the approach never came. Others tipped and approached about the role were highly rated, rugged film star Stuart Whitman and singing actor Robert Goulet, but he was unable to take the part due to his commitment to Richard Burton and the musical *Camelot*, which was still running on Broadway. Possibly out of desperation, the names of respected Hollywood stars Jack Lemmon and John Gavin were then thrown into the ring, but they were dismissed by Marilyn almost as soon as they were uttered.

The casting of Steven 'Adam' Burkett, the man with whom the actress's character has spent five years on a desert island, was also proving difficult. In mid-January, Marilyn suggested Gardner McKay, the 29-year-old star of ABC Television's highly popular children's series, *Adventures in Paradise*. Insider information reveals that Marilyn even rang the actor personally urging him to accept the offer. Director Cukor also spoke with Fox, the producers of the show, with a request for him to be given leave from their programme to appear in *Something's Got To Give*. Considering that the majority of *Adventures in Paradise*'s filming took place on the studio's own back lot, he believed this factor would also enable McKay to continue shooting his programme without any significant disruptions. Cukor was certain that they would agree to his request. They did. But McKay did *not*.

His reasons were soon forthcoming. 'The script is very funny,' he announced to the American trade papers, 'but the part they wanted me to play was just plain pathetic.' And in an interview published a year later, he revealed more about the proposition. 'They wanted me to do the old-fashioned, Randolph Scott role in the original [*My Favorite Wife*]. I figured if I had acquired any value in three years of television, I was worth more than that.' (The role would eventually be filled by 36-year-old American film and television actor Tom Tryon, a man best known for playing the Walt Disney television character Texas John Slaughter.)

Nunnally Johnson, an invaluable eyewitness to the incessant problems in getting Monroe's latest movie off the ground, remarked to the American press at the time, 'It is still all up in the air. So far they still do not have a finished script and no definite leading man. They can't do anything until Marilyn says "yes" to anything.' He concluded by saying, 'They are running around like a lot of rabbits.'

Less than a month after making these remarks, Johnson was to become another casualty of the unfolding chaos when he was fired from the movie. Already infuriated by the time the writer was taking to complete his script, director George Cukor called time on his employment when he read Johnson's (Monroe influenced) new version and noticed it had strayed too far away from the original charm of *My Favorite Wife*. In Cukor's opinion, 'The original film was now totally unrecognisable.'

Walter Bernstein was drafted in as Johnson's replacement. Cukor instructed him to rewrite entirely his predecessor's script, but in stark contrast to Cukor's directive producer Henry Weinstein told Bernstein not to make many changes to the script but just do 'a little polishing here and there'.

During one such conversation, Bernstein suggested introducing a scene whereby, when the wife (Marilyn) arrives back and finds her husband remarried, she goes off and attempts to sabotage the honeymoon. To this, Weinstein disconsolately shook his head and replied, 'Marilyn won't play it that way.' The scriptwriter naturally enquired why. 'Well,' Weinstein replied, 'she says Marilyn Monroe doesn't chase after the man. The man chases after *her*.' Bernstein then suggested that, since the actress did not have script approval, they should press ahead with the changes anyway. It was a fruitless suggestion. 'You don't understand,' Weinstein retorted. 'Marilyn doesn't need script approval. If she doesn't like something, she just doesn't show up.' Throughout the week, Weinstein would call Bernstein on a daily basis to enquire how the script changes were progressing and catechise how many pages he had rewritten.

To date, these numerous script revisions (now from *seven* different writers) had cost Fox a hefty $300,000, money they could barely afford. Between 1959 and 1962, 20th Century-Fox had lost $61 million, of which $22 million came in 1961 alone. Shareholders were aghast at these figures, and were soon threatening to depose the board and dethrone studio president Spyros P. Skouras. To make matters worse, Fox was currently haemorrhaging $150,000 on day on *Cleopatra*, an epic movie currently being shot on location in Rome. From the off, it was always intended to be the most expensive film in Hollywood history. Its star, Elizabeth Taylor, was on an extortionate $1 million salary, the highest wage of any star at the time. Originally expected to cost $5 million, however, the film's production costs had spiralled to $40 million.

Fox were also reeling from the spiralling costs of Darryl F. Zanuck's *The Longest Day*, the all-star Second World War epic about the Allied invasion of France on Tuesday 6 June 1944, which was currently being shot in CinemaScope on location in Europe. Its ten months of filming, one of the biggest and certainly one of the costliest projects since the war itself, had cost $10 million.

Fox were just one short step away from bankruptcy. Marilyn Monroe was one of the studio's last remaining bankable stars and they were desperate to milk her for every dollar they could while she was still at the peak of her popularity. So, as 1962 rolled on, despite her bravest attempts to do otherwise, Monroe knew she *had* to work on another movie for the studio, and she knew there was absolutely no legal way out of it.

Chapter Four

Marilyn and the Kennedys – The Unequivocal Truth

Saturday 23 September 1961 and beyond

For many years, the majestic Santa Monica home belonging to London-born Rat Pack actor Peter Lawford and his wife, Patricia, had been the site of many private parties and numerous all-star gatherings. And, since Patricia was the sister of both the President, John, and the Attorney General, Bobby, the Kennedys were, naturally, regular attendees.

On the evening of Thursday 1 February 1962, the coast-front building at 625 Palisades Beach Road played host to a crowd honouring Bobby on the eve of his six-day goodwill tour of Tokyo, Japan, a trip to be made on behalf of the President's 'New Frontier' programme. Hollywood luminaries such as Judy Garland, Angie Dickinson, Gene Kelly, Dean Martin, Tony Curtis and his wife Janet Leigh were in attendance, as were many respected newspaper reporters. In other words, those regarded as close or important enough to Kennedy.

Marilyn Monroe had known the Lawfords for a number of years. She and Peter had become friendly and even dated in 1953, soon after meeting in his agent's office – although, in his eyes, the thought of taking their relationship just that one step further was killed the moment he stepped into the excrement left by her small pet chihuahua at her Sunset Boulevard residence. Marilyn, too, was present at the Lawfords' house that evening; however, she was not regarded as so important. 'Sometimes I'm invited to places to kind of brighten up a dinner table,' she despondently admitted to *Life* magazine, 'like a musician who'll play the piano after dinner. I know you're not really invited for yourself. You're just an ornament.'

Lawford's home, a $95,000 purchase in 1956 from MGM magnate Louis B. Mayer, had been the setting for Marilyn's only previous encounter with Bobby Kennedy, just four months earlier on Wednesday 4 October 1961. This previous occasion had also been a party to honour the Attorney General.

As part of the Justice Department's crackdown on organised crime, Bobby was in town to talk with local law-enforcement officials about the rise in mob activity in Los Angeles. Following his brother John's favourable account of his first real meeting with Marilyn just 11 days earlier (which we will examine shortly), Bobby was keen to meet the great Hollywood star himself. The dinner was assigned as the perfect time to do it, and a request to that effect was placed through Lawford. Monroe, seeing this as the ideal occasion to quiz Bobby about why he had chosen to act against MCA, happily accepted. So excited was the Attorney General to meet her that evening that, in order to give him more time to prepare, he even cancelled that day's 1pm cabinet luncheon appointment with the Postmaster General, J. Edward Day.

Marilyn was busy composing herself too. Over at 882 North Doheny Drive, following a special, $170 hair makeover, her personal beauty expert, George Masters, was on hand to put the finishing touches. 'I did an extra-special make-up job on her,' he recalled in 1979. 'She looked like a fawn, innocent and wide-eyed. Then she brought out this dress.' It was a black, eye-catching, figure-hugging, floor-length, strapless peek-a-boo creation by American fashion designer Norman Norell. The sheer eyelet cutouts on the outfit barely covered her breasts. 'Aren't you embarrassed?' he asked. 'Of course not,' she replied. 'At least I'll be noticed.'

The actress spent so much time beautifying herself that she arrived at the party two and a half hours late. The joyous evening, moreover, ended on a low point when she practically passed out due to the amount of alcohol she had consumed and, as a result, had to be bundled into the back of Bobby's car, driven back to her apartment and carried inside by him and his aide, Edwin O. Guthman, the Pulitzer Prize-winning reporter and journalist and now the Justice Department's Chief of Information.

After ensuring she was safe and well, they shut the door behind them and left. Under his ruthless exterior, Kennedy possessed a compassionate heart. 'She asked Bobby to drive her home,' Guthman recalled to writer Maurice Zolotow in 1973. 'He asked me to go along so they wouldn't be alone. He knew damn well that there had to be gossip and he didn't want to build it up. We drove her home and helped her into the house.' It's safe to say Marilyn made a big impression on a Kennedy brother that night, but regrettably it was the unintended kind. Four months on, when the offer to meet the Attorney General came up again, she was determined to be more well-mannered.

For the sumptuous meal that evening in February 1962, Bobby strategically found himself seated between Marilyn and another top Hollywood actress, Kim Novak. Undoubtedly recalling their first infamous encounter and no doubt impressed by Marilyn's beauty, impeccable conduct, revealing dress and eye-catching horn-rimmed glasses, the Attorney General obviously took immense interest in the actress from the start and practically ignored Novak.

The gathering no doubt gave the Attorney General the perfect opportunity to learn from the actress more about Hollywood and its star system. At the time, 20th Century-Fox were planning to make a big-screen adaptation of his controversial 1960 book *The Enemy Within*, a chronicle of his investigation into the convicted (but later pardoned) American labour leader James 'Jimmy' Hoffa and the Teamsters Union while he was Chief Council for the Senate Subcommittee. But Monroe captivated him further when she began asking him a number of highly intelligent, thought-provoking questions. Eager to make amends after her previous debacle, she had spent much of the day with Henry Weinstein, producer of *Something's Got To Give*, preparing a wide-ranging set of queries, which varied from enquiries about his thoughts on the House Un-American Activities Committee to what his department was going to do about civil rights. The quizzing ended when the Attorney General caught sight of the actress peeking at the typed-out questions which she had secreted inside her handbag. He laughed at her endeavours and promised to answer Weinstein's questions personally.

The actress's famous, long-lost red diary has been an integral part of the mysteries surrounding her untimely death later that year. Many of those close to Marilyn denied that she had a diary of this sort. However, the party for Bobby Kennedy on Thursday 1 February 1962 proved conclusively that she *did* own a notebook like this and used it to jot down the answers he gave to her questions. The Associated Press's Hollywood correspondent, James Bacon, who was also in attendance that night, innocently and revealingly corroborated the fact in his column the following day. 'Listening attentively to every word he uttered,' he wrote, 'she frantically scribbled his answers in her small diary book . . . Marilyn came on like a High School reporter, asking RFK a batch of political style questions and jotting down the answers in longhand . . . Bobby was apparently delighted by Marilyn's interest in global matters.'(As Bacon himself would admit, she did this with most people, even during conversations with him.)

Hollywood and television columnist Erskine Johnson was another at the party to see at first hand the actress scribbling down Bobby's responses. So too was show business reporter Mike Connolly, who noticed that, besides taking the notes, Marilyn also scribbled a get-well message to the Kennedys' ailing father, Joseph, who was fighting the paralytic effects of a cerebral haemorrhage suffered on Tuesday 19 December 1961.

So why was she jotting down the Attorney General's replies? 'To remind herself of what was said,' explained those close to the actress. Even she was forced to remark how forgetful she often was. However, I tend to believe the theory that the diary was symbolic of something more important to her. I am certain that her handwritten scrawls – research notes if you like – were intended to form the basis of her next memoir. Her previous, largely inaccurate (and, at this point, still unfinished) biography, ghost-written by Ben Hecht, had concluded at the point when she visited Korea in February 1954, and she was keen to bring her life story up to date.

The person she eventually chose to help her do this was the photographer and writer, George Barris, the man who in June and July 1962 would take some of the actress's very last pictures. As Barris himself commented at the time, 'She said, "I'd like to set the record straight, all these lies that have been said about me."' On Wednesday 8 August 1962, the *Daily Mirror* announced, 'She had asked Barris to write her biography and to illustrate it. She had posed for him; she had talked to him for ten weeks about her past and her future . . . She talked more freely and frankly than she had ever talked to anyone before.'

Unsurprisingly, thanks to their mutual fascination, Marilyn and Bobby's hushed discussions continued throughout dinner. Once the meal had been consumed and the exchanges exhausted, they moved to the floor space assigned for dancing. Another guest at the party, Gloria Romanoff, wife of the great Los Angeles restaurateur, Michael, recalled the couple dancing to Chubby Checker's 'Let's Twist Again', which played repeatedly on Lawford's record player. As the disc spun, Marilyn took great pleasure in trying to teach Bobby the rudiments of the twist. 'She danced with Bobby several times that evening,' Edwin Guthman recalled. 'Marilyn loved dancing and was a good dancer.'

Kennedy was apparently so pleased she had attended the party that, later that evening, he excitedly phoned his father Joseph to tell him the news. Clearly an admirer of the Kennedy brothers, Monroe with equal excitement recalled that night's events to friends for several days afterwards. 'He was very nice,' she told her friend Norman Rosten, 'sort of boyish and likeable. Of course, he kept looking down my dress. But I'm used to that. I thought he was going to compliment me, but he asked me while dancing, who I thought was the most handsomest man in the room. I mean, how was I going to answer that? I said he was. Well, in a way, he *was!*' In a conversation with Pat Newcomb, who had accompanied her that night, Marilyn remarked that the Attorney General 'had such a wonderful sense of humour'. She reiterated this opinion the following day in a typed letter to her former father-in-law, Isidore Miller, in which she also gushingly described Bobby as being 'rather mature and brilliant for his thirty-six years'.

Unsurprisingly, the sight of the Hollywood star and the Attorney General engaged in deep, secretive conversations and tied up in energetic dance routines soon made way for absurd conjecture and idle gossip about the pair. Many would cite the party as the start of their affair. Guthman was having none of it, vehemently declaring, 'There was not even the *faintest* overtone of a romantic interest on his side or hers.' During an interview for US TV show *Inside Edition*, he dismissed the allegations further by remarking, 'I travelled with Bobby, day and night for five years and I never saw him pay attention to *anyone* but his wife.'

Following Bobby's phone call to his father, however, news of a Kennedy brother twisting the night away with one of the world's most famous movie stars naturally spread like wildfire throughout the family. The excitement prompted his sister, Jean, to elatedly put pen to paper on the matter. Written on the Kennedys' Palm Beach house stationery, her humorous, sardonic letter to the actress read in part: 'Dear Marilyn, I understand that you and Bobby are the hot item! We all think that he should bring you with him when he comes back East.'

Three decades on, in May 1994, the letter was rediscovered and (incorrectly advertised as originating from 1961) put up for sale as part of a private collection of Marilyn's documents. But, unfortunately, it was misinterpreted and served only to give credence to the suggestion that Bobby and the actress were romantically involved. At the time of the sale, auctioneer Bill Miller, chairman of Odyssey Auctions, enthusiastically remarked to the press, 'This letter really does put an end to decades of speculation as to whether a relationship [between Monroe and Kennedy] existed or not.' However, an aide of Jean Kennedy Smith (who by then was US Ambassador to Ireland) insisted otherwise. When informed of Miller's conclusion, the aide retorted, 'This is *ridiculous*,' before describing the letter as a 'perfect example of Ambassador Smith's tongue-in-cheek humour. This was friendly banter that demonstrates exactly the opposite of verification.'

The elucidation was spot on. Despite Bill Miller's or anyone else's attempts to show otherwise over the ensuing years, evidence produced in substantiation of an intense, long-term love affair between Marilyn and the Attorney General would always prove to be unfounded. While he obviously noticed every attractive woman who came his way, a relationship with any female other than his wife Ethel would have been wildly out of keeping with his nature. 'Bobby had a Calvinistic moral sense,' Andrew Glass, the Washington-based news reporter and close friend of Kennedy, once remarked. 'He really believed in absolute right and wrong and this strict code guided his moral life.'

Although it is safe to say that the Attorney General did grow closer to Marilyn than his brother, John, extensive research on my part involving their personal schedules proves that Bobby did not have a fully fledged affair with Marilyn. Moreover, details of Marilyn's supposed encounters with Bobby's charismatic brother, John Fitzgerald Kennedy, the 35th President of the United States, were subject to a similar level of gossip and misrepresentation.

For example, three years after the sale of Jean Kennedy Smith's letter, in 1997, the world's media was in a high state of excitement over a curious cache of recently discovered documents supposedly pertaining to the former President. Going by the apt title of 'The JFK Papers', the assortment consisted of over 700 handwritten letters, notes and index cards which, if proved to be authentic, would provide the strongest evidence yet of his links to the Mafia, organised crime, the Chicago gangster, Sam Giancana and, importantly, Marilyn Monroe.

It was claimed by 47-year-old Lawrence 'Lex' Cusack that he had found the documents in 1985 while cleaning out the files belonging to his recently deceased father, the prominent New York lawyer, Lawrence (Larry) X. Cusack. (Between 1959 and November 1963, Cusack apparently privately counselled JFK on matters of the utmost sensitivity. Interestingly, Marilyn's mother, Gladys Baker, had also been one of Cusack's clients; the lawyer had supposedly handled her affairs from 1980 until her death in 1984.)

Interest in Cusack's collection was naturally huge. Although the majority of the papers in the collection focused on routine matters such as JFK's business and tax, the highlight of the assortment was a neatly typed agreement between him and Marilyn Monroe, in which, in an attempt to buy her silence over their affair and knowledge of his dealings with the underworld, he agreed to pay $600,000 into a trust fund for her mother. (The four payments by instalment, ranging from $100,000 to $250,000, allegedly started on Saturday 1 October 1960 and concluded exactly one year later, on Sunday 1 October 1961.) A handwritten letter from the actress relating to this matter was also found among the papers. It read, 'Dear Jack, I hope you understand. I only want to make sure that my mother is taken care of. This is difficult for me. I'm afraid she will not be cared for. I will be silent on this secret of yours about Sam G. and the others. Thanks M Monroe.'

Prior to the public announcement of 'The JFK Papers', Cusack's collection was put up for sale and soon sold for over $6 million to a party of 140 investors. However, hastened by ABC TV's quite damning verdict on the collection during its 20/20 programme (aired on Thursday 25 September), doubts soon grew about the papers' authenticity. Cusack naturally fought back, insisting they were genuine. But well-known document experts and Kennedy specialists were equally assertive, claiming they were not.

In response to the ABC programme, one day later, Cusack and his wife Jennifer filed a $100 million libel lawsuit against the station and other people in the news media, accusing them of 16 civil violations including fraud, libel, breach of contract and 'infliction of emotional stress'. In an attempt to prove the doubters wrong, Cusack then took his collection to rival network, CBS. It was a bad move. A special feature about the papers was aired by the station during its *60 Minutes* television show on Sunday 23 November. The true provenance of the documents became clear when, during the programme, respected handwriting expert Dr Duayne Dillon, a man recommended by the FBI, unreservedly declared that JFK's notes in the collection were forged. So too were Marilyn's tear-stained letters begging him not to cut off all contact with her.

The floodgates opened and further inaccuracies about the collection soon began to emerge. First, one of the letters in the collection had been typed on a model of typewriter not manufactured until 1971, nine years after Marilyn's death. Secondly, one of the papers (dated 1962) possessed the newer, general system American ZIP code, a method not implemented by the USPOD (United States Post Office Department) until Monday 1 July 1963, and thirdly, the bank account allegedly set up to pay Marilyn off simply did not exist. On Monday 16 March 1998, Cusack was charged with falsifying documents and released on bail. On Friday 17 September 1999, following another trial and three months of incarceration, he was found guilty of fraud and sentenced to a further ten years, three months in prison. He was also ordered to pay $7 million in compensation to the manuscripts' buyers.

Folklore has given us numerous other examples of supposed meetings between Monroe and John F. Kennedy. As I will explain, most of these prove on close examination to be logistically impossible. However, I can reveal that JFK's very first encounter with Marilyn had actually taken place on Tuesday 15 May 1951, at a party in Beverly Hills at the home of legendary designer and decorator Elsie de Wolfe and her husband, diplomat Sir Charles Mendl. As was her tradition, Elsie would invite to dinner a mix of 16 top-rated Hollywood stars and emerging politicians; once the meal had been consumed, they would be joined by some of

Tinseltown's budding, starry-eyed hopefuls. With her rise to film prominence, as Rose Loomis in the 1953 film *Niagara*, still some 20 months away, Marilyn was one of the latter.

Metro-Goldwyn-Mayer actress Arlene Dahl, a guest at the party that night, remembered she was sitting at the piano with the musician Cole Porter, singing 'You're The Top', when suddenly the door opened and, in her own words, 'in walked this blonde Venus in a white satin gown that was just fabulous. It hugged all her curves.' In a 2002 interview for CNN's *Larry King Live* show, she recalled that the actress 'shimmered over to a group of gentlemen who were standing in the corner talking about Walt Whitman, the poet, and Marilyn, anxious to get into the conversation, heard Whitman and said, "Oh, I just love his chocolates."' (She was inadvertently thinking about Whitman's, one of America's largest and oldest chocolate manufacturers.) Congressman John Kennedy was standing near Dahl when Marilyn made her memorable entrance. 'He couldn't take his eyes off her,' she recalled. 'No man in the room could.' Just 12 days prior to this encounter, at a dinner party hosted by their mutual friends Charles and Martha Buck Bartlett at their home in Georgetown, Washington DC on Thursday 3 May, Kennedy had met his future wife, the elegant 24-year-old *Washington Times-Herald* photographer Jacqueline Bouvier.

Monroe's first encounter with the President-to-be was brief. There would, in fact, be no further meetings between them for another ten years. That did not, however, prevent various people, usually individuals who had either never met the actress or the President or could tell you only what they had been told had happened, from insisting that the pair met several times during the intervening period.

It is said, for instance, that on Monday 1 February 1960, the couple spent a night together at Lake Tahoe's Cal-Neva Lodge. The story goes that Kennedy visited after stopping at Squaw Valley, the site of that year's 8th Winter Olympics, which were set to start in just 17 days' time. In fact, he did visit Nevada that day, but he certainly did *not* have time to visit or reside at the lodge. Following a talk to Nevada labour leaders in Reno and an address to the joint session of the Legislature that morning, he was quickly hustled on to a plane destined for San Francisco. His time in Nevada was just a few short hours. Furthermore, it was impossible that Marilyn was there to greet him since she was in Hollywood at the time, rehearsing and shooting scenes for *Let's Make Love* (shooting of which had begun on Monday 18 January). There is nothing else on record at Boston's JFK Presidential Library that identifies Kennedy, officially or unofficially, visiting Lake Tahoe or Nevada at any time before his assassination in Dallas, Texas on Friday 22 November 1963.

In fact, John F. Kennedy did not pay a single visit to the Cal-Neva Lodge. Marilyn's occasional getaways there were more to do with her intermittent relationship with Frank Sinatra, the future co-owner of the establishment, than with Kennedy.

Some historians have also suggested that Monroe was having a fleeting affair with Kennedy in 1960 at the time he was campaigning in the Los Angeles area, and especially at the time of his historic Democratic Presidential nomination on Wednesday 13 July. We are reliably informed that she was introduced to the President-elect backstage at the venue by Peter Lawford. Other well-known Hollywood celebrities, such as Shelley Winters, Sammy Davis Jr, Shirley MacLaine, Danny Kaye and Edward G. Robinson, *were* present that evening (as proven in news film shot that night), but Marilyn was *not*. I can reveal that, on the night that JFK was at the Los Angeles Memorial Sports Arena celebrating his appointment, the actress was in New York City undergoing make-up tests and hair restyling (by her personal beauty expert, George Masters) for her latest movie, *The Misfits*. Just prior to that, on Thursday 7 July, she was spotted at Idlewild Airport, in her Cadillac, sharing some caviar and a glass of Dom Perignon champagne with Yves Montand, her co-star in *Let's Make Love*. ('She bought a bottle of chilled champagne and we sat in the car and drank it and talked,' the actor disclosed in 1961. 'The reporters made it look like an affair. How ridiculous . . . The matter at the airport has been *so* misunderstood.')

Marilyn remained in the Big Apple until Monday 18 July, and after several delays, most notably at Los Angeles International Airport, finally arrived in Nevada at Reno Municipal Airport in a United Airlines airplane during the afternoon of Wednesday 20 July. (Her plane touched down at 2.31 pm. She disembarked at precisely 3.16 pm.) She was there to begin filming *The Misfits*, the shooting of which had already been in progress for two days. Marilyn was met at the airport by her husband, Arthur Miller, and a welcoming committee comprising hotelier Charles Mapes (parts of the movie were shot in his establishment), Mrs Grant Sawyer, the wife of Nevada's governor, and her daughter, Gail, who handed the actress a bouquet of flowers. The pleasantries continued when Marilyn was presented with a key to the City of Reno by Councilman Charles Cowen. Afterwards a motorcade escorted her to downtown Reno, where she posed for pictures under the city's world-famous arch, 'The Biggest Little City In The World'.

Another meeting between Monroe and Kennedy supposedly took place on Tuesday 20 September 1960, at a party to celebrate the official assumption of control of the Cal-Neva Lodge by Frank Sinatra and his pals. The singer's star-studded guest list that night apparently included Joseph Kennedy and his son John. But, once again, that was simply not feasible. On the day of the celebration, JFK was on a tour of New Jersey, West Virginia and Washington campaigning and promising that, if he was elected President of the United States, he would 'launch within 90 days three programs to bolster national defence, send more help to under-developed countries and attack poverty at home'. Later that Tuesday evening, while Frank and his guests were partying the night away in Lake Tahoe, Kennedy was on nationwide television outlining how, if nominated, he intended to deal with the Soviet Premier, Nikita Khrushchev. (It was impossible to miss. The live 30-minute coast-to-coast transmission began at 8.30 pm Eastern Daylight Time and was screened on 180 ABC-affiliated stations.)

The following day, Wednesday 21 September, Kennedy launched his second big campaigning tour with appearances in Tennessee and Iowa. It is absurd to suggest that he could travel all the way from the eastern seaboard to Lake Tahoe in a day or less, while at the same time managing to avoid any press coverage of his visit. However, Marilyn *was* at the Cal-Neva on the night of Tuesday 20 September. With husband Arthur Miller by her side, she joined in the festivities, watching performances by Sinatra and singer Andy Williams. It is therefore safe to assume that JFK's only presence in the Cal-Neva that night came by way of the television set when Frank and his patrons tuned into his coast-to-coast address.

Several times during the filming of *The Misfits*, Marilyn and the cast and crew travelled up to the lodge for the evening. One such visit took place on Saturday 13 August, when the actress was pictured sitting at a table chatting with Sinatra and Bert 'Wingy' Grober, the club's former owner. Watching a performance by Frank in the Indian Room at the establishment concluded her night. It was Monroe's very first trip to a club she was infamously to visit again in late July 1962.

Belief that Monroe and Kennedy were clandestinely seeing each other in late 1960 was actually born out of a short piece by Art Buchwald, the American humorist and long-time columnist for *The Washington Post*. In his article entitled 'Let's Be Firm On Monroe Doctrine', published on Saturday 19 November, he wrote:

> Who will be the next ambassador to Monroe? This is one of the many problems President-elect Kennedy will have to work on in January. Obviously you can't leave Monroe adrift. There are too many greedy people eyeing her, and now that Ambassador Miller has left she could flounder around without any direction.

Credence that Buchwald had some kind of inside knowledge on their liaison came from the fact that, during the late 1950s, he and Monroe were rumoured to be romantically involved. During this time, it was believed, he had introduced her to Judaism, to which she did later convert. Furthermore, it was said that Marilyn was the basis in part for a character in Buchwald's 1958 novel A *Gift from the Boys*. They had remained friends and therefore it was rumoured that the fact that Monroe was seeing the President-elect had originated from her own lips.

As we know, Monroe was a master of self-publicity and would often leak valuable inside information about herself to influential show business columnists such as Buchwald. However, in this case, she did *not*. Buchwald was nonetheless famous for his humorous, astute digs at Washington politicians and so, with the news that Marilyn's marriage to Arthur Miller had collapsed coming just four days after JFK had won the American presidential race, he obviously thought it was the perfect opportunity to link the two famous names together. What started off as a satirical, quite innocent, disposable remark went on to be used as evidence by rumour-mongers and conspiracy theorists to prove that Marilyn and Kennedy were romantically involved.

In the weeks leading up to Buchwald's piece, it was, once again, impossible for the two of them to be together. Filming of The Misfits wrapped in Reno on Friday 4 November 1960, after which Monroe flew back to New York and spent several days (until at least Tuesday 15 November) resting in her apartment and fending off questions from reporters about the break-up of her marriage to Miller.

At this juncture, Kennedy was away in Hyannis Port, Massachusetts and at precisely 2.30 on the afternoon of Friday 11 November, just two days after winning, by the slimmest of margins, the American presidential race, he flew out to Palm Beach, Florida for a working vacation. His private plane stopped in Washington to allow his pregnant wife Jacqueline to disembark and, once he reached his destination, he headed straight for his father Joseph's summer house. Five days later, on Wednesday 16 November, Kennedy flew out alone to the Texan ranch of the new administration's Vice President, Lyndon B. Johnson. Scandal-mongers influenced by Buchwald's piece and desperate to pinpoint a November 1960 rendezvous between Marilyn and JFK quite conveniently failed to locate this information.

Rumours that the actress and the President-elect met up in New York during January 1961 still persist. True, the two of them *were* in the city at varying times during this period, but the chances of them having clandestine meetings were once again extremely remote. Kennedy arrived on the East Coast of America for the first time that month on Wednesday 4 January to discuss with his defence chief, Robert S. McNamara, the critical background of broken Cuban-US relations. He remained in Washington at the White House for one full week until Wednesday 11 January when he flew out to Palm Beach. He returned to New York six days later, on Tuesday 17 January, and took up his obligatory residence in the Carlyle Hotel.

Marilyn meanwhile spent most of the month relaxing in her East 57th Street, New York apartment, receiving massages from Ralph Roberts, attending special screenings of *The Misfits*, approving stills from the film and enjoying nights further out with her former husband, Joe DiMaggio. Their reunion, following her separation from Arthur Miller, had taken place just two weeks previously, on the evening of Christmas Day 1960. It was a case of two former lovers finding themselves bereft of company for the festive period. She called him on the night of Sunday 25 December, immediately after receiving his gift, a large bunch of poinsettias. (The cluster of flowers was so huge that Marilyn jokingly referred to them as a 'forest'.)

DiMaggio knew instinctively she would call him after receiving his unexpected gift. 'Who in the hell else do you have in the world?' he asked during their conversation. 'I was married to you and know you're not bothered about friends or in-laws.' DiMaggio confirmed what the actress already knew: despite her worldwide fame, she was still an exceedingly lonely woman.

He then asked Marilyn out for a drink. 'But you don't drink,' the actress insisted. 'I occasionally drink,' he replied. 'Well, it would have to be a very, very dark place then,' she insisted. Joe asked Marilyn what she was doing on Christmas evening. When she replied, 'Nothing,' DiMaggio agreed to drive over. He ended up staying for several days and their friendship was rekindled. From that moment on, they were almost inseparable.

On Saturday 7 January 1961, she was seen relishing his company at a New York theatre and restaurant. Eight days later, on Sunday 15 January, one day past their seventh wedding anniversary, Marilyn and Joe made it public that they were once again seeing each other when they dined together at the Le Pavilion restaurant and attended the closing night performance of the play *The Hostage* at the Eugene O'Neill Theatre. The couple even sat in Row B so everyone could plainly see them. (Marilyn had phoned the auditorium's box office and booked the plum seats herself.) Curious onlookers walked up and down the aisles just to get a better glimpse of the reunited pair.

Two nights later, on Tuesday 17 January, the day that JFK returned to New York, Monroe was once more spotted at Le Pavilion, sharing steaks with her former husband. This time they were joined by George Solotaire, the Broadway ticket broker and long-time friend of DiMaggio. Earlier in the day, Marilyn and Joe were seen walking around Sutton Place and were pictured chuckling at pages in Maurice Zolotow's recently released biography of the actress.

News that she had seemingly renewed her acquaintance with the baseball legend naturally became a big story. 'Marilyn And Joe Are Dating', screamed *The Press Courier* newspaper. A close pal of DiMaggio's was even quoted as saying (in the *Lowell Sun* newspaper on Wednesday 18 January), 'They *will* re-wed,' although the actress's press agent, John Springer, was quick to play down the renewed romance, saying, 'She considers Joe a good friend and that's the status of their relationship.'

On Friday 20 January, Marilyn, her publicist Pat Newcomb and New York attorney Aaron Frosch flew out of New York en route to Juarez in Mexico where, at a special night session at Judge Miguel Gomez' court, she filed a Mexican (quickie) divorce from Miller. ('Arthur is a wonderful writer,' she remarked, 'but I think he's a better writer than a husband. I'm sure writing comes first in his life.' As an acquaintance of the couple commented, 'When she knew that she could never have a child, the marriage held no interest.') It came just one day after she had signed a property settlement with him. In an attempt to avoid any unwanted publicity, Marilyn chose the day of JFK's inauguration to put the wheels of her split into motion. (During the stopover in Dallas, the actress and her companions gathered round a television set at the airport to watch live coverage of Kennedy's swearing-in ceremony.)

Monroe touched down across the border at El Paso Airport at 7pm Eastern Standard Time (EST). The town's First Civil Court stayed open for three extra hours especially for the actress to file the complaint. She was represented at the 8pm hearing by the local lawyer, Arturo Sosa Aquilar. Miller did not attend, but was spoken for by Mexican attorney Areliano Gonzalez Vargas.

After the hearing, she and her two companions were driven around Juarez and shared a celebratory margarita in the city's Kentucky Bar. Dinner at attorney Vargas's home followed. Once the meal had been digested, Marilyn, Newcomb and Frosch returned to El Paso Airport, where they boarded a Continental flight, which took them through Albuquerque and then Denver where she had a stopover before her flight back to New York became available. Monroe's entourage arrived back in the Big Apple at noon on Saturday 21 January. The actress then headed back to her Manhattan apartment. Three days later, on Tuesday 24 January, her divorce became absolute when her papers were signed by Judge Miguel Gomez Guerra (though they would not become effective for another two days).

JFK meanwhile, was busy himself during this period. Preparing for his inauguration on Friday was naturally uppermost in his thoughts and obviously he had no spare time whatsoever in the days preceding it. On Tuesday and Wednesday, 17 and 18 January, from his base at the

Carlyle Hotel, he met important officials and entertained show business luminaries, such as actors Anthony Quinn and Laurence Olivier and singer Ethel Merman. His encounter with the latter trio concluded with personal invites to fly them up to Washington in his private Convair CV-240 plane for his main inauguration-eve gala event, a showcase of America's greatest talent, produced and hosted by Frank Sinatra, which was set to take place at DC's National Guard Armory during the evening of Thursday 19 January. In effect, by participating at such an event, the President was informally acknowledging his induction into Sinatra's Rat Pack.

Unfortunately, the joyous occasion was ruined by a rare snowstorm, the worst Washington had seen in years. Local traffic was harshly disrupted, which meant that, by the start of the concert, which had been delayed by two hours, less than a quarter of the 13,000 seats in the auditorium had been occupied. The local weather bureau announced later that, by midnight, the time Sinatra's glossy gala was coming to an end, six inches of snow had fallen. By the morning, JFK's inauguration day, the snow had stopped and been hurriedly cleared.

A large number of the country's finest entertainers were in attendance at the gala, including singers Helen Traubel, Ella Fitzgerald, Ethel Merman, Mahalia Jackson, Nat King Cole and Harry Belafonte, comedians Joey Bishop, Alan King, Jimmy Durante and Milton Berle, actors Bette Davis, Angie Dickinson, Kim Novak, Fredrick March, Sidney Poitier and Tony Curtis, dancers Gene Kelly and Juliet Prowse and composer Leonard Bernstein. But Marilyn was not. She did not even make the short-list. So why the rebuff? The answer was elementary. Regardless of the picture many previous biographers have tried to paint, by January 1961 Monroe's path had still not properly crossed JFK's. Each artist on the bill that night was either a close friend of JFK or of his family and, despite the fact he was obviously aware of Marilyn and a great fan of her work (a poster of the actress was once known to have hung on the wall above his bed), he was still a stranger to her. Furthermore, if the actress had met the President-elect in his room at the Carlyle Hotel, as many have implied, why wasn't it reported by the American press in the same way that Ethel Merman, Laurence Olivier and Anthony Quinn's quite innocent visits were?

To prove conclusively that Kennedy did *not* meet Marilyn during this time, we must fill in the other gaps in his timeline. On the morning of Thursday 19 January, shortly after dropping in to see his New York dentist, JFK was back at the White House for a two-hour meeting with the outgoing President, Dwight D. Eisenhower. His time on the East Coast had lasted just two days. In the period preceding his inauguration and, aside from visits to church (on Sunday 22 January), the CIA (between 2.35 and 4.30pm on Thursday 26 January), the Andrews Air Force Base (between 11.58am and 12.09pm on Friday 27 January) and the National Press Building (between 7.46 and 7.55pm on Saturday 28 January), Kennedy remained in Washington at the White House right up to Saturday 11 February, when, at 12.35pm, he and his wife Jacqueline boarded a helicopter heading for Glen Ora, Virginia. Punctuating these dates, at 6pm EST on Wednesday 25 January JFK appeared in the very first live, nationwide US TV question and answer session with an American president.

For the better part of the month, therefore, Marilyn and Kennedy were preoccupied with extremely different schedules and simply had no time to meet. Their lives were still taking extremely different paths.

Thanksgiving Day, Thursday 23 November 1961, is another date often put forward for a supposed meeting between the actress and the President. According to John Danoff, a technician engaged by Fred Otash, the so-called 'Mr. O, The King of Hollywood private eyes', an audio-tape of the couple having sex in one of the bedrooms at Peter Lawford's beach house on that day was recorded. On that day, the President was nonetheless with his family, ice-skating and relaxing with his ailing father, Joseph, at his home in Hyannis Port. He would not return to Washington until 10.11am on Monday 27 November.

So when precisely did they encounter each other again? I can reveal that the actress's first genuine, one-to-one encounter with the 35th President of the United States took place during the weekend of 23 and 24 September 1961, when she was invited by Peter and Pat Lawford to spend two days at the Hyannis Port home of JFK's father, Joseph. Aside from John and his wife, also in attendance that day were Marilyn's assistant, Pat Newcomb, her current date, Frank Sinatra, JFK's brother, Edward 'Teddy' Kennedy, and Dominican playboy Porfirio Rubirosa and his wife, Odile. Marilyn asked Broadway stylist Ernie Adler to create a new, Egyptian-style hairdo especially for the occasion.

Marilyn, Newcomb, Sinatra and the President's sister, Pat, had arrived by air on Friday evening (22 September), landing at New Bedford, about 50 miles away, when fog closed the airports on Cape Cod. They almost failed to get there. Their flight out of Los Angeles the previous day had run into serious trouble and was forced to return. In cable-speak, Marilyn outlined the events in a touching Western Union telegram sent to Joe DiMaggio at his room at New York's Lexington Hotel. 'Dear dad darling airplane developed engine trouble plus all oil ran out of same plane so we had to turn back and land in LA. Leaving again on another plane at 5pm arrive New York at 1pm. When plane was in trouble I thought about two things you and changing my will. Love you I think more than ever.' She signed it with one of her aliases, 'Mrs Norman'.

Marilyn arrived at New Bedford in her obligatory disguise and was even able to outwit the usually astute waiting news-hounds. In their report of Sinatra's arrival, the *Gazette-Mail* newspaper unwittingly described her as one of his 'unidentified guests'. The party were forced to drive to the Kennedy compound by taxi. Another followed close behind, ferrying their luggage.

On the first day, Saturday 23 September, at precisely 12.40pm, the entourage took a three-and-a-half-hour cruise aboard the presidential motor-cruiser, *Marlin*, which had been anchored off the beach at Cotuit, Massachusetts. The highlight was the First Lady's dazzling display of water-skiing. The trip concluded at 4pm. Ever the party man, Sinatra had been followed on to the boat by 12 pieces of luggage, which included a case of wine and a dozen bottles of carefully wrapped champagne. One day later, the entourage once more assembled for a jaunt on *Marlin*, but, due to the President's 5.40pm trip to New York City with Peter Lawford later that day, the boat journey and in fact the entire weekend came to an abrupt end at just 2.55pm. (The guests naturally headed home. On the morning of Tuesday 26 September, Marilyn and Frank flew on to New York.)

The actress's second genuine encounter with the President occurred on Sunday 19 November 1961. However seedy some previous Marilyn scholars may have tried to make it, the event was nothing more than a quite innocent, relaxed dinner party for specially invited close friends of both JFK and the Lawfords. Marilyn was of course a very good friend of Peter Lawford and of the Kennedys' sister, Pat, and the chances of a quick liaison between the President and Monroe during the get-together were very slim indeed. The luncheon kicked off at 12 midday and ended just over three hours later at precisely 3.08pm. For the record, JFK was in town for a meeting with the West German Chancellor, Konrad Adenauer, which was set to take place at 4pm the following day.

Monroe's next meeting with Kennedy took place two weeks later, on Tuesday 5 December. The locale was New York City. JFK was in the area for an address at the National Football Foundation and Hall of Fame banquet at the Waldorf-Astoria Hotel. After his 20-minute speech, he attended a black-tie party thrown at the Park Avenue apartment belonging to socialite Mrs Fifi Fell, the widow of a prominent investment banker, and it was during this short gathering that the President encountered Monroe for the third time. In an appearance orchestrated by Lawford, she had flown in from Los Angeles especially. Pretending to be the actor's personal secretary, clutching a legal pad and pen and sporting a dark-red wig, dowdy clothes and dark glasses, she was apparently secreted into the building through a side entrance. Set to arrive at 8pm, she in fact arrived at approximately 10.15pm. Her obligatory New York stylist, Kenneth Battelle, had been preparing her hair at her Manhattan apartment.

Interestingly, on Monday 12 July 1965, almost four years after the event, the evening featured in an FBI report which, according to the file, said there was a 'sex party' that night, borne out of a Mafia plot to smear the Kennedys, 'in which a number of persons participated at different times'. Among those apparently taking part were 'Robert F. Kennedy, John F. Kennedy, Peter Lawford and Marilyn Monroe'. However, the file was incorrect. The crowd at the Park Avenue event was a specially invited one, so the chances of the actress slipping away unnoticed with Kennedy were slim indeed. Furthermore, time was of the essence. Although widely regarded as a sex addict and a Lothario, the President was also an extremely conscientious man and was well aware that he had to prepare himself for another important address. His speech to members of the National Association of Manufacturers was scheduled for midday the following day, so a late night was never in the offing.

When JFK did return to his room at the Carlyle Hotel later that night, where the 'sex party' was alleged to have taken place, he did so alone. The FBI's long-serving director, J. Edgar Hoover, the most powerful and feared man in the United States, clearly possessed an overwhelming interest in the President's bedside manner and kept an ever-watchful eye on him both before and long after the 1960 presidential election. Regrettably, he, or his employees, would embellish many of their reports.

The fact is that Marilyn was intimate with John F. Kennedy only once, during the evening of Saturday 24 March 1962, when both he and the screen actress were guests at singer Bing Crosby's three-bedroom house in Palm Springs and the adjoining, remote conclave home belonging to songwriter Jimmy Van Heusen and writer Bill Morrow.

The houses, situated in a tiny community 100 miles southeast of Los Angeles, stood against a mountain in Palm Desert at a place called Silver Spur and were situated up a single dirt thoroughfare called Van Heusen Road. They had been a favourite of former US President Dwight D. Eisenhower and his men during his tenure. Surprisingly, details that the President was about to spend the night there were leaked to the American press on Wednesday 14 March. When asked why, JFK simply replied, 'I've been in both houses and they are not big mansions by any means but comfortable homes were built for sun, solitude and rest.'

As is well known, Frank Sinatra had been expecting JFK and his Secret Service man to stay with him at his Palm Springs home. Indeed, in readiness for the visit, extra land was purchased and an additional guest house was built, an ultra-modern phone service installed and a new concrete heli-copter landing pad constructed. Sinatra then learnt, probably through a small piece in *Variety* magazine, that Kennedy would be spending the night nearby at Crosby's home instead. Fury immediately engulfed him and the focal point of his rage was Peter Lawford, the man who had given his word that the President would be residing with *him* that evening.

Lawford soon learnt that his friend was angry and he started to panic. In a desperate attempt to appease his Rat Pack buddy, he explained the situation to the President who immediately agreed to call Sinatra personally. He informed Frank it was a security decision and asked him not to blame his brother-in-law.

Moments after finishing his conversation with JFK, Sinatra rang Bobby at his desk at the White House. His suspicions that the Attorney General was indeed behind the excuse were confirmed when Bobby told Frank unreservedly that his brother could not be seen residing in a building where the Chicago Mafia boss, Sam Giancana, had slept. Sinatra argued and pleaded his case, but Bobby was uninterested and hung up. Frank was incensed. He saw this as treachery. In a fit of fury, he picked up an axe and started to attack the prized items strewn around his house, many of which were purchased especially for the presidential visit. Once back at the Cal-Neva, Sinatra armed himself with a sledgehammer and ran up the lodge's stairs to the club's roof where he vented his anger on another of his prized possessions: the recently modified concrete helicopter landing pad, on which JFK's helicopter was one day expected to alight.

Legend has it that Sinatra's anger at the covering-up of the Attorney General's vendetta shifted from material items to individual people – namely Lawford and JFK – and that he never dealt or spoke to either of them again. However, at least with regard to the President, that is essentially incorrect. As surviving documentation proves, in June that year JFK penned a letter to the singer thanking him for the 'floral rocking chair that you had thoughtfully sent me for my birthday'. Furthermore, despite what other biographers have told us, communication between the pair actually continued for many months after the incident. In late August, Sinatra obsequiously called Pierre Salinger, the President's press secretary, inform-ing him that he wished to send him a copy of his recently completed movie, *The Manchurian Candidate*. Sinatra added that 'a print of it will be available any hour, night or day, for viewing by the President'.

For Lawford, however, the repercussions from Sinatra's rebuff were catastrophic. The actor soon found out that he had been excised from the Rat Pack, their movies and any subsequent nightclub shows in which Sinatra, Dean Martin or Joey Bishop were set to appear.

Marilyn uncharacteristically rose at eight o'clock on the morning of the get-together at Crosby's home. Despite her strictest instructions that no workmen be allowed into her Fifth Helena premises that day, her plan to specially coiffure her hair for her latest meeting with JFK was dashed by a visit from the plumber, Roy Newell, who had arrived early to install a new, much-needed, large water heater in the garage. When she was informed that there would be a delay with the hot water, Marilyn flipped and dashed over to Ralph Greenson's home to wash her hair. Later that afternoon, following several hours of setting and resetting her tresses, and numerous changes of clothing, the actress was finally ready to meet the President of the United States once again. (It would be their fourth encounter.) She had never hidden her admiration for him. He was, after all, the most powerful man on the planet, a man of whom she was once quoted as saying, 'Jack Kennedy is much better than the old uglies with no brains or beauty.'

Sporting her mandatory dark-coloured wig, she climbed into Peter Lawford's car and was driven to Los Angeles International Airport where the President's Convair plane was waiting to fly them the 109 miles to Palm Springs Airport. There a car lingered to whisk them to Bing Crosby's secluded home in the desert.

On a rare day off from presidential duties, JFK arrived at Crosby's estate at precisely 12.03 on that Saturday afternoon, directly after a 55-minute meeting with Eisenhower. Amazingly, aside from just one member of the Secret Service, J. Walter Coughlin, he turned up alone. (First Lady Jacqueline Kennedy was away in India and Pakistan at the time, on an ambassadorial holiday.) Besides the President and his aforementioned man, there were just four others in Crosby's house that day: Peter Lawford, his wife Pat, comedian Bob Hope and, of course, Marilyn Monroe.

According to quotes from reliable sources, including Ralph Roberts, that afternoon the President and the actress took a slow stroll around the swimming pool. Later that evening, during an exclusive dinner party in a secluded cottage on the property, JFK, now sporting a casual black turtle-neck sweater, sat and listened while the actress told torrid tales of Hollywood. As she did so, he slid his hand under the table and moved it across Marilyn's thigh. Encountering no resistance, he continued but stopped when he discovered she was not wearing any underwear. (She never wore any.) Immediately, he withdrew his hand. 'He hadn't counted on going *that* far,' Marilyn later joked. Later that night, and with the actress making an alcohol-induced move for him, the couple moved into a quiet room in the cottage and the inevitable happened.

Reliable evidence that the President and Marilyn shared a bed that night came in an interview with Ralph Roberts, the actress's long-time confidant and masseur. He revealed that Marilyn innocently, but no doubt proudly, called him to enquire about the soleus muscle. (A powerful muscle, this is situated in the back part of the lower leg and runs from just below the knee to the heel. It is involved in standing and walking.) Roberts was well aware that she had been invited to Crosby's home that weekend and that the President would also be attending. So when the call came late on Saturday night, he knew instinctively that she had been discussing with Kennedy his well-known muscle and back problems. The phone was then passed to Kennedy himself, who asked Roberts for some advice on how to ease the incessant pains in his body.

In 1993, Roberts announced that Marilyn had told him that this night was the *only* time in their association with each other that they had spent the night together. 'Marilyn gave me the impression that it was not a major event for either of them,' he remarked. 'It happened once and that was that.' In another exchange, the actress was known to have announced, 'He may be a good President, but he doesn't grab me sexually.'

As we can gather, Marilyn's night of passion with Kennedy was far from satisfying. She later complained to at least two friends that he was far too perfunctory. With regard to his premature ejaculation, the actress also remarked to Roberts that the President 'made love like an adolescent'. The other confidant was her former, short-term lover, newspaper columnist James Bacon. When she informed him about how disappointing Kennedy was in the sack, he screamed, 'But Marilyn. He's too busy running the country to be bothered about being good in bed.'

In truth, due to his excruciating back pains, intercourse and lengthy periods of foreplay were, regrettably, nigh-on impossible for Kennedy. The only time he could successfully carry out interaction with a female was when he was in the White House pool. The movement in the water was beneficial for the muscles in his back and groin. But during encounters in other locations, of which there were many, he was only able to partake in kissing and oral sex, of which he was frequently the receiver. To him, sex, as Marilyn would testify, was mechanical. Foreplay was too painful, he reached an orgasm too quickly and, since his desire for intimacy with a woman was borne more out of need than choice, he wanted the act to be terminated at the earliest opportunity.

Marilyn wasn't alone in feeling carnally unsatisfied after a night in the boudoir with the President of the United States. Stories corroborating his inadequacy in the sack are easy to find. In Sally Smith's book *Grace And Power*, the President's wife, Jacqueline, was quoted as saying he 'goes too fast and falls asleep'. Mob moll Judith Campbell was another to publicly testify, in both books and magazine articles, about Kennedy's sexual inadequacy in the bedroom. But perhaps the most humorous recollection came from film and television actress Angie Dickinson, who, when discussing JFK's extremely hasty lovemaking style, was apparently once quoted as saying it was 'the best 20 seconds of my life'. (She even wrote about it in her still unpublished memoirs.)

Fundamental to Kennedy's sexual inefficiencies were the persistent and well-attested problems with both his back and the rest of body. He suffered from osteoporosis, which seriously affected his spine and, from the age of just 20, forced him to permanently wear a brace. His back was damaged further when, on Monday 2 August 1943, during the Second World War, his torpedo boat was hit by a Japanese destroyer in the South Pacific. For 16 straight hours, Kennedy heroically managed to rescue his fellow seamen, but his bravery only managed to put more pressure on his already damaged spine.

By his early 30s, the cocktail of steroids he had been consuming for colitis had accelerated his osteoporosis. His thinning bones, which had been supporting his spinal column, were now collapsing and he was now unable to perform even the simplest of tasks. Due to the fact that his left leg was three-quarters of an inch shorter than his right (an obvious mechanical aggravation of the weakness along his spine), he even had sometimes to turn sideways just to ascend a standard flight of stairs.

In an endeavour to ease his incessant back pain, surgeons cut open Kennedy's back and inserted into either side of his lower spine two thin metal plates. Called Wilson plates, these were meant to hold his spine in place, reduce the amount of movement and subsequently reduce the amount of pain he endured. But just three days after the operation, Kennedy developed a staphylococcus infection. It spiralled out of control and he went into a coma. The last rites were administered by the church but he pulled through. Nevertheless within months, the back pain returned, tragically more severe than before. Doctors decided to remove the plates but, as a result, he was left with two gaping holes in his back, the size of an average-sized fist. Thanks to the operations, his back was weaker than ever.

When JFK moved into the White House in January 1961, he took with him eight personal physicians; doctors who would cater for his every medical whim and help keep alive the public persona of a young, vibrant, robust President. He basked in his image of vitality and extreme good heath. But in truth, it was a façade. His body was a crumbling wreck. Even the most menial of tasks would cause him great distress. By the one and only time he was intimate with Marilyn, in March 1962, President Kennedy, the most powerful man in the world, was in such disrepair that he had trouble even getting out of bed in the morning. Bending down to pull on his shoes and socks caused him immense discomfort. With his body in such disorder, the thoughts of any kind of sexual intercourse outside the realms of the highly therapeutic White House pool were a complete non-starter.

Marilyn and JFK would never share a bed or a sexually charged session again, and Marilyn never pursued it. Before they parted, however, on the morning of Sunday 25 March, knowing his penchant for cigars, Marilyn handed the President a gift, a Ronson Adonis chrome cigarette lighter. Produced by the company between 1949 and 1964, she'd had the initials 'J.F.K.' engraved on it. Kennedy handed her something too, a verbal invite to sing at his forthcoming birthday gala. Naturally, she accepted.

She soon brushed off the Kennedy bedroom disappointment. That afternoon, she arrived back at her Brentwood home to find Joe DiMaggio waiting. During the following week, the pair were regularly seen out together. On Tuesday 27 March, they were spotted at the nearby Brentwood Country Mart shopping for rotisserie chickens. The actress did so in her obligatory disguise, a wig, scarf and dowdy polo coat, and bereft of make-up. Ever the gentleman, DiMaggio refused to stay each night in Marilyn's home, preferring instead to sleep in his room at the Beverly Hilton Hotel. However, there *was* an exception.

At 7.30pm on Saturday 31 March, at a cost of $900, the actress clandestinely arranged for a limousine to pick her up from her Fifth Helena home and drive her to where Joe was staying. Once the totally surprised DiMaggio had climbed aboard, the car escorted the couple back to the actress's home. The limousine remained on standby throughout the night and was not required again until 10.30 the following morning, when the chauffeur drove DiMaggio back to his hotel. It was abundantly clear that the couple were immensely enjoying each other's company again, in more ways than one.

It seems astonishing now, but at the time of Marilyn's death in August 1962, only the select Hollywood clique knew that the actress might have been romantically involved with either of the Kennedy brothers or that they might have had a hand in her death. Frank A. Capell's *The Strange Death of Marilyn Monroe* was the first to change this. His 1964 booklet brought the knowledge to a new, albeit small audience. In his scant 70-page publication, costing a mere $2, he noted that, after announcing that she was going to make public details of her affair with the Attorney General, Marilyn was murdered on the orders of the Communist Party, with which Kennedy was closely associated.

His motive for producing such a booklet became clear from his 'About the Author' introduction. Aside from his abundantly clear anti-Communist credentials, we also discover that Mr Capell had been fighting the 'reds' since long before the Second World War and, at the time of writing, was still fighting. Unsurprisingly, the publishers of this glorified pamphlet, New York's Herald of Freedom, were, besides being right-wing Kennedy haters, also responsible for a national, anti-Communist, bi-weekly educational newspaper. It is also worth remembering that, at the time of *The Strange Death of Marilyn Monroe*'s publication, it was American election year and Bobby was running for the Senate. The book certainly worried those at the top.

On Wednesday 8 July 1964, the FBI's J. Edgar Hoover even drafted a letter to Bobby to inform him of the publication and warn him that the publication would 'make reference to your alleged friendship with the late Miss Marilyn Monroe', adding that Mr Capell had stated 'he will indicate in his book that you and Miss Monroe were intimate and that you were in Miss Monroe's home at the time of her death.' Now discredited for its right-wing bias, the book does nevertheless deserve some credit. The amount of 'insider' information in the publication – the reproductions of Marilyn's autopsy forms, drug prescriptions and doctors' invoices – is nothing short of remarkable and a godsend for researchers desperate to piece together an honest account of the actress's final months.

It wasn't until 1969, almost seven years after her death, and the publication of the book *Norma Jean: Life of Marilyn Monroe* by Fred Lawrence Guiles, that the general public became slightly more knowledgeable about the Kennedy rumours. Even then, the publishers, McGraw-Hill, fell short of directly naming either JFK or Bobby as a prominent romantic figure in Marilyn's life, instead cryptically referring to him as 'an unnamed leading political figure', 'a married man' and 'an Easterner with few ties on the coast'. Interestingly, Guiles's original manuscript had named the Kennedy brother with whom Marilyn was romantically involved as Bobby, but the publishers decided to remove it on the grounds of bad taste. The Attorney General had been assassinated just one year prior to the book's release.

By September 1972, ten years after Marilyn's passing, and the time of the publication of *Sincerely, Marilyn Monroe*, a book by her alleged second husband, Robert Slatzer, the public were left in no doubt that Bobby was the Kennedy brother with whom Monroe had been, apparently, sexually active . . . and not John. With the end of censorship came a flood of erroneous speculation, in documentaries, articles and books about the actress, that if she had slept with Bobby then surely she *must* have bedded his brother, John, too – and on more than one occasion.

And so, with the grainy footage of the actress singing a sexually tinged version of 'Happy Birthday' to JFK at his birthday gala in 1962 seemingly always to hand whenever programme makers wished to press home the point, Marilyn's disappointing one-night stand with President Kennedy suddenly escalated into one of the greatest, immensely illicit, extremely exciting, highly glamorous love affairs of the 20th century. Sadly, it seemed that the public had become preoccupied with credibility rather than with the truth; with the believable rather than the true.

Just ten years after her tragic death, it seemed that almost every low-life even remotely associated with the actress was queuing up to cash in on her memory and play their part in cruelly rewriting her story. In fact, the aforementioned Robert Slatzer was a classic example: with two books and numerous appearances in various reports and television programmes about Marilyn, just like the actress Jeanne Carmen he was able to turn a passing acquaintance with Monroe into a profitable, lifetime career.

According to Slatzer, he and Marilyn met at 20th Century-Fox in July 1946, dated for the next six years and got married, in Tijuana, Mexico on Saturday 4 October 1952. But, following an objection by her boss at the studio, Darryl F. Zanuck, their 72-hour wedding was annulled and their marriage certificate destroyed. Many have poured scorn on his allegations; unsurprising really, since the only evidence he could provide showing him with the actress, were five photographs taken of them together on the set of the movie *Niagara* in late 1952. So was this former newspaper reporter really Marilyn's second husband? And did he really spend the weekend of 3 to 5 October with her in Mexico, getting married to her on the day in between, as he so often testified?

The simple answer is no. He was just a fantasist. After meeting Marilyn just once, at Niagara Falls, he became totally besotted with her. Soon after, in August 1952, news of an alleged romance between the pair managed to find its way into one of Dorothy Kilgallen's gossip columns. As Kilgallen wrote, 'A dark horse in the Marilyn Monroe romance derby is Bob Slatzer, from Columbus, Ohio, literary critic. He's been wooing her by phone and mail and improving her mind with gifts of the world's greatest books.' However, the tip-off about it came from Slatzer himself.

Then, in a May 1957 interview for *Confidential* magazine, Slatzer unashamedly gave fabricated details of his sexual affair with the actress, claiming he had slept with her in between her dates with DiMaggio. And his connection to the actress went up another echelon four years later when, in his 1961 book *The Agony of Marilyn Monroe*, author George Carpozi Jr inadvertently reiterated Kilgallen's tale about Slatzer's fruitless attempts to woo Monroe with phone calls and gifts. Slatzer's fixation was incessant. In June 1968, with the real Marilyn no longer around to chase, he began dating lookalike Paula Lane, who had impersonated the actress in Jerry Lewis's 1961 comedy *The Ladies' Man* and appeared in the 1964 movie *What a Way to Go*, ironically a vehicle once earmarked for Monroe herself.

In a desperate need of help to finish his own book about Monroe, on Monday 2 October 1972 Slatzer approached journalist Will Fowler with a theory that her death had been the result of a political cover-up. But Fowler was unconvinced. In his 1991 book *Reporters: Memoirs Of A Young Newspaper Man*, he disclosed that he remarked to Slatzer, 'Too bad you weren't married to Monroe. Now that would really make a good book.' Days after Fowler had started work on the first draft, Slatzer reappeared, declaring that he had indeed been married to Marilyn, but only 'for a weekend'. Fowler naturally became apprehensive and requested his name to be removed from the subsequent June 1974 publication, *The Life And Curious Death Of Marilyn Monroe*. In 1991, Slatzer's lies even formed the basis of the American movie *Marilyn and Me*, starring Susan Griffiths and Jesse Dobson. He died in Los Angeles on Monday 28 March 2005 after a long illness.

So where exactly was Marilyn during that first week of October 1952? The answer: in Los Angeles, shopping, socialising, giving interviews and spending time with Joe DiMaggio. I can reveal that, on Wednesday 1 October, she was in Hollywood being introduced to both his family and his close pal, comedian Lou Costello. Two days later, on Friday 3 October, the day that Slatzer claimed she eloped with him to Mexico, she was actually in the 20th Century-Fox Commissary, being interviewed – as we have already seen – by Lydia Lane. Moreover, one day later, on Saturday 4 October, the actress was seen out shopping on Wilshire Boulevard with her drama coach, Natasha Lytess.

Marilyn herself attempted to dispel the gossip about these alleged affairs when, in a Monday 24 November 1952 interview with United Press's Hollywood correspondent, Aline Mosby, she forthrightly declared she 'hadn't dated anyone' since Joe DiMaggio the previous March, remarked she had 'no plans for marriage', would not get married until it was 'just right', and added she was 'not ready for it at this time'. Furthermore, it stretches credibility to the limit to believe that she could simply slip away from Joe DiMaggio, head off to Mexico with a man she barely knew and marry him. Ironically, during the weekend of the alleged Mexican marriage, rumours circulated in the papers that Marilyn had just secretly got hitched to Joe, her current date,. Either by accident or design, we have to wonder whether Slatzer's scheme was actually cack-handedly inspired by the title of Monroe's recently released comedy, which was running in some cinemas across America that October . . . *We're Not Married*.

But quite possibly the most damaging contribution to Monroe's post-life legacy was the publication in July 1973 of Pulitzer Prize-winning author Norman Mailer's biography, *Marilyn*. In one of the most infamous moments of American TV history, the writer foolishly accepted an invitation to promote his book on the top-rated CBS news and features presentation *60 Minutes*, hosted by Mike Wallace. As one critic remarked,

'Submitting to a television interview with Wallace is like opening your door to the Boston Strangler.'

In front of millions, and following a severe grilling from the host, Mailer admitted that he had carried out very little research (he wrote his book in just 60 days, acquiring most of the information within from Guiles' 1969 publication), could not vouch for any of the events mentioned in it, did not interview any of the key characters in Monroe's life and, owing to his gargantuan financial commitment to both his ex-wives and children, had written the book because he 'needed the money very badly'. (The publishers, Grosset & Dunlap, had handed him a $10,000 advance.) The segment was, quite aptly, entitled 'Norman Mailer and the Fast Buck'.

At the end of the interview, viewers were left in no doubt that they had just witnessed the sight of Mailer and his second-rate, severely flawed, highly fabricated, plagiarism-accused book being torn, ripped and mutilated in front of millions of television watchers. But sadly, so too had Marilyn's once impregnable legacy. For the multitude of inquisitive Monroe fans watching, unaware of the dark side of her life, the actress's once flawless, unassailable image had been irretrievably tarnished.

Chapter Five

Wednesday 7 February 1962–Sunday 22 April 1962

Early in 1962, no sharp-witted Hollywood publicist could hide the fact that Marilyn's two most recent films, *Let's Make Love* and *The Misfits*, had misfired at the box office. On Wednesday 7 February, news of this sudden lack of cinematic success inexplicably became a mainstay of several newspapers. The beliefs that Marilyn's fame 'may be on the skids' and that 'her fans are no longer faithful' were now common among many of the world's columnists. The recent announcement that mail at her fan club had dipped from 8,000 letters a week to just 50, only managed to emphasise the points further.

Additional, but more damning evidence of her apparent fall from favour came in the results of a new film poll, which listed the current, most eminent box-office stars of the United States. Amazingly, Marilyn Monroe was not among the top 25 names recorded. The revelation seemed to initiate a worldwide onslaught on the actress. An examination of her fading popularity was even carried out by New York columnist John Gold, who revealed in the London *Evening News*, 'A year or two ago, the appearance of Marilyn Monroe on the streets of New York, Los Angeles or London tied up traffic for blocks. But today it results in only a few turned heads . . . '

The bad press was incessant. An American magazine article, entitled 'Star at a Turning Point', pointed out that, 'In the 35th year of her life, she's now spoofing the pin-up girl she once was.' In an article in *Show Business Illustrated*, a leading entertainment writer solemnly speculated,

'It is apparent that Monroe is at the turning point in her career . . . Her personal popularity is diminished and her future in Hollywood, on the surface at least, does not seem bright.'

However, support for the actress was close at hand. When told about Marilyn's apparent decline in public admiration, Billy Wilder, the director of her smash-hit 1959 film *Some Like It Hot*, cryptically remarked, 'The idea that she may be slipping is like saying marble is out of fashion when 100 sculptors are just waiting to get their chisels in a choice piece.'

On Sunday 11 February, while pre-production work on *Something's Got To Give* was haphazardly rumbling on at Fox and negative press about her was continuing to permeate the papers, Marilyn was busy preparing for a trip to New York, delayed from the 8th thanks to the move to her new house and her photo shoot with Willy Rizzo. An unexpected guest at Fifth Helena that morning was actress Edith Evanson. A veteran of many film and television roles, in particular Universal's small-screen western series *Wagon Train*, she had been employed by Fox to teach Swedish dialect to Monroe for her part in the forthcoming movie as Ingrid Tic, the foreign maid whose identity the actress's character adopts after her return from apparent death. 'Director George Cukor, an old friend of mine, asked me to coach Marilyn for her role,' she recalled for the *Corpus Christi Caller Times* in 1962. 'I met her first at her home. Everything was dark, heavy and depressing. It had a creepy feeling about it but I thought nothing of it because she talked of her plans for decorating and especially landscaping.

'When it came time to leave, she pleaded with me to ride to the airport with her in her chauffeur-driven car. At the airport, she pleaded again that I accompany her to New York . . . She was so pleading but I couldn't leave my husband at home. She understood.' Her revealing recollections continued. 'I was amazed at how she looked for the flight east. Her hair was not combed. She wore a dingy pair of Capri pants that were much the worse for wear.'

The sharp-eyed New York columnist John Sampson was on hand to witness Marilyn's arrival at Idlewild Airport later that day. In his desire to perpetuate the 'Marilyn is no longer popular' rumour, he despondently remarked in his piece, published a few days later, 'There was nobody to greet her, nobody to take her picture, nobody to ask her for her autograph. Not even a solitary wolf-whistle.'

So how did Marilyn manage to go about her business in an extremely busy airport without being recognised? Were her fans really snubbing her, as the press believed? Well, *no*. The simple truth was that she dashed through the airport wearing her obligatory disguise: shades and a dark-coloured wig. (That day it was red.) In her desire for anonymity she had also booked herself on the flight under the pseudonym 'Marjorie Stengal'.

(Borrowed from a woman she once knew, Monroe had been intermittently using this alias for almost ten years. In an attempt to deter fans and newspaper reporters, the moniker was even used on the doorbell at her North Doheny Drive apartment.)

Tired of the endless jostles with the waiting press, Marilyn simply enjoyed being incognito, a fact that Sampson conveniently failed to point out in his article. He obviously recognised her, but no one else did. In the concluding months of 1961 and in early 1962, as we know, Monroe often used this form of dress when she travelled. (We can therefore disregard the oft-told tales of how the actress only wore such disguises when she attended clandestine meetings with President Kennedy. Incidentally, at this point in the month, he was away with his family in Glen Ora, Virginia and did not return to the White House until 9.42am on Monday 12 February.)

Marilyn's time in New York, which lasted until Saturday 17 February, was split between preparing files for Fox, flagging down cabs at 52nd and Madison, and visiting places such as the restaurant Sardis and the clothing stores Saks, Lilly Daché and Lord & Taylor. Trips to the Actors Studio, Carnegie Hall, the Lowe's State Theatre and Greenwich Village's Theatre de Lys, where she watched the off-Broadway show *Brecht on Brecht*, starring singer Lotte Lenya, were also slipped into her extremely busy schedule.

On Tuesday 13 February, she attended the premiere of Franco Zeffirelli's production of *Romeo and Juliet* at Manhattan's City Center. She was seen mingling among the star-studded crowd at the venue's after-show party, an invite-only event organised by Lee Strasberg. The City Center's manager, Jean Dalrymple, was naturally present, accompanied by her husband, Major General Philip Ginder. Lee introduced Marilyn to the General with the words, 'Meet a lady who is a general in her business.' The story goes that he appraised her, nodded, thought for a second and approvingly remarked, 'Yes, four stars.' The actress arrived back at her 57th Street apartment at precisely 2.30am.

While in New York she also received an inoculation for her forthcoming trip to Mexico, a visit arranged by Frank Sinatra through the country's former president, Miguel Aleman. Another pastime was perusing, with Strasberg's wife Paula, yet another unsatisfying draft of *Something's Got To Give*. The latest version of the screenplay had been completed by Nunnally Johnson the previous Monday, 12 February. Marilyn's scrawling across many of its 108 pages makes for very interesting reading indeed.

Across its front, she annotated the words, 'We've got a dog here.' On page 7, the actress queried the character Bianca's use of the term 'psychosomatic'.

'Would she come right out with this sort of thing?' she asked. On page 23, with regard to the sequence where Bianca takes hold of her husband Nick's hand, Marilyn scribbled the words, 'Let's remember she is frigid. We all know what Kinsey found out about most females. This is got to be in one way or another.' (The Kinsey in question was Dr Albert C. Kinsey, the author of two world-famous books on human sexual behaviour, *Sexual Behavior in the Human Male* (1948) and *Sexual Behavior in the Human Female* (1953). At the time of writing, he theorised that many women of a certain age – late twenties, mid thirties – possessed equal heterosexual and lesbian tendencies.)

Marilyn's markings make it clear she was a keen devourer of the doctor's work. Certainly, bothered by her lack of a good education, the actress was a voracious reader. The books in her 400-plus assortment confirmed she was passionate about a wide range of subjects and far from the dumb blonde she was frequently portrayed as by the world's media.

Volumes reflecting her intelligence and comprehensive interests, as well as children's publications, the Bible and books on literature, art, drama, poetry, politics, history, theology, philosophy, psychology and gardening, sat proudly on her bookshelves. Classic works of literature by authors such as Twain and Tolstoy, and publications including F. Scott Fitzgerald's *The Great Gatsby*, James Joyce's *Dubliners*, Ernest Hemingway's *The Sun Also Rises*, Lewis Carroll's *Alice's Adventures in Wonderland* and a two-volume set, *The Life And Times Of Sigmund Freud*, were also represented among her vast collection. So too were Mabel Elsworth Todd's classic 1937 study of physiology *The Thinking Body* and Sir James George Frazer's, *The Golden Bough: A Study in Magic and Religion.*

'I'm a bookworm and proud of it,' she exclaimed to Hollywood columnist Erskine Johnson on Tuesday 22 April 1952. 'Sure I'm a book girl. But I'm not an intellectual and I'm mot interested in being one. I read because I want to expand as much and grow as much as I can.'

Conflicts with Cherie Redmond, her lawyer Milton 'Mickey' Rudin's business secretary, also came to a head during this trip to New York. For some inexplicable reason, Marilyn had taken an instant dislike to Redmond immediately after she took up her $689-a-month post the previous year. Problems were ignited when Monroe learnt that Redmond's Christian name was the same as that of Marilyn's character in the 1956 movie *Bus Stop*. As Eunice Murray recalled in her 1975 book, *Marilyn: The Last Months*, 'Marilyn had a week (*sic*) in New York to observe her and had formed a sudden judgement. "I don't want her advice about *anything* but business matters."'

Marilyn's strange grievance even followed her back to Los Angeles, becoming so intense that she decided she did not want Redmond anywhere near her new home. It naturally caused problems. When Cherie needed the actress to sign various cheques, letters or legal documents, she would be forced to hand them over the gate to Murray at the front of the house. Redmond naturally became curious about Marilyn's hostility; however, no answer was forthcoming. Perhaps Monroe had the solution. In a remark to Murray, the actress once quipped, 'Cherie once drank the last remains of my bottle of Dom Perignon.'

However, Redmond did have her uses and, unlike so many of Marilyn's other associates, was actually quite diligent with the actress's finances. This was evident in a memo sent to Eunice Murray on Wednesday 25 April 1962, in which she noted how Monroe could have saved 'anywhere between $50 and $60' if she had purchased the refrigerator for her new Brentwood home directly from a recognised Hotpoint dealer instead of an appliance distributor. Furthermore, thanks to her close scrutiny of the invoice Marilyn received for her limousine hire during that February 1962 stay in New York, she noticed an overcharging of $10.50: $10 on Wednesday 14 February and 50 cents the following day. She forcibly pointed out the fact in a letter sent to Exec-U-Car Inc.'s secretary, Blanche L. Marshall, who, in a letter drafted on Wednesday 21 March, put the error squarely down to the fact that she was ill, working from her bed and 'quite unable to work at all, so evidentally didn't think very clearly'. Her grovelling concluded with the line, 'I will surely try to be more careful next time.' She was. The company could hardly afford to lose Marilyn's custom. Her total bill for ten days of limousine hire had come to a grand total of $830.26, despite the fact she only used the vehicle for seven.

The limousine didn't go to waste, though. The Strasbergs made full use of it prior to the actress's arrival. For instance, at 2.45pm on Thursday 8 February, while Marilyn was busy moving into her new home, a car collected Lee and Paula from Monroe's apartment and escorted them first to the Actors Studio and then to the Savoy Hilton Hotel. After that, following a luxurious sightseeing cruise around the city's streets, at 8.30pm they were dropped off at the Carnegie Hall to watch a vocal performance by American operatic mezzo-soprano Jean Kraft. The evening concluded at 12 midnight when the Strasbergs were dropped back at Marilyn's apartment.

While the actress fretted and socialised in the Big Apple, updates of how her Fifth Helena renovations were progressing were regularly fed to her. During one such telephone exchange, she was informed that the person now in charge of the makeover was Murray's son-in-law, Norman Jeffries, along with his brother, Keith. This naturally astonished Marilyn. Just prior to her trip to New York, she had personally employed local handyman Ray Tolman and carpenter Austin A. Innes to execute the necessary tasks. In her absence, they had been fired and the Jeffries brothers hired, at a combined cost of $360 a month. Marilyn's authority had clearly been undermined.

Their appointment as the actress's new handymen was a perfect example of Dr Ralph Greenson's growing influence on Monroe's life. Besides the appointment of Murray as Marilyn's live-in companion and so-called housekeeper, her lawyer, Milton 'Mickey' Rudin, had also been appointed on Greenson's recommendation; Rudin happened to be not only Greenson's own lawyer but also his brother-in-law. The doctor was now even offering advice on her business affairs. And in the case of her new movie, he had been instrumental in the hiring of his friend Henry Weinstein – who had superseded Fox's original choice, David Brown, at the end of December 1961 – as the picture's producer.

Since the main job of any producer on a Monroe film was to get her to the studio and set on time, Fox thought the connection between producer and actress a vital one. Brown, a former top executive for the studio, had first encountered Marilyn back in 1952 when their paths crossed on the steps of the studio's administration building, and later admitted he thought she was 'the most beautiful girl in the world'. As the studio's story editor, Brown had been responsible for purchasing the narrative featured in Marilyn's 1953 box-office smash-hit comedy, *How to Marry a Millionaire*. Nine years on, *Something's Got To Give* was set to be his first in the role as producer. So why was he replaced?

'Nobody thought that my first project would attract (director) George Cukor,' he later explained. But his conjecture was wrong. After all, Cukor had signed on to direct the movie while Brown was still engaged on the production. However, rumours soon began to circulate which insinuated that the order to dismiss Brown had emanated from Ralph Greenson, and the rumours proved to be true. Ominously, thanks to his appointment as both mentor and therapist on the film, Greenson's presence would continue to linger throughout the making of Marilyn's movie.

Away from *Something's Got To Give*, in New Milford, Connecticut, on Saturday 17 February, Monroe's former husband, Arthur Miller, married as expected for the third time. Marilyn was alerted well in advance of the nuptials, but to the outside world it was still a closely guarded secret. Even Miller's father, Isidore, was kept in the dark about it. According to Eunice Murray, the wedding made the actress feel like a 'neglected sex symbol'. Instead of returning to her Brentwood home that day, she chose to fly on to Florida. Her publicist, Pat Newcomb, and personal hair stylist, George

Masters, were there to meet her at Los Angeles International Airport to catch her afternoon flight.

The reasons for the actress's decision to visit Miami were twofold. First, moved by his touching, handwritten letter on Thursday 8 February, in which he expressed both his loneliness at the Sea Isle resort where he was staying and despondency that he had 'no one to enjoy all this beauty with', she wanted desperately to catch up with her former father-in-law. Second, realising he was oblivious of the fact, she wanted to convey news of his son's latest marriage. Monroe was extremely fond of Isidore and affectionately called him 'Dad'. He loved this pet name and would even sign his letters to her with it.

Marilyn's eleventh-hour visit was announced by way of a telegram, which read: 'Arriving Eastern Airlines Flight 605 at 9:05 tonight, have reservations at Fontainebleau. Love you, Marilyn.' As Isidore waited for the actress at the airport, a man in pursuit of small-talk enquired who he was expecting. 'Marilyn Monroe,' Isidore proudly replied. By the reaction on the stranger's face, Miller could see that he was shocked by this retort. The stranger clearly couldn't comprehend how an elderly, quite ordinary man could possibly be waiting to meet one of the world's most famous and beautiful movie stars. When the plane arrived and the passengers started to filter through into the airport's welcoming area, the stranger apparently strolled over to the actress and informed her, 'There's a tall, elderly man looking for you.' 'Oh, that's Mr. Miller,' she replied. 'I came to Florida to see him.' The man was speechless.

Immediately after leaving the airport, and after saying farewell to Miller senior, the actress and her colleagues climbed into a taxi and headed straight to the safe haven of Miami Beach's Fontainebleau Hotel. Upon her arrival, she checked in using yet another alias, this time 'Gloria Lovell', a name borrowed from Frank Sinatra's secretary. During her three-day stay, she resided in a $125-a-night suite situated on the 17th floor, just down the hall from the hotel's plush presidential suite. (Contrary to popular, long-standing myths, Marilyn did *not* meet up with President Kennedy during her stay at the hotel. During the weekend of 17 and 18 February 1962, President Kennedy was in Glen Ora, Middleburg, Virginia with his wife, and did not return to the White House until 10.10am on Monday 19 February.)

Later that evening, Marilyn joined Isidore for dinner at the Fontainebleau's Club Gigi restaurant and ended the night by watching a show in the nearby Cabaret Minaret night club at the Sea Isle resort, where he was still residing. Unfortunately, the performance was less than satisfactory and Isidore suggested they leave. 'We can't do that,' she protested. 'It'd hurt the performers' feelings.' Once the show had reached its natural conclusion, the actress and 'Dad' strolled along Collins Avenue where they came face-to-face with some pushy autograph hunters. He was aghast at such behaviour from total strangers and asked why she accommodated it. 'When they stop doing it,' she explained, 'I'm finished.'

The following day, Miller invited some of his friends to meet Marilyn at the Fontainebleau. While the guests chatted, the actress happily mingled among them serving snacks and drinks. In a further display of generosity she insisted on taking them all out for dinner. Later that evening, after the sumptuous meal had been digested and Miller's highly appreciative guests had departed, Marilyn and Isidore sat and relaxed in the actress's suite. Their conversation focused on Arthur Miller's marriage. Isidore made it clear he was upset at being kept in the dark about it. Noticing this, Marilyn quickly eased the situation by saying, 'I'm sure a letter must be on its way.'

They bid their goodnights and Isidore immediately returned to his room at the Sea Isle. Later, preparing for bed, he discovered that the actress had slipped $200 into a pocket of the coat which he had hung up in the closet in her room. He immediately called Marilyn and insisted she take back the money. But she was insistent. She wanted him to have it. 'I know you spent more than that on me,' she protested. 'Take it. I won't feel right if you don't.'

Three days later, Isidore typed a note to the actress to thank her for her visit. On Sea Isle Hotel notepaper, the letter, in part, read:

> Dear Marilyn, I can't tell you in mere words just how much your trip to Florida meant to me. I don't ever remember having such a good time! The guests of the Sea Isle Hotel can't get over how beautiful you looked the night you was there. They were so thrilled to see you in person. They are still talking about it. Your visit was the best excitement they have had all season and expect to have . . . Please let me hear from you soon. Again, many, many thanks for a <u>wonderful</u> visit. With love, Dad.

On Monday 19 February, Marilyn was on the move again. She flew out to Fort Lauderdale to visit Joe DiMaggio, who was with his former team, the New York Yankees, during their spring training session. In these turbulent and emotional times, she knew that Joe was one of the very few people in her life that she could truly rely on. She spent the first evening there in a secluded hotel under another assumed name. The second was spent with her former husband in his penthouse suite in the Yankee Clipper Motel, so-called in DiMaggio's honour. Atypically, she checked in using her correct name.

A reporter tipped off about Marilyn's low-key visit caught sight of the actress as she attempted to discreetly flee the building with DiMaggio on Wednesday morning. 'Is there going to be any reconciliation?' the journalist shouted. 'Reconciliation?' she asked, as she was hastily clambering inside DiMaggio's car. 'I don't know what you mean. We're still good friends. There's nothing to reconcile.' With Joe at the helm, the vehicle quickly sped away, heading for Miami Airport. Marilyn and her trusty companions would be taking a morning flight to Mexico City.

Marilyn was accompanied as she made her entry into La Ciudad de los Palacios ('The City of Palaces') by the ever-present Pat Newcomb and George Masters. (Her live-in companion, Eunice Murray, had already been in Mexico for a week, staying with her brother-in-law, Churchill, who had offered to be a guide for Marilyn and her guests during their stay.) Immediately following their arrival, Monroe and her entourage took up residence in rooms 1110 and 1111 of the colourful Continental Hilton Hotel on Paseo de la Reforma. (Other establishments, such as the El Presidente in Acapulco, the Monte Cassino in Genova and the nearby, decidedly old-fashioned, Americana Reforma had also been considered.) And it was there, one day later, at 3pm on Thursday 22 February, in the building's Grand Ballroom, to satisfy the press's demands for a meeting with the actress, that Marilyn participated in her first and only Pat Newcomb-arranged Mexican press conference.

Characteristically, she was late. The assembled crowd of more than two hundred photographers and reporters were kept waiting for almost an hour before she finally arrived. Looking decidedly tired and slightly red-eyed, Marilyn swanned into the cigarette smoke-drenched room wearing a tight-fitting, lime-green silk Gucci jersey dress and clutching a matching transparent lime-green silk scarf. Her blonde hair shone under the bright, unceasing camera flashes. Women as well as men excitedly clambered on to chairs just to get a better glimpse of the actress, who took the opportunity to proudly display her new slimline figure and in doing so, effectively kill off rumours that she had lost her battle with her weight. She had dropped over 25 pounds, reaching the lowest weight of her adult life, and naturally, everyone at the event remarked how wonderful she looked.

Marilyn's graceful poses for the cameras soon gave way to a brief but energetic demonstration of the twist, following which she positioned herself on a settee and began parrying, through an interpreter, a wide range of questions, some of which were quite personal.

'Would you pose again in the nude for a calendar?' a reporter cheekily asked in reference to Marilyn's notorious 1952 picture. 'Under the same circumstances, yes,' she replied, champagne glass in hand. 'I got $50 for the picture. I needed the money badly at the time.' A roar of laughter reverberated around the room when she added, 'I'm more particular now about who sees me in the nude.'

The questions were ceaseless. 'Are your measurements the same as they were when the calendar picture was taken?' asked another journalist. 'I never measure myself, but without wanting to boast, I think the measurements are better now than when that picture was taken . . . I think they're *larger* now,' she quipped. The actress was in fine form and frequently made the assembled crowd chuckle and cheer. When one newsman enquired whether she was dating any Hollywood actors, Marilyn pondered for a moment before replying, 'No, I'm not dating any actors . . . just intelligent Mexican businessmen!' The remark naturally prompted one reporter to enquire, 'What do you think of the country's men?' Her response, 'Mexican men are very warm and very intense . . . and Mexican women are very beautiful,' drew wild, enthusiastic cheers from the gathered crowd.

When the applause died down, a sharp-eyed reporter switched the focus to the actress's dress, which he observed was more clinging than usual. To which Marilyn quipped, 'You should see it on the hanger!' 'You were referred to recently as a female Charlie Chaplin,' asked another journalist. 'Any comment?' The actress replied, 'I consider that a flattering exaggeration.' One reporter then asked her if she thought Jayne Mansfield's recent headline-making stay on a remote island was a publicity stunt. 'Personally,' she wittingly replied, 'I wouldn't get lost on an island with a publicity man.' Laughter once more echoed around the room.

Unsurprisingly, questions relating to matrimony and men soon followed. 'What do you like best in a man?' asked one reporter. 'Masculinity,' Marilyn replied with a broad smile. 'Do you think you'll marry again?' 'I'm keeping my eyes open,' she responded. 'Even though my three marriages failed, I haven't given up.' 'Do you have anyone in mind?' enquired another journalist. 'I'm keeping my eyes open,' the actress reiterated, while taking another sip of champagne. 'Which of your marriages were the happiest?' asked a reporter. Marilyn thought for a second before replying, 'The last two.'

The interrogations now focused on the two men in question, and the atmosphere in the room became decidedly icy. Asked about the recent marriage of ex-spouse Miller, the actress retorted, 'I'm happy he remarried. I learnt a lot from him. I wish him all the best.' When approached about the recurring rumours she might wed Joe DiMaggio again, Monroe shook her head and interestingly replied, 'No. We tried that once and it didn't work.'

In between the quick-fire questions, Monroe continued to sip champagne, plugged her new movie, and innocently, though possibly not

unwittingly, gave credence to the rumour that she did not wear underwear. Unsurprisingly, the fact was not lost on some of the leering, eagle-
eyed reporters, one of whom decided to unashamedly press the actress on
the matter. 'I cannot see the colour of your underclothes,' the man
declared. 'Can you affirm that you do not use any?' To which the actress
took another sip of champagne and unapologetically confirmed that she
did *not*.

Following a rapturous round of applause, the conference was over.
Monroe returned to her hotel room where at 5pm, following a request by
their mutual friend, Martha Josefy, she was welcomed to the country by
American-born Frederick Vanderbilt Field and his wife, Nieves. The visit,
arranged through New York friends and based on his friendship with
Arthur Miller, lasted just an hour, during which time they arranged a
furniture-buying trip to Toulca for the following day. As Field informed
her, it was market day and would provide Marilyn with the perfect
opportunity to purchase the items she desired for her new home.

Over the ensuing four days, in the company of Field and his wife,
Marilyn toured Toulca and visited shops and markets in Cuernavaca and
Taxco. Items of ethnic, hand-crafted furniture, namely a wooden coffee
table, four wooden benches, a wood and leather handmade chair and a
specially ordered silver-plated, blue-stone hinged box were among her first
purchases. Many other items followed, including mirrors, chairs, maracas,
throw blankets, pottery, baskets, a straw hat, an oval copper bowl and hand-
painted ornamental clay doves, blue and clear glass platters, an assortment
of specially produced soda glass tumblers, and four wire wall-hangings of
Mexican musicians. Decorative, hand-painted wall tiles were also
acquired: blue, green and gold ones for her kitchen and orange and gold
flowered ones for her master bathroom.

Her spending was incessant. Other items acquired included a
beautiful painting of a naked woman (known as a *desnudo*) entitled
'Olga', a rosewood silver and gold chess set, a specially ordered woven
carpet, a wall-hanging tapestry entitled 'Chac-Mool', hand-carved living
room chairs, a large bright-red sofa (which would not arrive at Marilyn's
home until late August), some copper candelabras acquired at William
Sprattling's famous silversmith factory in Taxco, and a large, highly
valuable Mexican wardrobe. (Unfortunately, due to the limit on exports
set by the Mexican government to prevent priceless antiques such as this
from leaving the country, the wardrobe would not reach the Cheli Air
Force Base in Los Angeles for another two years.) Besides the
acquisitions for her new home, one purchase was decidedly less
decorative. As her personal physician Dr Hyman Engelberg testified, due
to Mexico's extremely lax law regarding tranquillisers at the time,

Marilyn was available to obtain, without prescription, a small consignment of Nembutal tablets.

Lunch each day was usually taken at the popular Sanborns Restaurant on the Paseo de la Reforma boulevard. Seated near her through most of her visits was the 37-year-old, New York-born artist Nick Scire. A veteran of the Second World War, he had attended art school at the Brooklyn Museum and later at the Esmeralda Art School in Mexico City. In 1952, he was introduced to Carlos Tornel, a member of a prominent Mexican family and the grandson of the Major General of the Mexican Army in the war of 1945.

'Being Tornel's close friend,' Scire recalled, 'I was privileged to meet and visit people and places the ordinary American would not have access to, and it was during the summer of 1962 that I was fortunate enough to meet Marilyn Monroe because Carlos and I were staying at his grandfather's home in Mexico City.

'She was staying in a hotel on Paseo de la Reforma, which was the main street in Mexico City and when she came out there was always a large group of photographers waiting to take pictures of her because she was front-page news. Just about every day that Marilyn was in Mexico City, she had lunch at Sanborns, which was a short walk from her hotel. She usually arrived between 1.30 and 2pm. To get a table in the VIP section there, in those days, you either had to have a standing reserved table and/or be a VIP. She was always seated at the table next to my friend Carlos, who had a reservation there. Marilyn always sat in the same seat with her back to the wall. When entering Sanborns, hers was on the right side of the restaurant, near the wall, away from the window. She was always accompanied by at least two or three people. No professional photographers were allowed in when Marilyn was dining although, if you had a reserved table in the VIP area, you were able to take a quick photo of her . . . Marilyn wore light coloured clothes and was always very well dressed.

'The first time I spoke to Marilyn, I was seated within three feet of her table. Being one of the few people in Sanborns that spoke both English and Spanish, I waved to Marilyn and said, "Hello" in English. She waved and said, "Hello" back. She asked me what I was doing in Mexico City and I replied I was an artist and sculptor. Marilyn was interested in art and invited Carlos and I to join her for lunch. We joined our two tables together. The times I met her, even though I was so close to her, we never were able to have a long conversation. However, Marilyn did say she was planning to visit Frank Sinatra in Acapulco where he had a house. I told Marilyn I was going to do a sculpture of her and she gave a little laugh. I also told her that I hoped she had a very nice time in Mexico City. Marilyn ordered Cuba Libre [rum and coke with lime] with her lunch and Carlos and I left.'

Her lasting impression on Scire was one of desolation. 'Her face was sad,' he recalled. 'You could see that the events in the past few weeks were not very nice for her. When I met Marilyn, you could see by her face and manners that she was like a defeated person. She looked tired and she was not the real image of her character. There was a great sadness to Marilyn when you spoke to her.'

As Marilyn's time in the city rolled on, her day in Cuernavaca was punctuated by visits to the home of actress Merle Oberon and, later, the 30-acre Japanese-style house belonging to the world-famous New York-born socialite Barbara Hutton. Monroe used the invites as the perfect opportunity for tips on how to furnish and decorate a Mexican-style home. She also attended a party thrown by Murray's brother-in-law, Churchill, and paid a visit to the Byrna Art Gallery where she purchased three paintings. She naturally couldn't escape work. During her stay in the city, she was interviewed by the local reporter, Eva Samano, and played host to the current *Something's Got To Give* scriptwriter Nunnally Johnson, who had brought with him the very latest version of the script for her to approve. During their short time together, the actress curiously asked Johnson, 'Have you been trapped into this too?'

On Saturday 24 February, Marilyn was the guest of honour at the Coyoagan home of Mexican actor, writer and director Emilio Fernández Romo and his actress wife, Colunga. His invitation had come on Thursday, just moments after the actress had checked into the Hilton Hotel. She accepted on the precondition that it was a private, low-key affair, with just a select few in attendance. When news leaked out that the great Hollywood actress would be visiting his home, however, the number of attendees at the party that night suddenly quadrupled. It seemed that every individual from the Mexican film and newspaper industry had been invited.

The plethora of cameramen that night excitedly hovered around Monroe and joyously snapped images of the actress being taught by Emilio how to sip her first tequila, the country's famed drink. To an accompaniment of cheers and applause, she successfully downed it Mexican style, with salt and lemon. Music at the gathering was provided by the Mariachis, a six-piece group of Mexican guitar-strumming, violin-playing street buskers. After just an hour, however, she and Eunice Murray bid the hosts a good night and headed back to their hotel rooms.

The gathering did nonetheless produce a new acquaintance in the actress's life. Earlier, as the party stumbled on, Marilyn was introduced to José Bolaños. The slim, dark-haired, sharp-dressed 26-year-old Mexican impressed Monroe when he informed her he was a noted director and screenwriter in Mexican and American cinema. (He had in fact considerably embellished his curriculum vitae. Jose's only notable movie credit up to this point was as the writer on the 1959 film *La Cucaracha*.) He won Monroe's affections further by telling her he was a huge admirer. With the actress no doubt touched by his adulation, as well as his knowledge of Mexican furniture, handicrafts and curios, Bolaños suddenly became Marilyn's self-appointed escort for the remaining three days of the trip.

The following day, Sunday 25 February, with Frederick Vanderbilt Field once more on her arm, Marilyn attended a reception in honour of Princess Antonia De Braganza of Portugal at the home of Mexican actor Dennis Bourke. She had enjoyed her time in Mexico so much that, on Monday 26 February, she cancelled her planned shopping excursion to Acapulco just so she could remain where she was. She spent the days shopping and sightseeing, inadvertently causing traffic jams when she stopped to sign her signature and chat to her adoring fans in the street.

On Thursday 1 March, in the company of Mexico's First Lady, Mrs Eva Samano de Lopez Mateos, Marilyn began her penultimate day in the country by visiting a Mexican food plant. This was swiftly followed by a tour of the nearby orphanage for Indian children, the Catholic National Institute for the Protection of Children. At the end of her hour-long visit, the actress walked into Lopez Mateos' office, sat down at the desk, opened her small purse, took out her cheque book and, in keeping with a ritual performed by previous visiting Americans, made out a $1,000 payment to the Institution's programme, which provided free daily breakfasts for the country's thousands of needy schoolchildren. Pictures of Marilyn happily handing over the donation to the First Lady were taken. The actress was clearly moved by the kids' plight. 'I know what it means to go without breakfasts,' she touchingly remarked to Lopez Mateos, the Institute's executives and the gathered reporters.

But once the reporters had left the room, she once more reached into her purse, extracted her cheque book and wrote out another draft, this time for $10,000. The expressions on the faces of those in charge at the orphanage had made it clear to her they had anticipated a donation far in excess of the $1,000 the actress had originally offered. So with guilt getting the better of her, she increased her gift, even though she was herself severely strapped for cash. 'This tour was the highlight of my stay in Mexico,' Marilyn commented to the reporters as she left the building. Her pleasant ten-day visit was almost at an end. Away from Los Angeles and free from pressures of work, she had been able to sleep each night without the aid of her recently purchased tranquillisers, the first time in almost 15 years that she had been capable of doing so.

Her final two evenings in the country were spent with Bolaños at the Garibaldi Plaza night club. Famed for its roving troubadours, the afore-mentioned Mariachis, it was a venue haunted by many of the city's budding artists and writers. Marilyn and Bolaños spent their time there drinking and watching performances by local musicians. On the evening of Thursday 1 March, the club hosted a special farewell party for Marilyn. Cameras clicked away incessantly at the sight of the actress as she smooched passionately with her new companion. At the conclusion of the evening, she thanked everyone personally and promised she would return on Saturday 15 September, the eve of the country's Independence Day festivities. Before checking out of the Hilton, she reserved a room for that weekend too.

Monroe flew out of Mexico early on the morning of Friday 2 March and arrived back in Los Angeles at the city's International Airport approximately one hour behind schedule. Despite her joyous demeanour as she posed and waved to the waiting crowd from the doorway of her Mexicana Airline plane, she was not happy. She did not relish the thought of being back in California. This became evident when, as she rushed through the airport, the actress grumpily remarked to a *Fresno Bee* newspaper reporter, 'I no longer consider Los Angeles my home . . . My home is in New York.' In stark contrast to her pleasant and friendly demeanour in Mexico, she resolutely refused to answer any questions. Queries about her possible remarriage to Joe DiMaggio were met with a stony silence, and when asked about *Something's Got To Give*, she curtly declared, 'The filming is *not* definite because of legal complications.' Marilyn's loneliness was evident once again. Not one friend, acquaintance or associate was there to greet her at the airport.

The official word on the actress's visit to Mexico was that it had been for 'a vacation' and to pick up items, mostly 'furniture and ornaments for her newly acquired home'. This was indeed the case: she had purchased a Mexican-style home and wanted to furnish it with items produced in that country. It made perfect sense. But not to the FBI's paranoiac J. Edgar Hoover, whose monitoring of the star seemed to be increasing almost on a daily basis. He took a far more sinister approach to her visit to the country, reporting that Monroe 'was seen mingling with certain members of the ACGM [the American Communist Group of Mexico]', an organisation that comprised past and present members of the Communist Party USA, and shared a common sympathy for communism and the Soviet Union. As is verified by the letters 'SM-C', standing for 'Security Matter – Communist', under Monroe's name on the FBI files pertaining to her visit to Mexico, the FBI had now labelled the actress as a communist sympathiser.

This categorisation was not entirely surprising. Marilyn had married Arthur Miller, a man with a strong communist background, in June 1956 and, in a secret memo dated Tuesday 16 August 1955, the FBI had reported (and later confirmed as true) rumours that she had applied for a visa to visit the Soviet Union. By the late 1950s and early 1960s, those who knew the actress were united in the opinion that her political ideology was decidedly 'leftist'. She would passionately express her concerns over matters of civil rights, feminism, poverty and the burgeoning youth culture. And in 1962 – a period when hostilities between America, Soviet Russia and the rest of the world were reaching perilous new heights – an individual even flirting with communist, 'left-wing' tendencies was classified by the FBI as 'dangerous'. Although such sympathies were not classified as a crime in the USA, the bureau often treated them as such. Yet without doubt, Marilyn was an innocent pawn in the thorny predicament she was getting herself into.

The people Monroe mingled with in Mexico during that ten-day period in February and March 1962 were already known to the FBI: José Bolaños because of his recognised 'left-wing' tendencies and Frederick Vanderbilt Field since he was a dedicated communist and long-time Marxist who had fled the USA in 1953 and had been in regular contact with other Mexican-based communists. Field served as Executive Secretary of the American Peace Mobilization, an organisation with ties to the Soviet Union that had been dedicated to keeping the United States from entering the Second World War. He had also been arrested during the McCarthy era for refusing to reveal names. As a long-time communist, he both supported and befriended Fidel Castro. The FBI feared that if Monroe did indeed know state secrets through her brief conversations with Bobby Kennedy, and shared them with Field, the Cuban leader would then hear them clearly, and in turn so would Nikita Khruschev, the leader of the Soviet Union.

FBI reporters on Marilyn's case were naturally greatly alarmed when Field made it clear to associates and friends that Marilyn had several times spoken to him openly, proudly and unreservedly about her two liaisons with the Attorney General. In the FBI's apprehensive eyes, Monroe was fast becoming a lady who spoke too freely to the wrong people about the President's brother. J. Edgar Hoover must have been pretty worried about Marilyn's pillow talk; indeed, after detailed examination, it becomes apparent that the bureau's interest in the actress gained extra momentum after her alleged, but unfounded intimacy with Bobby at Peter Lawford's home on Thursday 1 February 1962. Unfortunately, the bureau's classification of the actress as a communist had now increased to that of a 'liability'.

Of course, Monroe was at fault in being so liberal with delicate information at such a precarious time in American history. (Her monitoring by the FBI would increase another notch in May when she, quite innocently, allowed Field and his wife to stay at her apartment in Manhattan during their trip to America.) But those following and filing reports on the actress must also be held accountable for the inaccuracy of some of their writings. For instance, FBI files state that 'the subject' (i.e. Monroe) 'arrived in Mexico' on Monday 19 February. But that was just not possible. The journalist camped outside Joe DiMaggio's motel in Fort Lauderdale early on Wednesday 21 February provides us with reliable evidence that Monroe was still in Miami that morning. Furthermore, a photograph exists of DiMaggio kissing his former wife goodbye as she left his company at Miami airport that day. This information clearly demonstrates that some of the detail to be found within the FBI's ever-growing files on Marilyn can be thrown into question.

Meanwhile, interest in Monroe's alleged involvement with John F. Kennedy had caught the eye of some sinister organisations. Marilyn's activities were now being monitored by the corrupt Teamster Union leader, Jimmy Hoffa, and by the Mafia, in particular by the powerful Chicago mob boss, Sam Giancana. Alongside their obvious links to the American underworld, they also had one other thing in common – a strong hatred for the Kennedys, especially Bobby who, since his appointment as Attorney General one year earlier, had made it clear he was out to nail organised crime and eradicate all 'mob' activities in the country. Top hoodlums such as Giancana and mobster Johnny Rosselli were soon placed under heavy physical and electronic surveillance by FBI agents. Subsequently, some form of revenge was always on the cards.

So when news reached them of Kennedy's friendship with Monroe, the chance of obtaining incriminating, defamatory evidence against him, particularly with regard to sexual indiscretions, was an opportunity too good to miss. A plan to deposit secret listening devices inside Marilyn's new home was soon hatched. The order to do so originated from Hoffa (FBI reports dated Wednesday 16 August 1961 reveal he was 'out to bury the Kennedys . . . [by] every means possible' and set up 'listening devices on the Kennedys' wherever feasible). When he announced his scheme to Giancana, the mobster naturally offered to help.

Bernard B. Spindel, Hoffa and America's premier wire-tapper and eavesdropper, another zealous hater of the Kennedys, was placed in charge of the operation. Soon after his appointment as Attorney General, Bobby had ordered the IRS (Internal Revenue Service) to keep Spindel under 24-hour surveillance. Even his tax returns going back to 1957 were pulled off the shelves, dusted down and re-examined. Inaccuracies were spotted and a prosecution for 'criminal violation of the tax code' followed. As a result, by 1962, Kennedy had gained another enemy. When Hoffa came to Spindel with a deal to bug Monroe's home and to catch Bobby red-handed with the actress, Spindel leapt at the chance.

However, the man handed with the task of concealing the bugs in the property was the internationally known Hollywood private detective Fred Otash, who one year earlier had proudly hinted to anyone who would listen that he had had FBI approval since 1955. Spying on Marilyn was certainly not new to him. A bureau memo dated Friday 23 April 1965 disclosed that he had investigated the actress in 1954 at the behest of both Frank Sinatra and Joe DiMaggio, the latter to see if his then wife had been sleeping around with other men.

Nor was snooping on John and Bobby Kennedy a novelty. An FBI document dated Sunday 10 July 1960 showed he had contacted a 'high-priced Hollywood call-girl' for salacious gossip about her 'participation in sex parties' involving Senator John Kennedy and his brother-in-law, Peter Lawford. Nine months later, in April 1961, Hollywood tabloid magazine *Confidential* confirmed it had hired him to 'dig up dirt' on both the Attorney General and Lawford.

So, in late February 1962, while Monroe was out and about, shopping, socialising and generally enjoying herself in Mexico, Otash – accompanied in all likelihood by his assistant, John Danoff – gained access to her house and began secreting wires and small transmitters, some no bigger than the size of a small box of matches, in the building's loft space, her telephones and, naturally, her bedrooms. It was sophisticated, hi-tech equipment. The microphones, placed inside the mouthpieces of both of her phones, were so powerful that they were perfectly capable of eavesdropping on both her conversations and the activities in the room at the exact same time.

Proof that Monroe's house, and most prominently her attic, was indeed a maze of microelectronic eavesdropping wires amalgamated with standard telephone lines, came from a most unlikely source. In 1982, actress Veronica Hamel, best known for her role as defence attorney Joyce Davenport in the popular US TV crime drama series *Hill Street Blues*, revealed that, shortly after her purchase of Marilyn's home in 1972, a contractor called to modernise the property and repair, once again, its particularly leaky roof, discovered thin audio wires hidden around the house and behind a large bush on the estate. By a strange coincidence, the man had worked in the Central Corps of the United States Government before taking up his current occupation and was very familiar with wire-tapping and bugs. He recognised that these cables were not common house wires but 'dead-room bugs', the kind used for observations back in the 1950s and 1960s and capable of high-powered surveillance on any given property for any length of time. In the words of a retired Justice Department official, they were 'standard FBI issue'.

Oblivious to how involved she had become in a very dangerous game with equally treacherous people, on Friday 2 March Marilyn flew back to Los Angeles and once more took up residence at her now bug-infested home, where her attentions were drawn back towards *Something's Got To Give*. Just a day after returning, she was once again visited by her dialect coach, Edith Evanson. 'I spent many hours with her that day and many days afterwards,' she recalled. 'She never ate anything but chopped up steak [for] breakfast, lunch and dinner. Around the house, she always wore a ragged old red housecoat. She was unkempt . . . She only had two moods. One moment, she would be a little girl; the next, a serious, mature woman. There never was any young girl or young motherhood mood. Often she would dance around the house like a little girl. I remarked about it. She answered, "You know, my husbands all said that too."'

Work turned to the new film. 'As I spoke the lines,' Evanson remembered, 'she asked me to speak them as [Greta] Garbo would. "You know," she said, "I have never seen Garbo in a movie." So I spoke as Garbo. Marilyn loved it. After several weeks of coaching, Cukor auditioned her accent. You know, he had been Garbo's favourite director. After the audition, Cukor was ecstatic. "She's like a young Garbo," he said.'

Evanson continued: 'One morning, I was at her house for a lesson and Marilyn came in with a magnolia. I asked her where she got it. She said, "I was out walking with my boyfriend last night and this one hung low enough for me to steal it." I said, "The magnolia is so like you; so white, so soft and so beautiful." She answered, "Isn't it terrible that there must be always something in life to live up to?" She looked so sad, so tragic when she said it. Marilyn did not name the boyfriend by name. I just assumed it was José Bolaños, the Mexican writer whom she had been dating.'

Late that Saturday evening, Marilyn heard, after a gap of more than ten years, from her father, Charles Stanley Gifford. The contact came via a phone call from a nurse at the Palm Springs Hospital, where the man was recovering from a severe heart attack. The nurse misleadingly informed Monroe that his condition was 'grave' and that it was unlikely he would survive, going on to relate to the actress, 'His strongest desire is to see you. He keeps talking about you all the time.'

Marilyn had often attempted to track down her real father. The actress's room-mate and fellow Hollywood star, Shelley Winters, once recalled an incident when, in March 1950, on the night that shooting had wrapped on the film *The Asphalt Jungle*, Marilyn called a man called Mortenson living in Whittier, Los Angeles, details of whom she had obtained from the

Orphan Asylum. 'She was convinced that this man was her biological father,' Winters recalled, 'and she explained to the man who she was . . . A drunken male voice responded, "Listen you tramp, I have my own family, and I don't want anything to do with Hollywood bums. Don't you ever call me again," and he hung up.' It was a false lead, the wrong Mortenson.

Following confirmation by Grace McKee, she discovered Gifford was her real father and covertly passed the fact on to her trusted drama coach, Natasha Lytess. In early 1951, after discovering that Gifford was living near Palm Springs, she plucked up enough courage to drive there, accompanied by Lytess, and try to meet him. With nerves getting the better of her, she decided to stop and ring him from the area. 'She called him three times and finally got through to him,' Lytess recalled to show business columnist Ezra Goodman. 'A lady answered. "I will tell him you're calling," she said.'

Following several agonising moments of silence, the woman returned to the phone and announced, 'He says please see his lawyer in Los Angeles if there is some complaint.' Gifford suddenly came to the phone. 'His voice sounded cold and cruel,' Lytess recalled. 'He said, "I have a family and children." He took her number and said he would contact her in Los Angeles.' The call did not come and Marilyn was heartbroken.

It was only in 1961 that he finally made contact. In February of that year, while Marilyn was resting in the Columbia Presbyterian Center, he sent his daughter a get-well card. It read, 'Best wishes for an early recovery. From the man you tried to see nearly ten years ago. God forgive me.' But, by then, she was uninterested.

Now, after so many years of painful rejection, Marilyn's response to the nurse's call was to remain aloof. Her reply was short, direct and decidedly indifferent. 'Tell the gentleman I have never met him. But if he has anything specific to tell me, he can contact my lawyer. Would you like his number?' The nurse was initially shocked into silence and then declined to take down the attorney's details.

Despite displaying no visible signs of emotion, Marilyn was clearly distressed by the incident and wasted no time in discussing it with Dr Greenson during a counselling session later that day. Just a day after her return from Mexico, an emotionally scarred Monroe told the doctor that, thanks to the phone call from her supposedly gravely ill father and the uncertainty surrounding *Something's Got To Give*, her life was an 'emotional and out of control mess'. She added that, in her eyes, the film was heading for 'total disaster'.

Following her father's unwelcome intervention, on Monday 5 March 1962, in the International Ballroom of the Beverly Hilton Hotel, Marilyn was once more back in the public gaze. At the 19th Golden Globes ceremony, after a poll carried out by the Hollywood Foreign Press Association, the actress's apparent fall from prominence proved to be premature when she was bestowed with the Henrietta Award for the World's Favourite Female Movie Star. Now a pale-platinum blonde, Marilyn arrived at the event sporting a Norman Norell creation, a form-fitting, floor-length, backless emerald-green and black beaded, sequinned evening gown and a pair of matching, $35,000 diamond and emerald-green earrings, the latter a present given to her by Frank Sinatra during their brief relationship the previous September.

By the actress's side at the star-studded event was José Bolaños. Having arrived in the city just a few days before, he suggested he and Marilyn meet, and his presence naturally ignited rumours in the American press of a 'Latin lover' in Marilyn's life. Aside from a few short walks in the moonlight, however, there was no romance. Just days after the lavish ceremony, and with the actress clearly tired of his company and the language barrier, Bolaños was packing his bags, heading back to Mexico.

According to previous Monroe scholars, Bolaños had accompanied Monroe back to Los Angeles from Mexico. This was not the case. But he did arrive on a later plane; moreover, once more conflicting with the information presented in previous Marilyn biographies, I can reveal that he had an ulterior motive for travelling to LA, one that had nothing to do with the actress. Like Marilyn, he was planning to attend the Golden Globes ceremony, which when he landed was due to take place in three days' time. He took the pre-booked flight in the company of the acclaimed Mexican film director Ismael Rodriguez, whose picture, *El Hombre Important* (*The Important Man*), was up for a Best Foreign Language Film award (he would win).

Before the start of the ceremony, American show business columnist Jonah Ruddy managed to catch a few words with the actress. 'I'm very happy to be back in Hollywood and very eager to work again,' she announced. When asked about her approaching 36th birthday and her imminent forties, she put her arm around Ruddy, squeezed him gently and breathlessly said, 'I think it's very nice being a girl. But it's wonderful, just wonderful being a woman.' The reporter then asked her what she intended to do when she reached that period of her life. 'Oh, I shall travel,' she retorted. 'I want to travel in Europe. I've never been to Europe, only London and the suburbs.' Ruddy then enquired whether she had any thoughts about remarrying. 'I hope so,' Marilyn optimistically replied, 'I hope so.'

Regrettably, this piece of light-hearted banter would prove to be the calm before the storm. Just an hour or so later, mouths dropped when the actress materialised on stage to collect her award from fellow screen legend Rock Hudson. The form-fitting, floor-length backless dress Marilyn was wearing was so tight, she could barely move. For one short moment, the Hollywood A-list sat speechless at the sight of the actress and her new figure-hugging outfit, many of them climbing onto their chairs just to get a better view of her.

The film star Zsa Zsa Gabor was clearly not impressed by Marilyn's spotlight-grabbing appearance. Gabor, who had flown in especially for the occasion, became angry when Monroe naturally attracted the most attention from the gathered photographers. 'I don't wish to be catty,' she spitefully remarked to one reporter, 'but personally, I thought Marilyn gave an imitation of Jayne Mansfield.'

Monroe's acceptance speech was as memorable as her dress. Running to just seven words, it became one of Hollywood's briefest ever. 'Thank you,' she purred. 'I'm grateful to you all.' Unfortunately, for those near the actress, the evening would be remembered for other reasons. James Bacon, whose table was adjacent to Marilyn's that night, recalled, 'I sat near her. She gulped wine by the glassful and when her name was called, she had to be helped out of her chair onto the stage. She accepted the award almost in a caricature of herself.' Another recollection of the night came from her actress friend, Susan Strasberg. She confirmed what everyone had suspected: Marilyn was drunk. 'Her voice was slurred and she was out of control,' she recalled. 'She was in one of her armoured vapour clouds. She had arrived four sheets to the wind and proceeded to go for five.'

Charlton Heston, the winner of that night's World's Favourite Male Movie Star award, was standing at the podium when Marilyn arrived to receive her prize. Writing in his *Journals*, he recalled, 'Monroe was absolutely smashed, unable to say a word (*sic*). Probably just as well.' Her eccentric behaviour continued backstage at the after-show party. When Judy Garland's doting manager, Freddie Fields, sauntered up to Monroe, offering to be her new manager, the actress informed him she was now not in the market for one, toasted him high with a glass of tequila and then accidentally spilt some of the drink in her own hair.

However, the reason for her outlandish behaviour was not self-induced. It was later revealed that potent injections of Nembutal, Seconal, phenobarbital and, ominously, the knockout drops chloral hydrate, had been administered to the actress over the previous three days. Marilyn's uncontrollable behaviour had been the result of her reaction to this lethal cocktail of drugs, a state of affairs exacerbated by the fact that Dr Ralph Greenson had just increased her dosage of sleeping pills, as arranged by the pair during their stormy meeting just two days previously on Saturday 3 March.

Something's Got To Give may not yet have been heading for disaster, but turmoil surrounding the film still impregnated the air. To help alleviate the problem, during the afternoon of Tuesday 6 March, Marilyn attended a meeting at Fox with the studio's vice-president, Peter G. Levathes. In essence, the conference with the 26-year-old former lawyer was designed for one thing and one thing only: to declare her wholehearted support for the project. Amid sighs of great relief, plans to send costumiers over to the actress's Brentwood house to take measurements for her outfits in the movie were immediately made.

In an almost hermit-like existence, Marilyn spent the remainder of the month at the house, studying her recently acquired Mexican horticulture books, recovering from a mild flu-like virus she had caught during her recent trips and negotiating a pay rise to her housekeeper, Eunice Murray.

Work on the property continued. At a cost of $66, tiler Jose Paraeo was called to repair the building's notoriously leaky roof tiles. The actress even personally undertook the planting of some citrus trees in her garden. The local gardener, Sam Tateishi, was hired to assist her, at an exorbitant $939.55 a month. It was emblematic of how her spending was still completely out of control and of how her generosity was being abused. At a cost of $1,982.75 per annum, the Bel Air Patrol Company was hired to guard her property and the Landon Pool Services company, at a cost of $496.52 a year, was employed to take care of her swimming pool (even though she never personally used it). Closing her North Doheny Drive apartment and moving her furniture out of it proved to be another huge expense. At a cost of $2,021, furniture not transferred to her new home, including her white baby-grand piano, was shipped back to New York and put into storage at the large warehouse belonging to J. Santini & Bros Inc.

It wasn't just at Marilyn's that large sums of money were being squandered. By mid-March, an elaborate $200,000 set replicating George Cukor's mansion and the back yard of his Beverly Hills home was being assembled on Stage 14 at 20th Century-Fox. Overseen by the movie's associate producer, Gene Allen, the duplication was so precise that studio painters even managed to reproduce precisely the colour of the shrubbery found in his real back garden. Towards the end of the month, following several lengthy discussions about money ('I wanted $15, they offered $12,' he joked), Rat Pack star and crooner Dean Martin finally agreed to star as the movie's leading man. 'It's a first-rate script,' he remarked at the time. 'I read fifty pages and I signed.' At his agent's insistence, an interesting caveat was inserted into the contract, which stipulated that, should Marilyn be replaced, Martin would need approval of the understudy, or else he would not complete the picture.

Other top Hollywood stars soon enlisted. Following Marilyn's insistence, these included eminent Hollywood dancer Cyd Charisse and television entertainers Steve Allen and Phil Silvers. A new version of the *Something's Got To Give* script was completed by Nunnally Johnson on Thursday 29 March and, to the relief of the cash-strapped, highly stressed Fox executives, a new starting date of Monday 16 April was set. With a budget of $3,254,000 for 47 working days, an October 1962 cinema release date for the movie was even tentatively scheduled (conveniently just in time to pay for the post-production costs of *Cleopatra*). For once, everything seemed to be going to plan on the movie. Unfortunately, the optimism would prove to be transient.

In the second week of April, and against Monroe's sternest wishes, 42-year-old Hollywood screenwriter Walter Bernstein was drafted in as Nunnally Johnson's replacement. Following instructions from George Cukor, which included his insistence that any interference from Marilyn should be ignored, his first task was to rewrite entirely his predecessor's script and restore much of Bella and Sam Spewack's 1939 screenplay, since, in Cukor's eyes, 'No one had yet managed to improve upon it.' Producer Henry Weinstein was also forthcoming with suggestions. But in stark contrast to Cukor's directive, he told Bernstein not to make many changes to the script but just do 'a little polishing here and there'.

Naturally upset about Johnson's dismissal, Marilyn was keen to see the writer off before he flew home. Since his flight back to England was scheduled for early the following morning, a prompt 7.45 meeting at his hotel was arranged by the pair. Completely devoid of any make-up, as planned, the actress arrived at Johnson's hotel, but the building's ever vigilant staff refused to grant her access to his room. Immediately, she called Johnson and explained the predicament. 'Tell them you're a call girl and I sent for you,' he humorously suggested. At once, the actress laughed, took on the persona of a prostitute and proceeded to tell the desk clerk just that. As if by magic, the lift doors opened and she was free to ascend to Johnson's room.

The two bottles of Dom Perignon champagne Marilyn had brought with her were turned down by the screenwriter. It was far too early for him to consume alcohol, but he graciously accepted them anyway for consumption later. After exchanging several pleasantries, the actress agreed to escort him to the airport, where they said their goodbyes. Johnson returned to England pleased that he had been able to work with Marilyn again, and completely unaware that it was the last time he would speak to or see her.

Marilyn's first taste of the film's impressive new staging occurred at 9am on Tuesday 10 April when, on the day it was officially announced that she had been added to the bill of President Kennedy's forthcoming birthday gala show, the actress uncharacteristically arrived on time for costume and screen tests. When she pulled up at the studio in a chauffeur-driven limousine arranged by Henry Weinstein a huge sigh of relief could be heard coming from the movie's production office. As one studio employee remarked, 'The executives working on that movie were really living on their nerves. Marilyn had made them manic. If you banged on their door, they'd leap eight feet in the air!'

Monroe's first appearance on a film set in 17 months was accompanied by the obligatory wolf-whistles and wild applause from the assembled studio technicians. But to the astonishment of all Fox employees, the movie's director, George Cukor, was not present to welcome the actress to the set or supervise her tests. Citing 'production business', he had chosen to stay away on the day of her great movie comeback. It was apparent that his deep-rooted two-year-old anger towards the actress still flowed in his blood. His no-show was a serious breach of studio etiquette. Other major stars would have stormed off the set at such an occurrence. But not Marilyn. She just shrugged and laughed off Cukor's petulance. However, inside she was wounded. She secretly regarded his unprofessional, ill-considered action as an almighty slap in the face. It was a great shame, as Marilyn's appearance that day was simply unmissable.

In an attempt to be visually perfect for her celebrated return to movie making, besides the low-cholesterol diet she was now on, the actress had drafted in two of Tinseltown's finest exponents of beauty: Elizabeth Arden (who regularly administered soothing, top-to-toe 'hot wax' treatments to the actress at her home) and the late Jean Harlow's elderly hair-colourist, Pearl Porterfield (who, to make a woman's hair truly platinum blonde, still utilised the old and harmful method of covering her tresses with a mixture of hydrogen peroxide, liquid Clorox bleach and the special household detergent, laundry bluing).

Marilyn also travelled for her care, paying several visits at $100 a time to the Sunset Strip branch of the well-known New York dermatologist, Rena's. The beautifying did not end there. Her good friend Ralph Roberts was also on hand to regularly administer his therapy, a soothing massage following a relaxing ice bath, into which Chanel No. 5, the actress's favourite fragrance, had been poured. The excessive pampering worked. Marilyn looked simply sensational in her Fox tests.

For six straight hours, and with producer Weinstein at the helm, she posed, paraded, smiled and laughed in front of the Deluxe colour CinemaScope cameras wearing seven different hairstyles (including a thigh-length blonde wig intended for the start of the film) and 15 costumes designed by William Travilla, ranging from a glamorous black and white silk dress and a figure-hugging lime-green bikini to a skimpy 'castaway-on-a-desert-isle' garment and a pair of sailor's trousers, which had to be held up with safety pins.

This was a newborn Monroe. Aided by her new svelte 22-inch waist and eight stone four body weight, she was considerably more sophisticated and stylish than she had ever been before. Her stunning appearance was abetted by a range of 50 brightly coloured spotlights, which had been placed at various points and heights around the studio by Academy Award-nominated Fox cinematographer Franz Planer. Pink-tinted lights to help make Marilyn appear more youthful and amber ones to make her seem softer were also used. Specifically to highlight the key features on her face, shoulders, arms and hands, he strategically placed several beam-lights on the set. It came as no surprise when Henry Weinstein described Monroe's appearance that day as 'her best' and 'extraordinary'. Others in attendance were in agreement, admitting that she looked 'better than she had done in years'.

That evening, the 35mm colour footage of Marilyn's tests was hastily processed and dispatched post-haste to one of the studio's screening rooms where Philip Feldman, Fox's executive vice-president for studio operations, excitedly viewed it. So too did Peter Levathes, who enthusiastically gushed to the press, 'This will be the *best* Monroe picture ever. Marilyn is at the *peak* of her beauty and ability.' Freshly printed copies of the screen test were shipped off to New York where Fox supremo Spyros P. Skouras was scheduled to scrutinise them early the following morning. Everyone who witnessed Marilyn's latest, utterly flawless, supremely joyous celluloid performance was united in the opinion that the actress was back to her most glamorous, beautiful and exceedingly photogenic best. Unfortunately, looks would prove deceiving.

That same evening, Henry Weinstein was summoned to Marilyn's home in Brentwood, where he discovered her sprawled across her bed, unconscious from an apparent overdose of barbiturates. 'I called Rommy [Dr Ralph Greenson] and he came running over,' Weinstein recalled in a documentary for Fox. 'I knew then that we were in trouble.' He immediately pleaded with studio executives to delay shooting. But with the company teetering on the brink of financial collapse, they badly needed their most bankable star to help bail them out. 'I went to studio bosses and was told, "Don't worry. You're being melodramatic. She'll be OK." But I was insistent and told them I didn't believe she was up for doing the movie yet. I said to them, "If I came and told you that Marilyn had had a heart attack, what would you do then?" They replied, "Well, we'd wait." So I asked them, "What's the difference?" They said, "Well, if she'd had a heart attack, we couldn't get insurance. But with this, we can.'" A decision to press ahead with shooting resulted. Weinstein later admitted that he felt their actions were cold and heartless. He was right.

Did the extra pressure on Marilyn to return to work and deliver the movie push her dangerously to the edge, we wonder? When she returned home on the night of 10 April, she was painfully aware that hers was the only film in production on the deserted, huge 20th Century-Fox lot. (According to Donald Spoto's 1993 book, *Marilyn Monroe: The Biography*, Joanne Woodward was at the studio concurrently shooting *The Stripper*. In fact, work on this did not begin until Monday 28 May 1962, seven weeks *after* Marilyn shot her screen tests. Woodward was at the studio, on Stage 12, a few weeks prior to this date, but only for rehearsals.) The livelihoods of 150 underpaid Fox employees, as well as the studio itself, were entirely reliant on her vigour, reliability and ability to complete the picture. I suspect these demands on Marilyn were too great and she simply wasn't able to cope.

Two days later, on Thursday 12 April, pre-production on *Something's Got To Give* was thrown into further chaos when a surprisingly rejuvenated Marilyn suddenly, but not entirely unexpectedly, announced that she was off to New York to be with her mentor and drama coach, Lee Strasberg. She excused her decision by saying she needed to work with him before starting the new picture. Naturally, with the actress's legendary reputation for frequently going 'absent without leave' during production of a movie, Fox executives were reluctant to see her go. George Cukor remonstrated with her but knew he had no power to prevent her from travelling. But Fox did. So Peter Levathes was drafted in to firmly deliver the command, 'Marilyn will not be allowed to travel to New York.'

Pre-production continued and a script conference between the film's associate producer and art director, Gene Allen, Henry Weinstein, George Cukor, scriptwriter Walter Bernstein and Marilyn, was called for Friday 13 April. Due to arrive at Fox at 10am, she did not materialise until midday, breezing into the office breathless and apologetic. Despite strictest orders from the highest powers, she was still pursuing her idea of heading to New York. The taxi in which she had arrived, and which was to transport her to the airport, was still running outside. 'I'm sure you don't really mind the little trip,' she nervously told her seated, speechless colleagues. 'I'm just going, you know, to oil the machinery.'

The seminar started but concluded within 30 minutes, during which time Marilyn's main suggestion was that her character should be more exciting. Throughout, the actress sported large, dark sunglasses to shield her eyes, which were red and weepy due to the medication she was taking. 'She was in good spirits,' Bernstein recalled for *The Gleaner* newspaper, 'and full of energy, a trait I had not associated with her. Her enthusiasm seemed spontaneous and she included everyone in it . . . She was not glamorous. She was not even pretty. But her appeal was genuine, a child's appeal, sweet and disarming.' The meeting reached its conclusion when the studio doctor, Lee Siegel, arrived to give Marilyn a vitamin injection. Minutes later, she rolled down her sleeve and bid everyone a fond farewell. No one present tried to discourage her from leaving. They knew there was no point. Furthermore, with the actress away and the script needing another slight rewrite, it was agreed that shooting should be postponed until Monday 23 April.

Working from original source material previously thought lost, I can categorically state that Marilyn Monroe headed out to New York on the afternoon of Friday 13 April 1962 to see Lee and Paula Strasberg and did *not* meet or sleep with the President of the United States during that three-day period.

Close scrutiny of his White House diary corroborates this. It reveals that, at 6.20pm on the evening of Friday 13 April, JFK boarded the USS *Northampton* for an overnight cruise to Norfolk, Virginia. One day later – between 2.30 and 3.10pm – he watched military exercises with the Shah of Iran at Camp Lejeune in North Carolina and on Sunday 15 April – between 12 midday and 12.56pm – the President attended mass at the Community Center in Middleburg, Virginia. He experienced another typically full weekend and had no time whatsoever to spend with the actress. Marilyn spent the weekend of 13–15 April 1962 neither in JFK's bed nor in Manhattan at a 'super-private, ten-thousand-dollar-a-plate, fund-raising affair'.

Aside from meeting Lee Strasberg that weekend, however, Marilyn did catch up with English-born reporter William J. Weatherby, who had first encountered the actress in 1960 during his report for the *Observer* on the making of *The Misfits*. They became acquaintances and over the ensuing 21 months, she would be interviewed by him at length on at least three separate occasions. Their last-minute meeting took place during the afternoon of Saturday 14 April, in a small booth at the rear of a decidedly low-key, unglamorous bar on Eighth Avenue. Uncharacteristically, Marilyn was already there when Weatherby arrived.

'I could see the change in her as I walked toward her,' he recalled in his 1976 book, *Conversations with Marilyn*. 'Her body had lost some of the shape and sap of youth. Her face lacked some of its former fullness.' He noticed that her skin seemed more stretched over the bones and less shiny.

'She had some make-up on this time,' he said, 'but it didn't hide the tiredness or the lines, and she must have known it . . . I couldn't believe that the woman I saw had changed so much.'

They spoke about Arthur Miller's recent marriage and mentioned she might go the same way again. When asked whether she had anyone in mind, Marilyn replied, 'Sort of . . . only problem is, he's married right now. And he's married, so we have to meet in secret . . . He's in politics.' 'In Hollywood?' Weatherby asked. 'Oh no, in Washington.' If Weatherby's recollections are accurate, it was obvious she was embellishing her one-night encounter with President Kennedy at Bing Crosby's home.

The reporter noted that Marilyn reminded him of a 'star-struck girl' at the mention of Kennedy's name. As their conversation unfurled, the actress made it clear she was very supportive of the President. 'I think he's going to be another [Abraham] Lincoln,' she insisted. Conversation came to a halt when Weatherby visited the men's room. He returned to find a strange man bent over their table talking to the actress. Mistaking her for a prostitute, he was making a rather ungainly, alcohol-induced pass at her. Weatherby was naturally aghast at the confusion and shouted his anger at the man, who sheepishly walked back to his nearby table.

It was time for a change of setting. Marilyn and Weatherby climbed inside a taxi and resumed their conversation on a bench in Central Park. Watching squirrels play and pigeons search for food punctuated their latest exchanges. Their time together soon ended; Marilyn had a meeting with Lee Strasberg to attend, a movie script to discuss and a journal interview to finish. Weatherby walked her back to 59th Street and watched as the actress climbed aboard another taxi. Just as the vehicle was about to pull away, she informed him she wouldn't be returning to the Big Apple 'for a long time'. Marilyn's remark would unfortunately prove to be prophetic. This was her penultimate visit to New York.

The actress's day concluded back at her apartment when, after a gap of three months, she finally wrapped up her piece for *Redbook* magazine. Her banter with the writer, Alan Levy, was once more most enlightening. 'I'm looking forward to eventually becoming a marvellous, excuse the word, marvellous character actress, like Marie Dressler, like Will Rogers,' she exclaimed. 'I think they've left this kind of appeal out of the movies today.' Once again, she was extremely philosophical. 'I am trying to prove to myself that I *am* a person,' the actress declared, 'then, maybe I'll convince myself that I *am* a person. The most difficult task I have ever set myself is *know* thyself, and I would underline it.' This tone continued throughout most of the conversation. 'Acting is very important,' she announced. 'To put it bluntly, I seem to have a whole superstructure with no foundation. But I'm working on the foundation.'

As promised, Monroe returned to Los Angeles on Sunday 15 April and a chat with Henry Weinstein was uppermost in her mind. Their exchange, by telephone, took place late that night. It was a problematic one. Early on the morning of Monday 16 April, Weinstein called scriptwriter Walter Bernstein. His conversation with Marilyn had left him in a high state of panic. 'Lee Strasberg practically liked the script,' Weinstein announced. Bernstein was naturally pleased by this but confused as to why the producer was so clearly unnerved. His puzzlement ended when he was informed that the script Strasberg had given his tentative blessing to was the one Bernstein had just scrapped and was currently overhauling. Due to her incessant rewrite demands, Fox, and in particular Cukor, had decided to keep Marilyn out of the revised-scripts loop; she, inadvertently, had taken a woefully out-of-date version of it to New York.

Weinstein was naturally horrified by this predicament. His worries had intensified when, during the previous night's conversation, Marilyn also told him that she concurred with Strasberg's decision that the screenplay was generally OK but still needed a bit of work, in particular 'a few more jokes'. Weinstein passed this verdict on to his scriptwriter. 'That's *not* what it wants,' Bernstein angrily shouted. Weinstein agreed.

The bad news did not end there. With Bernstein listening attentively, the producer hesitantly revealed that Monroe had in fact requested other amendments to the script; for instance, she was now firmly insisting that her character met her husband by *coincidence*, rather than by running after him. She also desired changes in the scene where Marilyn's character unexpectedly arrives back home and encounters her two young children for the first time in seven years. The script's insistence that they treat her rather frostily now appalled the actress. In her new idea, she demanded that she should win them over instantly, without even having to tell them who she was. As Weinstein and Bernstein's conversation unfolded they became united in the belief that, considering the new version of the script had just been completed, this was now a major problem.

The news that Marilyn was demanding wholesale changes naturally spread like wildfire. Gene Allen, the film's associate producer, was enraged when told of her eleventh-hour revisions and agreed they would be disastrous for the picture. So did George Cukor, who angrily confronted Marilyn at her home on the Monday morning. But she was unyielding and insistent that her demands should be met. Heated discussions over the script raged on for hours. Arguments between Weinstein, Bernstein, Cukor, Allen and various Fox executives were fought out in the director's badly decaying mobile office and on Sound Stage 14, in full view of the startled studio employees. A stalemate was rapidly reached.

Marilyn was now so perturbed by the script that she became fearful of it and, in turn, of everything to do with the film. Allen soon realised that failure to make the actress's amendments would only cause further delays to the start of shooting. A compromise about the revisions was soon agreed by everyone and, during the evening of Monday 16 April, Bernstein was once again ordered to rewrite the script. Upset by developments, Monroe turned to her pills. During the evening of Wednesday 18 April, she was driven by chauffeur to the Prescription Center on Wilshire Boulevard in Beverly Hills to collect a fresh consignment of sedatives, one of which was Nembutal.

In an attempt to pre-empt any impending confusion, Bernstein began utilising the colour-coding system (a device commonly employed when revisions of a screenplay are made), whereby each subsequent adjustment to the script was printed on different-coloured paper to the one previous. The very latest version of *Something's Got To Give* began life as blue throughout. Within a day, the first revisions had been hastily sent out for everyone to read and approve. But Marilyn was *still* unhappy. In the sequence where her character, Ellen, ruefully announces that, after losing many of her items after the plane crash, she doesn't possess many clothes, she caustically scribbled, 'Too flat. It's painting black on black so to speak. We don't have to worry about heart. I have one believe it or not.'

She also queried how the script had been revised. 'What has been rewritten?' she asked. 'New pages will inhibit me. Some changes should be made but not like this. Either way they have to trust me to play the scenes with heart or we are lost.' The actress even took the opportunity to take a swipe at Bernstein's credentials. 'This writer may be good,' she scrawled, 'But not on this movie.' Marilyn complained, and he was forced to rewrite certain sections of it again.

As the revisions from both Monroe and the other notables involved in the film began to pour in, Bernstein hurriedly incorporated these on to differently tinted pages, first yellow, then pink, symbolising respectively the second and third sets of changes to the screenplay. The completed versions were then hastily dispatched to the individuals' homes. Either by accident or design, Marilyn would not usually receive hers until at least ten o'clock at night. (Bernstein's script underwent so much transformation that, in the end, hardly any of his original, blue-coloured sheets remained.) From the outset, to avert any further problems, Marilyn was kept in the dark about the colour-change operation.

By Thursday 19 April, the latest, hurriedly finished 149-page screenplay of *Something's Got To Give*, chiefly pink in colour, had been dispatched to everyone; everyone that is except for Marilyn. The copy she received was still *white*. It was an irresponsible decision. It was naturally becoming harder for her to see where the latest amendments had been made. Attempts to study and learn her very latest lines were now a forlorn hope.

Marilyn devoured the latest version of the script that weekend. Bar Irving Shulman's original, eight-month-old ending, every part of it had now been hastily rewritten and comprehensively restyled to suit everyone's specifications. Unsurprisingly, the actress still found a few faults. Alongside Ellen's line, 'You know . . . far away in the South Sea Islands, when a man hurts himself, but doesn't want people to see him cry, do you know what he does? He has someone cry for him,' Monroe scribbled the words, 'Sentimental schmaltz.' However, there was no time left for changes. There were now just two days left before principal shooting was set to commence.

It had been a truly frantic week. But this was nothing compared to the calamitous events which were set to unfold on Monday 23 April, when shooting of Marilyn Monroe's latest movie was finally set to roll . . .

Chapter Six

Something's Got To Give
(part one)

Monday 23 April 1962–Saturday 19 May 1962

On Monday 23 April 1962, following five months of setbacks, work on Marilyn Monroe's new movie, her first since *The Misfits* 15 months before, was finally set to begin. It was shortly before 7am and 104 extremely eager Fox technicians and stagehands were busily preparing themselves for the start of shooting. Lights were in place and the CinemaScope cameras were in position to capture the first scenes. Sound Stage 14 was a hive of activity and excitement impregnated the air. The film's leading man, Dean Martin, fresh from make-up, was already on the set, as were the movie's director, George Cukor, and producer Henry T. Weinstein. Everyone was geared up and raring to go – everybody that is apart from the film's leading lady, the great Marilyn Monroe.

As the minutes sluggishly ticked by, Cukor began pacing around the expansive staging, Weinstein sauntered around the set's swimming pool, looking ready to throw himself in, and Martin sat motionless in his chair, deliberating whether he should rehearse his lines or practise his golf swing. The film's current scriptwriter, Walter Bernstein, arrived on the set just after 9am. Noticing Monroe's absence and the distinct lack of activity, he approached the movie's assistant director, Buck Hall, and was immediately informed the movie's leading lady would not be coming. 'She's sick,' Hall announced incredulously. 'She caught a cold from Lee Strasberg.'

Although Weinstein had already subconsciously prepared himself for the inevitable – after all, colds and flu had brought about severe delays on many of Marilyn's previous films – he was still taken aback by the actress's no-show; not by what had happened but by how it was done. 'I didn't sleep all weekend,' the fatigued producer remarked to Hall. 'I was on the phone with her [until] two, three, four in the morning [reassuring her about the movie]. My wife is ready to divorce me. I asked her where her analyst [Dr Greenson] was and she told me he was preparing to go to Europe and it's not even August!'

Following Monroe's call late on Saturday evening, Weinstein dispatched Fox's staff physician, Lee Siegel, the so-called 'doctor to the stars', over to her home to ascertain the severity of her illness. Since he had been treating her for over six years now, he was conversant with the actress and her ailments. 'Marilyn throws so much of herself into her work,' he once remarked to Hollywood columnist Mike Connolly, 'it's lucky we're able to salvage her at all.'

That night, the doctor found Marilyn to be suffering from laryngitis and headaches, which in turn had precipitated blurred vision. His diagnosis should have postponed the movie for a month, but because of her past history of successfully feigning sickness, studio executives instantly began questioning Siegel's analysis. Nevertheless, he was adamant: the actress *was* ill. His joy in the role as Monroe's doctor diminished when he learnt that studio executives were intending to force her on to the set whether she was healthy or not. In an interview with show business writer Maurice Zolotow, Siegel remarked, 'They were only interested in finishing that film, and in finishing it quickly. Their attitude seemed to be, "Let Marilyn collapse after we finish." They were aware it was her last film for them in any case.'

Monroe's call to say she was unable to start shooting came in shortly before 7.30am. She partly reiterated Siegel's prognosis by announcing she was indeed suffering from a sore throat and a severe sinus infection. But to George Cukor, after working with her on *Let's Make Love*, this scenario was all too familiar. So, just as he had on their previous film together, he decided to reorganise his filming schedules and press ahead with shooting anyway. He announced firmly that he intended to shoot scenes *around* his leading lady.

Shortly after receiving Monroe's call, Weinstein phoned actress Cyd Charisse at her home and requested she come to the studio post-haste. She agreed and, just four hours later, the very first scenes of *Something's Got To Give* were captured on celluloid. The sequence involved Dean Martin's character, Nick, and Bianca, played by Charisse, returning to his house after their honeymoon and encountering his two young children, played by Alexandra Heilweil and Robert Christopher Morley, as they assembled a tree house in their back yard.

Unfortunately, one day later, Tuesday 24 April, Cukor was once more forced to rearrange his plans when Marilyn again reported in sick. Her time away from the set forced her to miss a visit to Fox by the Shah of Iran and his wife, Empress Farah Pahlavi, who were two weeks into their goodwill tour of the United States. The original plan had been to drop in on Stage 14 and watch Marilyn at work. She was, after all, the one star the dignitaries had expressed a real desire to meet. However, she was refusing to budge from her home. That morning, during the first of many visits that week by Weinstein to the actress's abode, he informed her of the royal visit and suggested she come to the studio to meet the Shah and his wife. He reeled back in shock when she replied, 'I don't know whether I can. I don't know what his relationship with Israel is.'

In a desperate attempt to learn, Weinstein hastily placed a call to a Hollywood synagogue and put Marilyn on the phone to Rabbi Max Nusbaum, the so-called 'Rabbi to the stars'. He reassured her that Israel *did* have a good relationship with the Shah and it would be a very good idea indeed if she turned up on the set to exchange pleasantries with him and his wife. Unfortunately, his opinion failed to change Marilyn's mind and she decided to remain cooped up in her home. Weinstein later admitted that Monroe's belief that the Shah of Iran was 'anti-Israel' was just a lame excuse; he thought the real reason why she wouldn't meet the dignitaries was because, compared to Empress Farah Pahlavi, she felt she wasn't pretty enough.

In a last-ditch attempt to compensate for the non-appearance, Levathes decided to chaperone his guests over to the vast Sound Stage 14. Once inside, he stopped, pointed down at the set's large, completely empty swimming pool and excitedly declared, 'Marilyn Monroe swims nude by moonlight in one scene here.' His grand announcement was met by a stony silence. The Shah and the Empress wanted to see the actress in person, not view a large hollow abyss where she was due to dip sometime in the future. With an icy awkwardness infusing the air, the Shah moved quickly to break the embarrassment by enquiring how the lighting technicians intended to recreate moonlight in the scene. Shortly after, the Shah and his wife bid their farewells and drove out of the studio to resume their goodwill tour. Thankfully, the unease soon passed. Fox executives had another worry on their mind: Marilyn Monroe.

The pattern of her calling in sick continued throughout the week. Bulletins on the actress's current condition were issued daily. Tuesday's optimistically (and perhaps sarcastically) read: 'Marilyn's fever is slowly sinking. It is now below 100 degrees.' The very latest information was relayed to the Fox executives and those employed on the movie by Weinstein, who throughout that week regularly made phone calls to the actress and scurried between the studio and the patient's sick-bed. On each visit to Marilyn's home he was bombarded with questions, most of which were focused on her female co-star and beauty rival in the film, Cyd Charisse. Best known for her spectacular dancing in classic MGM musicals such as *Singing in the Rain* (1952), Charisse was almost five years older than her co-star. But her impeccable beauty and unimpeachable, perfectly toned body made her look years younger, and Marilyn knew it.

Even though Monroe was away from the set, lying motionless on her bed under a thin covering of blankets, she still managed to keep up to date with matters regarding *Something's Got To Give*. 'I got a call from Marilyn and she said Cyd was padding her breasts,' Weinstein recalled for Fox in 2001. 'I said, "Marilyn, you haven't been on the set. How would you know?" She replied, "I have people watching." I said, "Well, how can she? She's wearing this negligee. It's a little negligee. You can't do it." She replied, "You don't know anything." And I said, "Well, if you think I'm gonna tell Miss Charisse to stop doing this, you're mistaken."' Marilyn then informed him she was going to pad her breasts too and warned him that he would have redo all of her costumes. To this, Weinstein screamed, 'You're not going to pad your dresses. That would be *criminal*.'

In another conversation, Monroe wanted to know the exact colour of Cyd's hair. As Weinstein announced in an earlier interview, this time from 1972, 'She was convinced that Miss Charisse wanted to be a blonde like her.' He assured her that Cyd was wearing her hair in its natural colour, which was light brown. Unfortunately his assurances fell on deaf ears. 'Her *unconscious* wants it blonde,' the clearly jealous and paranoiac actress retorted.

Later that day, once back on the *Something's Got To Give* set and following strict instructions from Monroe, Weinstein clandestinely checked Charisse's hair for any tell-tale glints of blonde and, just to be sure, had her light brown hair darkened a shade or two. (Close examination of the surviving footage reveals that Cyd's hair does indeed enigmatically turn darker midway through the shooting. In addition, to avert any possible further troubles, Weinstein also ordered the hair of the actress, Eloise Hart, who was playing a secretary in the film, to be blackened.)

The producer's travels between Marilyn's home and the Fox lot concluded for the time being on Friday 27 April. Three days later, on Monday 30 April, a week after shooting had started, Marilyn finally managed to make it to the studio. She was picked up from her Fifth Helena home by a chauffeur-driven black limousine funded by Fox and arranged by Henry Weinstein. At the wheel of the vehicle was Rudy Karensky. Clutching a wicker basket containing toast, hard-boiled eggs and a grilled steak for lunch, prepared by Murray just minutes before her departure, Marilyn uncharacteristically arrived for her 6.30am make-up call 25 minutes early. But this punctuality did not prevent her from failing to appear on the set until 11.20am.

Keeping a close eye on developments was director Billy Wilder, who wasted no time in cracking jokes about the scenario. 'It gets worse and worse,' he said. 'It used to be you'd call her at 9am and she'd show at 12 noon. Now you call her in May and she shows in October.' He didn't stop there. In another remark, he quipped, 'I would like to do another movie with Miss Monroe, particularly in Paris because, while we were waiting for her to show up on the set, we could all learn how to paint.'

Once again, Monroe's fear of cameras had kicked in and she remained holed up in her poky, freshly painted dressing room until she had plucked up enough courage to venture out. The bouffant blonde Hollywood actress Dorothy Provine explained, 'Marilyn's hairdresser once told me she was *never* once late for make-up. But because of some insecurity, she couldn't make it out to the set. She was just frightened.' Billy Wilder concurred, saying Monroe did indeed possess a fear of the camera. Behind the closed door of her dressing room, Marilyn would sit and repeatedly postpone the dreaded moment until she would have to face the director and cameras.

Other excuses were also forthcoming. 'She sits at the dressing table nude, fascinated by her own beauty. She can't bring herself to get dressed,' explicated one former press aide. It wasn't just in front of her dressing-room mirror that Monroe would encounter this problem. It was in front of *every* mirror. In a 1968 interview for the BBC, Arthur Miller explained, 'Due to her upbringing, she felt self-display, beauty itself was evil. Because she was so attractive and beautiful, she felt guilty looking in the mirror.' 'When she goes into the powder room to wash her hands,' one former press agent complained at the time, 'I have to send someone in to hand her out. She's just standing there, before the mirror, transfixed, as though trying to believe the beautiful dame staring back at her is really Marilyn Monroe.'

A graphic example of how insecure Monroe was on a film set had occurred during the shooting of *Let's Make Love* two years earlier. In the scene where she, as a chorus girl, sits to one side and carries out homework for the courses she is taking in high school, she makes notations in a composition book. After the scene had been shot to Cukor's satisfaction, Marilyn headed back to her dressing room, inadvertently leaving the pad behind. One of the cast members noticed this and glanced at the notes she had been making, all of which were addressed to herself. They read, 'What am I afraid of? Why am I so afraid? Do I think I can't act? I know I can act, but I am afraid. I am afraid and I should not be and I must not be.' The actor refused to read any more, declaring, 'It made her seem even more naked than she did on those calendars she once posed for.'

'I am nervous before a scene,' Monroe admitted in 1961, 'and I'd rather slight the people back screen than the audience who come to the theatre to see me. I'm not abnormally nervous. I want to do the best I can do and I have a lot of responsibility, so sometimes it makes me nervous. Louis Calhern told me in *The Asphalt Jungle*, "Being nervous is part of being an actor or an actress; never be ashamed of it."'

Monroe, however, did agree to let photographers record her grand return to the set of *Something's Got To Give* that morning. The sight of Cukor greeting her with a kiss on her cheek was among the many pictures taken. She worked for the rest of the day, shooting the scene where her character, Ellen, returns home and emotes silently at seeing her two young children for the first time in five years. Highly sensitive to facial features, Cukor insisted on filming the actress with her mouth slightly ajar since, in his opinion, she seemed 'a bit less determined that way'.

'She arrived on the set looking absolutely lovely,' Cukor recalled in 1963, 'and then [we] found she had frightful difficulty in concentrating. I used to tell her, "You do it so easily, you're so accomplished," and she'd perform some straightforward actions such as walking down a path and I'd say, "Oh, that's great, perfect," but then she'd reply, "Oh no, I've lost it." Her inability to concentrate got worse. At the end, she couldn't do anything and was quite incapable of sustained mental effort.' In another interview, this time with Los Angeles radio station KNX-AM, he confessed, 'Marilyn's a conscientious girl in her efforts to get it right. She's a little trying. All she thinks of is to get the stuff on the screen and make it good. That's her real, real motive.'

Due to her persistent sore throat, Monroe read very few lines. That afternoon, after noticing signs of her weakening, studio publicist Jon Campbell solicitously asked Marilyn how she was feeling. 'I'm fine,' she replied, 'except that I've got a temperature.' She was indeed running a temperature of 102 degrees. Following the children's dismissal at 4pm, she shot a short sequence with Dean Martin and then, at 5.20pm, left the studios.

Despite her apparently happy demeanour, the turmoil surrounding the movie and the countless script changes had infuriated Marilyn and, when she returned home that evening, she could not relax. Studying, learning and acting out the following day's script encompassed her every waking thought; as the evening drew to a close, instead of becoming sleepy, she became agitated, panicky and even more awake. On top of her virus and sinus complications, slumber naturally became a forlorn hope. A half-hearted form of sleep only arrived after she had consumed a handful of sleeping pills, washed down with a glass of champagne. 'She would say, "Call me tomorrow at 5am,"' Eunice Murray recalled at the time. 'I'd get everything ready in the morning but she just couldn't make it.' The actress had barely slept and by the time she arrived at the studio two hours later (at 7am on the morning of Tuesday 1 May), she was totally exhausted.

Fox staffers Allan 'Whitey' Snyder – the actress's make-up man since she started at Fox in 1947 – and costumier Marjorie Plecher took one look at the actress and instructed her to go to her dressing room and lie down. After a brief 30-minute respite, they roused her and began readying her for shooting, but Marilyn wasn't prepared for such a duty. She was clearly suffering. To help revive her, the actress drank cup after cup of assistant Hazel Washington's strong black coffee. It was a futile exercise. As Marilyn's dress was slid up and placed around her lithe physique, the actress began to wander aimlessly around her dressing room as if she was mesmerised. The final straw came when she passed out under a hair-dryer. Shooting anything was naturally out of the question and it was universally agreed at 7.35am that Marilyn should return home. Later that morning, her press agent Pat Newcomb justified the decision to the enquiring press: 'Marilyn's resistance is low since she had that gall-bladder operation. That was major surgery and takes three or four months to get over [the operation had actually been performed a year before]. She's on a sort of diet, nothing fried.'

In truth, it wasn't the changes to the script that had angered the actress so. It wasn't the revisions to the screenplay that had forced her to stay awake late into the night; it wasn't the last-minute alterations to the dialogue that had made her turn up for work in an unemployable, hypnotic state. It wasn't even the virus infections which she was clearly unsettled by. It was actually symbolic of her frail self-confidence and her complete inability to deal with any major changes that were suddenly thrust upon her.

'There's a phrase that's used by doctors,' Marilyn's physician, Dr Hyman Engelberg, once tellingly remarked, 'called Psyche and Soma, which means psychological things and body things; they usually affect each other. When she [Monroe] was depressed, her resistance dropped to infection.' And such was the case during the shooting of Something's Got To Give in April 1962.

In addition, for the first time during production on the movie, Marilyn was, once again, frighteningly alone. Fox chairman Spyros P. Skouras, a true Marilyn supporter, was ill and unapproachable and her trusted film friend, scriptwriter Nunnally Johnson, was back at home in London and inaccessible. With no real friends to hand, a script she had trouble remembering and a screenplay she was frustratingly unhappy with, the filming of *Something's Got To Give* quickly turned into one long arduous chore. As the days progressed, she would only go to the studio when she was called or able and, unfortunately, she was not capable of doing so again until Monday 14 May. The days in between were spent in an almost reclusive existence at her Fifth Helena home. Occasional trips, such as that on Saturday, 12 May, to Pearson's nearby Brentwood Fine Liquors & Wines store at 2530 San Vicente Boulevard to purchase – for $173.22 – a case of Dom Perignon champagne, punctuated her boredom.

With Marilyn once more absent from the set, Weinstein was forced to resume his daily ritual of posting updates on her condition. Towards the end of the second week's shooting, he burst on to the set with thrilling, but somewhat sarcastic news. 'Miss Monroe's temperature is down to 98.6, only two-tenths of a degree above normal.' Disgruntled Buck Hall was naturally unimpressed by the announcement. 'I get a higher fever than that walking up the stairs,' he cynically muttered.

In Marilyn's absence, director Cukor continued to film around her, scenes in which her presence was not needed. Over the years, reports have circulated that, by Tuesday 8 May, the 13th day of the movie's production, Fox completely shut down production on the movie because Cukor had run out of sequences to shoot. But that is untrue. Rather than being confined to the Fox lot and Sound Stages 8, 14 and 15, he took the movie away on location and, on 8 May, shot scenes with Dean Martin at the Balboa Bay Club in Newport Harbor. Remarkably, the actor remained upbeat throughout the early parts of the movie; in a reference to Marilyn's continual absence and the two young children working on the film, he humorously quipped to members of the American press, 'We had some little kids in the picture when we started. Now they're ready for *college.*'

By now, however, *Something's Got To Give* was four and a half days behind schedule and sadly, it was set to get far worse. Two days later, on Thursday 10 May, Marilyn's 16th day of absenteeism, the movie's daily production sheets noted that, in order to complete the film by Wednesday 27 June, her presence was required for every one of the remaining days of shooting. Since she was still phoning in sick, the chances of that happening were very remote indeed. Naturally, the Fox hierarchy were beginning to worry. But, thankfully, there was a glimmer of hope on the horizon.

With promises that she might be fit for filming on Monday 14 May, a story conference was called by the actress on the preceding Sunday afternoon. The movie's scriptwriter, Walter Bernstein, was the only person requested to attend and Marilyn's Mexican-style bungalow was the natural choice of setting. 'She met me at the door,' Bernstein recalled for

American journalist Scott Carson in 1973. 'Her hair was in curlers; her face was pale from her confinement. Her manner was friendly but she seemed to have little energy. Her smile was pallid.' An exceedingly brief tour of her new home followed. 'She apologised for the bareness of the house,' Bernstein remarked. 'She had bought furniture in Mexico, which had not yet arrived. The living room contained only one chair and she insisted I sit in it. She sat on the floor, her script before her on a low coffee table and we went over several of the scenes.

'She was very shy about her own suggestions, as though she felt they were unworthy. But she had obviously been working on her part and, like a good actor, had found insights that improved the character she played. On the other hand, also like an actor, many of her ideas were good for her and not so good for the story. But if I hinted at this, her face would go blank for a second, as though the current had been turned off, and when it was turned on again she would continue as though I had said nothing at all, not disagreeing with me, not even referring to what I had said, simply going on with what followed. I had met this reaction before. It is the normal, uncomplicated self-involvement of the movie star. It stems from a splendid and incorruptible narcissism.'

During their discussion about the script, Marilyn began referring to herself in the third person, rather like Caesar. 'Remember you've got Marilyn Monroe here,' she remarked when talks shifted to discussions about her wearing a bikini in the movie. 'Remember you've got to use her.' Monroe and Bernstein's quite harmonious conference lasted three hours, during which time she delighted in acting out her part, especially the sequence where she spoke with a Swedish accent for her role as her husband Nick's foreign maid, Ingrid Tic. The actress was naturally over-joyed by Bernstein's applause at the end of her demonstration. But, according to the scriptwriter, the meeting was futile. He regarded the conference as nothing more than an excuse for her to enforce her authority on both the movie and script.

'Before I left [Marilyn's home], she offered me a can of Mexican beer and showed me around the house,' Bernstein recollected. 'Then we went out into the garden and she showed me where she was going to plant trees. She was proud of the house. It evidently meant a great deal to her. She was eager that it be liked.' In his words, he left the bungalow feeling like 'a deck-hand on a ship with no one at the helm and the water ahead full of rocks'.

Conference over, an invigorated Marilyn decided that, to help ease any lingering doubts about the movie, she would call her long-time acting coach, Paula Strasberg, and ask her to fly in from New York at once and be a supportive hand on the set. It seemed an obvious and simple scenario but, as it transpired, it only manifested new problems, especially since the actress was now beginning to *despise* Strasberg. Since Marilyn doubted her own judgement on many things and possessed precious little faith in herself as an actress, she constantly came to depend on the opinion and judgement of others – in particular that of Strasberg, who had made herself essential to the actress, so much so that the actress became resentful of the fact.

Paula had been sitting by Monroe's side on the sets of her past five movies and had gained a reputation for quietly undermining any director's control over the star. It was a manner of working that had naturally made her extremely unpopular. Strasberg was tremendously defensive and explosively confrontational about her employer. Whenever a director said anything untoward to Monroe, Strasberg would antagonise him by saying things like, 'She's a great star. You *can't* treat her like that.' Employing her was not cheap. Her four-week stint on *The Misfits* in 1960 had cost Marilyn $10,000. In the following year alone, she billed the actress $20,000 for her services.

However, despite her loathing, Monroe was still amazingly generous to both Paula and her husband Lee. At a cost of $11,000, she purchased for Paula 100 shares in the American Telephone and Telegraph company (AT&T), while trading in her own bonds to pay for Lee's drama-study trip to Japan. Expenditure relating to their overseas trips was commonplace. Surviving records show that reverse-charge telephone calls were made by Paula to Marilyn during her 1961 trip to Paris, France, their purpose being to demand money for a plane flight home to New York. At a cost of $411, the actress duly obliged. That same year, the actress promised to hand to Lee's Actors Studio her entire $100,000 appearance fee for *Rain*. In January 1962, she gave them, completely free of charge, her 1956 Ford Thunderbird car and one month later, when a financial crisis threatened to bring down the curtains on Lee's studio, she made an anonymous donation of $12,500 towards it.

Paula's first stretch on the *Something's Got To Give* set came the very next day, Monday 14 May, when shooting resumed for the week. After spending close to two hours with Marilyn in the actress's dressing room, she appeared on set at precisely 7.30am. 'Weinstein arrived on the set with a small, dumpy woman wearing large, black-rimmed glasses and a black shawl over her head,' Walter Bernstein recalled. 'She looked like a matronly Russian witch or Dracula's assistant. The crew on the picture gave her the nickname Black Bart. Weinstein introduced her as Paula Strasberg, wife of Lee Strasberg and personal drama coach to Marilyn Monroe . . . later he came back alone and said with great relief, "Paula liked the set." He spoke as if the set would have had to be dismantled if Mrs Strasberg had not liked it.'

When filming finally resumed, Strasberg stood quietly to the side of the cameras and watched intently as Marilyn went about shooting her scenes. Whenever Cukor shouted 'Cut' to signify the end of filming of a particular sequence, the actress would sharply look across to Strasberg and receive a signal, by way of either a nod or a head shake, as to whether the scene she had just shot was OK or needed doing again. This scenario was most prevalent during shooting on Friday 1 June. One of Monroe's few requirements that day was to take the few short steps down the set's tiny staircase. But due to Strasberg's dissatisfaction with the way the actress was carrying out the action, Monroe ended up ascending and descending the staircase up to 12 times until her acting coach was satisfied and called time on the sequence. The fact that she was now overruling his directorship on the movie severely angered Cukor; naturally, he came to loathe her for it and bitterness between the two immediately flared. 'I don't think they [the Strasbergs] helped her at all,' producer Weinstein controversially recalled for Fox back in 1990. 'I think they just pumped her up full of lots of stuff so they could use her.'

Between scenes, Marilyn sat with Paula in a quiet area of the studio, where they conferred very seriously about how the filming was progressing. When shooting was ready to resume, the actress would carry this seriousness back on to the set. But since the movie they were producing was supposed to be a light-hearted comedy, Marilyn's staid demeanour was gravely out of place and Cukor had to forcibly point out the fact, much to the actress's and coach's annoyance. Moreover, despite Marilyn's genuine intention to successfully get through 15 pages of script each day, her targets were ironically hampered by Cukor's decidedly listless work rate. As Peter Brown and Patte Barham wrote in their book *Marilyn – The Last Take*, he 'squandered most of this time, expending almost twenty-seven hours and more than a hundred takes on two and a half pages of script, just nine lines of dialogue'.

To cover his slothful speed and in an attempt to undermine her confidence, Cukor clandestinely (and quite inaccurately) remarked to studio executives that Marilyn's performance in front of the cameras was 'useless' and that she was incapable of 'matching her takes', and that as a result, endless retakes were required. But close examination of the surviving footage proves they were not. It was obvious that the director's deep-rooted hatred of Monroe was manifesting itself in imperceptible sabotage of both her and her career.

In front of the cameras, Marilyn was, to begin with, often shy and diffident with her suggestions. But that soon changed. During one day of shooting, she strolled up to the director and asked for permission to change a word in the script. When he surprisingly granted her wish, she would, in the style of a chameleon, completely alter her mood and timid demeanour and excitedly clap her hands in sheer delight. Touchingly, Marilyn seemed thrilled that anyone would ever consider doing such a thing for her. With her confidence spiralling, the floodgates opened and Monroe-enforced script changes began happening almost on a daily basis, most of which were unsurprisingly directed at Miss Charisse. Marilyn insisted that any references to Cyd in the screenplay as 'beautiful, seductive or desirable', should be excised, along with any indication that the husband of both these glamorous women was, even for a moment, remotely attracted to anyone but Miss Monroe.

Another script change came in the sequence where, for the only time in the movie, Marilyn was set to wear a negligee. Eager to display her stunning new slimline physique, she wanted the scene to be rewritten to show it off more. Unsurprisingly, the director once again succumbed to her demands and, for the second time, the actress was truly elated. Seeing her immense pleasure, and simultaneously seeing a way to successfully press ahead with the movie's shooting, Cukor immediately announced to the cast and crew that, from that moment on, any suggestions and last-minute revisions to the script should be submitted to Monroe for her approval.

With her dislike of certain parts of the script so apparent, the actress was overjoyed by the suggestion, but suddenly she became apprehensive about her newfound role. Half of her was unnerved about the power that had just been thrust upon her; the other clearly enjoyed her newly acquired potency and soon made it clear that she would almost kill anyone who dared to take it away.

Despite Monroe's and Cukor's strong dislike of Strasberg, it was evident that the coach's presence was having a positive effect on Marilyn. For four straight days, from Monday 14 to Thursday 17 May, the actress arrived punctually on the set and participated (for the first three days at least) in every conceivable session of shooting. On the first day, she found herself pitted against a most uncooperative canine and its extremely frustrated trainer.

Once again, the scene focused on Marilyn's character as she returned home after five years away. This time, the sequence showed her reunion with the family's cocker spaniel. But surprisingly, the delays were not down to the actress; they were due to the dog, Jeff, who continually failed to obey the cues and commands of his owner Rudd Weatherwax, the eminent trainer of dogs such as Lassie. The animal would turn out to be more difficult to work with than the star.

Kneeling on the floor near the edge of the pool, the animal's perpetual disobedience made it impossible for Monroe to deliver her short line 'I used to come here a long time ago'. Take after fruitless take followed, during which the actress, her platinum-blonde hair reflecting the brilliance of the huge arc lights, repeatedly broke down into fits of giggles. The shooting of this short sequence (due to last just 15 seconds in the completed movie) dragged on for most of the day. But strangely, at no point during the shooting did anyone think about replacing the animal with a more cooperative one or scrapping the sequence altogether.

Over the years, it's been claimed that Marilyn was 'out-of-it' and lethargic on the set of *Something's Got To Give*. The truth was that, when she managed to drag herself to the set and appear before the cameras, the actress was, for the most part, simply *sensational*. She ascended to the occasion and acted like the true cinematic star she was. Reporter Vernon Scott of the *Fresno Bee* newspaper corroborated this. As a visitor to the set, he was able to see first-hand just how alert, talkative, informative and decidedly friendly the actress was.

'When the take [with the dog] was completed,' he wrote, 'MM returned to her dressing room and whisked from a form-fitting dress to snug Capri pants and sweater. She opened a bottle of champagne and said, "I feel wonderful." She looked it too.' He asked her if she was aware of the flurry of excitement that accompanied her activities in Hollywood. 'Gee, I never pay that much attention to that,' she replied. 'Maybe it's because I'm in such a hurry all the time trying not to be late that people are in a state of excitement around me.' His report concluded, 'Marilyn's eyes sparkled when she was asked if she planned to marry again. She came up with an answer no press agent could concoct. "I'm going to stay single forever . . . for now."' Without any possible doubt, the actress was back on form and truly excited about both the film and her future.

When shooting concluded for the day, and with Strasberg still stuck to her side, Marilyn climbed back into the Carey Cadillac Co. limousine and, after returning home to change, was driven to the nearby Brentwood market to do some shopping. Her chauffeur, Rudy Karensky, dropped them back at Fifth Helena at 9.15pm precisely. The car's hire charges for the day ($102.43 including a generous 15 per cent tip) served as proof of her propensity to spend cash at every available opportunity.

Via the pre-booked limo, Marilyn returned to the movie set one day later, and once more shot sequences which focused on her character's sentimental homecoming. In a memorable, heart-wrenching sequence, the actress was seen encountering her two young children, who, unlike the family's dog, failed to recognise her. Before filming began, in an attempt to put the young actors firmly at ease, the actress spent many moments interacting and playing with them. Everyone present on the set that day recalled how moved they were with Marilyn's actions. They all knew just how badly she wanted to be a mother herself.

Following a most enjoyable, trouble-free day of shooting, the actress left the studio. As folklore has it, she then headed for a series of dinner parties in the Hollywood hills, one of which was an event honouring Dr Timothy Leary, the Harvard psychologist and expert on consciousness-altering, mind-expanding drugs. The actress was ostensibly keen to meet him and during their brief liaison, and following her request, she was apparently introduced to lysergic acid diethylamide, a drug most commonly known as LSD. A sexual liaison supposedly followed. He later claimed that they 'Took a drive, walked by the sea, and took [the popular sedative] Mandrax.'

After examination of several highly respected notes, files, diaries and well-researched biographies about Leary, I can categorically announce that this never happened. The tale about his encounter with the screen legend actually grew out of one of his several, highly embellished LSD flashbacks, which he in turn passed on to his many disciples over the ensuing years. Ultimately, it appeared that Leary himself would end up believing his illusory encounter with Monroe actually happened. In truth, he was getting confused with President Kennedy's 41-year-old mistress, the socialite and painter Mary Pinchot Meyer, a lady who truly *did* contact Leary to try LSD. She had apparently turned the President on to marijuana cigarettes during their infrequent meetings at the White House.

In fact Marilyn returned home, where she spent the evening rehearsing her lines for the following day's shoot and her song for the important forthcoming birthday gala. A day later, on Wednesday 16 May, she returned to the Fox lot, but worryingly, her temperature had risen to 99.2. When the news of this sneaked out, Buck Hall, a self-confessed enemy of the actress, dejectedly muttered, 'Oh well, that takes care of the rest of the week.' He was wrong. Monroe managed to work throughout most of the day, and shot scenes with the children beside the pool. (During the afternoon session, following her lunch break, she returned to Stage 14 at 1.20 but did not arrive on the set until 2.55.)

She was continuing to take immense pride in the film and how she looked on screen. At the end of most of her days on the set, Marilyn paid a visit to David Bretherton, the movie's editor and therefore first viewer of the movie's 'dailies' (the first positive prints made by the laboratory from the negatives photographed during the previous day's shooting). She naturally enquired how she looked in her sequences and took great delight when he informed her she was 'wonderful, just wonderful'. The actress's publicist, Arthur Jacobs, recalled they always had a difficult time trying to keep her away from these screenings and remembered how she would sneak in at the back of the theatre, watch them and then, when the lights went up, begin to make preposterous judgements on how she might have been better lit or shot from a better angle. 'Of course, one simply *did not* do that,' Jacobs recalled in 1982, 'not if one wanted to stay on the right side of the director, crew and company.' To discourage her from such interventions, Cukor even went as far as to arrange screenings during the afternoons in a secret projection room.

Marilyn was back at the studio on Thursday 17 May but worked for just five hours. At 12.30pm, a helicopter arrived at the Fox lot, landing in the large yard just outside Sound Stage 14. Its mission was to collect Monroe, her press agent Pat Newcomb and coach Paula Strasberg, and whisk them to Los Angeles International Airport where they were set to catch a flight to the Big Apple. There, on Saturday at Madison Square Garden, Marilyn was due to participate in 'New York's Birthday Salute to the President', an all-star celebrity event with dual purposes as a fund-raising gala for the Democratic party and a celebration of John F. Kennedy's upcoming 45th birthday.

The announcement that Monroe had been added to the star-studded bill was made to the American press on Tuesday 10 April, a day after she had informed the Fox executives of her intention to appear. Regardless of what we've been told before, Marilyn's request to appear at the gala came directly from personality agent Earl Blackwell of the company Celebrity Service International, who had acted after receiving an order from the show's executive producer, the famed Broadway composer Richard Adler. Adler had liaised with Bobby Kennedy, who had moved after obtaining an order from the President himself.

When Adler rang Marilyn at her apartment in New York, on Friday 13 April, to tell her about the lyrics he had just penned for her, she had promised him she would be wearing an 'historical gown' for the occasion. It was an undertaking she did not forsake to deliver. The size 5 gown, a clone of one worn by entertainer Marlene Dietrich during one of her shows in London, was a second-skin, sheer, sparkling creation by 54-year-old French clothing designer and multiple Academy Award nominee Jean Louis Berthauldt. Once famed for the black satin strapless dress worn by the actress Rita Hayworth in her 1946 film *Gilda*, and for the figure-hugging stage wear used by Dietrich on her world cabaret tours, he would soon be best remembered for the gown which Marilyn would wear when she breathlessly serenaded 'Happy Birthday' to the President of the United States on Saturday 19 May 1962.

The actress ordered the full-length, silk soufflé creation from the Hollywood outfitters, Western Costume Co., situated at 5335 Melrose

Avenue in Hollywood, immediately after receiving the invitation. 'I want you to design a truly historical dress, a dazzling dress that is one of a kind,' Marilyn begged Jean Louis. As he remarked, the gown was designed to 'delicate in wholesome freshness her new and slimmer contour'.

Various estimates of its cost have been given over the years – $3,000 according to one author, $7,500 or $12,000 according to two others. In fact its cost, including tax, materials, labour charges and overtime, came to $1,404.65. The silk soufflé dress itself cost $1,027.36, its 2,500 intricately woven, hand-stitched rhinestones and mirrors came to $321.89, and its beading cost $55.40. To complete the dazzling outfit, Marilyn paid $35.68 for a pair of white stiletto shoes. The grand total of $1,440.33 was cleared by the actress by way of a handwritten cheque on Friday 8 June.

The actress kept the outside world totally in the dark about the gown. Even her housekeeper, Eunice Murray, was oblivious to it. The first glimpse she had of it came by way of one of Jean Louis' hand-drawn sketches, which he had brought over during one of his regular trips to Marilyn's home. During his visits, he and his assistant, Elizabeth Courtney, would be met at the door by Murray and escorted into the actress's inner sanctum, her bedroom, where, behind its firmly locked door, she would excitedly be measured.

In a 1973 interview for the *Winnipeg Free Press*, Jean Louis recalled, 'With a fitter, I went to her house. She was not always on time but she had champagne and caviar for us while we waited.' When she eventually appeared, she was barefoot and wearing a gown. 'She opened the robe, and she had no clothes on under it,' he remembered, '"If you are going to dress me," she said. "I want you to see what I look like." I was aghast. I am shy. Her behaviour was totally without guile or brazenness. She had no self-consciousness whatsoever about her nudity and simply thought it would be much easier for me to get her real measurements if she were unencumbered by clothes.'

'She was the most wonderful person,' Elizabeth Courtney remembered in 1962. 'She was very loving, and very appreciative of the least little things you would do for her. I've been in this business for 29 years and I've worked with a lot of stars, but Marilyn really was something extra. She would thank me a dozen times when I made her costumes, like I was doing something extraordinary.'

Marilyn had knocked herself out for three straight weeks rehearsing for her appearance at Kennedy's get-together. The actress would undertake painstaking run-throughs, both on the days when she was at Fox – where, during lunch breaks on *Something's Got To Give*, she would be coached by the studio's music director, Lionel Newman – and at her Brentwood home each night after returning from the studio. Friends of the actress touchingly recalled how she would be heard practising the song while she soaked in her bath tub. To hear how her rendition was shaping up, the actress even recorded her performances on a reel-to-reel tape recorder, which had been loaned to her by Dr Greenson.

Excitement was naturally engulfing her when Thursday 17 May finally arrived and it was time for her to dash out of one of Fox's soundstage doors and embark on the helicopter destined for Los Angeles International Airport. (Contrary to popular belief, actor Peter Lawford was not on board with her.) Besides her baggage and her colleagues, two other items accompanied her. The first was the 1954 book *The Little Engine That Could*, a moralistic children's story by Watty Piper about positive thinking, a present given to her by Joan Greenson, Ralph's daughter. The other was a chess piece, a knight extracted from the set she had purchased in Mexico in February. In a confidence-building exercise, Marilyn planned to wrap it in a handkerchief and clutch it as she sang at the gala. Unfortunately she would mislay it sometime during her stay in New York.

Once at the airport, Marilyn, Paula and Pat boarded a flight to New York's Idlewild Airport where the actress's rented limousine was waiting to whisk them to her 444 East 57th Street apartment. Shortly after their arrival, Marilyn's private secretary, May Reis, visited and later that evening, the actress was picked up from her residence by her New York press agent, John Springer, and driven to the nearby Savoy-Plaza Hotel at 767 5th Avenue at East 58th Street, where *Life* magazine columnist Richard Meryman and his assistant, Barbara Villet, were waiting.

Sitting at a table adjacent to the bar, Meryman ordered champagne and informed Marilyn that *Life* wanted to do an in-depth feature on her. Noticing her initial misgivings, he told her it would provide an ideal opportunity to talk unreservedly for the first time about her life, marriages, film bosses, fame and status as a screen icon, and provide a chance to silence the critics who insisted she did not create her own quotes. The actress listened intently while sipping Dom Perignon from her glass. After numerous questions, she warmed to the idea. A suggestion to carry out the interview at her home in Brentwood was agreed by all. Discussions about *when* exactly they should record the piece were interrupted when Marilyn suddenly announced, 'Peter Lawford is upstairs. Why don't we drop in on him? He told me to look him up when we reached town.'

The quartet agreed and, after finishing their drinks, walked across to an elevator which carried them up to the tenth floor of the 33-storey building. When they reached the actor's room, Marilyn knocked on its door. It was opened not by Lawford, but by a young man attired in only a bath towel. Appearing both shocked and embarrassed, the actress politely informed him, 'We're looking for Mr Lawford.' The man was lost for words. He just stood and stared. He was clearly shocked to find himself facing this world-famous movie star for the very first time while in a state of almost complete undress. Unperturbed, the actress continued, 'He must be in another room.' With his eyes still fixed on her, he eventually muttered, 'Yes, yes. He must be. He must be.' Marilyn politely thanked the man and the door slammed shut.

As the actress and her three companions began their long walk back up the corridor towards the elevator, she burst into a fit of giggles. 'He probably thinks he's drunk,' she theorised. 'He's seeing pink Marilyns.' The party ventured to the hotel's reception and enquired about Lawford. The desk clerk confirmed that he had checked into the hotel earlier but was out for the evening. No one bothered questioning whether his reply was the truth or part of a discreet cover-up.

After saying their goodbyes to Meryman and Villet, Springer – assuming she had no plans for the evening – invited Marilyn to join him and his wife for dinner. The actress declined the offer, insisting she was tired after such a long day. But the truth was that she loathed such acts of pity and knew they only ever came about via an inappropriate act of kindness. According to folklore, the actress then retreated to her apartment alone, a scenario she had acted out numerous times before, and forlornly faced an unappetising dinner comprising cold leftovers from her refrigerator. The truth was quite different.

In fact, earlier in the day, shortly after her arrival home, and before the visit of May Reis, Marilyn had called first the Beekman Market and then the A. Fitz & Sons Meat Market, situated three blocks from her home, to order a large quantity of food. The delivery, some of which the actress and her colleagues Newcomb and Strasberg tucked into that night after leaving Springer and his wife, included English muffins, lamb chops, steaks, chicken, artichokes, cucumber, eggs, radishes, strawberry jam, cheddar cheese, corn-on-the-cob, strawberries, endive and milk. A selection of liquor, delivered earlier in the day by Luria's Wine and Spirits Store at 1217 Madison Avenue, purchased at a cost of $129.85, helped wash down their feast. It was evident Marilyn was not watching her weight or depriving herself in the run-up to the President's ball.

Friday 18 May got off to a bad start when, shortly before 8am, the actress awoke to receive a 'Violation of Contract' note from 20th Century-Fox. The hand-delivered paper, which had originated from the studio's office in New York, charged her with 'failure to work' on her latest picture and warned her of 'dire consequences' if she failed to fulfil her obligations to the company. Marilyn was incensed by this. She knew Fox were aware of her intentions to travel and had actually given their blessings. With indignation filling her head, she soon began her day. Preparing for Kennedy's show was her *only* concern now.

At 9.30am, the actress and her colleagues stepped out of her apartment, travelled down in the lift and climbed into her waiting, chauffeur-driven limousine, hired once more from Exec-U-Car Inc. at 30 West 60th Street. Their first port of call was to make-up specialist Marie Irvine for a preliminary discussion at her home on Elbertson Street, Long Island. A trip to Monroe's regular New York hair stylist, Kenneth Battelle, followed. Later that night, at precisely 10pm, back at Marilyn's apartment, and with both Strasberg and Newcomb watching and supervising, the actress ran through another rendition of 'Happy Birthday'. However, her drama coach was becoming frustrated by it. 'It keeps getting sexier and sexier,' she remarked to her daughter, Susan, later that night. 'If she doesn't stop, it will be a parody.'

On the day of the concert, Saturday 19 May, the actress was escorted to Madison Square Garden, the gala venue, to participate in rehearsals with the other stars of the show. In charge of the preparations were producer Richard Adler and one of the event's co-organisers, the legendary English-born 'party-planner' Clive David. Set to arrive at 11am, Monroe did not appear until approximately 11.25. 'Marilyn was late,' David recalled. 'She was always late for things. Even though everybody was given a designated time [to attend], it still ran an hour behind schedule.

'The one artist I dreaded meeting was Maria Callas,' he continued, 'because she was known to be the most difficult woman opera had ever known; brilliantly talented but very difficult. I was dreading it. When she arrived in her limousine, I told her we were running behind schedule and she said, "Oh no, oh no." The air-conditioning inside Madison Square Garden had made it like a giant refrigerator and she said, "I can't sit in here. I won't have a voice. Can you find me somewhere that's not so cold?" So I found her a broom closet and I put her in there for one hour. She was very, very nice to me. [The comedian] Jack Benny was annoyed at being late. He was really angry, in fact. Marilyn arrived plainly dressed for the rehearsal.' Throughout her two and a half hours at the Garden, Monroe sported dark shades, a white headscarf, a tight-fitting, long-sleeved lime green Pucci blouse and white Capri slacks. At this point, a more grandiose idea for her rendition of 'Happy Birthday' was being orchestrated. 'As a gimmick, Richard Adler originally wanted Marilyn up on the top balcony with all the lights in the room surrounding her when she sang,' David remembered. 'But it never happened. Marilyn *hated* the idea.'

At approximately 2pm, after delivering a few brief run-throughs of her song with Newcomb by her side, she quickly departed the building, jumped into her waiting limousine and raced back to her apartment, where final preparations for the gala were *really* about to begin.

Since *Something's Got To Give* was now seven and a half days behind schedule, no one at Fox believed that Marilyn would be allowed to totally abandon shooting and fly out to the Big Apple. As Henry Weinstein sarcastically joked, 'It was enough to make Republicans of everyone on the set.' The incident could not have happened at a worse time for the studio. In New York, on Tuesday 15 May, just two days before Monroe's departure, at Fox's annual general meeting, president Spyros P. Skouras faced jeers, cynicism and disdain from a capacity crowd of over 300 shareholders who were angry about the studio's plummeting stock price, the rising costs of the still unfinished *Cleopatra* and the inflated wages of its star, Elizabeth Taylor. Their fury intensified when Skouras meekly informed them that, in their previous year of business, the company had incurred a loss of $22.5 million. Even an offer to screen excerpts from several of Fox's newest movies failed to quieten the unruly attendees. 'We came here on business,' screamed one irate stockholder, '*not* to be entertained.'

Unrest seemed to be everywhere. So, when Marilyn announced to the studio that she was intent on travelling, in turn heaping more delays on the studio, attempts were made to dissuade her from doing so. In the week leading up to her exodus, studio chief Levathes pleaded with her several times not to go. He even firmly declared to everyone concerned that the actress would *not* be permitted to leave.

Such was the seriousness of his declaration that on Friday 11 May a letter was drafted by the studio. In part it read:

> Marilyn, as you know we are behind schedule with our picture. We
> have a great deal of money already invested in it and we cannot afford
> anymore delays. While I realise that this social function may be
> important to you, we cannot consent to or acquiesce in your absence
> and I must, on behalf of 20th Century-Fox, insist that you will be
> available at our studio to render your services during the week of May
> 14 to 18 inclusive . . .

Milton S. Gould, one of New York City's most accomplished litigators, was on the board at 20th Century-Fox at the time, and was also insistent that the actress should remain in Los Angeles and committed to the film. In an interview for the book *The Dark Side Of Camelot* by Seymour H. Hersh, Gould recalled that Attorney General Bobby Kennedy rang him personally and asked him to waive his objection. He told Bobby, 'Look, General, in no way can we do this. The lady has caused all sorts of kinds of trouble. We're way behind budget. I just can't.' He continued to say no. Then, according to Gould, Kennedy got very abusive, called him a 'Jewish bastard' and slammed down the phone. The Attorney General never apologised for his rude behaviour.

Dean Martin was also angry at Marilyn's decision to travel. He had reluctantly rejected an invitation to appear at the illustrious event due to his commitments on *Something's Got To Give*. Additionally, he didn't wish to be held responsible for throwing an entire crew out of work for two days. George Cukor was another livid at Marilyn's choice. He told scriptwriter Walter Bernstein he felt helpless in the situation and believed that whatever he or the studio said, she was always going to get her way. The movie's producer was irate too. 'She just didn't have any sense of responsibility or respect for them [the studio bosses],' Henry Weinstein dejectedly remarked. 'She had no feeling for them.'

However, Marilyn was uninterested. She had set her heart on singing to the President of the United States and nobody on earth could dissuade her from doing so.

With hindsight, Weinstein admitted that he felt that this was a wasted opportunity and that Fox should have travelled to New York with her and used the trip as a promotional exercise for the movie. Speaking to the studio for a documentary about the film in 1990, he remarked, 'We should have gone with a sign saying *Something's Got To Give* instead of worrying about whether she had gone or what the studio thought . . . Immediately, the studio should have been alerted, we should have had our own cameraman there, with her and the President. That's what you would do. Instead, they said, "How could she go?"'

Of course, the Fox hierarchy *were* aware of and (before shooting had commenced and run into serious trouble) *had* given their blessing to the actress's trip. In an interview on Tuesday 15 May with movie and television writer Bob Thomas, Marilyn partially confirmed this when she remarked, 'I told the studio six weeks ago [on Monday 9 April] I was going,' adding, 'I consider it an honour to appear before the President of the United States. Besides, I *am* a Democrat.'

But either way, with the film's leading lady now in the Big Apple and with all viable filming options completely exhausted, work on *Something's Got To Give* was now completely impossible. It came as no surprise to anyone when a 'shut down' sign was tacked on to the doors of Sound Stage 14. In the words of Hollywood columnist Dorothy Manners, 'The studio had finally thrown in the towel . . . '

October 1960, Pyramid Lake, Nevada. Marilyn and her third husband, the playwright Arthur Miller, take a break during the filming of *The Misfits*.

11 November 1960, New York. Marilyn attempts to leave her apartment following the announcement that she was divorcing Arthur Miller. 'Arthur is a wonderful writer,' she would remark, 'but I think he's a better writer than a husband.'

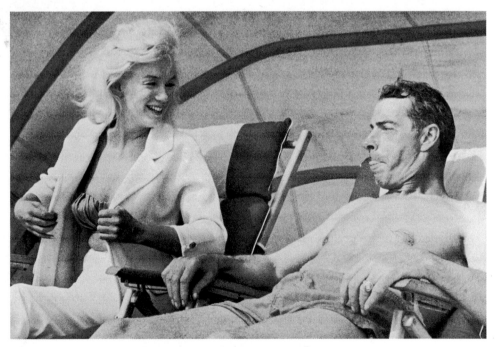

22 March 1961, Reddington Beach, Florida. DiMaggio sticks his tongue out to waiting journalists who were attempting to disrupt his and Marilyn's rest on the beach.

14 June 1961, Sands Hotel, Las Vegas. Dean Martin's surprise belated 44th birthday celebration, midnight. Marilyn was seen seated at the very edge of the Sands' stage, champagne glass in hand, gently swaying along to the music, enthusiastically applauding each number and gazing up adoringly at Sinatra as he performed. Seated alongside her were Martin and her great screen rival, Elizabeth Taylor.

15 June 1961, Idlewild Airport. Marilyn arrives back in New York following her flight out of Los Angeles. Amid tidal waves of wolf-whistles and flash bulbs, she remarked 'No comment' to reporters who enquired why she had suddenly returned.

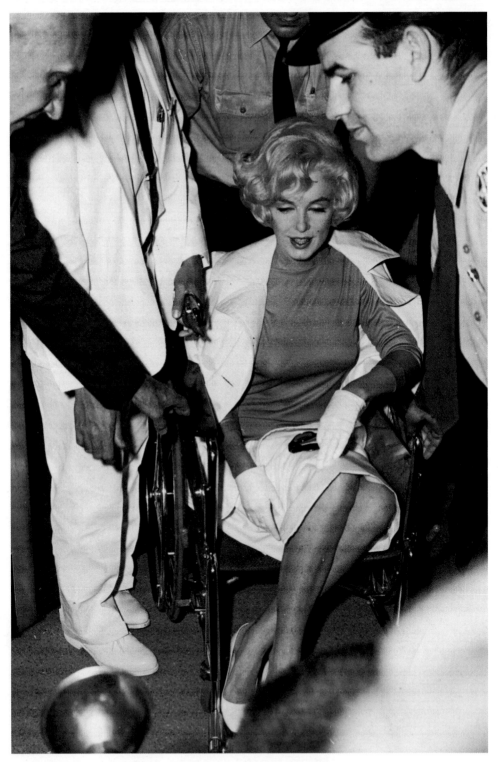

11 July 1961, the Polyclinic Hospital, New York. After two weeks of recuperating, Marilyn was wheeled out of hospital following gall-bladder surgery. Before doing so, her obligatory New York hairstylist, the eminent Kenneth Battelle had been urgently summoned to fix her tresses. 'I had flown in from Europe that day,' he recalled. 'I flew to New York for three hours just to do Marilyn's hair.'

11 August 1961, Beverly Hills Hotel. Marilyn fulfils the wishes of 14-year-old Barbara Heinz, who was dying of incurable bone cancer in Wisconsin's Appleton Memorial Hospital. With just a month to live, the young girl, a keen collector of toys, penned a letter to the actress requesting a picture of her with Maf. Marilyn duly obliged. This photograph arrived at the girl's bedside on Wednesday 23 August inscribed with the words, 'From Marilyn Monroe to Barbara Heinz. With love.'

5 March 1962, Golden Globes ceremony. By Marilyn's side at this star-studded event was the Mexican-born Jose Bolaños. His presence naturally ignited rumours in the American press of a 'Latin lover' in Marilyn's life. However, aside from a few short walks in the moonlight, there was no romance. Just days after the lavish ceremony, and with the actress clearly tired of his company and the language barrier, Bolaños was packing his bags, heading back to his motherland.

5 March 1962, Golden Globes ceremony, the International Ballroom of the Beverly Hilton Hotel. After a poll carried out by the Hollywood Foreign Press Association, Marilyn's apparent fall from prominence proved to be premature when she was bestowed with the Henrietta Award for the World's Favourite Female Movie Star. She is pictured here with the actor, Rock Hudson.

10 April 1962, Twentieth Century-Fox Studios, Los Angeles, screen-tests for *Something's Got To Give*. Marilyn's first appearance on a film set in 17 months. This was a newborn Monroe. Aided by her new svelte 22-inch waist and 8-stone 4lbs body weight, she was considerably more sophisticated and stylish than she had ever been before.

10 April, 1962, Twentieth-Century Fox Studios, Los Angeles, screen-tests for *Something's Got to Give*.

For six straight hours, Marilyn posed, paraded, smiled and laughed in front of the Deluxe colour CinemaScope cameras wearing a total of 7 different hairstyles and 15 different costumes.

19 May 1962, Madison Square Garden, New York. During a break in rehearsals for the JFK Gala, Marilyn sits and chats with one of the event's co-organisers, the legendary English-born 'party-planner' Clive David. 'She was the high-spot of the evening,' he admitted. 'The guest-list was incredible but she was the true highlight of the whole thing.' (From the collection of Clive David.)

As a keepsake from the event, reproduced here for the very first time, Marilyn inscribed a wall-tile for David with the words, 'To Clive love & kisses Marilyn Monroe'. An inscription by the Strasbergs (Lee and Paula) can be seen at the bottom of the image. (From the collection of Clive David.)

19 May 1962, Madison Square Garden, New York, 11.30 p.m. In front of 12,000 loyal Democratic Party members, Marilyn half-sang, half-talked an extremely sultry, sexually charged, super-slow rendition of 'Happy Birthday' in a way that no one had ever heard it sung before. Before she did so, she thought to herself, 'By God, I'll sing this song if it's the last thing I ever do.'

TO RENTAL FROM

WESTERN COSTUME CO. 5335 Melrose Ave.
HOLLYWOOD 38, CALIF.   HOllywood 9-1451
THEATRICAL COSTUMES · PROPERTIES · EQUIPMENT · WIGS AND HAIR GOODS · COSTUME JEWELRY

ORIGINAL INVOICE   Invoice No. 69778

	CUST. ORDER NO.	PRODUCTION	DATE
700			5/29/62

TO.
Miss Marilyn Monroe
12305 Fifth Helena Dr.
Los Angeles 49, Calif.

TERMS: NET 10 DAYS E.O.M.

SHIPPING SHEET NO.	QUAN.		UNIT PRICE	TOTAL
82692	1	Made to Order Dress Labor and Material including necessary Overtime		1,027.36
		Cost of Rhinestones & Mirrors (not including the actual beading)		321.89
	1	Pr. Shoes		35.68
				1,384.93
		Sales Tax		55.40
				1,440.33
		Less Deposit		300.00
dw		PURCHASE	Balance Due	1,140.33

Ck #16.59
JUN 8 1962

102	202	201	203	204	205	206	207	112	28	221	345
								55.40		(1,384.93)	

The foregoing articles are rented from Western Costume Co. upon the terms set forth in the shipping sheet heretofore signed by the representative of the lessee to which shipping sheet reference is hereby made.

The original invoice for Marilyn's world-famous dress she wore that night. (From the Keith Badman collection.)

19 May 1962, Upper East Side townhouse at 33 East 69th Street, New York, a private after-show gathering. In this world-famous picture, Marilyn, still wearing her legendary dress, stands in the library between John and Bobby Kennedy. In the palm of her left hand is her present for JFK, an 18ct, $5,000 gold Rolex 'President' watch (pictured below) inscribed with the words, 'Jack, with love as always from Marilyn, May 19th, 1962.' Tucked inside the timepiece's box was a poem, which read, 'Let lovers breathe their sighs / And roses bloom and music sound / Let passion burn on lips and eyes / And pleasures merry world go round / Let golden sunshine flood the sky / And let me love / Or let me die!' This is the only known picture of the actress taken with either of the Kennedy brothers.

Exec - U - Car Inc.

30 WEST 60TH STREET
NEW YORK 22, N. Y.

DATE May 22, 1962

ACCT. Miss Marilyn Monroe (Account)

444 East 57th Street & 12305 Fifth Helena Dr

New York City, N. Y. Los Angeles 49,
California.

DATE	VOUCHER NO.	CHARGES	BALANCE
		BALANCE FORWARD ➡➔	
5-17-62	#62-1870		$21.60
5-18-62	#62-1871		101.15
5-19-62	#62-1875		142.60
5-20-62	#62-1876		37.30
			$302.65

Thank you again for letting Exec-U-Car Inc.
serve you. Do tell us if the service is not
satisfactory at any time.

Incidently, we attended the Birthday Party of
President Kennedy, and surely enjoyed it all.
You were certainly wonderful, Miss Monroe.

JUN 1 1962
CR# 1639

May 1962, Marilyn's Exec-U-Car Inc. limousine hire invoice, covering the period 17 to 20 May 1962, the entire time she was in New York for JFK's birthday gala. (From the Keith Badman collection.)

1 June 1962, Chavez Ravine Stadium, the home of the Los Angeles Angels baseball team. In front of a record-breaking 51,584 crowd, Marilyn blew kisses and made an appeal for donations for the Muscular Dystrophy Association. Throughout the evening, with the wind blowing hard through the stadium, the actress fought hard to keep her hat attached to her head. The Angels' smallest player, outfielder Albie Gregory Pearson is amongst those pictured alongside her. Besides being Marilyn's 36th birthday, it was also her very last public performance.

FRANKS

NURSERIES AND FLOWERS

12424 WILSHIRE BOULEVARD

WEST LOS ANGELES 25, CALIF. 8-1-1962

DELIVER TO: Miss Marilyn Monroe

ADDRESS: 1230 - 5th Helena Dr.

THIS IS A CONFIRMATION OF YOUR ORDER

3337-40

Thank You

4 August 1962, 12305 Fifth Helena Drive, Brentwood. At approximately 4 p.m. on the day of her death Marilyn received a delivery of, amongst other items, petunias, begonias, sedums, terracotta pots, a Mexican lime tree, a hanging begonia basket and some hummingbird feeding stands from Franks Nurseries & Flowers shop at 12424 Wilshire Boulevard. This is one of the actress's receipts from the sale, made on 1 August. (From the Keith Badman collection.)

August 1962. Eunice Murray didn't like being called Marilyn's housekeeper. 'I guess there's no word in the dictionary to exactly describe what I was,' she admitted. 'I was her chauffeur, her cook, her real estate agent, her social secretary.' In truth, she was a house-spy, sent by Dr Greenson, and never once did she let on to the actress she had a background as a psychiatric nurse. It was a vocation she had been employed in since 1951.

5 August 1962, rear of Marilyn's home, 12305 Fifth Helena Drive, Brentwood, morning – two baubles, one a tiger, the other a lamb, lay abandoned on the grass, at the exact spot they landed the night before, at the conclusion of a game of 'fetch-ball' between Marilyn and Maf.

8 August 1962, Westwood Village Mortuary chapel in the grounds of the Westwood Memorial Park Cemetery, 1 p.m. Pacific Daylight Time (4 p.m. Eastern Daylight Time). Dr Ralph Greenson (Marilyn Monroe's psychiatrist), his wife Hildi and their children, Daniel and Joan, in attendance at Marilyn's funeral.

DIMAG CLAIMS MARILYN'S BODY

Joins Star's Sister; Rites Set

August 1962. Coverage of Marilyn's death featured prominently for several days in newspapers right across the globe.

8 August 1962, Westwood Village Mortuary. A decidedly distraught DiMaggio, alongside his son, Joe Jr. at Marilyn's funeral.

Chapter Seven

The JFK Gala/Something's Got To Give (part two)

Saturday 19 May 1962–Tuesday 12 June 1962

'**M**ost politicians, when they come to New York, make their headquarters at the Waldorf, mine is Madison Square Garden,' President Kennedy quipped on the afternoon of Saturday 19 May, just hours before his fund-raising gala. Besides the small matter of his impending 45th birthday, the main purpose of the event was to wipe clean the debt left from the Democrats' 1960 presidential campaign. Fortuitously, it was New York City's hottest day for five years and, at that time, the hottest May temperature on record. In the late afternoon, it peaked at a blistering 99 degrees.

Before travelling on to the Garden, at precisely 7.05pm JFK avoided the heat by hosting a dinner party in Manhattan's opulent Four Seasons restaurant. While there, he showed his gratitude to the 375 individuals who had purchased the highest-priced $1,000 tickets to his show by stopping at every one of their tables and personally pumping each of their hands. Although Marilyn Monroe was one of those purchasers, she was not at the restaurant. She was busily beautifying herself for the big night.

Five hours earlier, after returning briefly to her condominium (where a home-movie enthusiast caught a glimpse of her signing her autograph and hugging and chatting to an elderly female fan), the actress had been driven round to the Lilly Daché building. There, at a cost of $150, her hair stylist Kenneth Battelle was ready and waiting to mould her hair into his most famous creation, parted to the side with a flick. (Contrary to the insistence of many historians, the hairstyle was not done by hairdresser Mickey Song.

Not only did he have no connection with the actress, he was a complete stranger to the Kennedy family too.) Afterwards, with Pat Newcomb still by her side, Monroe gingerly climbed into her limousine again and was rushed back to her apartment where her make-up lady, Marie Irvine, was lingering to give her a special $125 beautification. When it was completed, with the aid of her personal maid, Hazel Washington, the actress was painstakingly hooked and stitched into her stunning new Jean Louis gown. Throughout all this, her rented black limousine sat idle on the road outside.

Kennedy meanwhile left the Four Seasons at 8.50 and arrived at the Garden shortly after 9.10. He travelled happy in the knowledge that, for the first time since November 1960, the party was solvent. 'All we have now is the federal deficit,' he joked to waiting reporters. With tickets for the gala priced in a range from $100 and $500 to $1,000, the Democratic Party had easily surpassed their gross target of just $11,300 for the night. (In total, their coffers were sweetened by $1 million. However, despite the long-held belief that it was a full house that evening, only 12,000 of the 17,500 ticket-holders turned up to see the night's entertainment.)

Waiting to greet Kennedy as he entered his private box was his Vice-President, Lyndon B. Johnson. The crowd within the arena gave the President a rousing standing ovation and roared 'Happy Birthday' to him at every available opportunity. Coinciding with his arrival, the orchestra played 'Hail to the Chief', the official anthem of the President of the United States. The notoriously drab venue had never looked so festive. Red, white and blue bunting hung everywhere and hundreds of balloons, adorned with the American flag, rained down from the ceiling several times during the night.

Another long-believed myth about the gala was that Kennedy's brother-in-law, Peter Lawford, was the MC for the entire show. In fact, for the first half, the host was radio and television comedian Jack Benny. At approximately 9.30pm, a full hour after the allotted starting time, the comic got the presentation off to a cracking start when he quipped, in a reference to his notoriously tight-fisted public persona, 'The greatest compliment I could pay the President was the fact that I flew all the way from California at my *own* expense and I'm not even a Democrat.' When the laughter died down, another joke followed. 'The amazing thing to me is how a man in a rocking chair can have such a young wife.' (This was a satirical nod to Kennedy's 1955 P & P Chair Company rocking chair, in which he would sit to help relieve the pains in his lower back.)

Benny was followed by the dance troupe Jerome Robbins' Ballet USA, actor Henry Fonda, comedian Jimmy Durante, and singers Ella Fitzgerald, Harry Belafonte (a last-minute replacement for comedy actor

Danny Kaye), Peggy Lee (who climbed out of her sick-bed to appear), Maria Callas (who flew in from Europe to deliver songs from the musical *Carmen*) and Judy Garland (who had flown in especially from Shepperton Studios in Surrey where she was shooting *I Could Go On Singing*).

The President watched the entire show from his box. Throughout, he sat sandwiched between his mother, Rose, and Anna Rosenberg, the former Assistant Secretary of Defence and co-sponsor of the presentation. Clearly relaxed, he was determined to enjoy himself. With his feet perched high on the enclosure's rails, he serenely puffed away on his cigars and happily laughed and clapped along to the evening's entertainment.

The artists performing on the bill that night had been requested to assemble backstage and be ready to take their seats in the hall by 8pm. Characteristically, Marilyn was late, arriving at precisely 8.40pm, in the company of Pat Newcomb and her date for the night, Isidore Miller. Just prior to her arrival at the Garden, the actress had insisted on performing her rendition of 'Happy Birthday' to Miller at her apartment; rather than being influenced by JFK, as has sometimes been claimed, the real inspiration behind the rendition was in fact Miller. The version she would perform that night was actually orchestrated by *his* directions.

Attired in her stunning new, underwear-free creation, Marilyn slid out of her stretch limo and immediately headed backstage where, for the next two hours 50 minutes, she was seen chatting and mingling with the other big-name stars on the bill. Her casual, Dom Perignon-induced demeanour was superbly captured in stills form by the multi-talented Broadway performer and photographer Victor R. Helou. Fearful of adverse publicity, Marilyn made it clear to everyone, including Kenneth Battelle, that she did not want to be seen at the event with *any* specific male on her arm, aside from the relatively safe Isidore Miller.

At 11.30pm, approximately two hours into the gala, co-MC Peter Lawford once more strolled on to the podium. His mission this time was to herald the actress on to it.

Each of his initial attempts appeared to be met with failure. 'Mr President,' he announced. 'On this occasion of your birthday, this lovely lady is not only pulchritudinous but punctual. Mr President, Marilyn Monroe.' He turned to greet the actress. A spot of light instantly illuminated the area at the back of the stage where she was due to materialise. A roll on the drums followed. But she failed to appear. Laughter rang out from the audience.

Lawford walked four paces away from his lectern, clutched his chin and stared in bewilderment at both the audience and the empty abyss at the rear of the platform. Though many in the audience failed to see the joke, it was an obvious satirical nod to the actress's legendary tardiness in both her social and professional life, a caper Lawford and Marilyn had concocted between them in the days leading up to the event. Contrary to the assertions of some previous Monroe biographers, she was never scheduled to appear earlier in the show and, because of her tardiness and drunken behaviour, continually shunted down the bill until she was ready to perform. As the surviving running-order notes from the gala clearly demonstrate, the actress's rendition was always set to be the twenty-third – and final – part of the programme.

The actor returned to his stand and attempted the introduction again. 'A woman about whom, it truly may be said, she needs no introduction. Let me just say . . . here she is.' Another drum-roll followed but there was still no sign of Monroe. Once more, the audience laughed.

However, she *was* nearby, standing motionless, visibly trembling and noticeably tipsy, in the darkness at the very edge of the Madison Square Garden stage, waiting patiently for her cue in Lawford's apparently rambling introduction. When it came, Marilyn took a deep breath, straightened her shoulders, pushed out her chest, stuck out her buttocks, coyly clutched at her white ermine jacket (borrowed from Fox's wardrobe department), ascended the short flight of steps and strode into the bright glare of the spotlights.

Her arrival was met by rapturous applause and a spectacular tidal wave of flashing photographic light bulbs. Her premature emergence cut short Lawford's corny, 'Mr President, because, in the history of show business, at best, there has been no one female, who has meant so much . . . who has done more' speech. When the audience caught sight of Marilyn skittering, tippy-toe, geisha-like, across the stage to stand alongside Lawford under the brightest spotlight in the building, their gasps soon turned into a thunderous roar. 'She mounted the stage in the tightest, slinkiest, ankle-length silk and sequin creation ever seen in the Garden,' wrote Robert S. Bird of the *Herald Tribune*. 'She was the high-spot of the evening,' admitted event co-organiser Clive David. 'The guest-list was incredible but she was the *true* highlight of the whole thing.' The last words of Lawford's introduction would, regrettably, prove to be prophetic. 'Mr President. The *late* Marilyn Monroe.' He then collected the jacket from her torso and exited stage right.

Monroe was now alone on stage. But no one noticed. Everybody was transfixed by her seemingly transparent, flesh-coloured, rhinestone-decorated dress, which sparkled incessantly. 'There was a hush over the whole place when I came on to sing,' she remarked to *Life* magazine later in the year. 'I thought, "Oh my gosh, what if no sound comes out?"' She flicked the microphone to check if it was working; it was. Amid the sound of another drum-roll, she lunged at it, shaded her eyes from the strong Madison Square Garden lights, fleetingly glanced up at the President in his box and waited before starting to sing.

Fifteen seconds passed. Anticipation filled the air; momentary bursts of applause punctuated the calm. Rightly milking every last moment, she pursed her lips, caressed the microphone, stared seductively into the vast crowd and then, in front of 12,000 loyal Democratic Party members, half-sang, half-talked an extremely sultry, sexually charged, super-slow rendition of 'Happy Birthday' in a way that no one had ever heard it sung before. Before doing so, she thought to herself, 'By God, I'll sing this song if it's the last thing I ever do.' Each and every line of her performance was greeted with overwhelming critical and audience approval. Her words were like a caress of pleasure. She had successfully managed to breathe sexual innuendo into a simple, innocent, age-old refrain. She sang it so breathily, so gaspily, so erotically that even the coldest, most reticent people in the house were moved.

'With Marilyn whispering "Happy Birthday" and the crowd yelling and screaming, it was like mass seduction,' Richard Adler recalled. Politician Adlai Stevenson remarked, 'I don't think I have ever seen anyone so beautiful as Marilyn Monroe that night. She was dressed in what she called skin and beads . . . I didn't see the beads.' Historian Arthur Schlesinger Jr reiterated this, writing in his journal, 'I do not think I have seen *anyone* so beautiful.' The UPI columnist Merriman Smith recalled, 'Her low-cut, skin-tight evening dress was such a form-fitting creation that the crowd paid little attention to what she said.' Clive David's reaction to Marilyn's performance was simple. 'Wow! She created the biggest smile *ever* in history,' he confessed. '*Everyone* in the audience just beamed.' The actress had unintentionally managed to steal the night right from under the President's nose.

She concluded her dazzling but brief performance with a unique rendering of the classic song and Bob Hope theme tune, 'Thanks for the Memory', rewritten by Richard Adler with lyrics directed at Kennedy. 'Thanks, Mr President,' Marilyn sang, 'For all the things you've done, The battles that you've won, The way you deal with US Steel, And our problems by the ton, We thank you so much . . . ' The new lyric referred to a speech made on Thursday 12 April, in which Kennedy had denounced US Steel Corp chairman Roger M. Blough's planned $6-a-ton rise in steel prices as 'unjustifiable and irresponsible defiance of the public interest'.

'Everybody, happy birthday,' she then shouted, frantically waving her arms as she introduced a rendition of 'Happy Birthday' by the house orchestra. On cue, the audience rose to give the President yet another standing ovation.

Marilyn quite rightly regarded her performance as one of the most triumphant moments of her career. The gala had been an elite gathering of America's finest, and the fact that she was thought of as the highlight of the evening confirmed the power and recognition she still wielded as an international celebrity in 1962. Furthermore, it showed that, despite the harsh words of some newspaper critics, she was still the most exciting and desired woman on the planet.

Everyone seemed to love her – everyone that is except for Jacqueline Kennedy. Fully aware that Marilyn was going to hijack the show, and no doubt still incensed by her husband's one-night liaison with the actress two months previously, the President's wife decided to miss the event, instead choosing to take herself and her children away. At the very last minute, as the *Independent Press-Telegram* noted on Sunday 20 May, she was a shock attendee at a two-day horse competition in Leesburg, Virginia. 'Mrs. J. F. Kennedy was a surprise participant in the Loudoun Hunt Horse Show Saturday. Mrs. Kennedy, accompanied by her young daughter, Caroline, came here from the Kennedy leased estate, Glen Ora . . . Clad in riding habit, Mrs. Kennedy rode Minbreno in three classes and took third place in the Maj. Larry Lawrence Memorial Trophy event for owner-riders.'

At the conclusion of Monroe's brief but scenic performance, after a five-foot high, multi-tiered cake studded with 45 sparkling blue candles had been carried out from behind the stage by two toque-wearing chefs, and following the briefest of introductions by New York Mayor Robert F. Wagner, the President mounted the stage and humorously remarked, 'I can now retire from politics after having had "Happy Birthday" sung to me in such a sweet, wholesome way.'

Plans to follow Monroe's performance with a lengthy, pre-prepared speech about his programme of action and Republican opposition were swiftly discarded. Protocol had been cast to the wind. Clearly relishing the birthday party spirit, he instead used the opportunity to jest and personally thank those who had one way or another played a part in the night. 'To Jack Benny,' he said, 'who came to help an older man celebrate his birthday. Danny Kaye, whom I talked to in a hospital, I feel sorry for him. Harry Belafonte, I don't feel sorry for him though, because he interrupted his tour in Columbus, Ohio and I can tell you, there is no city in the United States where a Democrat gets a warmer welcome and less votes than Columbus, Ohio . . .'

With applause both for herself and the President still ringing in her ears, Marilyn left the stage. Waiting to meet and congratulate her as she descended from it was Brooklyn-born opera diva Maria Callas. Monroe then headed for her dressing room where she collapsed and, in an attempt to lower her temperature, bathed with cool hand towels. She then briefly took her front-row seat next to Miller and her three other associates. Judy Garland was seated nearby and, as Marilyn passed by, she inclined forward to embrace her.

The historic dual Kennedy/Democratic Party event concluded at precisely 11.55pm, having run for precisely 2 hours 25 minutes (rather than four hours, as some researchers have insisted). A crowd in excess of 10,000 excitedly lined the streets and cheered as JFK's car departed from the Garden, making its way across town to Park Avenue and up to the Upper East Side townhouse at 33 East 69th Street belonging to Arthur B. Krim, where Kennedy was to be the guest of honour at a private gathering for the dignitaries, friends and performers who had worked tirelessly to put the evening's show together.

Photographers from the world's press were banned. However, snapper Cecil N. Stoughton was not. He had been chosen by the White House to exclusively document the private affair.The party for 75 people, which also included a short performance by entertainer Diahann Carroll, was a truly joyous occasion. In an interview with *National Geographic*, Stoughton recalled, 'Everybody was there, Maria Callas, Jimmy Durante, Shirley MacLean. And when Marilyn showed up. I got a shot of JFK, Bobby and Marilyn all in the same frame when they were packed in the library with a whole bunch of other guests.'

The picture he referred to has since become world-famous. It shows the actress, still wearing her famous dress, standing in between John and Bobby in front of a large bookshelf and clutching, in the palm of her left hand, her present for JFK, an 18ct, $5,000, gold Rolex 'President' watch inscribed with the words, 'Jack, with love as always from Marilyn May 19th, 1962.' Tucked inside the timepiece's box was a poem, which read, 'Let lovers breathe their sighs / And roses bloom and music sound / Let passion burn on lips and eyes / And pleasures merry world go round / Let golden sunshine flood the sky / And let me love / Or let me die!'

Introduced in 1956 at the Basel Watch, Clock and Jewellery Fair, the 'President' turned out to be one of the company's flagship models. A version of the watch presented to President Eisenhower to celebrate his re-election to the White House in November 1956 featured the new, so-called 'President' bracelet and the name remained with it; hence, six years later, Marilyn chose to purchase one for JFK.

It's worth noting that a fourth individual, historian Arthur Schlesinger, is also seen in the original photograph, although, so as to add credence to the belief that Marilyn, Bobby and John had slid away from the others for a discreet, private discussion, his presence is excised from practically every subsequent reproduction. The image however does perfectly corroborate Schlesinger's recollections that he and Bobby had 'engaged in mock competition' for Marilyn's attention at the party. The Attorney General – of whom she would later remark, 'It was good to see a smiling, friendly face' – apparently startled her by discussing politics, something that no one had ever attempted doing with her before.

Marilyn's escort that evening, Isidore Miller, tellingly recalled in late 1962 the get-together at Krim's. 'She [Marilyn] took me along to meet the President. She said I was her date and when she went up to the President, instead of saying, "I am pleased to meet you, Mr. President," she said, "I want you to meet my former father-in-law." I'm sure she was thinking about the thrill I was getting instead of etiquette.' His remark provides us with reliable evidence that, following their brief liaison at Bing Crosby's house just seven weeks earlier, Marilyn felt she knew the President well enough to avoid the standard introductory protocol, and that she had failed to divulge to Isidore even the remotest details about her intimate tryst with Kennedy.

For the few remaining years of his life, Miller would treasure a photograph taken at the party, which showed Monroe and the President laughing spontaneously at one of his humorous remarks. Aside from the time when they watched Diahann Carroll perform, everyone at the gathering stood but, despite his protestations, the actress insisted he should sit. When he did, she knelt down beside him. 'She was very beautiful and caring,' he recalled. Marilyn never strayed far from him or that area of the house for the entire night, causing her to miss the fine range of delicacies which had been laid out on a table in an adjacent room.

When the party came to a close, the actress insisted on taking Miller home. At the elevator of the building where he was staying, they kissed goodbye. But, just as she was about to climb into her waiting limousine, she turned round, walked back inside and asked him to travel with her to Los Angeles the following day. He declined the offer but suggested he would make the trip sometime in the future, possibly in November. They would talk many more times on the phone but sadly, this would be their penultimate outing together.

Much has been written about the actress's apparent clandestine meeting with the President (or his brother) immediately after (or during or prior to) Krim's party. Some authors have suggested that she spent that night with JFK in his bed at the Carlyle Hotel. New York columnist Earl Wilson fuelled this myth when he announced that, shortly after 1am, Secret Service agents escorted Marilyn and the President to the basement of Krim's apartment house and through a maze of tunnels which led to the

Carlyle Hotel, where JFK regularly maintained a penthouse. 'I learned from an FBI agent that they remained in the suite for several hours. It was the last prolonged encounter between them,' he sensationally remarked.

I can reveal that these accounts are fictitious and, moreover, unfeasible in practical terms. Is it possible that the President and the world-famous actress could slip away from Krim's private, three-hour party without anyone noticing? It's also worth remembering that Marilyn's close friend Ralph Roberts went on record by saying that a meeting between JFK and Monroe that night was 'impossible' because he was waiting to give her a massage at her apartment following the party and departed in the region of 4am while she was asleep.

Furthermore, Marilyn was pictured leaving Krim's party and climbing into her waiting limousine still wearing her skin-tight dress, a creation she had to be sewn into. Is it likely that, after Monroe had been intimate with JFK in his room at the Carlyle Hotel, he, the President of the United States, the most powerful man in the world, was responsible for sewing and hooking her back into the outfit? Marilyn's stand-in and close friend, Evelyn Moriarty, concurred with this view. 'So many people said she left the party and went to meet Kennedy, so please answer me, how could she get out of that dress and back into it? The dress had all those little hooks in it. She was sewn into it . . . The rumours about Kennedy started *after* she died, *not* before. Nothing was said. Nobody said *anything* about it [when she was alive]. She went to a few parties and he was there. She was a friend of his sisters.'

In addition, Marilyn's date that night was Isidore Miller. Did she just abandon him while she went off to be intimate with Kennedy? Of course not.

Instead, Marilyn spent the concluding hours of the night in the platonic company of Ralph Roberts and James Haspiel at her East 57th Street apartment. As the latter wrote in his 2002 book, *Marilyn: The Ultimate Look at the Legend*, 'I can tell you with *authority* that I was with Marilyn at her apartment ten minutes to four in the morning.' This is confirmed by recently recovered receipts from the day of the JFK Democratic gala (19/20 May). Aside from the drive by her publicist, John Springer, Marilyn's entire journeying around New York and to and from Madison Square Garden (between the evening of Thursday 17 May and the morning of Sunday 20 May) was aided by a limousine hired from the city's Exec-U-Car Inc. Her invoice clearly shows that Marilyn's rented car left its base at 11.15am and returned to its garage just over 17 hours later, at 4.30am. This, along with the recollection of Ralph Roberts, confirms that Haspiel's announcement was entirely accurate.

*

Basking in the fame of her performance at the President's bash, Marilyn flew back to Los Angeles the very next day, Sunday 20 May. Waiting to greet her at 10am at the city's International Airport was another chauffeur-driven limousine. Hired by her at a cost of $17.00 (including tax) from the Carey Cadillac Renting Co. of California of 9641 Sunset Boulevard, Beverly Hills, its mission to whisk both her and her luggage back home to Brentwood.

Once there, desperate to learn of any new developments with Fox while she had been away, the actress immediately called Milton Rudin, who informed her that, as from the following day, the studio would no longer be footing the bill for her limousine hire. If she wanted a car to pick her up and take her to the studio each morning, she would have to pay for it herself. It was a petty act of revenge by a corporation still smarting over her decision to defy their wishes and fly out to New York. In just a few short hours, her feeling of utter euphoria had been replaced by one of sheer despair. Now completely demoralised, yet simmering, the actress remained holed up in her home for the rest of the day, trying to rest and preparing for the next day's shooting.

At precisely 5.30am on Monday 21 May, as arranged the previous afternoon, Marilyn's limousine pulled up on the driveway outside her home. Determined to demonstrate how unruffled she was by the studio's vindictiveness, Monroe agreed to assume responsibility for the vehicle's charges, but, in comparison with the previous arrangement, her directives for it were far more majestic.

A good example of this took place later that week. At five o'clock on the morning of Thursday 24 May, the actress's car (leased as normal from the Carey Cadillac Renting Co. of California) once more came to a halt at Marilyn's house. However, instead of merely taking her directly to and from the studio, as Fox had previously demanded, the actress instructed her chauffeur, the ever-reliable Rudy Kadensky, first to escort her to the film studio and wait while she shot her scenes and then, at lunch time, to drive her to Beverly Hills and wait while she carried out her shopping (which, that day, included a visit to the Martindale's book store where she purchased three publications, the novel *The Skin of Our Teeth* by Thornton Wilder, the war book *Captain MD* by Leo Calvin Rostein, and the new publication *The Tempering of Eugene O'Neill* by Doris Alexander).

Her limousine then drove her back to Fox, waited while she filmed further sequences and then escorted her back home to Fifth Helena when shooting had wrapped for the day. However, her use of the vehicle did not end there. After changing into casual clothes, she was then driven to the local Brentwood Country Mart, where her limo waited while she carried out her errands. A return trip to her home wrapped up both her and the car's day. A total of 43 miles was covered during that 15-hour period from 5am to 8pm. Her $81.43 bill was rounded up by an $11 tip. This scenario was repeated many times during the remainder of the shooting.

It wasn't just cars she was hiring. Almost three weeks earlier, on Saturday 5 May, for a period of precisely one month and at a cost of $18, she had rented, from the Hans Ohrt Lightweight Bicycles store in Beverly Hills, an English-style bike. Her idea of *cycling* to and from Fox each day was soon shelved.

As we can see, Marilyn's spending was still out of control. In a memo the following month from her Los Angeles secretary, Cherie Redmond, it was calculated that, between Monday 1 January and Monday 11 June 1962, among her other costs, Marilyn had spent a total of $6,401.71 on her wardrobe, $6,741.03 on hairdressing, make-up, beautifications and supplies, $10,131.23 on drugs and a colossal $15,411.18 on the services of Paula Strasberg. As the charges clearly demonstrate, the actress was still spending unwisely whatever money she had at her disposal.

With such a grave disregard of her finances, it came as no surprise when, on Monday 25 June, Milton Rudin was propelled to draft a note to her saying he felt obliged to 'caution' her on her disbursements since, 'at the rate you have been making these expenditures, you will spend the $13,000 [the sum she had remaining in her accounts] in a very short period of time and we will have to consider where to borrow additional monies.' Soon after, in an inter-office memo, the ever-assiduous Redmond touched upon the actress's spending habits and fast-dwindling bank accounts when she ominously noted, 'The fewer people who know about the state of Marilyn Monroe's finances the better.'

On Monday 21 May, the actress's car pulled up inside the Fox lot at precisely 6.05am. With wicker basket in hand, Marilyn climbed out and immediately headed to her dressing room where, 25 minutes later, she underwent make-up. To all intents and purposes, it seemed that filming of *Something's Got To Give* was ready to resume for another week. And since it was the first time during the shooting that the movie's three main stars, Monroe, Charisse and Martin, were all set to feature together in one sequence, for George Cukor in particular this was a most significant day. The clearly excited director relayed this fact to Charisse. 'Don't be so sure,' she ominously retorted.

With no sign of Marilyn on the set, fear began to course through the director's body. 'When we were waiting for her,' Charisse recalled, 'he [Cukor] would say, "Now, look, this is the way she's always worked. We must have patience and we'll just work like she usually does."' After an hour of waiting, Cukor finally plucked up enough courage to venture to the actress's dressing room. But within minutes he was trudging out, shaking his head like a shell-shocked prize-fighter who had just been knocked out of commission but still couldn't believe it. The actress had informed him that she was suffering from fatigue and unable to shoot any close-ups. She suggested they shoot them the following day. Cukor reluctantly agreed. At 10.40am Monroe was coaxed out of her room by Paula Strasberg, but the actress's tiredness plagued the rest of the day's shooting. At 5pm, she was dismissed with many of the day's key sequences with the children remaining unfinished.

One day later, Tuesday 22 May, Marilyn returned to the set. She was still suffering from exhaustion, while her co-star, Dean Martin, had reported for work suffering from a bad cold. His temperature was 100 degrees. Fearing she would inherit his germs, the actress informed Cukor and then Henry Weinstein, in no uncertain terms, that she would not participate in any scenes with the star while he was unwell. She was deaf to medical testimony that Martin's condition was not contagious. Cukor reluctantly once again caved in to Marilyn's demands and, while her co-star was dispatched home to bed, she reluctantly filmed a sequence with Cyd Charisse and heavily filtered, soft-focus close-ups of the actress with child actor Robert Christopher Morley.

Monroe's maternal instincts were apparent during the shoot. When she noticed the young boy shivering, following the shooting of a scene where he had to repeatedly swim back and forth across the pool, she refused to film any more sequences until an electric heater was brought on to the set to warm him. Aside from a brief interlude when Marilyn took part in an interview with Hollywood movie and television writer Bob Thomas, shooting continued through most of the day and wrapped at 5pm.

Her journey home to Fifth Helena was delayed when she instructed her driver, Kadensky, to stop at Jorgensen's Food Store, at 353 North Rodeo Drive in Beverly Hills. She needed to purchase a case of 1953 Dom Perignon champagne. (Her bill, including tax, came to $173.22.) The shop was unable to fulfil her order but promised they would be able to do so the following morning. Marilyn was happy about this but insisted on a caveat: delivery must be made to her home first thing.

On Wednesday 23 May, Marilyn once more appeared on the *Something's Got To Give* set. The trouble over Dean Martin's cold rumbled on when she hand-delivered Cukor and Weinstein a memo, which read: 'I cannot work with Mr. Martin until he's well. I take this action upon the advice of my physicians.' Since she was not up to remembering and delivering many lines or shooting anything with her cold-riddled co-star, Cukor thought it would be best if she had a crack at shooting the film's swimming pool sequence. It was 10.40am.

In an attempt to entice her husband Nick (Martin) away from the bed he was sharing with his new wife, Bianca (Charisse), and encourage him to tell her that his first wife had returned home, the script called for Monroe to gambol nude in the house's pool while he watched above from his bedroom window. 'Come on in, the water's so refreshing,' she shouts to Martin's absent character. (Later, when asked where Dean was during the shoot, Marilyn whimsically replied, 'Oh, I think he was out playing golf.' He was.)

Filming began modestly enough. In a brave attempt to fool the cameras, Marilyn started the scene by donning a flesh-coloured body-stocking cum invisible bikini, which had been produced by Jean Louis out of material left over from the actress's stunning JFK gala gown. But, at least according to folklore, the endeavour was thwarted when the eagle-eyed cinematographer, Harry Daniels, remarked that the cameras were picking up too clearly the material adorning the upper part of Monroe's torso. 'Cut,' Cukor shouted. A discussion between the camera operators and the director followed. Marilyn was alerted to the problem and informed something had to give.

The decision to film the actress sans brassiere was reached. She agreed to these provisions, but *only* if the set was cleared of everyone bar essential personnel. Security around the set was tightened as Sound Stage 14 was hastily swept free of rubber-neckers and non-essential employees. 'The set was closed, all except for members of the crew,' Marilyn recalled. 'They were very sweet. I told them to close their eyes or turn their backs and I think they all did.' Uniformed guards even stood sentry at the stage's entrance. 'It looked like the inner sanctum of Cape Canaveral,' a reporter for *Hush Hush* magazine remarked. 'Not even a top US security clearance could get anyone through that door on that particular day.'

A minimum crew of about 12 men were allowed to remain on the set. As the actress revealed, the few electricians that were allowed to linger were humorously instructed to keep their gaze away from Marilyn's. After the disgruntled, less essential Fox employees had been speedily shepherded out of the building, the actress slid back into the water, removed the offending brassiere, re-emerged and perched herself on the pool's edge, with her back facing towards the cameras.

But yet again, the cameras were not fooled into believing Marilyn was in the nude. Daniels announced that the line of her bikini briefs was now clearly visible. A further discussion between Cukor and his cameramen followed and once more, something had to give. The director then politely asked Monroe whether she would consider filming the sequence in the nude. She needed little persuasion. She bounced off to her dressing room and returned a few minutes later sans briefs but now wearing a blue, terry-cloth bath robe.

Marilyn then employed her make-up man, Allan 'Whitey' Snyder, to stand guard beside the main camera to ensure that revealing sights of her unclad body were kept to a minimum. She instructed Cukor that she wanted the outline of her figure to show, and nothing more. Feeling slightly apprehensive about his decision, Marilyn then enlisted the services of a trusted female, her wardrobe girl Marjorie Plecher, to work alongside Snyder to ensure her demands were met.

With Snyder and Plecher standing firm on either side of the main, pool-side camera, Marilyn felt comfortable enough to disrobe. After doing so, she slid back into the pool and began shooting a much more satisfactory sequence. She looked totally exquisite. 'It was a scene of sheer voluptuousness, raw, unveiled desirability. Vesuvius erupting,' *Hush Hush* magazine excitedly gushed. 'It was the first time I'd ever worked in a movie without any clothes on,' Marilyn later remarked.

Curiously, as shooting continued, she became more bashful about showing off her limited swimming strokes than her figure. 'All I can do is dog-paddle,' she shouted to Cukor. 'That will be just fine, darling,' he replied. 'I was a little embarrassed by the fact I don't swim very well,' Marilyn jokingly admitted. 'I only dog-paddle but I'm buoyant and I can float. I once went under but I popped right back to the surface. There was a lifeguard on the set to help me out if I needed him. But I'm not sure it would have worked. He had his eyes closed too.'

As the cameras rolled, Monroe frolicked up and down the pool, simultaneously teasing the cinematographers with tantalising, exceedingly brief glimpses of her magnificent naked body. A year earlier, Marilyn had been 15 pounds overweight and would have thought twice about doing such a brazen scene. But in May 1962, she had trimmed down and was back to her most famous, truly sensational, highly photogenic 37-22-35 best. 'Why, she looks exactly the same as she did when she posed for that calendar,' one startled spectator was heard to remark. 'She looks like a girl of 20, not a woman of 35.'

News that Marilyn was shooting a sequence in the raw unsurprisingly spread like wildfire across the Fox lot and naturally, everyone wanted to get a better view of it. Security guards fought hard to keep out all uninvited personnel. However, close scrutiny of the 'unofficial' shots, taken at the end of the shoot, reveals that, contrary to what we've previously been told, a large number of bystanders *did* manage to gate-crash their way on to the supposedly impermeable sound stage.

Realising that images from the sequence would be good for the movie's worldwide publicity, Marilyn allowed three photographers on to the set. Celebrity snapper Larry Schiller was one; the others were William Read Woodfield and Fox's still-pictures expert, Jimmy Mitchell. Once more, for their benefit, and once filming had wrapped, she doggy-paddled up and down the pool and playfully posed on the poolside edge. Gambolling over, the actress clambered out of the water and for one extremely brief blurred moment, posed in the altogether before vanishing into the swirl of a bath towel. Paula Strasberg, however, refused to watch any of it, preferring instead to sit out of the way, in a quiet room, alone, and eat her lunch off a tray. 'If she wants to be taken seriously,' she blasted to friends, 'she can't jump into a pool naked anymore.'

Though Monroe's flesh-coloured bikini *was* clearly evident through the camera's highly sensitive lens, clever editing and complex shooting could have easily camouflaged the lines of the attire. Cukor chose instead to mislead her into doing it for real. However, she was wise to his scheme. In July of that year, Marilyn recalled, 'I did it because George Cukor asked me to. I have confidence in his good taste. When he said the swimming pool scene would look more realistic if I did it in the nude, I agreed. I did it only because I was told it would make the picture more of an artistic and commercial success. That picture meant a lot to me. I really wanted it to be great.' When asked about her second nude appearance before the cameras, Marilyn giggled and quipped, 'My birthday is June 1, and I thought I'd celebrate a little early by acting in my birthday suit.' Elsewhere she joked, 'I hope it doesn't end up on a calendar.'

The scorching, colour 35mm footage of Marilyn's four-hour swimming pool shoot was developed later that day, in the humorous words of one Hollywood columnist, 'behind doors locked tighter than Jack Benny's safe'. The processed photographs from the session were confiscated by the actress for censoring. (Negatives of those she disapproved of were immediately destroyed with a pair of scissors.) Larry Schiller excitedly remarked, 'Miss Monroe looked 1,000 per cent better than I had imagined. She looked slim and well proportioned.'

Although it is not unusual for leading female stars to pose au naturel for a feature film, Marilyn's cinematic nude shoot was believed to be the first time that a star of her calibre had done so for a domestic movie release. In fact, on Monday 5 March, approximately 11 weeks before Monroe shot her sequence, Elizabeth Taylor had filmed a rather rude – at least for its time – nude bathing scene for *Cleopatra*, as well as a back massage sequence with exposed flesh. News that she had filmed these sequences was, surprisingly, kept under wraps by Fox and therefore failed to attract any attention until the movie was released in June of the following year. By shooting and announcing her own scene in the way she did, Marilyn had managed to pre-empt her rival's quite racy performance by several months.

With so many critics unaware of Taylor's sequences, the question as to why exactly Monroe had appeared in the nude began to circulate around

Hollywood and the film-loving capitals of the world. The general consensus was that, since her last couple of movies had not been particularly successful at the box office, her career needed something of a jolt. In recent years she had seemingly lost her 'queen of glamour' title to French actress Brigitte Bardot. When hearing of this accusation, a spokesman for Monroe at 20th Century-Fox moved quickly to deny the actress had done the scene purely for publicity for herself or the movie. This, of course, was completely untrue.

In fact, there were two reasons why Marilyn shot the sequence. First, she was desperate to regain her rating as the world's number-one sex symbol and canny enough to realise that flaunting herself was the best way to do it. Second, as she forthrightly told a reporter, and as we can safely guess, she did it because she wanted to 'knock Elizabeth Taylor off the front of every magazine cover'. (In recent months, Marilyn's great Fox rival had appeared on the face of practically every magazine around the world through coverage of her starring role in *Cleopatra* and it annoyed her.)

Monroe was successful in her second aim. In total, pictures of her nude swim would feature on the covers of 72 different magazines. Many of the globe's biggest magazines and newspapers, including the American magazines *Saga* and *Life* (who paid $10,000 for the US rights alone), the Italian publication *L'Europeo*, Swedish magazine *Se* and Australian publication *Everybodys* would all outbid each other to scoop a selection of the pictures. In the UK (in the edition published on Monday 18 June), the *Daily Mirror* perfectly summed up the situation by printing a small selection of the images under the heading, 'It Was For A Film . . . It Was Also Her Idea . . . But The Pictures Rocked Hollywood And Are Exploding Across The World!' (*Playboy* paid $25,000 but, out of respect for both the actress and *Life*, delayed publishing the shots until January 1964.)

Selected photos from Marilyn's swim were published in a total of 32 countries, collectively earning Messrs Schiller and Woodfield alone a hefty $200,000. A proviso was included in all their deals: a publication deadline of approximately 30 days after the shoot had taken place. The reason was simple. In order to gain the maximum exposure, Marilyn wanted the pictures to appear around the world simultaneously.

Pictures of a modern-day, unclad Marilyn were of course priceless, but strangely, she was uninterested in the money. Publicity was all she craved from the deals. Amazingly, she even managed to thrust this view on to Fox who, albeit reluctantly, relinquished their rights to the images. When Schiller asked the actress what she wanted from his windfall, she solemnly replied, 'A slide projector to show them on.' Her request moved him to tears.

The actress's nude sequence naturally became a major selling point for the film and Fox were overjoyed. As one Los Angeles-based press agent correctly remarked, 'A lot of people are going to want to see the film now.' Marilyn's plan had worked.

Monroe reported bright and early for work on the *Something's Got To Give* set for the next two days, Thursday and Friday, 24 and 25 May. Dean Martin's lingering cold was the only black mark on two otherwise highly successful days of shooting. Surprisingly, in a brave attempt to catch up on the schedule, Monroe was an active participant when filming was hastily pencilled in for Saturday 26 May. Finally working with both Charisse and Martin, whose cold had now thankfully subsided, the actress shot the sequence where her character, Ellen, pretended to be her husband's Swedish maid and child-minder, Ingrid Tic. It was a superbly acted, humorous scene and as the surviving footage shows, the time Marilyn spent with her language coach, Edith Evanson, had not gone to waste. The actress managed to seize the American–Swedish-tinged dialect with charming, heart-warming accuracy.

A tentatively arranged day of filming on Sunday 27 May failed to materialise when Monroe once again phoned in sick and was treated for an ear infection by her replacement doctor, Milton H. Uhley, a medic acting on call for Dr Hyman Engelberg. The following day, Marilyn's run of reporting in sick continued when she informed Fox she was still suffering from her ear virus; stories suggesting that Marilyn appeared on the Fox set that day but was in bad shape and all the footage she shot had to be scrapped are erroneous. Dr Uhley was forced to pay another visit to the actress's home late that evening.

A day later, Tuesday 29 May, Marilyn returned to Fox but regrettably her legendary tardiness had come back to haunt her. Repeating a ritual she had acted out hundreds of times before, she was driven around aimlessly for hours until she was finally able to pluck up enough courage to enter the studio's gates. Once more, the thought of standing and acting before a cast and crew horrified her. The instant she did muster enough courage to enter the studio, Marilyn headed straight for her room where, according to a Fox make-up woman, she sat 'nude at the dressing table, staring at herself in the mirror. She couldn't bring herself to get dressed.'

Later that morning, in a scene intended to follow straight after her nude midnight swim, Marilyn participated in a sequence with Martin, their first alone together since shooting began, where his character implied that his wife was unfaithful during her five years away on the island. Due to Monroe's continued exhaustion, filming wrapped at 5pm. But instead of travelling home, the actress followed her co-star back to his home at 601

Mountain Drive, Beverly Hills. Once there, wearing dark sunglasses and a headscarf, she sat and watched him and his daughter, Deanna, perform the twist to the 1960 Bobby Darin recording, '(Up a) Lazy River'. As Deanna recalled in her 2005 publication, *Memories Are Made Of This*, Marilyn 'smiled shyly, applauded and thanked us. She was very sweet and polite.'

Since Wednesday 30 May was Memorial Day, there was no shooting and the movie's cast and crew were given a day's holiday. Marilyn spent the day at home finishing a painting she intended to give the President, a watercolour on paper featuring a symbolic red rose. Intended for Kennedy's 45th birthday, the actress was planning to hand it to him personally during a party to be held at the White House on her own birthday. Her handwritten inscription in blue and black ink in the bottom left corner of the painting touchingly read: 'Happy Birthday Pres. Kennedy from Marilyn Monroe. Happy Birthday June 1, 1962, My Best Wishes, Marilyn, Marilyn.' (She had inadvertently signed her name on it twice.)

Filming on *Something's Got To Give* reconvened a day later, when, in the much smaller Sound Stage 8, Marilyn and Wally Cox shot a sequence in a fabricated shoe store. In the scene, Monroe's character, Ellen, tries to persuade the naïve, somewhat nerdy salesman (Cox) to pose as the man she was marooned on an island with. As the surviving footage demonstrates, the actress was in fine form and managed to deliver her lines impeccably. But unfortunately, Marilyn's flawless acting skills were in evidence far too late. Production on the movie was now 11 days behind schedule.

On Friday 1 June, at precisely 9.37am, and following a brief hair-trim by Marilyn's stylist, Sydney Guilaroff, shooting on *Something's Got To Give* resumed on Sound Stage 14. Today's humorous sequence focused on attempts by Marilyn's character to pass off the shoe salesman as the man she had spent the previous five years with, while completely unaware that her husband (Martin) had already encountered her 'real' island cohabitant, played by Thomas Tryon. 'What kind of an island was it?' Nick asks the patsy. 'I'd say it was an ordinary one,' the shoe-seller unwittingly replies. 'Small island?' Nick enquires. 'Not small, not large,' Cox offers. 'Medium,' Marilyn's character interjects. 'Water?' Nick asks. 'Oh yes, water all around,' the shoe-seller responds.

While the light-hearted banter unfurled, Monroe looked on, smiling and interposing where necessary. During a break in the shooting, for one brief moment, she stood sideways on to the camera, her posterior facing towards Martin's face. Noticing this, he jokingly formed his hand into the shape of a gun, aimed it at the actress's rear and quipped, 'Haven't I seen that some place before?'

Her demeanour throughout the day was happy and, apart from a lunchtime visit to the studio canteen with Paula Strasberg, Marilyn remained on the set throughout. It was also the actress's 36th birthday, a day that she had been dreading. At a recent party, Hollywood stars Natalie Wood and Warren Beatty both recalled how Marilyn walked up to them murmuring the words, 'Thirty-six, thirty-six, thirty-six. It's all over.' For a girl whose appeal was primarily based upon her youth, beauty and sex appeal, she knew it was not a good age to be. Throughout the day, presents for the actress from stars such as Marlon Brando, Jack Lemmon and Frank Sinatra, ranging from bunches of flowers to bottles of champagne, arrived in droves.

There were numerous telegrams too. The first was from Joe DiMaggio, who was currently away in Madrid, on holiday with blonde jazz singer and Monroe lookalike Choo Choo Collins. His note, sent by way of Western Union, read 'Happy birthday. Hope today and future years bring you sunny skies and all your heart desires. As ever – Joe.'

'I like celebrating birthdays,' Marilyn once remarked to film and television writer Bob Thomas. 'I enjoy knowing I'm alive.' Due to the severity of the delays in filming, however, George Cukor was reluctant to celebrate the actress's birthday until shooting had wrapped for the day. Aside from the supplying of free coffee to the cast and crew during breaks (which Fox miserly charged to Monroe's account), the first official recognition of the birthday did not come until 5.30pm when the director called time on the day's activities. A bottle of champagne was cracked open to signify the start of their small party. Thirty minutes later, following a suggestion by Dean Martin, the crew presented Marilyn with a special $7 sheet cake, purchased by the actress's stand-in, Evelyn Moriarty, from the bakery at the Farmers Market, at Third Street and Fairfax Avenue, a day earlier. It was adorned with seven Fourth of July-type sparklers and a bikini-clad miniature doll, an obvious reference to her impressive new svelte figure.

As the actress blew out the sparklers, the cast and crew, including Cukor, huddled together and sang a rather halting version of 'Happy Birthday'. A picture was taken of the moment, showing Marilyn wearing a false smile and with tears evident in her lifeless eyes. Naturally, she would grow to hate it. She managed to perk up when she was presented with a hand-drawn birthday card, signed by everyone in the movie's entourage, which featured a cartoon drawing of a nude Monroe holding up a towel to cover her modesty. As a humorous nod to her legendary nude swimming pool sequence, the words 'Happy Birthday (Suit)' had been drawn in large letters across the front. However, according to Weinstein, due to all the troubles they'd gone through during the making of the movie, it was a 'pretend celebration'.

Compared with Elizabeth Taylor's recent, lavish birthday celebration, it was indeed a subdued affair. When the *Cleopatra* star celebrated her 30th birthday, in Rome back on Tuesday 27 February, she had taken a day off from shooting and spent it relaxing in her villa near Rome's old Appian Way. Later that night, along with her husband, Eddie Fisher, and some of the film's cast and crew, she attended a dinner party at the swanky 14th-century Roman-themed restaurant, Hostaria dell'Orso (Hostelry of the Bear), the city's oldest eating establishment. The centrepiece of their table was an assortment of orchids provided by Fox's president, Spyros P. Skouras. A visit to a plush night club followed. At midnight, when she and Fisher were attempting to leave the venue, the in-house orchestra promptly struck up a rendition of 'Happy Birthday'. Their attempt to flee was hindered once again when, approximately ten minutes later, she was presented with a surprise cake, adorned with three candles.

And how did Marilyn celebrate her big day? She worked all day, was forced to pay for the crew's coffee, drank champagne from paper cups and shared, with her colleagues, a simple, $7, one-layer frosted cake, which had been purchased by a friend from a local market. It was no wonder that she had tears in her eyes.

After 30 more minutes of unenthusiastic goodwill-gesturing, cake-eating, alcohol-sipping and perfunctory posing for pictures with colleagues in Martin's dressing room, the party finally began to peter out. Marilyn gathered her belongings and prepared to leave the studio. Before doing so, she brushed off her disappointment by returning a phone call to her good friend, Hollywood movie and television writer James Bacon. During the exchange she informed him, 'Well, I'm finally going to see the New York Yankees tonight. I don't think I'll see the whole game, though. I would if Joe [DiMaggio] were playing. He's the only ball-player I care about.' Rather than attending the White House, at the eleventh hour she had apparently agreed to make an appearance at the game between the Yankees and the Los Angeles Angels in aid of an appeal for donations for the Muscular Dystrophy Association.

With the fur-trimmed mink beret she had worn during the day's filming still attached to her head, Marilyn walked out of the studio and headed straight to her chauffeur-driven limousine. Sitting behind the wheel was the ever-reliable Rudy Kadensky. Her new best pal, Wally Cox, accompanied her. Following a gentle wave to a waiting photographer and a shout of 'Goodbye, I will see you on Monday' to her friends and work colleagues, she was driven out of the studio gates.

'That does it,' assistant director Buck Hall remarked as he caught sight of Monroe's car leaving the studio. He was convinced that this was the end of the movie. Executives had even begged the actress not to go to the baseball game and told her that if she *really* wanted to do something for charity she should stay at home and do it for Fox. Threats from Cukor and Weinstein that the notoriously damp and cold Californian nights might be bad for her health had failed to dissuade her from going.

Regrettably, Hall's remarks would be prophetic. As Marilyn's car drove out of the Fox lot that night, however, no one could possibly have known that the actress had just completed her final day of work on *Something's Got To Give* (out of the 33 shooting days, she had showed just 12 times) and finished the last sequence of filming in her career. The actress would not appear on a motion picture set again.

After picking up Dean Martin's son, Dino, at the Martins' family home, the actress journeyed on to Chavez Ravine Stadium, the home of the Los Angeles Angels baseball team. Marilyn's hastily arranged address was set to take place in front of a record-breaking 51,584 crowd. 'You'll make the speech from home plate,' an Angels executive whispered to her upon her arrival at the park. 'Oh, that's wonderful,' she enthusiastically remarked, before asking, 'Where's that?'

With the beret still sitting delicately on her head, Marilyn took to the field on the arm of the Angels' smallest player, outfielder Albie Gregory Pearson. To even things up, she was then joined by the opposing side's star player, Roger Maris. Her pre-game talk was brief. Aside from the appeal, she also playfully attempted to distance herself from any favouritism towards the New York Yankees by announcing, 'I'm for *both* teams.' Marilyn concluded her appearance by blowing kisses to the crowd, signing autographs, speaking with young children in wheelchairs, watching a school choir perform and throwing out the opening ball of the game. Throughout the evening, with the wind blowing hard through the stadium, the actress fought hard to keep her hat attached to her head.

With Joe DiMaggio Jr acting as her escort, Marilyn clearly enjoyed herself and was to some extent successful in her attempts to put the problems surrounding her new movie behind her. Nor, contrary to previous reports, was she the only star in attendance that night. Sitting alongside her in addition to Wally Cox, were Hollywood film and TV celebrities Bob Hope, Sid Cesar, Doris Day, Ann Blythe, Lucille Ball, and director Stanley Kramer.

After her appearance, Monroe, DiMaggio Jr, Dino and Cox were driven to the world-famous celebrity restaurant, Chasen's, at 9039 Beverly Boulevard in Beverly Hills, where she tucked into her regular dish of sliced artichokes placed in a shape of a star with soba noodles in the middle and topped off with three succulent shrimps. After the meal, the actress asked Rudy Kadensky to drop her guests off. But Marilyn was in no mood to end her day yet.

The actress was escorted back to her home on Fifth Helena where she called her favourite eatery, the Italian gourmet restaurant La Scala, located nearby at 9455 Santa Monica Boulevard. She wanted to know whether her regular cubicle was available. When told it was, she walked back to her limo and promptly instructed Kadensky to drive her there. Once inside, and after exchanging low-key pleasantries with the manager and staff, she lackadaisically tucked into her second meal of the day, her favoured choice at the restaurant, a small portion of fettuccine leon and veal piccata. After eating, she was escorted back home – although, contrary to the claims of previous Marilyn biographers that she returned early that evening, the surviving limousine-hire receipts show that she actually enjoyed a rather full day and did not return home until 12.30am.

Even though it was Monroe's birthday, this did not prevent her tactless doctor's family from hand-delivering Ralph Greenson's latest invoice. Marilyn found it waiting for her on a table when she re-entered her home. (The sum of $350, for his 'professional services', was dutifully paid by the actress, by way of a cheque – no. 1647 – one week later, on Friday 8 June.)

At this point, the first major confusion in the actress's final months begins. It is still not entirely certain how, precisely, Marilyn spent that weekend. For producer Henry Weinstein, though, whatever *did* happen was a defining moment in Monroe's life. Speaking to Fox in 1990, he remarked, 'What happened that weekend? I don't know. To me, that's more interesting than what happened the day Marilyn died. To me [that weekend] was the turning point.'

Legend has it that, between that Friday night and the opening hours of Monday 4 June, the actress spent the entire time holed up in her Brentwood home. And that is indeed what transpired. On the evening of her 36th birthday, shortly after arriving back home, Marilyn once again found herself alone with no one to love, no one to care for, and absolutely no one to speak to. So she reached for her pills. She instinctively knew that, in times of despair, she could always rely on them. With Dr Greenson out of the country on a five-week combined business and holiday trip to Switzerland and Tel Aviv, Marilyn returned to her old habit of consuming her pills on a round-the-clock basis. As a result, she suffered an emotional relapse. But was her deterioration precipitated by some other incident?

An event in Washington that Friday evening might hold the key. At 8pm on Friday 1 June, President Kennedy and his wife Jacqueline hosted a private dinner and dance at the White House, its last of the social season. The black-tie gathering had been organised by the First Lady as an act of thanks to the United States Ambassador to India, John Kenneth Galbraith, for his helpfulness during her recent visit there. Fifty-one specially invited guests were in attendance. But Marilyn was not one of them.

Believing she was now an accepted part of that crowd, and no doubt going on assurances from Peter Lawford that she would receive one, she had expected an invite would be forthcoming. As we have seen, she was even preparing a gift to present to Kennedy that night. But the summons did not arrive. A phone call from Lawford corroborating the snub obviously followed and an appearance at Chavez Ravine was swiftly arranged by Joe DiMaggio in an attempt to brighten her spirits. Coming on top of the news that her former husband, Arthur Miller, as well as both Lee and Paula Strasberg, had on Friday 11 May attended a dinner party at the White House, held to honour André Malraux, the French Minister of Cultural Affairs, she rightly regarded this as an almighty slap in the face. On Marilyn's birthday night, just 13 days after she had been the star, the showpiece, the grand finale of Kennedy's big birthday gala, she had been unceremoniously snubbed by him, his wife and his associates.

Did this rejection, while she sat alone in her bedroom, brooding, seething and staring at the painting on her birthday night, tip her over the edge? I suspect it did.

Early on the morning of Saturday 2 June, with Greenson out of the country, a substitute doctor had to be summoned to Marilyn's home. Many previous Monroe biographers have suggested that, once again, she was treated by Milton Uhley. However, I tend to side with the belief that the actress was looked after by Greenson's close colleague, the charismatic but tenacious 46-year-old psychoanalyst Dr Milton Wexler. Greenson had shared offices with Wexler for several years and was greatly influenced by his co-worker's notions about the importance of closeness between analyst and patient.

During his visit to Marilyn's home, after observing the huge stockpile of tablets which had accumulated on her bedside table, Wexler promptly scooped them all up and dropped them into his black medical bag. Unlike Greenson, he was strict about multiple drug use. Seeing her pills vanish into a deep, dark abyss, Marilyn began to panic. They were symbolic of her refuge. With her drugs no longer to hand, she found herself in a quandary; if she couldn't rest, she couldn't recuperate, and if she couldn't recover, she had absolutely no chance of returning to work. Full of anxiety, she now needed Dr Greenson's help (and prescriptions) more than ever.

Despite requests to the contrary from Greenson's family, Marilyn set about contacting him. Due to the nine-hour time difference between Los Angeles and Switzerland, Eunice Murray's long-distance conversations with the doctor had to take place in the middle of *his* night. She read out a list of the actress's hastily prepared questions, in particular where she could obtain her pills at short notice. His negative answers did little to ease her predicament, so Pat Newcomb was forced to move in to the actress's home. Her own supply of tranquillisers, enough to tide Marilyn over until Greenson's return, accompanied her. Over the ensuing 48 hours, Newcomb watched over Monroe during the day and slept in a berth erected at the foot of the actress's bed at night. The pair rarely left the bedroom, the door of which was largely kept locked throughout. With Marilyn now suffering from withdrawal symptoms, she was in bad shape. Newcomb and Murray knew instinctively she could not be left her own.

Producer Weinstein announced he was desperate to know what happened to Monroe that weekend, describing it as a 'defining moment' in her life. In truth it *was*. It was the moment when the actress and everyone close to her became frighteningly aware of just how addicted Marilyn was to Nembutal. As the well-informed Hollywood reporter Donald Stewart wrote shortly after the actress's death, 'She had been taking about 20 pills a day, enough to *kill* a non-user.' The sad truth was that, for that entire first weekend of June 1962, the actress was, as Eunice Murray recalled in her 1975 book, 'in a comatose state'.

With Monroe inevitably incapable of work, at 8am on Monday 4 June, Paula Strasberg phoned Fox and delivered the message that the actress was once again sick and 'unable to travel to the studio'. It was the 17th time she had done so. Learning of her absence, Milton Rudin paid Marilyn a visit. When he confronted her about it, a half-hearted, heated exchange ensued, and when he tried to persuade her to return to work, she accused him of being on Fox's side. Producer Weinstein managed to get her on the phone and told her he would be more than willing to send a car for her or even come and pick her up personally and escort her to the studio. But she was uninterested. She wasn't going to film anything today. Moreover, with listlessness running through her entire body, it was impossible for her to do so.

When he heard the news, director Cukor flipped and immediately announced that he refused to shoot any more scenes without her. Regrettably, it wasn't only the director who had had enough. Actress Cyd Charisse remarked that, for the first time ever during the filming, Dean Martin became angry when he was told his leading lady would not be coming. At 3pm, he stormed off the set for the final time. His tenure on *Something's Got To Give* had just come to an end.

One day later, Tuesday 5 June, it was the turn of Eunice Murray to put in the dreaded 8am phone call to Fox and deliver the same message: the actress was 'ill and unable to appear before the cameras'. Studio doctor Lee Siegel was dispatched to the actress's home and swiftly informed studio executives that Marilyn's sinuses had flared and her temperature was 102. However, mistrust was erupting everywhere. No one at Fox believed him or accepted the severity of her illness. Importantly, Cukor had had enough. 'This was a sick woman,' scriptwriter Walter Bernstein controversially recalled for Fox in 1990, 'but also a movie star. This was a movie star who was getting her way. She was doing this because she *was* a movie star and didn't give a damn about anybody else and being destructive or self-destructive.'

However, contrary to what he and numerous others have said about the matter, Marilyn was desperate to sort out the mess she had helped create. That same day, the actress managed to place a call through to Spyros P. Skouras, even though he was recuperating from surgery in New York's St Luke's Hospital. Trumpeter Dick Ruedebusch was visiting Skouras when the call came through. Incensed by how the actress was misbehaving on his film set, Ruedebusch recalled, the Fox chief immediately jumped out of his bed and ripped down her famous nude calendar picture, which was hanging on his hospital wall.

On Wednesday 6 June, work on *Something's Got To Give* officially shut down. Fox claimed they had no more scenes to shoot without their leading lady. When told this, Pat Newcomb was quick to point that this was incorrect. 'There *are* other scenes to shoot,' she insisted. 'They can't shoot them because there *isn't* a completed script.' The war of words had begun.

That afternoon, an anonymous studio insider announced to the American press, 'Something has to be done with these unprofessional people. We have to sit down on them or else forget about the industry. They're running it.' In another statement, producer Weinstein worryingly remarked, 'There had to be an agonising appraisal of the situation. We have to decide whether Marilyn can recover in time to continue with production and if the studio can stand further delays.' When told of this utterance, Pat Newcomb partly reiterated her previous remark by saying, 'There would not have been delays if there had been a completed script.' Almost immediately, Fox responded by insisting there *was* a completed script but 'Marilyn insisted on rewriting it *every* night!'

Back at Fox, studio executives, huddled together in a hastily called emergency meeting, listened intently as George Cukor firmly announced, 'Marilyn Monroe *must* be fired and replaced.' They agreed but knew that they were powerless to make such a decision. This rested with Peter G. Levathes, Fox's plain-speaking, no-messing executive vice-president, who was away on a troubleshooting trip to Rome trying to resolve the unending mess surrounding Elizabeth Taylor's ill-fated epic, *Cleopatra*. Her continual absence from the set had helped raise the cost of the film to a colossal $30 Levathes's no-nonsense method resulted in the sacking on Friday 1 June of the movie's Academy Award-winning producer, Walter Wanger, whom Levathes held accountable for the debacle. As a result, Wanger never worked in Hollywood again.

Executives at the Fox meeting chose to delay any announcement about Marilyn until Levathes had returned and been consulted, and a suitable replacement had been found. However, Cukor was in no mood to wait and clandestinely passed the news on to two highly influential Hollywood gossip writers, Hedda Hopper and Sheilah Graham. The former's article, for her 'Looking At Hollywood' column, appeared the next day and was entitled 'Marilyn To Be Replaced; Is She Finished?'

The latter's damning piece, which appeared in the first editions of *The New York Mirror* later that evening, was entitled 'No Show, Marilyn Getting The Bounce', and read in part: 'The studio is fed-up to the teeth with Marilyn Monroe. She hasn't shown up for work for the past three days. But when she does, she'll find out that she has been fired and replaced . . . 20th Century-Fox doesn't want her anymore.' Alternative versions of the report carried even more information: 'Kim Novak has been asked. As soon as officials here can get an okay from Peter Levathes, head of production, who is now in Rome, they will make it official.' Dean Martin meanwhile stayed well clear of the unfolding turmoil, calling himself 'the highest paid golfer in history'.

So where was his leading lady amid all this verbal hostility? Keen to continue her home-based activities and avoid being photographed, Marilyn began her day by holding a relaxed phone conversation with her long-time associate, UPI Hollywood columnist Vernon Scott. 'I'm really sick,' she informed him. 'I have a temperature of over 100 degrees and my throat is terribly sore. I want to get back to work and I hope the studio understands.' Later, with the help of Pat Newcomb, the actress began preparing her dog Maf for his inaugural visit to the City of Los Angeles Department of Animal Regulation, where he was due to have his first rabies vaccination.

The following day, Thursday 7 June, while the actress listlessly sauntered around her Brentwood home, Newcomb rang Fox and incorrectly informed them her client was still 'unwell but improving'. She concluded by optimistically remarking that the actress would be 'fit and ready for filming' by the start of the following week. When quizzed by the hovering reporters who had started to gather like vultures outside Marilyn's property, Newcomb remarked, 'People *do* get sick. She doesn't like it anymore than the studio. She still wants to do the picture and there is every justification she will.'

When the quote reached the news wires, Fox immediately refuted it. '*Look* at the star's attendance record,' a spokesperson at the studio raged,

'12 out of 32 days. On her show days, she was usually on time for her 6.30am make-up call but then we had to wait around for her to emerge from her dressing room. That can be 10.30 or 11. After the lunch break, it's another hour or two until she comes out. Then she quits at 4.30 or 5.' Cold-war conversations between Marilyn's camp and the studio were not to end there.

That day, moments after receiving yet another transatlantic phone call from Murray, Ralph Greenson abruptly cut short his trip, booked himself on the first available flight and rushed to the actress's home where he found her lying in bed, unresponsive and partially sedated. (She was still consuming Newcomb's tranquillisers.) Following a heated discussion by phone, Greenson then headed over to Fox for a hastily arranged personal tête-à-tête in Fox's conference room with the studio hierarchy, as represented by executive vice-president Phil Feldman and manager Frank Ferguson.

With attorney Milton Rudin by his side, as the minutes of the meeting reveal, he began by admitting that his trips to Tel Aviv and Switzerland were 'a part of the cause of what happened'. In an attempt to appease his disgruntled colleagues, he promised to excise troublesome drama coach Paula Strasberg from the actress's life and career and insisted that he would 'wean Marilyn off barbiturates and get her fit and ready for work by the following Monday'. In worryingly Svengali-esque tones, Greenson then notified them he would 'be able to get the actress to go along with any responsible request' and 'persuade her to do anything reasonable' that he wanted in order to complete the film. However, Fox weren't listening. They were already pressing ahead for a replacement and were well on their way to calling 'every actress in and out of town'.

The meeting came to a sudden halt when Rudin requested a private discussion with Greenson in another room. At once, they rose from their chairs and walked to an unoccupied room nearby, returning a few minutes later. Deliberations resumed immediately. Feldman began by telling Greenson he was unconvinced that Marilyn would be able to complete the movie. 'Since her past history indicated nothing of the sort,' he remarked, 'and since I am a layman in the field, I am not convinced.' The doctor retaliated by asking, 'What *would* convince you?' Feldman refused an answer, instead suggesting, 'If you wish to progress the conversation further, you should allow a doctor of our own to consult with you about Marilyn's problems.' The name of Dr Karl Von Hagen, chairman of the Department of Neurology at the University of Southern California was suggested. Greenson immediately dismissed the idea and put forward several other names. Feldman vetoed the offer. A stalemate had been reached and, shortly afterwards, the meeting was adjourned. Greenson began his journey back to Marilyn's home on Fifth Helena.

So where was Marilyn when her doctor was making these outlandish claims? We have been reliably informed that she was still resting in bed. This is partly true. However, Fox documentation reveals that, during the afternoon of Thursday 7 June, just moments after Greenson had returned from his emergency meeting at the studio, she left her home and was driven to her 52-year-old plastic surgeon, Dr Michael M. Gurdin, at his clinic in Beverly Hills. Fearful that her nose had been broken, she informed him that, between 2 and 3am, she had slipped in the shower. But her home did not possess such a device. The truth about the incident was very different indeed.

During Greenson's first visit to Marilyn that day, hot-foot from his plane journey, and shortly before he left for his meeting at Fox, discussions between him and the actress became so intense that he struck her hard across her face. With Monroe now seriously undermining his position at the studio as one of the country's most eminent psychoanalysts, he vented his anger in the only way he knew: violence.

Examination of Gurdin's original case notes reveal there was 'No nose bleed, no loss of consciousness and mild laceration of the nasal dorsum, the bridge of the nose, and swelling of the right lower lid.' As normal in circumstances such as these, Gurdin sent her for X-rays. The distressed actress was driven by Greenson to doctors Conti and Steinberg at 416 North Bedford Drive, Beverly Hills. Photographs showed her nose was not seriously damaged but the black and blue marks on her face were very prominent. Reporters camped outside her Brentwood home naturally caught sight of the contusions as the heavily camouflaged actress dashed out of her doctor's car. When asked about them, she repeated the tale that she had taken 'too much medication and had fallen in the shower'. Greenson was naturally desperate to keep his outburst a secret. He knew that, should news of it leak out, his career as one of the country's finest psychoanalysts would be well and truly over.

Ominously, however, his reappearance in the actress's life seemed to have the desired effect. Less than 20 hours after his return, he intimidated the actress into ringing Fox herself. At 8am on Friday 8 June, Monroe (completely unaware of the plans to replace her) called Weinstein and excitedly announced she was 'ready and eager to go back to work', reiterating both Newcomb and Greenson's promise that she would be 'back on the set first thing on Monday morning'. Unfortunately, the declaration failed to appease the producer, who flipped uncontrollably when he heard the news. 'She is *not* ill,' he exasperatedly announced in a private call to the always-listening Hollywood gossip columnist, Hedda Hopper. 'I have no official notification of illness. All I have is that she's coming but she *never* does.'

Monroe's no-show on Friday, despite the fact that the movie was now 16 days behind schedule and almost $2 million in debt, meant that the totally innocent, hardworking crew on *Something's Got To Give* had lost another week's salary. That was what really angered Weinstein. The *Los Angeles Herald Examiner* concurred. 'Marilyn Monroe's wilful irresponsibility,' they wrote, 'has taken the bread right out of the mouths of men who depend on this film to feed their families.' Oblivious to the ensuing troubles, that afternoon Marilyn dashed to the nearby Vicente Pharmacy at 12025 San Vicente Boulevard, where, with lack of sleep and her facial bruises still causing her immense distress, she purchased a sleep shade and an ice bag.

Across Los Angeles, the actress's troubles were about to escalate further. Fox's vice-president, Peter Levathes, had arrived back at the studio. Seeing severance with a troublesome player as the most obvious way to solve the company's unending problems, when he was informed of the actress's obstructive tactics on *Something's Got To Give*, he became agitated and, after discussing the matter with studio board member Milton S. Gould, immediately instructed the studio's manager, Phil Feldman, to concede defeat and cancel her contract. At 3pm, Marilyn was officially sacked. At 3.45pm, Feldman called Rudin at his office and informed him of their decision, adding that Marilyn was in breach of contract and that they would be pursuing the matter in that regard. Rudin fought back, reiterating that his client *was* unwell and would be 'fit to return on Monday morning'. His claims fell on deaf ears.

Immediately after finishing the call, Feldman advised the studio's legal department to press ahead with a Superior Court 'damage' suit against the actress and announced he was not going to waste any more of 20th Century-Fox's money on 'uncertainties'. Despite solid promises from Greenson, Newcomb, Marilyn and now Rudin that she would be 'fit and ready' in three days' time, it was too late. Levathes, Cukor and Weinstein had reached the end of their tether and were united in their opinion that Marilyn Monroe, one of the world's most celebrated movie stars, must go.

A statement to that effect was hastily prepared and released. It read:

> Marilyn Monroe has been removed from the cast of *Something's Got To Give*. This action was made necessary because of Miss Monroe's repeated breaches of her contract. No justification was given by Miss Monroe for her failure to report for photography on many occasions. The studio has suffered losses through these absences and the 20th Century-Fox Film Company will take legal action against Miss Monroe.

A $500,000 lawsuit was registered by the studio at the Los Angeles

Superior Court with just two minutes to spare before filings were due to close for the evening. Studio attorney Jesse R. O'Malhey had signed the action on Fox's behalf. Speaking on the day of the lawsuit, he stated that 'Marilyn Monroe had signed a "Four-pix pact" on December 31, 1955 for $100,000 per picture and received $142,000 on the execution of the agreement. She had completed two pictures (for Fox) up to January 16, 1961 and since April 16, 1961 (*sic*) has refused and neglected to render her services under her contract. Fox at all times performed all conditions of the agreement and has been damaged to the tune of $500,000.' The time difference between the actresses's sacking and the registering of the lawsuit was just three hours.

'No one was more surprised than I when I heard on Friday night that I was fired,' Marilyn remarked to James Bacon. 'How could they expect me to work when I was sick?' When *The New York Post* asked him for a quote about her axing, Dean Martin remarked, 'Gee, that's a shame. I'm really sorry. If they'd kept Marilyn in the cast, I think it would have made a very fine picture. But she was too sick to go ahead with it. So that's it.'

News that the actress had been handed her pink slip soon reached Spyros Skouras, who was still recuperating in his bed at St Luke's Hospital. Immediately, he called Levathes and attempted to dissuade him from carrying out his actions. But it was far too late, and Skouras was too weak to engage in any such negotiations.

Henry Weinstein naturally moved quickly to uphold the studio's action against Monroe, remarking in a statement, 'She has completely flouted professional discipline and is responsible for putting 104 crew members out of work. And when she *did* turn up for work, the most she could deliver was a page and a half of script a day compared with three or four pages from the other actors. Yet she was fit enough to jet off to New York to sing "Happy Birthday" to President Kennedy and fit enough to go to a baseball game.'

Meanwhile, in an interview with *Variety*, Peter Levathes announced that he had been warned before shooting commenced that Marilyn would 'cut a caper or two' and he'd be sorry. 'She convinced me that she would come through like a sound trooper and that I had nothing to fear,' he dejectedly remarked. His comment came at a time when the price of Fox's stock had dipped from $39 to $20 and their great rivals, United Artists, were expected to announce, at their annual general meeting on Tuesday 12 June, an *increase* in earnings for the first quarter of the year. It was a dire time for Fox.

When the announcement of Marilyn's sacking reached the news wires, a pack of information-hungry, bloodthirsty journalists unsurprisingly descended upon the studio gates, desperate to get their hands on the latest news. Keen to offer his take on the matter, a front office spokesman was heard to remark, 'It's sad. But no one studio these days can afford to have Liz Taylor and Marilyn Monroe working at the same time, especially a studio that lost $25 (*sic*) million last year.' Fox's forthright spokesperson continued, 'Marilyn claims she couldn't work because she was sick. I actually believe she *is* sick. It's all in her mind, of course, and maybe her mental condition makes her physically ill. I don't think she can control herself. She wants to work, wants to be a great actress and *is* a great star. But whatever her ailment is, it just won't let her work.'

However, possibly the most poignant remark about the actress came from an unnamed source at Fox. In an interview with Hedda Hopper for her weekly 'Hedda Hopper's Hollywood' column, the source, described as 'one of the most knowledgeable men in the industry', remarked, 'I believe it is the end of her [Marilyn's] career. She wants to do the picture but she has no control of herself. Her performance is not good. It's as though she's acting underwater. And she's intelligent enough to realise this.'

Hopper herself even joined in the onslaughts, theorising forlornly:

> Marilyn Monroe is at the end of the road. As a movie star who could write her own ticket and command fantastic salaries, she has had it . . . Marilyn, I feel, is mentally or emotionally disturbed and I feel desperately sorry for her. But there was ruthlessness about her behaviour in the last months that it is impossible to forgive . . . At 34, she had not only failed at marriage she had lost the Hollywood people who helped her. [Director] Billy Wilder vowed he never would work with her again [and] Orry-Kelly, the designer who fashioned her wardrobe swore he would never do another thing for her. She ripped the lining out of his gowns so they would cling closer to her body.

Her tirade raged on (although her final comment, as we know from the surviving footage, is completely unwarranted):

> Her fans deserted her. *The Misfits* lost money . . . I don't think *Let's Make Love* ever earned back the cost of the negatives. Marilyn even lost Yves Montand, who was her romantic interest after the Miller divorce . . . I think Marilyn fell for him pretty hard. But she was in the hospital for a week and he wouldn't even talk to her on the phone . . . On the few days she showed up for work in *Something's Got To Give* her performance was bad. She behaved as if she was in a trance.

Attacks from Monroe's contemporaries were commonplace. 'I was proud to be part of this industry when Marilyn was fired,' declared actress Joan Crawford, a self-confessed Monroe hater. 'I don't think she has a friend. She hasn't taken time to make a friend in this industry. And many people have tried to befriend her.' Surprisingly, even Billy Wilder, one of the actress's few true supporters in the industry, joined in the onslaught. Early that month, he was quoted as saying, 'The question really is, whether Marilyn is a person or one of the greatest synthetic products ever invented. She has breasts like granite and a brain like Swiss cheese, full of holes. She defies gravity. She hasn't the vaguest idea of time. She arrives late and tells you she couldn't find the studio, although she's been working there for years.'

While the American press, her enemies and her so-called best friends were continuing their diatribe against the actress, 20th Century-Fox unsurprisingly became defiant that Marilyn's firing did not mean the end of *Something's Got To Give*. On the afternoon of Friday 8 June, while the lawsuit against Monroe was being prepared and filed, 26-year-old blonde thespian Lee Remick was hastily approached by Fox executives to be the movie's new leading lady. First Kim Novak and then Shirley MacLaine had already been briefly considered but since Remick still owed the studio two more movies and shared her predecessor's dress size, she was the obvious choice.

Just hours after Marilyn's sacking, Remick was whisked to the Fox lot and pinned into several of the actress's costumes so that the studio could take pictures of her smiling and reading a copy of the movie's script alongside George Cukor. Plans for her to recreate Marilyn's famous naked swim were apparently even discussed. In an interview with *New York Post* reporter Don Forst, Henry Weinstein announced, 'I expect her to duplicate the nude bathing scene. I expect her to follow the script and, where it calls for that scene, she will be asked to fulfil the role.'

In 1992, however, the actress revealed that, in fact, her tenure on the film had been just '20 minutes', adding, 'I certainly wasn't interested in it. Marilyn and I were as different as two actresses can be. But the studio told me, "We have a contract with you, and we want you to fulfil your obligation."' True, she did have a commitment to Fox, but in reality, it was highly unlikely that the studio would ever hire her to fill Monroe's shoes. Fox were well aware that, several weeks before the actress was approached, she had signed with Columbia Pictures to make the suspense drama *The Running Man* for director Sir Carol Reed in Spain and Ireland. Although the film was not set to start rolling until July, Remick didn't pull out. She had guessed all along that she would never make *Something's Got To Give* and only agreed to do the film if they agreed to pay her $80,000 whether it was made or not.

'No star is bigger than the studio,' 20th Century-Fox proudly announced at the time of Marilyn's sacking. But the truth was that, in June 1962, the ailing, cash-starved studio was in a bind. They knew in their heart of hearts that she was irreplaceable. (For the record, *Something's Got To Give* would resurface in December 1962 as *Move Over, Darling*, starring Doris Day and, ironically, James Garner.)

And bombshells continued to detonate. On the evening of Friday 8 June, Dean Martin surprised everyone by declaring that he had no interest whatsoever in working with Remick. Hours later, he announced he had quit the film. In comments later reiterated in a press statement, he paid his compliments to Lee Remick and made it clear to her it was nothing personal, but he had signed to be in a Marilyn Monroe movie and since the actress was no longer involved, this was no longer the case. Director George Cukor managed to avoid the ensuing troubles when, days after supposedly welcoming Lee Remick to the fold, he flew off to Honolulu for a holiday.

Word soon reached Marilyn about Remick and the cancelling of her Fox contract. Almost immediately, from her home in Brentwood, she placed a call through to Bobby Kennedy in Washington to notify him of the news. Rather than thinking of a tryst with the Attorney General, as some biographers have testified, she was hoping for a favour. As reporters Paul Scott and Robert S. Allen wrote in the *Post-Tribune* newspaper on Friday 12 June 1964, 'If you are a world-known actress in distress, it's mighty helpful to have Attorney General, Robert Kennedy to take a keen personal interest in your welfare. As head of the Justice Department, he is in a powerful position to solve problems with a dispatch and thoroughness that a veteran diplomat can't equal.' Just like many other film stars before (and after) her, Monroe was now turning to Bobby for help.

Due to Kennedy's ongoing plans with Fox to shoot a big-screen version of his book *The Enemy Within*, Bobby wielded some power at the studio, and Marilyn knew it. According to FBI documents, 'Robert Kennedy told her not to worry about the contract. He would take care of everything.' Unfortunately, this time he could not. He made just one call, to 66-year-old Judge Samuel I. Rosenman, a close friend of his family and a recent appointee as chairman of Fox's board of directors, and asked him for assistance in getting the actress reinstated. Rosenman was sensitive to his pleas but told him the only person capable of doing such a thing was Milton S. Gould – a man instrumental in Marilyn's sacking and an individual whom Kennedy, just a month earlier, during the run-up to his brother's gala, had labelled a 'Jewish bastard'. The Attorney General was powerless to assist.

On Saturday 9 June, Marilyn placed another call through to Bobby in Washington. He had promised her he would sort out the problem, but he clearly had not and she was angry. According to FBI reports, 'When nothing was done, she again called him from her home . . . and on this occasion they had unpleasant words. She was reported to have threatened to make public their affair (*sic*).' With regard to the matter of an affair, the FBI was clearly confusing its Kennedys.

The death-knell for *Something's Got To Give* had come with Dean Martin's decision to quit. But, contrary to what we've been previously led to believe, Fox did have one further, desperate plan up their sleeves to resurrect the movie. In between Martin's announcement late on Friday 8 June and the studio's declaration on Monday 11 June that they had irrevocably shut down production and served the crew with notices, the studio toyed with the idea of replacing the actress with glamorous 35-year-old blonde singer, actress and comedienne Edie Adams. Well known for her frequent impressions of Monroe, she recalled at the time, 'I dressed myself up like Marilyn Monroe and everybody bought it.'

In 1962, Adams, the wife of legendary comic Ernie Kovacs, was carrying out her parodies on her weekly, Emmy-nominated ABC television comedy show, *Here's Edie*. When it became known that Marilyn would not be completing *Something's Got To Give* and Lee Remick would not be replacing her, Edie was a perfectly natural, if desperate eleventh-hour alternative. Her appointment was even approved during a rushed, highly secretive Fox meeting. Their original plan was to either reshoot the movie from scratch and let Adams impersonate Marilyn throughout or allow her to appear as a double in long shots, or from behind in scenes that the actress had not yet shot. The plan became so advanced that she was even summoned to the studio and asked to wriggle into several of Monroe's costumes.

'It was eerie,' Edie announced in 1962. 'We wear the same size and everything.' (They were even almost the same age. Monroe was just ten months her senior.) Unsurprisingly, when this scheme reached Marilyn, she immediately called in her attorney, Rudin, who at once informed Fox that, by employing Adams in this way, the actress could sue them over rights to her 'image'. Predictably, Fox soon shelved the plans. (As a footnote to this story, on Tuesday 3 July 1962, following several warning letters from Rudin, Adams publicly announced that she had given up doing impersonations of Monroe.)

Conspiracies surrounding the movie's final days did not end there. Contrary to what we've been informed many times over the ensuing years, Dean Martin actually retracted his original announcement and said he would *return* to *Something's Got To Give* if a 'suitable replacement' for Marilyn was found. Original, recently unearthed reports reveal that he had even given the green light to Adams' hiring.

These documents reveal that, on Monday 11 June, just three days after Martin's announcement of his resignation, a Screen Actors' Guild (SAG) fact-finding committee comprising actors Charlton Heston, Dana Andrews and George Chandler met with his associate in Hollywood to discuss his problems at Fox. Since the possibility of Marilyn not finishing *Something's Got To Give* had strangely not been anticipated (or so Martin claimed), he was not protected contractually, so he turned to the SAG for help. The meeting concluded with the dilemma unresolved.

The following day, Tuesday 12 June, after another long discussion with the actor's representative, the Guild issued a statement which read, 'Dean Martin has now stated categorically that he has *not* closed the door to a suitable replacement for Marilyn Monroe.' Fox immediately countered with a statement of their own, which read:

> Despite the statement issued today by the Screen Actors' Guild, Martin has *never* advised 20th Century-Fox that his publicly stated position concerning Miss Monroe has changed. Miss Remick is an established star in the motion picture industry and has co-starred with James Stewart, Glenn Ford and Jack Lemmon and others. Martin's original announcement insinuated he would *not* work with *any* other leading lady in *Something's Got To Give*.

The flurry of statements concluded as fast as they had started and suddenly it seemed that Martin was being unduly and unfairly criticised for a situation that was not of his making. Unsurprisingly, with the actor now refusing to speak to anyone regarding the matter, his doting wife Jeannie entered the scene and moved swiftly to deflect the criticisms directed at her husband. Her original remarks, which have gone unpublished since 1962, paint the most honest account of Martin's decision.

'Dean's actions were not based on any undying love or eternal friendship for Marilyn Monroe,' she remarked to journalists who had camped on the front porch of the Martin family home on Mountain Drive in Beverly Hills. 'Fact is, we have seven kids and we need the money. But the picture is no good without Marilyn or a reasonable facsimile [an obvious reference to Edie Adams]. This girl has got to be the sexpot queen of the world. She has to make Cyd Charisse look like a wall-flower. What Marilyn would add to the story with all her wiggling and personality can't be replaced. Dean signed a contract in good faith. He's not some old second-rate thing that 20th can push around. Marilyn is not his responsibility. What's more he should not have to go and look for leading ladies.'

And so, just days after their last fruitless search for a replacement for Miss Monroe had bitten the dust, the studio felt they had no alternative but finally to once more call time on *Something's Got To Give*. The dismantling of the movie's impressive set on Sound Stage 14 was the symbolic gesture that time had finally run out on the ill-fated film. 'That's all there is to it,' Fox's publicity man dejectedly remarked. 'No quotes. No amplification. Nothing.'

What he failed to say was that the studio believed that, if they had continued at the rate they were going on the picture, they would have had an American version of the already costly *Cleopatra* on their hands. As another unnamed source at Fox remarked, 'It was better to shut down and lose $2 million than keep on and maybe lose $10 or $12 million.'

Marilyn took this closure as an opportunity to wire the movie's director, producer, workers and stagehands to express her sympathy about what had happened. It read: 'Please forgive me, it was not my doing. I had so looked forward to working with you.' They were unimpressed, and quickly announced – though the threat was never carried out – that they were intending to place an advert in the trade papers headed: 'Thanks Dean and Marilyn, for putting us out of work.'

So, five decades on, the question still remains: what caused Marilyn to act as she did? Why did she vanish for days on end? Was she really that sick? Besides the factors explored in this and the previous chapter – her illnesses, her frustration over script changes and her lack of allies at 20th Century-Fox – I believe there were several other reasons why Monroe apparently flouted the rules and seemingly showed such disrespect for her fellow professionals.

First, before shooting had even begun, her studio doctor, Lee Siegel, remarked that, due to laryngitis and headaches, Marilyn was truly incapable of starting work. These are traits familiar to Nembutal users. Mixing those with her other likely symptoms – drowsiness, agitation, nervousness and anxiety – and the fact that she *was* suffering from the persistent effects of an obscure virus infection which she had picked up during her trip to New York, the doctor was entirely accurate when he proposed that Fox 'should postpone the movie for a month'. They failed to do so.

Second, friends close to the star – the same friends who had also secretly advised her not to turn up on the set until she had a satisfactory script to hand – suggested that her failure to show on the set was precipitated by her unhappiness at how Fox were treating her. The actress was disappointed by the non-appearance on *Something's Got To Give* of the noted cinematographer Charles B. Lang. A great favourite of Marilyn's, he was engaged elsewhere in Hollywood at the time, shooting the new Warner Brothers comedy *Critic's Choice*, starring Lucille Ball and Bob Hope. Insiders suggested that she had actually tried delaying production on

Something's Got To Give until his commitment to Ball and Hope had concluded.

Another factor was the movie's producer, Henry T. Weinstein. Despite the valiant efforts to show how amicable their working relationship was, in truth it was far from that. Monroe and Weinstein were at loggerheads from day one. Early on during the making of the film, troubles intensified when, for unknown reasons, the actress refused blankly to deal with him, except when absolutely necessary. Subsequently, for Monroe, the shooting quickly turned into one long gruelling chore. Underpaid and under-valued, she vented her feelings in the only way she knew, by staying away.

Third, realising the actress's inability to perform first thing in the morning, Fox apparently promised Marilyn during pre-production that she would not be required to appear at the studio until 10am each day. However, when filming got under way, the pledge was dropped and starts at around 7.30am soon became the norm. Knowing she was incapable of working at such an early hour, studio doctor Lee Siegel even proposed a plan to allow the actress to shoot her scenes between noon and 8pm, as was frequently done in Europe. Fox dismissed the idea, even though, in Rome, Elizabeth Taylor was working a regular 11am to 7pm shift on *Cleopatra*.

Other explanations for Monroe's behaviour can be found. On Thursday 14 June 1962, the noted Hollywood film and television columnist Mike Connolly, a close associate of the actress, confirmed what already seemed evident, that she possessed a mental block against showing up on time. In addition, after her empty weekends, he announced that Mondays (she failed to show for three in a row) were always a bad time for her. A little-known fact is that around this time Marilyn had also been increasingly worried about her mother, Gladys, whose condition at the time of shooting had suddenly worsened. Naturally this affected her.

It is also worth addressing the over-emphasised point that the actress only turned up at the studio on 12 of the 33 shooting days. Aside from the fact that Marilyn *was* indeed ill during the filming, it has been conveniently overlooked since 1962 that she was not required on every one of those other 21 days. For instance, on Tuesday 8 May she was not scheduled to appear on the set, since her co-star, Dean Martin, was away from Fox with George Cukor that day shooting scenes on location. It is also important to recall that, regardless of what other historians may tell us, most of Marilyn's absences from the set actually fell in line with the Screen Actors' Guild's description of the 'excused absences' rule.

Fox were also at fault for another reason. Studio executives clearly overlooked a proviso in her December 1955 contract that, due to the severe stomach pains she suffered, she was not expected to work at the start of her menstrual cycle; in this case, Thursday 17 May, the date when she flew off to New York. The pain she experienced during her cycle was so excruciating that she would sometimes have to remain in bed for days on end or crumble to the floor in agony through the onset of her period. It is significant that, knowing of their legal obligation to the actress, permission to fly to Kennedy's bash was naturally granted by the studio before shooting had even started.

Moreover, with regard to the funding of *Something's Got To Give*, as producer Henry Weinstein remarked, knowing how troublesome Marilyn was, Fox should have budgeted for 16 weeks instead of eight. By doing so, the movie would have easily been completed. With regards to the accounts, Marilyn had, as we know, agreed to her contractually obligated $100,000 fee regardless of whether she actually received the fee (which she didn't), or how long the film would take to produce. Consequently, and in complete contrast to the picture painted by Fox at the time, Marilyn's absenteeism did not add to her costs to the studio at all.

And one more detail regularly overlooked is that Elizabeth Taylor was actually absent from the set of *Cleopatra* far more times than Marilyn was from that of *Something's Got To Give*: 99 out of 101 days in one instance. Filming started on Friday 30 September 1960, but she did not appear on the set until almost a year later, on Tuesday 12 September 1961, by which time shooting had shifted from Pinewood Studios in Iver, England to Rome in Italy. The ostensible reasons included food poisoning, suicide attempts, and a supposed automobile accident in Rome on Friday 27 April 1962, actually invented to account for damage to her nose suffered thanks to a beating she received from her new lover, Richard Burton. The bruises on Taylor's face were so severe that she was forced to miss 22 straight days of filming, far more than Marilyn ever managed.

But we also have to wonder whether Monroe's apparent disruptiveness on *Something's Got To Give* was influenced by Taylor's scandalous behaviour on her 1960 movie, *Butterfield 8*. From the start, Taylor, like Monroe had made it clear she wanted to make the film, yet seemed to do everything she could to get out of it, even announcing several times that the script was poor and insisted on changes being made to it. Desperate like Marilyn, to break free from her studio – in Taylor's case, Metro-Goldwyn-Mayer – she gained agreement that, if she made the movie, they would grant her wish and end their pact with her. Before shooting commenced, Taylor, like Monroe, insisted on a long list of provisos, in her case a final say in costumier, hairdresser and actors employed on the production. With regard to every one of those points, Marilyn followed suit.

Monroe always appeared to regard Taylor as a rival. Fury must then have engulfed her when, on Monday 17 April 1961, several months after completing *Butterfield 8* and just six weeks after almost dying of pneumonia, Taylor was awarded the most notorious 'pity Oscar' in Hollywood history. Marilyn was never even nominated for the award. As I revealed earlier, her decision to 'give away' her rights to her nude swimming pictures was inspired by her overwhelming desire to knock Taylor off the front of the world's magazine covers. Furthermore, was her decision to go au naturel influenced not by George Cukor but by Taylor's revealing nude bath sequence in *Cleopatra*, which she had shot just 11 weeks earlier? I suspect it was.

Much of this information has been hidden for almost 50 years. But the sad fact is, should it have been uncovered, released or published at the time of the movie's cancellation, it would probably have fallen on deaf ears. As far as the industry was concerned in mid-1962, Marilyn's movie career was well and truly wrecked, and it seemed that no one in the industry was prepared to save it.

Marilyn spent the first eight days of June 1962 in seclusion behind the high walls of her white-bricked Brentwood hacienda, refusing to open her door or answer questions about her future from anyone, especially journalists. She slept until noon and when she did venture out, which was seldom, she wore her obligatory black wig and dark shades. Hardly any of her neighbours reported seeing her.

Sitting within her sparsely furnished home with associates such as Pat Newcomb and Lee and Paula Strasberg, Marilyn knew she was facing the biggest challenge of her adult life. She understood better than anyone that, following her dismissal by Fox, the company that helped create the 'Marilyn Monroe' image, she could be virtually washed up as a big money star. Furthermore, she knew full well that if any producer wanted to gamble on her again after this latest fiasco, he would be playing with loaded dice. She also understood that very few insurance companies would be willing to cushion a producer's fall should the unpredictable and seemingly uncaring actress once again spin into one of her prolonged states of fragility.

Marilyn's life was seemingly at a crossroads and her existence as a world-famous celebrity apparently hung on a knife's edge. Or did it? Not according to some. On Sunday 10 June, Hedda Hopper announced in her 'Hollywood Today' column that the actress had been invited by Fox president Spyros Skouras to appear as one of the stars of his 'Star Spangled Ball' gala, to be held at New York's Waldorf Hotel on Thursday 8 November. The person accepting the role of Honorary World Chairman at the event was none other than President John F. Kennedy . . .

Chapter Eight

Despondency, Rebirth, Photo Shoots and the Cal-Neva

Saturday 9 June 1962–Monday 30 July 1962

'**B**eing fired from *Something's Got To Give* was hard for her to take,' Eunice Murray admitted in 1962. With despondency engulfing her life, Marilyn was unexcited by the prospect of sharing another stage with the President. Following the White House rejection, she knew that in any case it was a hollow promise.

Her appearance was suffering too. 'Her hair was unkempt,' wrote the Hollywood reporter Martin Buckley, 'her nails were longer than usual.' The actress's consumption of alcohol, in particular champagne, was also increasing. Daylight was almost a luxury for her now. She would get through the days, but it was the nights that were too long. Suddenly, she was at a loss about what she should do with herself. Fox had fired her for tardiness, but now she had no reason to be on time. Yet she found herself watching the clock. Murray would suggest she eat something. She didn't answer. 'She would get quiet, stay quiet for hours and hours,' the housekeeper recalled. In her 1975 book, *Marilyn: The Last Months*, she revealed that the actress 'spent a lot of time musing with a far away look in her eyes. Some might have seen this as depression.' In the words of her good friend, the Hollywood publicist Rupert Allan, Marilyn was 'facing the dark tunnel of her career'.

She used to enjoy the idea of staying at home all day. But not any more. The interior decorating ideas that had once engaged her no longer seemed important. Ornaments she had purchased for her Mexican-style bar cantina still lay in the box. She had no desire to open it. On the occasional nights when she *did* go out, she would go for a drive with Murray in the housekeeper's green Dodge car. Her favourite was along the Santa Monica beach where she would trail the curve of the sand, without having to ponder where she was going. Sometimes she would drive past Peter Lawford's house. Many times she thought about stopping. She rarely did.

Saturday 9 June was spent holed up in Beverly Hills in her white brick apartment at 882 North Doheny Drive. Far from the party spirit, and with the bruises still prominent on her face, she failed to show that evening at Dean Martin's special bash for her. The eleventh-hour get-together at his home in Beverly Hills was intended to cheer her up following her sacking. Instead, as the rain fell, Marilyn sat alone, contemplating her future. Her solitary companions were her dog, Maf, and the Sinatra records that spun continuously on her player. Fruitless calls to the Attorney General and her fan club secretary, Madge Inman, punctuated her banal proceedings. The actress's despondency increased when the latter informed her that, once more, she had just 50 letters waiting for collection.

It was a far cry from September 1953, when Fox assigned 20 girls from the script department just to help catch up on the actress's mail, which was piling up at the rate of 10,000 letters a month. With her bank balance dwindling fast, she naturally began to question whether the $262.65 it was costing her to run the club each month was worth it. Earlier in the day, when the sun started to shine, she had ventured to Coldwater Canyon, where she sat for hours, watching the children play in the park. The hurt of not being able to mother a child of her own had returned to haunt her. 'Marilyn no longer felt the struggle was worth the try,' one New York columnist correctly theorised at the time. 'She simply refused. She refused to even get excited about scripts. An offer for a musical arrived. It stayed on her table unread.'

The proposal in question, sent by telegram on Friday 15 June, was from Natalia Danesi Murray, the New York representative of Anita Loos, the author of Monroe's smash 1953 movie *Gentlemen Prefer Blondes*:

Dear Miss Monroe: On behalf of Anita Loos, now in Europe, we would like to know if you would be interested star role new musical based on French play 'GoGo'. Book by Anita Loos, lyrics by Gladys Shelley and entertaining music by Claude Leville. Can send you script and music if you express interest. Natalia Danesi Murray.

The musical was set to earn Marilyn $5,500 a week, the highest such offer for an entertainer at the time. But, as her attorney, Milton Rudin, revealed, 'She turned down the offer from Las Vegas, even though she needed the money, because she couldn't take getting up in front of people.'

Author George Carpozi Jr was another observer of the actress. 'Few friends saw Marilyn. She retreated behind the walls of her [Brentwood] Spanish bungalow . . . She lived alone with her poodle. She didn't socialise except for her doctor, lawyer and Eunice. People about town seemingly washed their hands of her . . . Her days were unbearably aimless. During the long afternoons, Marilyn pottered around her garden, sat by her pool in her back yard, occasionally read and seldom spoke to friends on the phone . . . '

However, on Thursday 14 June, her telephone *did* ring. It was Walter Winchell, the so-called dean of Hollywood gossip columnists, innocently calling to invite Marilyn to the Coconut Grove night club to see a performance by singer Eddie Fisher. 'We thought maybe Marilyn could use a friend or two in her moment of need,' he informed the actress's press agent, Pat Newcomb. Before slamming the phone down, Newcomb abruptly declared, 'She's not talking to *anyone!*' Marilyn did not receive the invite. She would not have gone anyway. Fisher was Elizabeth Taylor's husband and the last thing she needed at that moment was to see her arch-rival's smiling face, gloating at her current misfortune.

Four days earlier, on Sunday 10 June, following a highly inspirational early-morning visit by Joe DiMaggio, Marilyn had surprised everyone by making a decidedly low-key, but action-packed trip to her adopted homeland of New York. One of her many appointments was to see Isidore Miller. When she told him about what had happened at Fox, she began to sob. He asked her, 'Why are you crying?' She replied, 'Dad, because you are such a wonderful man and you are interested in what will happen to me.' She also caught up with her trusted friend, the writer Truman Capote, and attended a meeting with Fox's veteran Hollywood executive Darryl F. Zanuck, who had just flown in from Paris. But the main reason for her visit, following a request from Peter Lawford, was to see the President of the United States.

With rumours of an affair between him and the actress now gaining momentum in the presidential circle, no doubt triggered by her sultry performance at his gala, Kennedy felt that Marilyn was a luxury he could not afford. He knew their one-night liaison had put the administration in great jeopardy and was well aware that, through the stringent bugging of his brother-in-law Lawford's beachside home (eavesdropping equipment had been secreted under carpets, in chandeliers, on the phones and in ceiling fixtures) and the illicit recordings of conversations carried out there, any one of Kennedy's enemies could have amassed damaging information about the President.

With regard to his connection to promiscuous women, the heat was already on. On Tuesday 27 February, the FBI's Director, J. Edgar Hoover, had sent a memo to top Kennedy aide Kenneth P. O'Donnell, notifying him that the President had been involved with 26-year-old Judith Campbell, a woman known to frequent mob circles and, prior to her involvement with Kennedy, recognised for her relationships with both Frank Sinatra and Mafia leader Sam Giancana. With no alternative in sight, JFK was warned by Hoover he could not risk the scandal of yet another extramarital connection, however innocent, becoming public, especially one with someone as famous as Monroe. At once – knowing moreover that the decision would please his wife – he decided to cease communication with Marilyn; hence her White House dinner party snub on Friday 1 June. He had, in her eyes, for the want of a more suitable expression, cut and run.

So he wished to explain. Following examination of the President's diaries, I believe his decision to clarify everything to the actress came during the evening of Sunday 10 June, following his stopover in New York to visit, with Peter Lawford, his ailing father Joseph, who was still recuperating in the Manhattan rehabilitation centre, Horizon House. Discussions between Kennedy and Marilyn took place later that night at his regular New York base, the Carlyle Hotel, sometime after 6.55pm. It was their final encounter. Amid a feeling of disappointment, she returned to her apartment shortly after. (For the record, the President left the hotel at 8.55 the following morning and flew on to New Haven, Connecticut where, at 11.30am, he received an honorary degree from Yale University. He returned to Washington that afternoon at precisely 3.42 by helicopter, arriving back at the White House exactly ten minutes later.)

His decision to excise the actress from his life was then relayed to his brother Bobby, who in attempt to ease her obvious disappointment, and to apologise for his failure to help her at Fox, rang the actress at her Brentwood home during the evening of Wednesday 13 June and passed on his number at the Justice Department. A disclosure about this came from Pat Lawford, who in her 1988 book, *The Peter Lawford Story*, sensationally claimed that Bobby had apparently informed Marilyn she was 'not even a serious affair for the President' and was 'just another of Jack's fucks (*sic*)'.

Bobby's action in handing over his number, however, was in itself not an unusual one. Other film stars, such as Judy Garland and Richard Burton, had the number and often called the Attorney General when they were in distress or just needed someone to talk to. Bobby was a compassionate man and above all, a good listener.

Evidence for this final meeting between Marilyn and the President can be found in an excerpt from *Answered Prayers*, the partially unpublished memoir by the highly flamboyant Louisiana-born writer Truman Capote. Best known for *Breakfast at Tiffany's*, he had grown very close to the actress and was heartbroken that she lost out to Audrey Hepburn in the movie version of his book. On Monday 11 June, the actress had lunch with Capote at the posh Manhattan restaurant La Fonda Del Sol. During their get-together, she covertly informed him of what had transpired between her and the President. Noticing a new maturity about her, and detecting she wasn't so giggly any more, he told her, 'Why cry over Jack? Between him and Bobby, they can't raise a decent hard-on and I know a lot about cocks. I've seen an awful lot of them and if you put all the Kennedys together, you wouldn't have a good one.' His claim of familiarity with their genitalia stemmed from the time when, during his stays in Palm Beach with financier Loel Guinness and his wife, style arbiter Gloria, he would frequently witness the sight of the Kennedy boys, who lived nearby, going for a swim in the nude. (It was no secret that Capote had no time for the Kennedys. In the book *Conversations*, he remarked, 'The Kennedy boys are like dogs. They can't pass a fire hydrant without pissing on it.') Capote's comment made Marilyn laugh, but it wasn't quite the response she was looking for.

In a further attempt to make amends for the President's decision, and to explain in more comfortable surroundings the precise reasons why he had chosen to retreat, during that call to her Brentwood home on 13 June Bobby also invited Marilyn to a gathering at Peter Lawford's beachside house, which was set to take place the following Sunday evening. Concerned by the contusions that remained visible on her face, and still smarting over the rebuff, she declined the invite by way of a cryptic Western Union telegram, which was sent later that day, at 10.15pm, to Bobby and his wife Ethel at their country home in Hickory Hill, McLean, Virginia. It read:

> Dear Attorney General and Mrs Robert Kennedy: I could have been delighted to have accepted your invitation honouring Pat and Peter Lawford. Unfortunately, I am involved in a freedom ride protesting the loss of the minority rights belonging to the few remaining earthbound stars. After all, all we demanded was our right to twinkle. Marilyn Monroe.

Once deciphered, it appears that her enigmatic message was in fact a cleverly disguised, snide yet astute below-the-belt attack on the Kennedys. The party in question was *not* to honour the Lawfords (their eighth wedding anniversary was actually six weeks earlier, on Tuesday 24 April) but to salute the 12th wedding anniversary of Bobby and Ethel Kennedy. The actress had shrewdly notched up a small, self-satisfying if vindictive victory against both the President and his family.

Marilyn's visit to the Big Apple was brief. On Wednesday 13 June she headed back to Brentwood, where she visited her physician, Dr Hyman Engelberg, and received anaemia shots and tablets for her increasingly jittery nerves. In the middle of the month, fed up with her nondescript, clinging existence, she suddenly decided that she was no longer prepared to lie down. After being tossed to one side by Fox and now the mighty-powerful President, she concluded she didn't want to just fade into the distance. Instead, she was ready to retaliate. She had worked long and hard to reach her position as one of the world's most famous film stars and she was not ready to throw it away.

Two people were instrumental in this decision. As we can guess, one was Joe DiMaggio. The other was Frank Sinatra. Since Marilyn's sacking by Fox, Sinatra had taken an increasingly active hand in her affairs and had even been advising and consoling her, usually by phone. On Saturday 16 June – just a day after returning to Los Angeles from a two-month world tour in aid of children's charities – concerned at her absence the previous evening from his surprise 'Welcome Home' bash, held in the recently completed new wing of Dean Martin's home, he called Marilyn and invited her out to dinner. (A tip-off that Juliet Prowse was in attendance had played a huge part in her decision not to attend.)

Marilyn gushed with joy when Sinatra called. Following his severance from Prowse, Frank was ready to resume his relationship with the actress. He picked her up at her Brentwood home, his only visit there (before leaving, the actress insisted on giving him a guided tour). During dinner that night, at his jointly owned Villa Capri restaurant in Hollywood, Frank put his lawyers at her service and informed her his film production company, Essex, would be prepared to produce her next movie. In fact the pair discussed starring in two movies together: *How To Murder Your Wife*, a comedy especially written for them by George Axelrod, and *What a Way to Go*. The latter, a comedy-musical about a woman who is a fatal jinx to her husbands, greatly impressed the actress and was soon touted as the follow-up to *Something's Got To Give*. J. Lee Thompson, director of *The Guns of Navarone*, was even suggested as the movie's director.

When news of Frank and Marilyn's clandestine meeting and planned movie collaboration reached the Hollywood news wires, Sinatra remarked, 'I think it would be good for Sinatra. It is good company. It is good chemistry. The public would find it exciting.' However, the announcement did not excite everyone. In a reference to the actress's legendary on-set antics, critic Dorothy Manners sarcastically suggested in one of her columns that one of the movies they had in mind should be retitled *How To Murder Your Co-Star*.

Clearly invigorated by Sinatra's support and persuasive coaxing, Monroe took a rejuvenated interest in everything around her, especially the transformation of her home. On Sunday 24 June, at a cost of $65.50, Louis Alatorre of the Patios-Block Walls company at 1959 Corinth Avenue, Los Angeles, arrived to cut and fit a new Inca red tile on the property, acid clean her brick patio walls and drill a hole through one of the walls in the kitchen to improve its drainage. Marilyn regularly toasted this new-found euphoria. Six days earlier, on Monday 18 June, for instance, she had sent Eunice Murray out to the Briggs Wines & Spirits store, at 13038 San Vicente Boulevard, to purchase (for her) a $14.43 bottle of Dom Perignon and (for Murray) one bottle of Smirnoff vodka and one of J&B Scotch whisky (total cost $15.11). With the recent arrival of her first shipment of Mexican furniture, she became absorbed in plans to turn her Fifth Helena home into what she called 'Mexican-modern'.

The actress, naturally, also became obsessed with kick-starting her career. She began by gathering the press and anyone who was keen to listen to her story about how she had been betrayed by the Hollywood star system. She also instigated a campaign to win back her job at 20th Century-Fox. Fellow actress Cyd Charisse, angry that Fox had welched on their agreement, immediately agreed to be part of the effort. 'Of course, Marilyn,' she replied, 'whatever you do is fine with me.'

Hollywood's best known hair stylist, Sydney Guilaroff, was another individual summoned. In the third week of June, hot on the heels of Bobby Kennedy's surprising lack of success in the matter, Guilaroff rang Fox executives and said, 'If I can get rid of the people around her and get her back on the set, will you take her back?' They replied with a resounding 'Yes!' But in fact, by the time he called, the wheels to re-employ Marilyn were already well in motion.

The first meeting to discuss Monroe's rehiring had actually taken place during the afternoon of Saturday 23 June. In a clandestine, previously undocumented encounter, Marilyn had a personal face-to-face discussion with Fox vice-president Peter Levathes at her home on Fifth Helena.

Levathes had contacted the actress after receiving a call from Spyros Skouras; the Fox president had in turn called Levathes following his meeting with Darryl Zanuck, whom Marilyn had met for lunch during her brief stay in New York. With his Second World War epic *The Longest Day* now completed, and with problems at the studio continuing to concern him, on or around the afternoon of Friday 15 June Zanuck had arranged a clear-the-air meeting with Skouras in New York at his hospital bedside. It was during that conference that he suggested, for the long-term benefit of both the studio and its stockholders, that they should rehire Monroe. Since Zanuck was a major investor at Fox, Skouras was forced to agree. Although no one said as much, they had agreed that there was no substitute for Marilyn.

Suspicious of Levathes' motives that Saturday afternoon, Monroe astutely secreted Pat Newcomb in an adjoining room, door slightly ajar, to eavesdrop and take notes of what he said and promised during the meeting. That way, as the actress believed, he and Fox would have to adhere to every pledge he made.

As their conversation unfolded, Levathes politely informed Monroe of one of their provisos for her return: she must replace key members of her staff, those known to have a disruptive influence over her on the film set. Besides the obvious names of Ralph Greenson and Paula Strasberg, the one other he put forward was that of Newcomb herself, who Fox felt wielded too much control over the actress. The example of George Cukor sometimes having to endure Newcomb in order just to speak to the actress was brought up. While Levathes spoke, Marilyn merely sat and listened.

The discussion soon ended, although another was planned. Her next and more widely known meeting with Levathes took place five days later, on Thursday 28 June. Once more, her home in Brentwood was the setting. This time, however, her attorney, Milton Rudin, and not Pat Newcomb was in attendance.

Guilaroff partly assented to Fox's beliefs. In a 1966 interview for the magazine *Films and Filming*, he bluntly declared that, in his opinion, the people that had prevented Marilyn from completing *Something's Got To Give* were indeed Strasberg and Greenson. So, determined to make a fresh start in her life and unburden herself of her money-draining sycophants, Marilyn took on board both the studio's and Guilaroff's advice. In late June, she began formulating plans to sever her professional ties to Paula Strasberg, as well as her husband, Lee, although she was unsure about cutting her links to Newcomb. Due to her drug dependency, she knew freeing herself from Greenson's overpowering grasp was going to be another matter entirely.

Almost immediately, once the bruises on her face had subsided, Monroe was back at work. Through Newcomb, she had made herself available to three major magazines and for three straight evenings, beginning on Saturday 23 June (shortly after her meeting with Levathes) and concluding on Monday 25 June, she took part in the first of two lengthy photo shoots.

The first turned into an in-depth session for the high-fashion magazine *Vogue*, her first for this kind of publication.

A fact overlooked by every previous biographer of the actress is that, in order to prepare for the shoots, and in particular that for *Life* magazine, Marilyn had made a nostalgic, low-key trip to see Emmeline Snively of the Blue Book School of Charm and Modelling Agency, the first that she had ever belonged to. At the age of 19, Norma Jeane Dougherty, as she was known then, had signed with the bureau on Thursday 2 August 1945. Snively revealed to reporter Milton Shulman in 1956 that 'Marilyn hadn't enough money to pay for the course, so I paid for it. She paid me back later.' Marilyn never forgot this generosity so, on or around Tuesday 12 June, during her short stay in New York, she met up again with Snively, who was working in the city at the time, and asked if she could pose for one of her classes. Her request was naturally granted, although most of Snively's students that day were prominent, off-duty businessmen.

The photographer commissioned to carry out the first of Marilyn's June 1962 shoots, meanwhile, was 31-year-old, Brooklyn-born *Vogue* photographer Bert Stern. He had first encountered Marilyn at a Manhattan cocktail party in 1955 and had always harboured a desire to photograph her. 'I really wanted to be alone with her in the bedroom,' Stern declared. He was about to get his wish.

After discussions with both the actress and her publicist, Arthur Jacobs, arrangements were made not to use a studio, but instead to shoot the pictures in the improvised setting of Suite 261 at the Bel Air Hotel in Beverly Hills, at that time the most secluded and sexy hotel in Los Angeles. Long before Marilyn's arrival on 23 June, Stern was preparing for the shoot like a man anxiously awaiting his lover. He knew his desires for the actress went much further than his yearning to capture her in stills form. His camera was loaded, lights were in place, hi-fi was ready, Chanel No. 5, Marilyn's favourite perfume, had been sprayed into the air and a case of 1953 Dom Perignon champagne was chilling in the refrigerator. Props in the form of several transparent scarves were strewn across the bed. All that was needed was the subject. Marilyn said she would appear at two o'clock. But because her meeting with Levathes overran, she did not appear until seven.

Tipped off about her eventual arrival by a phone call from the hotel's receptionist, Stern immediately rushed down to greet the star and was surprised to find Monroe, the world famous Hollywood film star, completely alone. As the photographer recalled in his 1982 book, *The Last Sitting*, 'I was surprised to see a girl walking towards me on her own. No PR agent, no bodyguard, no secretary. Totally alone.' (Although not according to Allan 'Whitey' Snyder. Shortly after her death, Snyder submitted an invoice for $600.00 to Marilyn's estate to cover three days of his services at the Bel Air Hotel on this day as well as the following two.)

However, Stern recalled Marilyn did show with an entourage during the second day of shooting, humorously describing Snyder as a 'husky guy who looked like a bodyguard'. Surprisingly, the actress's regular Los Angeles hair stylist, Agnes M. Flanagan, was not hired for the shoot. She had been employed by the actress to help her prepare for almost every major (or minor) engagement she attended, such as her meetings with Fox, her forthcoming photographic session with George Barris (due to start the following Friday) and the dinner parties at Peter Lawford's house. But not today.

When Marilyn reached the suite, she greeted her chosen hair stylist for the day, George Masters. Having been introduced to Stern's 22-year-old, Swedish-born assistant, Leif-Erik Nygards, she walked into the bedroom, her makeshift make-up room, to prepare. She sat down in front of the mirror, removed her shawl and started to comb out her hair. 'What do you want to do?' she asked Stern.

'Are you in a hurry?' he enquired.

'No, why?' she responded.

'I thought you were going to have just minutes,' he insisted.

'Are you kidding?' she responded.

'How much time have you got?' he asked.

'All the time we want,' she solemnly replied. She had plenty to kill. She had no other plans. She had no social life in Los Angeles. As she made it quite clear, she had all the time in the world.

As the shoot unfolded, glasses of champagne were poured and albums by the Everly Brothers were spun. (Stern had inadvertently failed to bring any by Sinatra, much to Marilyn's umbrage.) Against a white paper backdrop, the actress began by posing in dresses and even in a dark wig. Then, once the champagne had taken effect, Marilyn mellowed to posing almost nude. She walked into the bedroom, stripped off her clothes and enacted a sort of fan dance with various diaphanous scarves which exposed nearly all of her body. At one point, she attempted to cover her breast with two chiffon cloth roses.

'I'm not going to take my pants off,' she firmly stated. More alcohol was consumed. Further persuasions to pose without the scarves ensued. As dawn broke, she relented. Although the resulting shots could never be described as explicit, Marilyn did display more than she had intended. The session had lasted almost 12 hours and at 7am, after bidding their fond farewells, Stern caught his flight back to New York and rushed to develop his pictures. Colour shots were sent out for processing, black and white he printed himself. *Vogue*'s Ukrainian-born art director, Alexander

Liberman, was elated with the results and wanted more, particularly in monochrome. Stern agreed. An offer to do another shoot was immediately made to Marilyn. She too concurred.

So, just hours after concluding their first session, Stern was heading back to California to prepare for another. A much larger, three-roomed bungalow (number 96) at the Bel Air was hastily rehired and further bottles of Dom Perignon plus a case of 1955 Chateau Lafitte-Rothschild were hurriedly purchased. Due to arrive at 2pm, Marilyn arrived at the hotel at 4.30. But this time, Pat Newcomb and Allan Snyder were in tow. Such was the excitement over the session that *Vogue* even flew in their picture editor, Babs Sampson, and America's premier hair stylist, Marilyn's obligatory New York stylist Kenneth Battelle.

Vogue felt the only elements missing from the first day's shoot were images that focused on fashion, an integral ingredient of a magazine which was, of course, a leader in the field. To make good the deficiency, stacks of furs, robes and diamonds as well as a floor-length chinchilla coat and a brunette wig were sent along. But after six hours of posing and several changes of costume, at precisely midnight Marilyn grew tired. The idea of being a fashion model and posing in this kind of attire had started to bore her. In an attempt to goad a smile, Newcomb started taunting her about her transitory Mexican acquaintance, José Bolaños. Despite its promising start, the manipulation soon waned. With the session beginning to flag, Stern decided to lace Monroe's champagne with neat vodka and naturally, the actress soon became intoxicated. It was around midnight when he asked her, 'How about if we went to bed?'

The room was cleared of all personnel. As his camera kept clicking, Marilyn lay across the bed and romped with erotic playfulness on a bed of white linens. Stern soon joined her. He slid his hands below the bed sheets and attempted to kiss her, but she turned away and Stern was deflated. He did not pursue intimacy and he withdrew his hand. In *The Last Sitting*, he explained why. 'I think the real reason was that I cared too much for her. My desire for Marilyn was pure, it bordered on awe.' Stern left the recumbent actress as she woozily attempted to descend into a deep, alcohol-induced sleep. A couple of empty champagne bottles and a half-empty glass of Dom Perignon lay strewn on the floor beside the bed. As he ventured into the outside world again, he caught sight of two Japanese cooks in their tall hats peering through the crack of one of the window's shades.

However, for Stern's assistant, Leif-Erik Nygards, the shoot still had one small surprise in store. 'At the end of the session, I was alone in the studio with Marilyn,' he recalled in 2006 for the PBS *American Masters* television show, *Still Life*. 'She [got up and] sat on the bed, wrapped in a sheet. Her head stuck out of the sheet. She looked like she was a mummy. I thought, "I must have a picture of Marilyn." My friends in Sweden would just laugh at me because if I said I had met her . . . they'd say, "Tell us another story." So I asked Marilyn, "Can I take just one frame of you?" She said, "Of course," and when I turned round, she had unwrapped herself from the sheet and [was] lying totally nude on the bed. The first thing I thought was, "Jesus! I can't show this to my mother." I acted like it was nothing, took the picture and when the flash went off, she lifted up her head and smiled. I should have taken two pictures. I was very stupid. I asked for one picture, got it and I should be very grateful.'

Stern's third day with the actress was decidedly subdued. He took black and white images of her lying down on purpose-built scaffolding made from a table and chairs, wearing a necklace and covered with sprinkle, as well as shots of her holding one of his Nikon cameras. Stern also managed to obtain the one shot of Marilyn he truly wanted; a close-up of the actress looking straight up into the eyes of the beholder, as if he was making love to her.

Three days after the session, Newcomb called Stern to enquire about the pictures. (In total, 2,571 were taken during the three-day shoot.) He told her he was pleased with the results. To this, she reminded him of Marilyn's rights to approve each and every one of the pictures he had taken. *Vogue* did not usually grant such a wish. But at once, with the magazine's publishing deadline fast approaching, contact prints of the photos and a third of the colour ones were sent over to Marilyn for her endorsement.

Three weeks later, she returned them, but more than half had been defaced. She demonstrated her dislike of some of them by either scratching them with a hairpin or defacing them with a large 'X', made by a red magic marker pen. This act of vandalism took the photographer by surprise and he was naturally furious. 'Not that she didn't like the pictures,' he announced in 1982, 'but [because] she'd been so destructive about it. Why couldn't she have picked up the phone and said, "Let's go over these together?"'

'I never expected her to destroy them or do anything to them,' he remarked in 1992. 'She said she just wanted to see them. As she could not express her rage to others, she took it out on herself . . . I don't think it was because she really disliked the pictures, but the mutilation was just because she was terribly angry at the time.'

Thankfully, through the wonders of modern technology, the damaged images were later restored. It seemed that the only images Marilyn objected to were the ones in which she disliked her facial expressions.

Vogue featured a selection of her approved images in an eight-page spread in September 1962, while a selection of the nude photos was published in the quarterly art magazine *Eros*, before it went out of business, having been banned by many postal authorities due to its often salacious contents. Stern's pictures would become known as 'The Last Sitting', even though her last session, or at least her last poses before the camera, would not take place for another two weeks.

The final day of Stern's shoot, 25 June, coincided with Marilyn's very first call to Bobby Kennedy at the Justice Department in Washington, during which she was informed by his secretary, Angie Novello, that he was in Chicago and on his way to Los Angeles as part of a nationwide tour to fight organised crime. (Bobby's arrival in the city, during the afternoon of Tuesday 26 June, on United Airlines flight no. 737 B-720, would be delayed by 2 hours 10 minutes. After disembarking at 4.25pm, he was met by a colleague, William G. Simon, and the US Attorney for the Southern District of California, Francis C. Whelan. Immediately afterwards, Kennedy was escorted to the Beverly Hills Hotel, a journey which lasted approximately 35 minutes.)

In all probability, she rang the Attorney General to impart to him how pleased she was with Stern's session and to confirm his presence at Peter Lawford's beachside home the following evening. Due to her recovered telephone records, we discover that she dialled the general switchboard (Republic 7-8200) and was transferred, via the operator, to Bobby's secretary. The actress would repeat this scenario right up until her death. Between the aforementioned date and Monday 30 July 1962, she would dial that number eight times. This information indicates that, despite claims to the contrary, Bobby never passed on his private number to the actress. Why would she call the switchboard, after all, if she had Bobby's private number? Reports suggesting that, prior to their first date, Marilyn had been using that line to contact him are therefore unsubstantiated. This is corroborated by her personal telephone book (which was sold by the Heritage Auction Galleries for $11,950 on Friday 13 April 2007).

On the evening of Tuesday 26 June, Marilyn was due to attend Peter Lawford's latest dinner party. During the afternoon, therefore, she once again called on the services of Agnes M. Flanagan and Allan 'Whitey' Snyder, who both visited the actress at her Fifth Helena home. President Kennedy was not in attendance at the 7.30pm party. (He spent the day in discussion with the Oregon Senator, Wayne Morse, and in meetings with the National Security Council and the Foreign Intelligence Advisory Board.) But, as Monroe anticipated, his brother *was* there. At the gathering, according to FBI reports filed on Thursday 26 July 1962, the actress 'asked the President (*sic*) a lot of socially significant questions concerning the morality of atomic testing and the future of the youth of America'. Informants at the party described her questions and views as 'positively and concisely leftist'.

During the course of the evening, those in attendance also discussed a number of government secrets, including the disastrous Bay of Pigs invasion, civil rights, the Peace Corps and organised crime. Their most significant topic of conversation, however, concerned recent Mafia attempts to assassinate the Cuban leader, Fidel Castro, of which Bobby had just learnt via a secret CIA memo prepared on Monday 14 May by Colonel Sheffield Edwards, the director of its office of security.

While Kennedy spoke, Marilyn innocently took notes of his utterances in her small red pocket book. It was during this evening that Bobby's friendship with the actress, albeit brief, began to develop. Instead of retreating from the Kennedys' lives, as the President had wanted, Marilyn had successfully managed to substitute one Kennedy brother for another. But rather than becoming social intimates, their alliance would be – excluding his visit to her on Thursday 27 June – entirely based on exceedingly short, infrequent phone conversations.

Bobby was an easy target for someone wanting favours from the President. He was more emotional, self-conscious and serious than his brother. Marilyn meanwhile was a brilliant seductress. She wanted him because he was the closest to JFK. Their relationship, however, was entirely platonic. Though she would soon regard him as a friend, he wasn't her sort. 'He's not my type,' she told her masseur friend, Ralph Roberts. 'I think the word she used was "puny",' he recalled.

When we examine closely the information about Marilyn's alleged sexual relationship with Bobby, it becomes clear that, as I touched upon in Chapter 4, those tales began life as a political smear against him when he was running for the United States Senate in 1964. Four years later, in 1968, the rumours were given a new lease of life when he was tragically assassinated. By that time, no doubt emboldened by the fact that families of the deceased cannot sue for libel, those with axes to grind felt free to begin embellishing their tales about the two legends. For instance, there was the occasion when, on Wednesday 27 June 1962, a day after Lawford's dinner party, the Attorney General accepted an invitation to peruse the actress's new home.

As surviving documents testify, seeing Marilyn that day was not high on Bobby's list of priorities. The Attorney General's first appointment was an 11am meeting at Fox, with producer Jerry Wald and writer Budd Schulberg, to discuss again the big-screen version of his book *The Enemy Within*. This meeting was an integral reason for Monroe to invite Kennedy to her home. Since her position with Fox was still decidedly precarious and Jerry Wald was a long-time, close personal friend, by summoning Bobby she was able to obtain the very latest gossip about both her and the studio.

Bobby's itinerary for the remainder of Wednesday 27 June was as follows. At 12.30, immediately after his conference at Fox, he had a cold-food luncheon at the Federal Judge's court house. He faced a press conference at the United States attorney's office one hour later, met his staff at 2pm and the heads of investigative agencies at 3pm. When his duties for the day were concluded, he and his assistant, Edwin Guthman, decided to drive over to Marilyn's home in Brentwood, arriving there at precisely 4.30pm. Neighbours remembered seeing him driving up Fifth Helena in his white, open-topped Cadillac convertible.

Eunice Murray greeted Bobby at the door and recalled him as being 'casually dressed, looking almost boyish in slacks and open shirt'. When Marilyn came to the entrance, she formally introduced the pair. 'She did not seem bubbly or excited by his visit as she might have at a romantic interest, just posed and gracious,' Murray recalled in *Marilyn: The Final Months*. Instead of her usual Capri slacks and blouse, Monroe greeted Kennedy in a long, flowing hostess gown. While the actress continued with her tour of the house, Murray returned to her sewing. 'Marilyn loved showing off the house,' Eunice Murray once remarked. 'It was like it was her baby. She was so proud of it. But she didn't go sneaking around with Mr. Kennedy . . .'

By 6pm, Bobby was gone. However, before leaving, he left a message thanking the housekeeper for being so kind in opening the door and for 'greeting him with a warm hello and a smile'. He returned to his base at the Beverly Hills Hotel and checked out the following morning, Thursday 28 June. At 10.30am, he was boarding his plane, American Airlines flight 126, en route to his next destination, Oklahoma City. As he drove away on that hot, sunny afternoon of Wednesday 27 June, he would not see Marilyn again until the afternoon of Saturday 4 August.

Patricia Seaton Lawford informed us in her book that the visit was to 'tell her once and for all to stop contacting his brother, Jack'. But that is chronologically incorrect. As we can see, the chief reason for Bobby's visit that day was to look over the actress's new home, in particular her kitchen. That afternoon's rendezvous between Marilyn and Bobby was, as he saw it, just a meet-up between two new friends. Furthermore, if he had wished to keep his visit to Marilyn's home a secret, he most certainly would not have arrived, as the neighbours recalled seeing him, in an open-topped car.

With this in mind, therefore, we can safely dismiss the numerous other erroneous tales told about the couple. According to past conjecture,

Marilyn's whirlwind, albeit exceedingly fleeting romance with the Attorney General came to a grinding halt on the Fourth of July weekend 1962, while they were attending a party at Peter Lawford's beach house. Bobby and the actress were reportedly seen strolling along the water's edge, hand in hand, like two young, starry-eyed lovers. And, somewhere during that walk, so the story goes, thanks to fears of entrapment by American gangland, Bobby told Marilyn their relationship must cease with immediate effect. As legend would have it, the announcement that she had been ditched by the Attorney General apparently ended her deluded dreams of marrying into the highly revered Kennedy family and aspirations of becoming America's First Lady. Marilyn supposedly retaliated by telling Bobby that she was pregnant with his child.

But, once again, I must take issue with this long-believed scenario. Research shows that whenever the actress had a rendezvous with one or more of the Kennedys, be it a dinner party or special engagement, she always booked an appointment with Agnes M. Flanagan, her personal hairdresser, and the *only* bookings around this period she had with the actress occurred on Saturday 30 June and Friday 6 July. These could only pertain to two events, Marilyn's photographic sessions with George Barris and *Life* magazine respectively. Furthermore, as irrefutable evidence clearly shows, both the actress and the Attorney General were preoccupied elsewhere on Wednesday 4 July: Marilyn with her *Life* magazine interview (which we will focus on shortly); Bobby with the 11th birthday party of his and Ethel's first child, Kathleen Hartington, at the Kennedy compound in Hyannis Port.

So, despite the picture previous Monroe scholars have painted, the best way to describe the liaison between Marilyn and Bobby Kennedy is that they were infrequent dinner party friends and occasional phone buddies but *never* sexually active. As Guthman remarked, 'They never had any dates alone. There was *always* a group around when Marilyn was present.' Washington reporter Andrew Glass, a man who grew to know Bobby very well over the years, echoed these sentiments: 'He really believed in absolute right and wrong and this strict code guided his moral life. In truth, just like any other red-blooded male, RFK just noticed and watched the pretty girls. But he never went beyond that.'

And the most conclusive proof came from Marilyn's friend, Hollywood gossip columnist James Bacon. During a conversation with Bacon, she once remarked, 'I like him [Bobby], but *not* physically.' In truth, it was his mind that appealed to her.

During the morning of Thursday 28 June, the day that Bobby flew to Oklahoma and just hours before she attended another meeting at Fox,

Marilyn once again met up with José Bolaños. He was a visitor to her home on Fifth Helena. However, their time together was brief. After a heated exchange, he soon left and was seen drowning his sorrows over breakfast at the Beverly Wilshire Hotel. With language barriers between the pair clearly a problem, Marilyn's interest in the well-mannered Mexican had completely faded. It would be their last physical encounter, although they would speak on the phone once more, in early July, and on Monday 13 August he would visit her grave. Coincidentally, sitting near Bolaños at the Beverly Wilshire that morning, in a booth quietly drinking a cup of coffee, was Joe DiMaggio.

It has been reported by several Monroe scholars that on Friday 29 June, she accepted Frank Sinatra's invitation to travel up to his Cal-Neva Lodge for the weekend on the pretence of discussing further their upcoming film projects. But, once again, that is untrue. On that day, Monroe actually began her second lengthy, three-day photo session, this time with freelance snapper George Barris, the plans for which had been drawn up the previous Sunday, 24 June, during a face-to-face encounter at the actress's home.

The two had first crossed paths in New York in the autumn of 1954, when Barris was assigned to take photographs of the actress on the set of *The Seven Year Itch*. On Tuesday 9 November that year, alongside 4,000 thousand other star-struck onlookers, he stood outside the Trans-Lux Theater, situated at 52nd Street and Lexington Avenue, and watched as Marilyn repeatedly shot the sequence in which her white skirt was blown high above her ears. Monroe and Barris's friendship was cemented several days later at a thank-you party for those employed on the movie. He sat with her as she desperately tried to contact her husband, Joe DiMaggio, who had flown back to California in disgust following the shooting of the skirt-blowing scene. Marilyn tearfully confided in Barris how lonely she was. 'We became friends instantly,' he recalled. She enjoyed his company immensely and was captivated by him further when he promised to introduce her to reclusive actress Greta Garbo. 'She became speechless and wide-eyed with excitement,' he recalled.

The session also provided an opportunity for Monroe and Barris to resume work on her autobiography. Following ten weeks of intermittent discussions, beginning on Friday 1 June, when he dropped by the set of *Something's Got To Give* to wish her a happy birthday, she had finally decided to set the record straight about her colourful life. In the 1987 book *Marilyn* by Barris and Gloria Steinem, the actress is recorded as remarking to the photographer, 'Lies, lies, lies, everything they've been saying about me are lies . . . This is *the* first true story; you're the first one I've told it to.' She intended to tell Barris everything: her childhood, career, marriages and divorces. No stone would be left unturned. She also spoke optimistically about resuming work on *Something's Got To Give*. 'I hope we can continue . . . It can be a great picture. I know it can and so does everyone else. But all I can do is wait until they let me know.'

Intended for *Cosmopolitan* magazine, the first two days of the shoot took place at 1506 Blue Jay Way, in the Bird Streets area of Los Angeles. The spacious, four-bedroom, 3,891-square-foot home had been completed by San Francisco-born property magnate Walter H. 'Tim' Leimert just weeks before the session took place and, despite its furnishings, was actually still uninhabited. During the stint, Marilyn paraded in front of a mirror, lounged on a settee and sprawled across a bed. The future owner's housekeeper, Louise, who allowed them access to the property, was pleased to meet the actress. 'Are you really Marilyn Monroe?' she asked. 'I can't believe it.' 'Well, I can't believe it too,' the film star replied. 'I guess I am. Everybody says I am.' At the tail end of the day, location moved to the quiet street outside, where Marilyn posed behind the wheel of a car.

On Sunday 1 July, the third day of the shoot, the location shifted to Peter Lawford's beachside home in Santa Monica. The image of Marilyn standing on a balcony at the house, champagne glass in hand, toasting the ocean, would become one of the shoot's most memorable. As Barris recalled for the *Daily Mirror* in August 1962, 'Champagne was a symbol to her. Every time she had a glass she was saying to herself, "Here's to the future." The champagne girl drank nothing else. Zest for living. That is what Marilyn had in the last nine weeks that led to her death.' Her optimism was a recurring theme throughout the session. 'The happiest time of my life is now,' she excitedly declared. 'As far as I'm concerned, there's a future and I can't wait to get to it.'

With a chill filling the air and dark clouds beginning to punctuate the skies, the session concluded on the deserted beach. Sporting a tangerine-coloured bikini, and with Pat Newcomb watching on, the actress bravely cavorted in the cold sea and even fooled around with some dead seaweed. While she laughed, Barris excitedly clicked away. Marilyn even suggested some of the shots and angles. 'It was as if Marilyn Monroe was directing Marilyn Monroe,' he said. He handed her a beach towel and instructed her to do something with it. At once, she wrapped it around her, snuggled her chin into it and pulled a face at him. She kept running into the water until Barris protested she was going out too far. 'Oh, take your shoes off,' she shouted. At once he followed her command, rolled up his trousers and waded into the water to continue taking pictures.

Satisfied with the images he had captured, Barris and Monroe slowly paddled their way back up to the beach. When they reached it, he discovered that one of his shoes was missing. It had been carried away by the tide. 'What can you do with only one shoe?' she humorously asked. In response, he picked up his remaining shoe and threw it into the sea. Catching sight of this, Marilyn laughed, held aloft a glass of champagne and remarked, 'Well, you can't take it with you.' With the temperature now icy, the actress put on a short, light blue terry-cloth hooded bath robe. Observing the events from her own beachside property was Hollywood legend Mae West. Although keen to meet Marilyn, she failed to walk over and introduce herself to the actress.

As the sun went down, an increasingly chilly wind began to permeate the air and Marilyn reached for her thick, hand-knitted Mexican jumper. She also draped a blanket over her knees. The session had reached its conclusion. 'She stayed out there posing and working for hours,' Barris recalled in 1962. 'She was so cold that she was actually shivering. That was a pro.' He finished by asking Marilyn what she wanted out of life more than anything. 'I want to have children,' she responded. 'I used to feel that for every child I had, I would adopt another . . . But I don't think a single person should adopt children. There's no Ma or Pas there and I know what that can be like.'

Although the actress was tired and her teeth were beginning to chatter, she still posed for him one last time. It was now 8.30pm. 'Just one more shot,' he pleaded. 'I have got one left. It will be the last one.' With a smirk, she replied, 'I have heard that before.' She pursed her lips and blew a kiss at the photographer. 'OK, George,' she said, 'and it's just for you.'

Shortly after the session, on Wednesday 18 July, Barris dropped by Marilyn's home in Fifth Helena to show her the fruits of their labour. Sitting barefoot on the floor, for five straight hours she scrutinised each and every one of his images under a magnifying glass. To the ones she endorsed, she was heard to say, 'Yes, that's me,' affirming this by scribbling the word 'Good' over the top. The ones she didn't, she defaced with a large 'X', again made with a thick red marker pen. After perusing closely every one of the pictures, Marilyn looked at Barris and told him, 'I'm in your hands now, I trust you.' 'Don't worry,' he reassuringly replied. 'I'll never hurt you.'

Before exiting the bungalow, Monroe curiously admitted she had no regrets with her life. 'If I've made any mistakes,' she declared, 'I was responsible.' She added, 'There is now and there is the future. What's happened is behind . . . As far as I am concerned, there *is* a future and I cannot wait to get to it. It should be very interesting.' Barris bid his farewell and departed to the strains of the Judy Garland song 'Who Cares', which was blaring out of Marilyn's record player.

By the opening week of July, the actress's newfound optimism was running freely through her body and, for the first time in a long while, she was genuinely excited about her future. This became evident when, early in the month, following seven weeks of discussions with Pat Newcomb, she finally arranged a date to be interviewed by *Life* magazine's associate editor, Richard Meryman.

The notion of being taken seriously in such a highly regarded magazine appealed to her immensely. She warmed further to the piece when she was informed that it was not to be one of their regular Hollywood glamour-type assignments. Set to be called 'Marilyn Lets Her Hair Down About Being Famous', the objective of Meryman's expansive, down-to-earth piece was to capture and embed Monroe's personality deep in the pages of the magazine. As the publication's photographer, Allan Grant, recalled, *Life* wanted 'Marilyn *without* the Monroe attached'. It was a superb idea but, as usual in publishing, time was of the essence. Since actor Cary Grant, the original choice of subject for the magazine, had declined their request, Marilyn's spread was already being earmarked for the Friday 3 August edition.

On Wednesday 4 July, and with time running out fast, work on the article hastily got under way when Meryman arrived at the actress's home in Fifth Helena. As he admitted, his heart was pounding and he did not know what to expect from her. Having been met at the door by Eunice Murray, he entered the premises to find Pat Newcomb inside. 'The house was saturated in paranoia,' he later recalled for the 1965 book, *The Tragic Venus*. Meryman reeled back in shock at the sight of a virtually empty living room. There was nothing in it except for a couple of chairs. He placed his tape recorder on the floor and knelt down in front of it trying to make it work. Suddenly, in front of him, he saw yellow Capri slacks and heard a voice saying, 'Is there anything I can do to help?' It was Marilyn.

Meryman admitted he found her extremely likeable and very smart, but not in the slightest bit sexy. He didn't find her particularly attractive either, largely down to, as he put it, her 'large head and jaw'. But he *was* enchanted by her, especially her innocence. In an unprecedented move for an interviewee, in order to prepare for the session, the actress had requested Meryman's questions in advance. As the discussion unfurled, she displayed her full range of emotions – rage, wit, bravado, kindness and unhappiness – and discussed her childhood, films, Hollywood, fame, ambitions, dreams and ideas as effortlessly as she had ever done. It was an insight not accorded to anyone but her closest friends. But, despite this, Meryman still sensed she was suspicious of him and was walking on eggshells throughout. 'I really felt that she needed to control the interview,' he recalled in another interview. 'She wanted to be in control of it, you know, on top of the situation. And she was!'

In a June 2001 interview for CNN's *Larry King Live* show, Meryman recalled, 'The minute Marilyn started talking, I knew instantly that I wanted to reproduce her words like a monologue on the page. She talked with just this tremendous gusto, images tumbling over each other, sometimes not making a lot of sense . . . I felt that she was terribly vulnerable, terribly needy, terribly distrustful. She felt betrayed right and left. She felt betrayed by her friends.'

At a suitable point in the discussion, the actress suggested she should go into her kitchen and cook a steak for them both. But when she peered into her refrigerator, she found that it was completely bereft of food. Eunice Murray had, once more, omitted to do the household shopping. With no sustenance forthcoming, Monroe proceeded to give Meryman a guided tour of her home and outlined her plans for it. She also proudly showed off her garden, which was now blooming with a wide range of multi-coloured flowers. Back inside, the champagne continued to flow and Meryman's interview resumed. The actress spoke about the way businessmen and others misunderstood the actor, adding that actors and actresses were not machines, as so many people thought, and that a performance depended on many factors.

When the conversation began to drift away from this most interesting subject, Meryman attempted to bring it back. 'Now, what was it like, confidentially, when Marilyn was cranking up for a scene?' he innocently asked. But the actress was unimpressed with the query. She froze and the room became icy. 'I don't crank anything,' she screamed. 'I'm not a Model T. Excuse me but I think that's kind of disrespectful to refer to it that way. I'm trying to work as an art form, not in a manufacturing establishment.' Meryman apologised for his ill-conceived joke and she accepted it. But the frostiness remained and he was forced to reconsider any subsequent inappropriate jokes or questions.

A 30-minute telephone call from her *Something's Got To Give* co-star, Wally Cox, punctuated the first day's session. One from Joe DiMaggio interrupted the second. When it came, Marilyn shouted to Murray, 'If it's an Italian, tell him I'm not here.' Her doctor, Hyman Engelberg, was a visitor to the house that second day. Entering via the key secreted in the fuschia pot by the front door, he had arrived to administer a $25 liver injection.

Following two days (and over eight hours) of interviewing, the lengthy session was over. Marilyn clinched it by curiously remarking, 'Fame will go by and, so long, I've had you, fame. If it goes by, I've always known it was fickle. So at least it's something I experienced, but that's not where I live.' The banter concluded with a request from the actress, '*Please* don't make me a joke.' The actress walked Meryman to the door and said goodbye. As he walked down the driveway, he turned back and glanced back at Marilyn, who was still standing in the doorway. Noticing his action, she waved and called, 'Hey, thanks.'

Meryman immediately headed back to New York to type up the piece. 'I only think she did the piece to get her voice out in the world,' he recalled in 1986. 'She had just been fired from Fox and she wanted her side told.' In the 1992 television programme *Marilyn: The Last Interview*, he most tellingly remarked, 'I never saw *any* sign that this was a woman giving her last interview, on the verge of committing suicide.'

Set to arrive at 2pm, *Life*'s photographer Allan Grant arrived 15 minutes early at Fifth Helena on the afternoon of Friday 6 July. (Contrary to the widely held belief, the session did not take place on the Saturday.) He thought arriving before the allotted time was a good idea since the magazine was expecting a roll of his 'Marilyn-at-home' snaps to be on board a flight to New York later this evening.

Once inside the actress's bungalow, he was introduced to Pat Newcomb, make-up artist Allan Snyder and Eunice Murray. Marilyn, meanwhile, was in another room, being attended to by her hairdresser, Agnes Flanagan. Grant immediately set to work loading his cameras and positioning his lights. Tasks completed, he sat and waited for his subject to appear. Approximately 20 minutes passed before Marilyn appeared, sporting a bathrobe and clutching an obligatory glass of champagne. The actress was visibly far from ready and Grant naturally began fearing he was going to miss his already tight airplane deadline.

Monroe immediately offered Grant a glass of champagne, which he accepted. The two began discussing what she should wear for the photographs. He instructed her to dress casually. With these thoughts mulling around in her mind, she left to prepare with Snyder and Flanagan in tow. About 25 minutes later she reappeared in her obligatory tight-fitting Capri pants and a dark V-neck sweater. 'There was nothing about her that reminded me of the lush, laughing Marilyn Monroe of the big screen,' Grant later recalled. 'To me, she seemed somewhat thinner and much more fragile than I expected . . . I detected sadness about her. She had become the Marilyn they [*Life*] asked for.'

The photographic session began. Grant captured the actress's expressions at the article's questions, which Newcomb read out aloud. During the brief shoot, Marilyn perched herself on the arm of her antique chair in front of the sunlit window, inadvertently piercing its lime-green fabric with her stiletto heel as she did so, and at one point playfully hung from one of the beams on the ceiling to show how she used to hang from a tree as a youngster while the boys looked on.

The frivolity ended when the actress became concerned with the lights

Grant had put up in the room. 'She asked me if the light was OK,' he recalled, 'and I said, "To tell you the truth, this is the first time I've done a portrait and I don't really know where the lights should be."' He was joking. But Marilyn did not realise this. She was horrified and began to panic. Noticing her distress, Newcomb swiftly interjected by saying, 'For God's sake, Allan, don't fool with Marilyn that way.'

Grant apologised – 'It's a joke,' he announced, 'I'm sorry' – and the session continued. Within two hours of its start, as planned, Grant's film was on board an airplane heading for New York.

A copy of the completed *Life* article was sent for Marilyn's approval on Saturday 14 July. Aside from quotes which referred to her clandestine donations to disadvantaged individuals and lines which she feared might upset her stepchildren, she gave her thumbs-up to the piece the following day. As her sister Berniece remarked, Marilyn described the interview as her most 'accurate and gratifying'. (As scheduled, the article appeared in the edition published on Friday 3 August.) As a preview to the piece inside, the words 'Marilyn Monroe Pours Her Heart Out' appeared on the magazine's front cover. Strangely, a picture of the actress did not; instead, this honour went to Major Bob White of the US Air Force and his son, Greg.

As July progressed, the actress oversaw more decorating work and happily devoured some recently received film scripts. She also found time to see Ralph Greenson on an almost daily basis, not merely for counselling but also for companionship. Despite her newfound optimism, loneliness was still an immense problem. Sessions at the doctor's home in nearby North Roxbury Drive would usually last a minimum of 90 minutes; those when the doctor visited the actress's home two hours. (Despite being seen by Marilyn as a friend, his charge to the actress was still $50 an hour.) Between Sunday 1 July and Saturday 4 August he saw her a total of 28 times.

She also spent some of this time in and around the vicinity of Sunset Boulevard. On one such visit, during the afternoon of Wednesday 11 July, she bumped into an old acquaintance, Hollywood show business reporter David Lewin, who remarked, 'She was wearing firmly fitting white slacks and a loose purple top. She had come into town unexpectedly in her white, chauffeur-driven convertible to do some shopping for lunch.' (In fact, though Lewin was obviously unaware of this, the actress was there to do some shopping and to purchase items for her next meeting with Fox, which was set to take place at the studio the following day.)

When he asked for an update about her seemingly floundering film career, Marilyn paused for a moment before announcing, 'I am ready to go back to work quickly, but I'm prepared to face lawsuits or almost anything else that may happen to me. I'm flexible and I can go it alone. My philosophy is still, "Enjoy the day" and the only difference between now and the last time we met is that I am single again and I have to enjoy the day alone. No, I'm not sad about it. After all, you can be alone, even with a husband.'

Marilyn was extremely relaxed and eager to talk off-the-cuff with an old friend, and after a brief interlude when the actress had to dash off to pick up chopped liver from the nearby delicatessen, she was more than willing to resume their conversation. Lewin continued by asking her about the Hollywood star system and the executives' well-used phrase, 'the inmates have taken over the asylum'. She replied, 'I don't understand the line. It is just some incompetent executive seeing how daring a slogan he can find.'

Obviously angered by the question, she continued, 'The public makes a star. The studios made the system. I don't lose any sleep over what is said. I lost sleep over much more important things like the H-bomb long before this.' She paused for a moment before saying, 'An actor isn't a system. I just have me and I carry my ability wherever I go. I can work anywhere there is a part to play. I'd like to come back to England. What I do is to try to keep informed and up to date and learn about life. I do not rush, which is maybe why I'm late a few times. You rush and you just run yourself down. That's why I like being in my thirties. It's so much better than being in the rushing twenties.'

The conversation concluded when she remarked, philosophically and cryptically, 'I don't go in for this entire American pace. I take my time and I try to care and take effort about things. I take care to be a human being. *That* is important, *not* being a human being.'

One day later, on Thursday 12 July, Fox summoned Marilyn to a second official meeting to discuss her reinstatement on *Something's Got To Give*. The actress arrived at the studio to be greeted by the sight of the lot still resembling a ghost town. Just one of the studio's 16 sound stages was occupied, for the shooting of the new Joanne Newman movie, *A Woman Of July* (a film originally intended for Monroe when, at the start of 1961, it was called *Celebration*). No one could disguise the fact that the studio was in decline, its glory days seemingly behind it.

In the build-up to the 3.30pm conference, Monroe called on Sydney Guilaroff and Allan 'Whitey' Snyder to create a startling, severe look for her. Dressed in a conservative, beige Norman Norell dress and horn-rimmed spectacles, the actress turned up looking the antithesis of America's dumbest blonde. It worked. She walked away from the meeting with a verbally agreed $1,000,000 deal; $500,000 to complete *Something's*

Got To Give and a further $500,000 for one additional movie. The long-mooted musical comedy, *What a Way to Go* (also known as *I Love Louisa*), featuring production by Marilyn's publicist Arthur P. Jacobs, was the leading contender.

As she anticipated, provisos were to be inserted into the pact. Fox demanded that Paula Strasberg and Pat Newcomb be banned from the set of *Something's Got To Give* and Ralph Greenson be excised as her negotiator on the movie. In addition, they insisted that she relinquish all rights to her say as to the director, cameramen and co-stars employed on the picture. Their demands did not end there. Insistences that she give up her rights to script approval and desires to view the 'dailies' were also heaped upon her.

However, aware that it *was* after all included in her December 1955 contract with the studio, Marilyn shrewdly counteracted by exercising her right of director approval, insisting that George Cukor be supplanted by Romanian-born Jean Negulesco. (The latter had successfully directed her in the 1953 smash *How to Marry a Millionaire*.) An agreement to tailor the screenplay to meet her specifications was also begrudgingly approved by the studio.

There was one final proviso up Fox's sleeves. They wanted Marilyn to sign a highly embarrassing, pre-prepared public apology letter. On Tuesday 10 July, two days before the meeting, at the behest of Charles Enfield and Phil Feldman, the heads of promotion and business relations at the studio respectively, one of the secretaries in the legal and publicity department typed a grovelling admission-of-guilt note from the actress, in which she apparently acknowledged her 'barbiturate habit' and begged for 'forgiveness' for her 'tardiness and lack of discipline' during the previous period of filming. Realising the intensive nature of it, on Sunday 22 July Fox publicist Jack Brodsky drafted a second, less austere note of excuse. (Although it still resides on microfilm in the 20th Century-Fox archives, it was highly doubtful that Monroe was ever made aware of this rather malicious piece of underhanded spin-doctoring.)

The meeting came to a pleasant conclusion when it was announced that all lawsuits between Fox and Marilyn would be dropped. A major point in Fox's decision to re-employ the actress had been her refusal to name the studio specifically in any of her newspaper outbursts. This loyalty impressed them. But for the actress, aside from the improved pay offer, she had now received from the studio and the industry what she really craved . . . respect.

Marilyn was now spectacularly happy. Two days later, on Saturday 14 July, her rush of optimism was once again evident when she sent a telegram to Ralph Greenson to acknowledge his wedding anniversary. It read: 'Dear Dr. Greenson: I hope all your roses are in bloom today including the blackest red ones. Happy Anniversary to you and Mrs. Greenson. Marilyn.' As recent events demonstrated, she was buoyant and evidently in complete control of her career. Work around her house was also progressing. On that day, reminded by her associates that the locks on the filing cabinet in her cottage were still not functioning, the actress called locksmith Austin A. Innis, of 6919 North Figueroa Street. (At a cost of $71.55, his employee, Edward P. Halavaty, carried out the repair three days later, on Tuesday 17 July.)

Marilyn spent the remainder of the month in and around Los Angeles. That much is true. However, several substantial inconsistencies have arisen in the various accounts of this brief period of the actress's life, which I am now able to clear up.

To begin with, there is biographer Donald Spoto's claim that, on Sunday 15 July, she travelled to Palm Springs in the company of her old friend and confidant, the newspaper columnist and movie producer Sidney Skolsky, to discuss a movie based on the life of screen legend Jean Harlow with the late actress's mother, 'Mother Jean' Harlow Carpenter Bello.

This visit simply could not have taken place. Harlow senior had passed away, aged 67, four years earlier, on Saturday 7 June 1958, precisely 21 years after and in the very same hospital as her daughter. Furthermore, the chances of Marilyn appearing in a movie such as this in 1962 were extremely slim. By this time, the idea of producing *The Jean Harlow Story* was already ten years old. First mooted in March 1952, stories about it had reverberated around the industry for years. Marilyn first became aware of the project one month later when she was informed about it by top Hollywood columnist Louella Parsons, who just happened to be the author of the 1937 publication *Jean Harlow's Life Story*. In June 1954, Fox announced they would settle for no one else but Monroe in the lead role and even offered her a slice of the profits if she accepted the part. She didn't.

Work on the project started afresh in late November 1957, when the great Hollywood scriptwriter (and Marilyn's original biographer) Ben Hecht began penning a new version of the screenplay. But, contrary to the belief of some Monroe biographers, and despite the fact she was a big fan of the star, she wasn't keen on appearing in the project. As she remarked to the movie's intended producer, Jerry Wald, in 1958, she wanted to star in the 20th Century-Fox film *Blue Angel* first. (She would ultimately lose out in the role as Lola-Lola to Sammy Davis Jr's future wife, May Britt. The story of screen legend Jean Harlow would eventually hit the cinema screens in July 1965 as the Paramount picture *Harlow*, starring Carroll Baker.)

What's more, the suggestion that the actress was still seeing Sidney Skolsky in 1962 is highly implausible. The two parted company in less than amicable circumstances in December 1954, just weeks before Marilyn flew out of Los Angeles en route to New York where she was about to embark on a new life and, on Friday 7 January 1955, launch her new company, Marilyn Monroe Productions. This void in the actress's life was soon filled by her new business partner, photographer Milton H. Greene.

The second and possibly more damaging lie told about Marilyn at this period of her life concerns Friday 20 July, when it is claimed she spent three days in Miami's Cedars of Lebanon Hospital and apparently left, looking wan and exhausted, four days later, on Tuesday 24 July. Many of her so-called confidants hinted that she checked into the hospital under an assumed name and was there to abort President Kennedy's (or Bobby's) baby. Author Fred Lawrence Guiles originated the myth in his 1969 book, *Norma Jean: The Life of Marilyn Monroe*, when he wrote,

> Marilyn discovered she was pregnant. Those few who knew Marilyn's secret were horrified. While friends were told that Marilyn had gone for a long weekend to Lake Tahoe, she was secretly hospitalised on Friday, July 20 in Cedars of Lebanon Hospital, and remained there for four days . . .

A surgical termination of pregnancy was decided upon by a doctor on the Cedars' staff. The pregnancy was tubular, as was her first pregnancy with Miller, and could not have gone beyond its fifth or sixth week without the gravest complications.

It is highly likely that the instigator of the malicious abortion rumour was an employee of Arthur Jacobs.

According to other sources, on Thursday 19 July Monroe slipped away from her friends and colleagues and did not reappear until three days later. Hollywood gossip columnists at the time insinuated that she had 'slipped into LA's Cedars of Lebanon hospital to abort Robert [Kennedy]'s child'. In another story, allegedly picked up from illicit tapes recorded in her house, Marilyn was accompanied across the border to Mexico – since abortion was still illegal in America at the time – for the termination by an unnamed 'American doctor'.

While it is true that Marilyn was angry with JFK (and later became so with Bobby) for dispensing with her, the same cannot be said about her aborted pregnancy. The sad truth is that, on Saturday 21 July, Monroe *was* admitted to the Cedars-Sinai Medical Center (as it was correctly called at the time), but only for treatment for endometriosis, a common disease affecting an estimated 89 million women of reproductive age around the world and occurring in one in every five females, but one which often causes severe pelvic pain, irregular menstrual bleeding, infertility and sometimes bowel and bladder symptoms. The ailment was said to have developed as a result of the 12 abortions she was rumoured to have had when she was a starlet starting out in Hollywood, a period when the studios felt they had complete and utter ownership of their stars – although, according to Leon Kohn, a doctor at the Cedars-Sinai Medical Center, and a medic to Frank Sinatra, she did not even have *one*.

As we know, however, the actress did spend much of her short life in chronic pain, suffering miscarriages and becoming addicted to painkillers; moreover, the condition would have severely impaired her chances of becoming a mother. For example, in August 1957, she suffered an ectopic pregnancy, which occurs when the fertilised egg attaches itself outside the cavity of the uterus (womb). She suffered a new miscarriage one year later, in 1958. (In his 2009 biography, *The Making of Some Like It Hot*, the actor, Tony Curtis, Marilyn's co-star in the 1959 movie of the same name, sensationally claimed this baby was his.) However hard Marilyn tried, medical evidence proved that she could not successfully carry a child for most or all of the full nine-month duration and the chances of her doing so in 1962, at the age of 36, were very remote indeed.

One Marilyn book even claimed that she went into Cedars for a 'D & C' (Dilatation and Curettage), a procedure to scrape and collect the tissue (endometrium) from inside the uterus, used both as a means of ameliorating certain gynaecological conditions and as a method of abortion. The same publication claimed that Eunice Murray was oblivious to why the actress had been hospitalised and that 'Marilyn called Bobby (from her home) to report everything had gone as planned and that the pregnancy was terminated.'

With such matters to discuss, it's safe to assume that any conversation between the two at the time would have been a lengthy one. But not according to the actress's phone records. The only date near her departure from the hospital on which Monroe called the Attorney General was Monday 23 July and the duration of the call was just *one* minute. So, if not to talk about the termination of her pregnancy, why did she contact him?

Well, on that day, between 3pm and 3.30pm, President Kennedy faced a press conference at the Department of State Auditorium. Parts of the event were relayed to the UK and Europe via the orbiting Telstar satellite which, just 13 days earlier, had been launched by NASA from Cape Canaveral in Florida. Since this was the first live transatlantic television signal from the United States to the UK, it was naturally a momentous event. History was being made in front of every viewer's eyes, including those of Marilyn, who watched the transmission from her living room at Fifth Helena. Without doubt, the call she placed to Bobby that day was to excitedly speak to him about his brother's ground-breaking address.

In any case, he wasn't there. He was away with his family at his summer house in Hyannis Port. (Pictures of him water-skiing with the First Lady appeared in many of the following day's newspapers.) Instead, the actress once again found herself conversing with his secretary, Angie Novello.

The question still remains, what exactly happened to the actress that weekend? Working from original letters, notes and invoices, I can now lay to rest the lies about her alleged termination and reveal her precise activities during that five-day period.

On the morning of Thursday 19 July, clearly feeling homesick, Marilyn began the day by authorising a three-month subscription to *The New York Times* (both daily and Sunday editions). Afterwards, she was driven to see Ralph Greenson at his North Roxbury Drive home. Later that afternoon, she hosted a special birthday dinner party in honour of his daughter, Joan. (It was the only time that Marilyn's home would host such an event.) Later that evening, no doubt because she knew she would be elsewhere on Saturday, Marilyn received her regular weekly massage from Ralph Roberts. A day later, on Friday 20 July, the actress once more visited Greenson at his home for another 90-minute counselling session.

In the company of Joe DiMaggio, during the morning of Saturday 21 July, Monroe travelled to the Cedars-Sinai Medical Center in Los Angeles, where she was admitted to receive treatment for endometriosis. But she left just hours later, and spent the remainder of that day and the whole of the following one recuperating at her home on Fifth Helena. On Monday 23 July, she was visited at her home by both Greenson and Dr Hyman Engelberg (who administered two anaemia injections: one costing $20, the other $10). Later that day, after watching Kennedy's speech, the actress felt well enough to pay another visit to Greenson. She was driven there by Eunice Murray. It's therefore clear that Marilyn did not stay in the Cedars hospital for up to four days. Four *hours* was the most likely duration.

However, there is still an element of truth to be found among the stories about her final month. For instance, in the last weekend of July, Marilyn *did* pay a visit to Frank Sinatra's Cal-Neva lodge.

Built in 1926 by the wealthy businessmen Robert Pierce Sherman and Harry O. Comstock on the beautiful north shore of Lake Tahoe, in the picturesque lakefront community of Crystal Bay, the Cal-Neva was so-called because the dividing border between California and Nevada runs through the middle of the property. As Sinatra himself once joked, 'It's the only place where you can walk across the lobby and get locked up for violating the Mann Act.'

The retreat, located high in the mountains, began life as both a guest harbour and an illegal gambling joint. Its unlawful activities were short-lived, however when, just a few years later, in March 1931, it obtained one of the first casino licences and subsequently became a desirable attraction for A-list celebrities and the wealthy alike.

Having been rebuilt after its destruction by fire in 1937, the status of the venue was elevated a notch further when, in September 1960, American singing sensation Frank Sinatra purchased a substantial share in the resort. (In August 1960, at a cost of $100,000, Nevada State records show that he owned a 25 per cent stake in the operation. One year later, on Tuesday 15 August 1961, his stake in the premises had increased to 35.6 per cent and by Tuesday 15 May 1962, his interest had risen to 50 per cent.) The first public declaration about Frank's involvement in the Cal-Neva came on Wednesday 13 July 1960. On the day that John F. Kennedy won the Democratic nomination in Los Angeles, papers announced that Sinatra, along with his Rat Pack buddy Dean Martin, pal and business partner Hank Sincola and convicted white slaver Paul 'Skinny' D'Amato had applied for permission from the State of Nevada to take over the running of the establishment. They soon got their wish.

However, a fact omitted from official reports was that the Chicago mobster Sam Giancana and his outfit had also acquired a small slice of it. By the time the news reached the papers, sensing trouble was in the air and after realizing the extent of Giancana's involvement, Martin had wisely withdrawn his interests and distanced himself from both the project and the mobster.

It was a prudent move. Before the age of 20, the Mafioso leader had already been quizzed about three separate murders. Killing was not a problem for Giancana and his intimidating demeanour upset many people. In 1999, the former Chicago police detective, Chuck Adamson, spoke for many when he remarked, 'Sam Giancana was the lowest form of human being . . . He was a little, mousey, rat-looking bum.' However, as George Jacobs noted in his excellent 2003 biography *Mr S.: My Life With Frank Sinatra*, 'Marilyn had total respect for Sam, and he always treated her like a lady. To her, Sam was no fearsome killer figure . . . She liked him a lot.'

Because he was listed in the State of Nevada's black book of persons forbidden to enter a casino, Giancana's involvement in the new operation was, naturally, kept under wraps. Owing to the fact he couldn't even be seen *driving* through Las Vegas, he would be forced to arrive at the Cal-Neva in a helicopter; Sinatra therefore constructed a landing pad for one on the building's roof.

Even before Sinatra's involvement, the place had a history. In the mid-to late 1950s, the President's father, Joseph, had supplied liquor to a previous owner, receiving hospitality for himself and his family in return. Now Sinatra wanted to create a warm and welcoming environment in which he could entertain his friends and attract customers who wanted to sample his affluent lifestyle. The venue would become a Mecca for gamblers, gangsters and entertainers alike – major stars, many of whom, his close personal friends, were booked into the new Celebrity Showroom. It was Sinatra's own piece of paradise, a private world awash with ample supplies of girls, gambling and booze. It was also a venue bereft of rules.

Sinatra's Rat Pack acquaintances were, naturally, frequent visitors. However, regardless of claims that she and the Kennedys stayed so frequently, they were presented with their very own cabins (Monroe's apparently being chalet 3, originally numbered 52; John's and Bobby's numbers 1 and 2 respectively), Marilyn Monroe visited the Cal-Neva only occasionally – and, as we saw in Chapter 4, neither JFK nor his brother ever went there at all.

At the Cal-Neva's opening night on Tuesday 20 September 1960, Sinatra's guests supposedly included Joe Kennedy and his son John. In fact, not only did JFK never visit the establishment, but Kennedy senior's only verified travels there came during the summers of 1957 and 1958. Marilyn, though, *was* present, along with the mobster Johnny Rosselli. Unsought and secreted up in the hills surrounding the casino that night were men from J. Edgar Hoover's FBI.

Over the intervening years, we've been reliably informed that the chief reason for Monroe's visit to the Cal-Neva during that final weekend in July 1962 was because Bobby Kennedy was in Los Angeles on business and wanted the actress well out of the way. Previous Monroe authors have added to the myth by announcing that, during that three-day period, '[Bobby's] speech to the National Insurance Association was broadcast on all three television networks.' Meanwhile Louis McWillie, an outfit-related gambler who worked for Sinatra at the Cal-Neva, remarked, 'There was more to what happened up there than anybody has ever told. It would have been a big fall for Bobby Kennedy.' Another Marilyn scholar confidently announced that Marilyn's weekend trip to Lake Tahoe was to 'ensure her silence about the Kennedys' and that 'Robert Kennedy was a guest at the Cal-Neva that weekend and was hurriedly secreted out when activities that weekend turned decidedly repulsive.'

In fact these claims are entirely unsubstantiated. The Attorney General did *not* pass the weekend of Friday 27 to Sunday 29 July in Los Angeles. He actually spent that period, at the very least, 2,591 miles away in the company of his brother John at the White House and with the rest of the Kennedy clan in Hyannis Port, where on Sunday 29 July they celebrated the birthday of America's First Lady, Jacqueline Kennedy. Such was the importance of the day, she even posed for her first official White House portrait. That weekend was a true family affair. As *The New York Post* reported, 'A flock of Kennedys got together today for a birthday celebration – the 33rd for First Lady, Jacqueline. The family made arrangements for a party tonight after taking it easy yesterday, aboard boat and water skis, at the scene of many Kennedy reunions.' Later that evening, Jacqueline's birthday was celebrated at a sumptuous dinner party. It is inconceivable that, as some previous Monroe biographers have claimed, Bobby would fail to show at such an important Kennedy family event.

True, Bobby had spent some in Los Angeles that week. On Thursday 26 July, shortly after his 5am arrival in the city, he made a speech at the National Insurance Association and took up residence in room 227 at the Beverly Hills Hotel. But his stay was suspended by an anonymous call that had come through to the Los Angeles office of the FBI, in which plans to assassinate him were announced. The Attorney General hastily flew out of the city at 9am on Friday 27 July, and headed back to Washington. Presidential diaries clearly demonstrate that, later that morning, Bobby was in attendance at a 10.25am US arms control meeting at the White House. His only appointment during that birthday party weekend was on the morning of Saturday 28 July, when he attended a 9.30am White House meeting with the Department of Justice's Assistant Attorney General, Nicholas de Belleville Katzenbach. Working from this information, it is quite clear that the suggestion that Marilyn was ushered out of Los Angeles to the Cal-Neva simply because Bobby wanted her out of the way is entirely erroneous. The Attorney General had left Los Angeles a good two days before the actress set foot in Lake Tahoe.

It was actually for three reasons that Marilyn chose to visit the lodge that weekend. First, she naturally wanted to celebrate her revised, much-improved 20th Century-Fox contract. Her updated agreement with the studio was currently being prepared and was due to be delivered to her attorney's office in three days' time, on Wednesday 1 August.

Second, it provided an ideal time to catch up again with Dean Martin, who was headlining in Cal-Neva's biggest room, the plush and elegant Celebrity Showroom. There has been much confusion about who exactly was performing at the lodge that weekend. It was even suggested in one Marilyn book that singer Jack Jones (or even Frank Sinatra) was the Cal-Neva's main attraction. Examination of the club's concert calendar for this period, however, confirms that it *was* Dean Martin. His residency began on Friday 27 July and concluded on Thursday 2 August.

Knowing that he was performing at the venue, Marilyn thought it was the perfect time to travel there to show him the new, hot-off-the press *Something's Got To Give* screenplay, which had been completed by the veteran variety writer Hal Kanter on Wednesday 25 July. A bound edition was hand-delivered to Fox vice-president Peter Levathes two days later, during the morning of Friday 27 July. Immediately after receiving it, he excitedly drove out to Marilyn's home in Brentwood to hand it over to her. With shooting of the problematic *Cleopatra* finally finishing on Tuesday 24 July, Fox were keen to resume Monroe's movie as soon as possible. Plans to recommence it on Monday 23 July were even optimistically discussed. But with interruptions still blighting the picture, it was a short-lived scheme. However, delays this time were not down to the actress; they were due to Martin.

Before starting work on his next movie, the United Artists production *Toys in the Attic*, and although his six-month commitment to *Something's Got To Give* did not officially end until Monday 17 September, he had signed up for an interim booking on the lucrative night-club circuit, of which his Cal-Neva appearances were a part. (Recently uncovered documents reveal that Martin had actually planned to delay restarting Marilyn's movie until the opening week of 1963, or at the very latest, February. When Fox discovered he was unavailable, the studio became impatient and began toying with the idea of replacing him. According to Hollywood gossip columnist Earl Wilson, the name of Paul Newman was even touted.)

When Monroe was informed of the new script, no doubt by way of a phone call from the studio on the morning of 25 July (the day that Darryl F. Zanuck was elected the new president of Fox), apprehension began to set in. The thought that she would soon be returning to work, with a new boss to answer to, horrified her. Paula Strasberg was hastily summoned from New York and a reservation at the nearby Bel Air Sands Hotel was immediately made for her. An extra appointment with Dr Greenson was also arranged. Marilyn saw him twice that day, once at his office, on the other occasion at her home. Dr Hyman Engelberg was another visitor. Anxiety about resuming the movie was now engulfing her and extra medicine, to help ease her emotional turmoil, was requested from both of them.

Besides writing out a prescription for sulfathalidine to help ease her colon problems, Engelberg also wrote out one for Nembutal. Greenson, in an attempt to wean her off that drug, approved one for the hypnotic sedative chloral hydrate. The order was for a bottle of 50. It was a deadly combination. As medical testimony shows, the latter slows the metabolism of the former and together they act adversely. (Greenson would write out a prescription for 40 more chloral hydrate tablets six days later on Tuesday 31 July. Providing she took them all – which she more than likely did – between 25 July and Saturday 4 August, in addition to the Nembutal capsules Engelberg was prescribing her, Marilyn would ominously consume approximately eight chloral hydrate tablets *a day*. Without a shadow of a doubt, Greenson's attempts to deter her from Nembutal had been nullified.) Oblivious to these perilous actions, the actress felt it unnecessary to inform each doctor about what the other had just prescribed.

The actress collected her two sets of pills from the Vicente Pharmacy during the afternoon of 25 July. Afterwards, she paid a visit to Dean Martin at his home in Mountain Drive, where they discussed resuming their movie. Their get-together concluded with Marilyn promising to show him the latest version of the script at the Cal-Neva that weekend.

The third reason for Marilyn's getaway trip to the lodge, as suggested by Sinatra, was that it would also provide the actress with a chance to see her intimate and discuss with him again their long-proposed film plans. It would also enable her to get the hell out of Los Angeles, a city she truly detested. However, due to her Friday morning appointment with Peter Levathes, her obligatory end-of-day 4pm rendezvous with Greenson (as his invoice supplied to Marilyn's estate on Monday 15 July 1963 testified) and her regular Saturday engagement with masseur Ralph Roberts, it was agreed that Marilyn would drop by the club only on Sunday 29 July 1962, and *not* earlier as we are informed by many biographers.

Further evidence that she was at home on Fifth Helena that Saturday comes from her phone records, which reveal that, on that day, she made two telephone calls – one lasting four minutes, the other ten – to Florida and New York City respectively. The former was to Joe DiMaggio, the latter to Isidore Miller. 'Your voice is very clear,' Miller informed her. 'I know you feel well.' She replied, 'Dad, I feel fine.' With this information to hand, I feel safe in speculating that her time at the Cal-Neva Lodge was just 19 hours. Furthermore, realising she would be away that weekend, Marilyn arranged for Paula Strasberg to fly home to New York on the first available flight (via American Airlines during the morning of Monday 30 July). The first-class, one-way ticket, booked via the Rand-Fields Inc. Travel & Theatre Ticket outlet at 9406 Dayton Way, Beverly Hills, cost the actress $205.59, which she paid by way of a City National Bank cheque (no. 1800) on Thursday 2 August.

So, in all certainty, Marilyn flew out of Los Angeles International Airport in Sinatra's luxurious twin-engined private plane, *Christina*, so-called after his daughter, Tina, on the morning of Sunday 29 July. She was met at Reno Tahoe Airport by the singer's 300-pound aide-de-camp, Ed Pucci, who proceeded to escort her the 35 miles to the lodge. Since there was nowhere safely to land it, she did not fly up in Sinatra's private heli-copter, as has been claimed. As we saw in Chapter 4, he had smashed up the heli-pad on the Cal-Neva roof in March during a fit of anger following the President Kennedy/Bing Crosby fiasco. Furthermore, with fears that heavier helicopters might damage the building's roof, Sinatra had taken the pad out of service.

Moreover, Peter Lawford did not accompany Marilyn during any part of her journey and, contrary to another long-held belief, neither did his wife, Pat. She was still in Hyannis Port with the rest of the Kennedy clan celebrating Jacqueline's 33rd birthday.

That final weekend of July 1962 is a date etched in Monroe folklore for all the wrong reasons. As 'Skinny' D'Amato, Sinatra's close friend, manager of the lodge and owner of Atlantic City's popular 500 Club, once remarked, 'There was more to what happened [that weekend] than anyone has told.' We will examine what exactly transpired shortly. Despite the claims of many biographies, however, which said the actress was out of commission for most of the day, she actually began Sunday in fine fettle and even managed to put in a lunchtime appearance at the lodge's regular, ladies-only, 'Bingo & Brunch' event.

On the door that day was James Gray-Gold, the son of major league baseball player Lefty O'Doul. In an interview for the *Hollywood Nostalgia* website he recalled, 'There are some dates that are seared into one's memory forever. The last hot Sunday of July 1962 is one of those days. My roommates and I took jobs as parking attendants at Cal-Neva Lodge after graduating high school . . . Since we parked the cars at Cal-Neva, nobody came in or out that we didn't see. Peter Lawford, Dean Martin, Sammy Davis . . . In other words, whoever showed up at the lake paid their respects at the Lodge sooner or later.'

His most interesting recollection continued. 'It was ladies "Bingo & Brunch" that Sunday as the black Lincoln pulled in. As I happen to have been by the front doors, I took the next car matter-of-factly. A woman stepped hesitantly out of the back, head down. I took her hand to steady her. At the time I remember thinking "another one of Sinatra's imports." As she rose her head, that thought quickly faded. Old memories welled up inside of me. It was Marilyn Monroe and I hadn't seen her in eight years. She smiled at me and was whisked away by Ed Pucci, a Sinatra bodyguard. I stood there for the longest time wondering if Marilyn had remembered me. After all, I was only a young boy the last time I had seen her.'

Going by Gold's impeccable memory, we can be assured that Marilyn *did* arrive at the venue at that time. Dressed in a matching green headscarf, blouse, slacks and shoes, she was in good spirits and, following her arrival, rushed to meet the others. A mix of friends, acquaintances and rivals, these included Sinatra, Martin, Juliet Prowse and Sam Giancana, plus the actress Rhonda Fleming, jazz pianist Buddy Greco and hair stylist Jay Sebring. Black and white pictures of Marilyn playfully posing in the sun with Sinatra and Greco, who was performing in the club's new casino-lounge, were taken by his then wife and manager, Sally Baionno. Further pictures of the actress standing, glass in hand, with Peter Lawford on the balcony of his cabin were also taken. Afterwards, Marilyn rushed back down to the club to catch the buffet and participate in the 1.30pm bingo session.

However, events later that night do have a ring of familiarity about them. Working from educated supposition, extensive research and reliable, first-hand accounts, I can reveal the true chain of events for the latter half of the day.

First, after finishing her drinks, food and game, Marilyn settled into her room (cabin 52), freshened up, rested, changed into a swanky evening dress and then walked through the lodge's underground tunnel, which led to the venue's Celebrity Showroom. There, from Sinatra's favourite table, situated in the third booth from the entrance, she watched a performance by Dean Martin and his regular support act, the dance duo Brascia and Tybee.

Sitting alongside them were Sam Giancana (who, through his state ban, had no right to be there), the venue's manager, the criminal, Paul 'Skinny' D'Amato, the mobster and Giancana associate, Johnny Rosselli and, most surprisingly, Peter Lawford. Since their almighty falling-out over the JFK/Crosby fiasco in March, he and Sinatra had not spoken once. But this weekend was different. The Kennedys' brother-in-law had an ulterior motive for being there.

During dinner, once the free-flowing alcohol had started to take effect, he politely informed Marilyn she had to stop contacting Bobby Kennedy. He told her, in no uncertain terms, that the Attorney General had reluctantly severed his ties to her and that her calls to him had to cease. (This was indeed harsh since, up to this point, the actress had placed just seven through to his number at the Justice Department.) Just like the President, he had decided to disconnect himself from her. Reiterating the fears of his brother, the Attorney General knew that there were many individuals who hated their guts and possessed an agenda to do anything they could to remove them from the White House. No doubt acting on a direct order from JFK, who had once again found himself in the position of fearing recriminations thanks to his association with one of Hollywood's sassiest yet most unstable women, Bobby knew that he had no alternative but to cut his ties to the blonde bombshell. Other reasons for this soon became apparent.

Around this period, the Attorney General had learnt from Lawford that his conversation with the actress, during the dinner party on Thursday 26 June, had been recorded by the surveillance equipment secreted into the actor's beachside home. At the same time, FBI director J. Edgar Hoover, no doubt led by Bobby's clandestine conversations with Marilyn, was loosely making references to colleagues concerning an 'especially hot' file on RFK and the actress. Coincidentally, brother Ted's senatorial primary election in Massachusetts was looming in September and so, without doubt, Marilyn was considered a liability to Bobby and his family's political aspirations. According to some sources, the decision to drop her quickly had in fact originated from his mother, Rose, and other family members. Sadly for Marilyn, she had once more turned into an unaffordable luxury for the Kennedy clan.

Bobby's rejection reawakened memories of Monroe's father's abandonment of her and she was naturally devastated and inconsolable. Furthermore, she was enraged that, unlike the President, the Attorney General did not possess the courage or the gallantry to explain or say his goodbye personally and instead had to rely on the family's ever-dependable bagman cum lapdog, Lawford. As everyone plainly knew, he was besotted with the Kennedys and there was *nothing* he would not do for them, legal or otherwise.

While she was at the table, a lethal mix of Dom Perignon and vodka was incessantly poured into her glass by her so-called 'live-it-up' associates, and she became drunk. Precipitated by Lawford's news, she began to speak unreservedly to D'Amato about matters of which, as he told her, 'people ought not to speak'. In her alcohol-fuelled outburst, she made it clear that she had been 'seeing' or had been 'intimate' with one of the Kennedys and, as she did so, after many months of ambiguous speculation, the gangsters finally had their proof. She had unwittingly confirmed their long-believed suspicions about her and the two men.

As the drink continued to flow, Marilyn became uncontrollable and, in full view of the hundreds of guests at the club, practically passed out. She was carried up to her cabin and, when she reached it, was molested. Her dress was removed, she was showered with alcohol and a dog collar was placed around her neck. Her humiliation continued when the Cal-Neva low-life forced her to half-heartedly crawl around the floor on all fours and reluctantly participate in a lesbian sex act with prostitutes. Obtaining ladies such as these at a moment's notice was easy. Individuals from the sex industry regularly littered the lodge. D'Amato was known to be operating a prostitution ring out of the building, bookings for which could even be reportedly made quite openly at the hotel's front desk. Investigators suspected that the women involved in the operation were flown in especially from San Francisco.

Due to the amount of alcohol she had consumed, the actress was oblivious to most of what was unfolding. It was therefore no surprise that, in a conversation with her close friend Ralph Roberts just one day later, she would describe the parts of the weekend she *did* remember as a 'nightmare' and disclose that she felt more like a 'prisoner' than a guest.

Legend has it that Giancana even took his turn with her. Soon after Monroe's death, an FBI wire-tapper apparently recorded a conversation between Giancana and Rosselli, discussing a sex orgy at the Cal-Neva. On the tape, Rosselli allegedly told Giancana, 'You sure get your rocks off fucking the same broad as the [Kennedy] brothers, don't you?' However, that scenario is highly doubtful since Giancana would never dare share or get sexually involved with any of Sinatra's women. Sam's daughter, Antoinette, waded into the debate by adding, 'I knew my father's taste in women. Marilyn was wiry, too active for him.'

Therefore, it seems highly likely that 'Skinny' D'Amato and Johnny Rosselli, who had a strong, predatory interest in the actress, worked alone in orchestrating the half-hearted debauchery. A motive? Rosselli was another individual who was increasingly angry at the Kennedys for giving the Mafia a hard time and frequently bragged about 'friends in high places' who were going to knock off the President. It's also feasible that the spiritless orgy was intended to teach Marilyn a lesson for bestowing, as they believed, her sexual favours on the Kennedys. As Sinatra's valet, George Jacobs, wrote in *Mr. S.: My Life With Frank Sinatra*, 'She was *their* girl, *not* the Micks.'

Marilyn had arrived at the lodge hoping to get away from the horrors of Los Angeles and relax with friends such as Sinatra and Martin. Instead, she found herself substituting one traumatic situation for another. When the effects of the liquor started to wane, it began to dawn on her what had happened. Now alone in her chalet, depressed and too frightened to leave, Marilyn frantically called Joe DiMaggio who, following the actress's announcement that she was going to be in Lake Tahoe that weekend, had instantly made arrangements to be in the vicinity too.

He had spent the first part of that day watching a Timber Little League baseball game. Later that evening, he travelled on to the five-star nightclub and gambling establishment Harrah's, situated at the south end of the lake, to see a concert by movie star and entertainer Mitzi Gaynor, who was performing in the venue's South Shore Room. (The story that he had booked himself into the Silver Crest Motel, approximately eight miles away in Kings Beach, is inaccurate.) When Gaynor announced to the crowd that the baseball legend was sitting among them, he stood up and received a rapturous ovation.

Marilyn's frantic call to the hotel came at the tail end of Gaynor's presentation. When a waiter discreetly informed DiMaggio that he was urgently required on the telephone, he rose, walked to the manager's office, picked up the receiver and listened intently to the actress's highly emotional tale of despair. Immediately after concluding the call, he dashed out of the hotel, climbed into his car and sped the 20 miles round to the north end of the lake to the Cal-Neva, his intention to fly home immediately after Gaynor's concert forgotten. News of his unexpected stopover even managed to reach the news wires of the ever-watchful Dorothy Kilgallen, who suggested in her column, 'DiMaggio was held-over, either by the scenic beauty or one of the chorines [chorus girls] in the show.'

Engulfed by unhappiness and humiliated by what had just happened, Marilyn was in a frightful state. Unable to rest, she reached into her bag for her pills. Sick of being used, and aware that she had just been sexually mistreated, the actress popped several Nembutal capsules and, worryingly, a few chloral hydrates. Mixed with the large quantity of alcohol she had consumed, it was a deadly cocktail. Miscalculating the amount she had swallowed, Marilyn inadvertently took more than her body could handle. However, it was *not* a suicide attempt. As Dr Hyman Engelberg would later explain, 'Marilyn had too much to drink, and had taken possibly slightly more than she should have.'

Fortuitously, at the end of her call to DiMaggio, she left her line to the lodge's switchboard operator open. The connection would save her life. The operator raised the alarm when she overheard arduous breathing sounds emanating from the actress's room. A maid sent up to her chalet found Marilyn now slumped across the floor, next to her bed. She was almost comatose. Lawford was notified and he rushed to the room.

Ted Stephens, a kitchen worker at the Cal-Neva, told the Sinatra biographer J. Randy Taraborrelli, 'We got a phone call from Peter Lawford. "We need coffee in chalet 52," he screamed into the phone, then he hung up. He sounded frantic. No less than two minutes passed and it was Mr. Sinatra on the phone, screaming, "Where's the goddamn coffee?" I learned later they were in 52 walking Marilyn around, trying to wake her up.' Regrettably, many of her friends assumed that it was just another cry for attention.

Contrary to reports, the actress was *not* rushed 20 miles to the nearby Carson-Tahoe hospital to have her stomach pumped. Neither was she attended to by a doctor. Desperate to keep a tight lid on the situation, the actress was in fact treated only by Sinatra, Lawford and various Cal-Neva employees, and sadly, her only form of medicine came in the shape of several cups of black coffee. Evidence that no doctors were summoned to the lodge is provided by the fact that there were no medical reports of the incident, as Dorothy Kilgallen discovered when she researched the incident in August 1962. Furthermore, despite the compulsory order to do so, news of what was believed to be Marilyn's believed suicide attempt was not even reported to the local police authority.

Before the night was over, completely oblivious to the lackadaisical orgy that had just taken place, Sinatra was discreetly handed a roll of film. Someone had unashamedly decided to capture a photographic record of the event. There are many who believe that it was in fact Sinatra himself who took the pictures. He didn't. But his camera *was* the one used. The singer handed the film to *Life* magazine photographer Billy Woodfield and asked him to develop it. Within minutes Sinatra was reeling in shock at nine freshly processed images of a semi-unconscious Marilyn, in complete disarray, being sexually fondled in the presence of mobsters Rosselli and D'Amato. Reports soon came to light claiming that Sam Giancana was seen in one of the pictures. But, considering how respectful he was of the actress, I suspect he was an innocent bystander in the proceedings and was seen only at the tail end of the incident, attempting to haul Marilyn up off the floor.

Sinatra immediately ordered the pictures and negatives to be destroyed. However, I can reveal that, even though eight of the images were scrapped, one *did* escape the furnace. In an attempt to maximise the scandal and totally discredit the actress, one incriminating image was dispatched to Dorothy Kilgallen. In her Hearst-syndicated column, published on Friday 3 August, she wrote, 'In California, they're circulating a photograph of her that certainly isn't as bare as her famous calendar, but is very interesting. Marilyn's dress looks as if it was plastered to her skin and the skirt is hitched higher above the knees than any Paris designer would dare to promote in the fall showings.' Accompanying the picture was an anonymously written note, which implied that Monroe had been rather intimate with the Kennedys. (The fact that she had indeed spent the night with the President at Bing Crosby's home back in March was, at this point, still a closely guarded secret, known only by those in JFK's and Marilyn's elite circle of friends.)

Early the next morning, the roof truly caved in on the actress's life when she discovered that the grapevine had picked up and begun speculating about the previous night's events. Now sporting her dark shades, and bereft of both sleep and her shoes, the actress had managed to drag herself out of her hell-hole and was seen alone, wandering aimlessly in a drunken stupor, by the resort's fog-covered swimming pool, looking up the hill to where Joe DiMaggio was now standing and watching. Neither spoke. They just glanced at each other. No speech was necessary. They were still close and the actress realised it. His attempt to rescue her this time, however, was futile, thanks to a years-old rift between Sinatra and DiMaggio.

Inevitably, Marilyn was at the core of it. On Friday 5 November 1954, in an attempt to catch his wife in a passionate clinch with another individual, Joe DiMaggio, along with Sinatra and the private detectives Barney Ruditsky and Phil Irwin, had broken into the Warring Avenue apartment belonging to Florence Kotz. But Marilyn wasn't there. They had burst into the wrong lodgings. In May 1957, Kotz filed suit against Messrs DiMaggio, Sinatra, Ruditsky and Irwin to the tune of $200,000 but eventually settled out of court for the sum of $7,500.

Frank and Joe's friendship plummeted from then on. In the early 1960s, even though DiMaggio had been separated from Marilyn for several years, the former baseball star began insinuating that his former wife was having an affair with the singer – as she was, albeit briefly – and Sinatra naturally became angry that the baseball legend was spying on him, hoping to find proof that a tryst was taking place. Their mutual dislike of each other never relented, with the result that Sinatra had banned the so-called 'slugger' from coming anywhere near his lodge.

Oblivious of what had actually happened, Sinatra was furious about Marilyn's apparent overdose and participation in an orgy. So much so that, early on Monday morning, shortly after seeing the recently developed pictures, he ordered her off his property and instructed George Jacobs to drive her (and the alcohol-ridden Lawford) back to Reno Tahoe Airport. Upon their arrival there, she was reportedly seen stumbling barefoot out of the car and climbing aboard Frank's hastily summoned plane. With Lawford still in tow and with Santa Monica Airport still closed, they flew back to Los Angeles International Airport where Pat Newcomb and Eunice Murray were waiting to meet her and drive her back to her Brentwood home. Jacobs stated in *Mr. S.: My Life With Frank Sinatra*, 'In the car, the thing that bothered her most was that her drugged-out behaviour had offended the straight-laced Mr. Sam, who was united with Mr. S in a hatred of drugs.' This tends to corroborate my belief that Giancana played no part in the Cal-Neva debauchery.

The whole scenario had left a nasty taste in the mouths of those running the Cal-Neva and bridges to those involved were quickly burnt. The S&M orgy-party, with Marilyn as the unwitting participant, marked the end of their association. Although still fond of her, Sinatra was now through with the actress. He'd slept with screen legends such as Ava Gardner, Kim Novak and Juliet Prowse and knew there were plenty more to come. He didn't need an unbalanced individual like Marilyn dangling over his head.

As she correctly guessed, Giancana was through with her too, as were Joseph Kennedy and his two spoilt sons. The Mafia boss had personally pulled strings in Chicago to help squeeze Kennedy past Richard Nixon and into the White House in January 1961 and even shared good-time girl Judith Campbell with the President. The Chicago gangster had even, supposedly, been a witness to meetings with Joseph Kennedy at the Cal-Neva; now, with his son Bobby consistently making noises about bringing down the heat on organised crime in America, the hypocrisy of it all angered Giancana. Like Sinatra he was finished with the whole damn caboodle. It was the end of an era.

Early on the morning of Monday 30 July, with an intoxicated Lawford still by her side, Marilyn left Lake Tahoe. Naturally upset about what had just happened with Sinatra, Rosselli and D'Amato, and displeased that Bobby had used the actor to tell her their friendship had ended, she began making threats; warnings that, given her highly unstable condition, could not be taken lightly. The most disconcerting of these was her stipulation that if Bobby did not contact her personally and explain why he had dispensed with her, she would front a press conference at which she would make public details of her brief tryst with President Kennedy and announce how badly she had been treated by the brothers.

Later that day, immediately after completing her journey home from Los Angeles Airport, the actress attempted to place another call through to the Attorney General at the White House. Reiterating the scenario with his brother, John, the actress once again wanted to know precisely *why* she had been unceremoniously ditched. She had put her career on the line to appear at his brother's gala and now she had been dumped again by another member of his family. And it *hurt*. In an exchange lasting precisely eight minutes, Bobby's secretary, Angie Novello, correctly informed her he was out of the office. (In fact, he had been in a meeting with the President and wasn't due to return to the bureau until the following morning.) Requests to be put through to him were allegedly rejected and she supposedly became angry. From that moment on, as we have been led to believe, she began referring to Bobby as 'that little midget bastard'. As legend would have it, Marilyn was now a woman scorned.

Or was she? There is an alternative side to this story. As many historians believe, instead of ringing to ascertain why he had dispensed with her, what if Marilyn was actually trying to contact Bobby to warn him about a possible assassination attempt? As we know, the actress had just stayed the night at Sinatra's Cal-Neva Lodge, an entertainment and gambling establishment awash with notables from enemy territory. While rubbing shoulders with these undesirables, did she perchance overhear tales of a planned assassination attempt on the Attorney General or the President? From the low-life hoodlum Skinny D'Amato to the parasite Johnny Rosselli, everything about the Cal-Neva reeked of conspiracy.

As we have seen, on Thursday 26 July 1962, three days before Monroe's arrival there, the Los Angeles office of the FBI received an anonymous call warning about 'gangland types' who were plotting to murder Bobby Kennedy. Furthermore, the last proven date that Marilyn tried to contact Bobby at the Justice Department in Washington was Monday 30 July. Was she just desperate to pass on to Bobby the disturbing news she had heard about him or his brother? Many believe that Marilyn might even have been murdered because of what she'd accidentally overheard during her momentous stay at the Cal-Neva, although this is untrue.

Whatever is the case, the actress was understandably disturbed by her rejection and the incidents at the lodge. As surviving receipts show, upon her return to Fifth Helena that Monday, and immediately after attempting to contact Kennedy, she called two of her friends in New York, one of whom was Norman Rosten. Desperate for a friend to talk to in her time of need, their discussion lasted for 13 minutes. At its conclusion, she was hastily driven to Dr Greenson's office in nearby North Roxbury Drive for another session. When her anxieties had alleviated, Marilyn ordered a $43.31 delivery of food and alcohol for herself and Eunice Murray from the Briggs Wines & Spirits store. Her eventful day concluded with a hastily arranged early-morning massage at 2.15am from her ever-reliable friend, Ralph Roberts.

She was in a high state of panic. The Nembutal pills Dr Hyman Engelberg had prescribed were failing to work. Within 15 minutes, with the aid of the front door key, still hidden in one of the fuschia pots by the front door, Roberts had arrived and was busy carrying out his work in her darkened bedroom. (This detail never concerned Roberts. Having been there many times to administer a soothing massage, he knew the layout of the actress's sleeping quarters well. 'Marilyn hated light and loved dark,' he recalled. 'If it was at night time, she insisted on having the lights off. She loved to have a massage to relax her. Sometimes she'd fall asleep on my table.') His visit to the actress's house lasted just under an hour. He left as discreetly as he had arrived.

Lawford, meanwhile, was naturally apprehensive about Marilyn's plans for revenge. He knew she could be a powder keg to both the Kennedy brothers and his family. After parting company with her at the airport, he interrupted his drive home to Santa Monica by ordering his driver, the pilot Frank Lieto, to stop a few blocks away from his beachside house. He needed to make an urgent, pay-booth telephone call to the White House. He knew his home was bugged so he could not ring from there.

During the course of the call, Lawford fawningly informed the President that, as she had told him on the way back to the airport, Monroe was planning to front a tell-all press conference. No doubt referring to her small red pocket diary, he apparently informed JFK drunkenly that the actress had documentation to substantiate her claims. (White House telephone records indicate that Kennedy received an 18-minute call on Monday 30 July at 8.40pm – 5.40pm West Coast time. By this time, he was relaxing back at his mansion. Bobby was still with him. Earlier that afternoon, the Attorney General had been in attendance at a meeting about nuclear testing involving the President and 23 other high-ranking officials.)

In Lawford's alcohol-befuddled mind, Marilyn had become an angry woman who was not prepared to fade away into oblivion. He believed she was ready for a fight. As he saw it, she knew how America would want to hear about her tryst with the world's most powerful man, learn about the Kennedys' political secrets, discover how badly she had been treated by the brothers and learn about her revealing, politically sensitive conversations with the Attorney General.

However, her off-the-cuff claims to him during their trip home that she would tell all at a press conference were entirely hollow. As the timeline of her ensuing days testifies, she had no plans whatsoever to follow the threat through, but only *she* knew this. Her decision to declare an intention such as this was inspired by the President's historic, televised, Telstar satellite-broadcast speech just a week earlier. Regrettably, she was unaware of the ramifications her threats would bring.

At the end of July and beginning of August 1962, Marilyn's world-famous face and figure were once more featuring prominently on many magazine covers. Her name was being dropped in several noted newspaper columns, her work diary was once again beginning to fill and her future looked decidedly rosy. But regrettably, she had also become entangled with too many powerful individuals and was about to push her luck one step too far. The final tumultuous events of her tragically short life were about to commence.

Chapter Nine

Tuesday 31 July 1962–7.55pm, Saturday 4 August 1962

With Dean Martin unable (or unwilling) to resume work on *Something's Got To Give* until, at best, early in the New Year, Marilyn knew she had no reason whatsoever to stay in Los Angeles. So, on the morning of Tuesday 31 July, she decided to return to New York. Informed by Pat Newcomb that her first-class return flight via United Airlines, at a cost of $411.18, had been reserved, the actress made an 11-minute call to her housekeeper, Florence Thomas, and told her to clean and dust her apartment in Manhattan ready for her return the following week. September trips to Washington, and to Mexico on Saturday 15th, to celebrate the country's Independence Day one day later, were also planned.

The same afternoon, once she had concluded her phone call to Florence Thomas, Marilyn was driven over to the Sunset Boulevard office of her publicist, Arthur Jacobs. Desperate to resolve his client's career and kick-start his vocation as a movie producer, Jacobs was keen to sell to the actress the directorial expertise of J. Lee Thompson. Mindful of the hang-ups she had about certain people in their profession, Jacobs had earmarked Thompson to direct her and Gene Kelly (rather than Frank Sinatra) in the long-mooted First World War musical *I Love Louisa* (later retitled *What a Way to Go*). Before he could push the project further, he naturally needed Marilyn's approval, so, in an attempt to do this, he summoned the actress to a meeting to see a taster of Thompson's work.

In Jacobs' small private cinema, a clip of Thompson's recent movie, *The Guns of Navarone*, was screened. Even with its wartime flavour, it was a still a bad choice for the actress. 'Excellent,' she said at the end of it. 'But it's *not* a comedy.' At once, Jacobs arranged for excerpts of two other Thompson movies to be projected, namely *Flame Over India* and *Tiger Bay* (both from 1959). Despite the fact that neither was humorous, Marilyn was impressed by what she saw. So when Jacobs enquired whether she would consider working with the director, she replied, 'I'll do it, *unless* I dislike him on sight.' A meeting between the pair was suggested and a rendezvous at 5pm on the following Saturday, at her home in Brentwood, was swiftly arranged.

Meeting over, Jacobs immediately called Fox's Phil Feldman and elatedly informed him the actress was interested in starring in *I Love Louisa*, confirming that the studio had thus obtained a second title for their new, two-picture deal with Marilyn. The actress meanwhile interrupted her journey home by attending a 90-minute session with Dr Greenson at his office in North Roxbury Drive. At the end of this, with concerns about work once again getting the better of her, Greenson wrote out another prescription for her, a refill of 10 chloral hydrate tablets. She collected it at once from the Vicente Pharmacy.

On Wednesday 1 August, the onslaught of bad press against the actress reared its ugly head again when she found herself on the receiving end of reporter Erskine Johnson's caustic wit. On this day, in his weekly 'Hollywood Today' column, he launched the first of his off-beat, impudent ripostes to the Oscars, entitling them 'Marilyns' since, as he put it, 'Marilyn Monroe is one of our top winners.' In his sarcastic piece, Johnson proceeded to award the actress a 'Marilyn' in recognition for her 'classy "Beat Dialog" when Fox bounced her out of *Something's Got To Give*. "How can they do this to me?" she said, after becoming the year's most celebrated no-show.' His quirky, make-believe awards ceremony continued when, in recognition of her infamous non-attendance on the film set, he cheekily bestowed Marilyn with the 'Best Song' award, 'Never on Sunday, Monday, Tuesday, Wednesday, Thursday, Friday or Saturday'.

Aside from the wisecracks, the actress continued to oversee the work on her Fifth Helena home. That morning, new wooden Reece Period furniture gates were hung at the front of the property. (With seven hinges, the total cost, including labour, materials and tax, came to $313.92.) 'Marilyn was getting things done around the house,' Pat Newcomb recalled at the time. 'She loved it. She was so excited about it, just like a little girl with a new toy.' No expense with the renovations was spared. She even paid $29.38 to the Film City Ornamental Iron Works Company at 5851 Sunset Boulevard for nails with specially made heads for her front door.

While the work was carried out, Marilyn spent time on the phone. One call was from Phil Feldman. Following Jacobs' buoyant call the previous afternoon, he was ringing to confirm the studio's offer of a $1 million, two-picture deal ($500,000 for the resumption of Something's Got To Give and a further $500,000 for I Love Louisa) and to inform her that a contract to that effect had been sent to her attorney, Milton Rudin, for his and her approval. She agreed in principle to the plan immediately. Now on a higher rate of pay, the actress had just won a major personal victory against the studio and she was ecstatic. However, their conversation was still peppered with caveats. The studio agreed to hire her choice of director, Jean Negulesco, for Something's Got To Give, but only on the condition that she excised Paula Strasberg from her professional life. She requested time to think about it. He agreed.

Word that Something's Got To Give might restart soon spread. Following a tip-off from the studio, Marilyn's stand-in, Evelyn Moriarty, rang the actress at her home. They spoke excitedly about it for 45 minutes. 'I heard we were going to do the picture,' Moriarty recalled, 'so I called her on the Wednesday and I talked to her. The conversation was, "We're going to go back, we're going to go back and work." She was really up . . . She was happy. We were going to start in September.' She was mistaken. With Dean Martin both busy and aloof, they were not.

Sensing a story, Hollywood journalist James Bacon was a surprise visitor to Marilyn's house early that afternoon. 'She was in very good spirits,' he recalled. 'She was laughing. Maybe the champagne helped her, I don't know . . . I think she downed about two bottles while I was there . . . and maybe four or five pills. I said, "Marilyn, that combination is gonna kill ya." She took another pill and defiantly said, "It hasn't killed me yet."'

Once he had left, the actress placed a call through to Elizabeth Courtney, the veteran dress designer and assistant to Jean Louis. She wished to order a formal $1,600 dress for the world premiere of the new Irving Berlin musical Mr. President, which was set to take place in Washington DC on Tuesday 25 September. The show in question, at the National Theatre, was to be a charity event hosted by the White House as a fundraiser to benefit the Kennedy Child Study Center For Retarded Children and The Lt. Joseph P. Kennedy Jr. Institute For Mental Retardation. Given that the joint honorary chairmen for the event were Jacqueline Kennedy, the President's mother Rose and brother Bobby, Marilyn's acceptance of the invitation showed not only an element of defiance but also perhaps a reluctance to allow the family to deprive her of the chance to be present on a truly momentous night. After all, this would be Berlin's very last Broadway production; it was billed by many as 'the social occasion of the year'. Marilyn desperately wanted to be there looking her very, very best and keen, no doubt, to sassily upstage the President's wife.

'She said she had a sketch of a gown Jean had drawn,' Courtney recalled, 'and she wanted me to talk it over with him and then come to her place for a fitting. "Come any time," she said. "I'll have time whenever you're free. Maybe you can make it Saturday?" But because of the pressures of business, I was unable to get to Miss Monroe's house. She also told me that someone from the studio had gotten in touch with her and talked about getting the film back in production. "Just keep your fingers crossed," she told me. "I'm sure that I'm going to do the picture."' Immediately after finishing the call, amid fears that she might be lacking suitable attire for the Washington show, Marilyn placed a call through to Saks' flagship department store at 611 Fifth Avenue in New York and ordered a $382.62 Gucci dress. (She would write a cheque out for it, no. 1782, two days later, on Friday 3 August.)

Once the work on the gates had been completed and her calls had been concluded, the actress paid a visit – with Eunice Murray once again acting as her chauffeur – to the architect, designer and bit-part actor William Alexander Levy at his art and antique store, The Mart, on Santa Monica Boulevard. During her stay, she chose a coffee table and a wall design depicting the images of Adam and Eve. When she went to purchase the items, the shop's 53-year-old owner, realising immediately who she was, lurched forward and offered a proposal of marriage. 'I'll think about it,' Marilyn laughingly replied before walking out of the shop.

From there, she and Murray travelled on to the Pilgrim's Furniture store at 12217 Wilshire Boulevard where she purchased a Roman-style white chest of drawers. The shop assistant promised to deliver the item to the actress's home on Saturday 4 August and agreed to let her pay for it upon its arrival. Marilyn and her companion then climbed back into their car and drove the short journey to Franks Nurseries & Flowers shop at 12424 Wilshire Boulevard, where (at a total cost of $93.08) she purchased from the proprietor, Robert K. Goka, a range of items including various sized tuberose plants, a Mexican lime tree, a hanging begonia basket and a Valencia orange. Remembering she would be busy with director J. Lee Thompson when the delivery was due to be made, late on Saturday afternoon, she instructed the salesman to ask for Murray's son-in-law, Norman Jeffries, when he reached her home. Immediately after completing her acquisitions, the actress returned to the car but realised she had forgotten some other items. She walked back into the store and bought (at a cost of $63.53), among other items, some tomatoes, hummingbird feeding stands and food, plus petunias, begonias (in various sizes and quantities), sedums and terracotta pots.

As we can see, her spending was still out of control. On that first day of August, her City National Bank of Beverly Hills account ominously showed she was overdrawn to the tune of $4,208.34. Her others were only slightly better. Her savings accounts at the Excelsior and Bowery banks boasted balances of just $1,171.06 and $614.29 respectively, while in her cheque accounts at the Irving Trust Co. and the First National City banks, there were sums of $2,334.65 and $84.67. 'Marilyn kept in her checking account only enough for current expenses,' Milton Rudin explained at the time, 'but she was to have received half-a-million dollars over the next two years alone as part of her percentage from the fabulously successful movie, *Some Like It Hot*.'

Later, back at her Brentwood home, after paying another visit to Dr Greenson and following a $25 injection from Dr Hyman Engelberg, she took a phone call from Gene Kelly. With news that they would be starring together in *I Love Louisa* now beginning to circulate, he thought it would be a good idea to make contact with the actress personally and arrange a time to discuss the project further. They agreed a meeting in four days' time, on Sunday 5 August, to which director J. Lee Thompson would also be invited. A steak and baked potato barbecue on her patio, with Ralph Roberts doing the cooking, was proposed by the actress. 'She was in excellent spirits,' Kelly recalled, 'very happy and very excited about her future projects.'

At precisely 7pm, the actress settled down in front of her television set to watch President Kennedy's live, 32-minute, televised news conference. By now, however, she was feeling rocked after a confrontation with Joe DiMaggio.

Over in Virginia, several hours earlier, troubled by the events at the Cal-Neva, DiMaggio had resigned from his lucrative, $100,000-a-year job as vice-president of V.H. Monette Inc., a firm specialising in military post exchanges. He did so for one reason only, to be near his former wife. Remarriage was on his mind. This was substantiated by an old-timer at the DiMaggio family restaurant at 235 Jefferson Street, Fisherman's Wharf in San Francisco. In July 1962, a close, unnamed friend of DiMaggio's remarked, 'Joe never sold his home [there], the one he wanted for Marilyn. He has never stopped talking about her over the years. I think he believes she'll eventually find herself and return to him. He's in no hurry. He'll wait.' The chairman at V.H. Monette gave credence to this when he announced to an *Oakland Tribune* reporter at the time, 'DiMaggio told me he was going back to the West Coast to live there the rest of his life,' adding, 'I couldn't see any other reason for DiMaggio's quitting other than the personal troubles of his ex-wife.'

During the afternoon of 1 August, now tired of waiting, DiMaggio excitedly flew out to Los Angeles and headed straight to Marilyn's home in Brentwood where he asked for her hand in marriage. But although appreciative, she dismissed his offer outright and told him she wished to remain a friend only.

Though there were no doubts that DiMaggio was her best and most trusted friend, the chances of them ever remarrying were very remote indeed. In truth, Monroe's marriage to the baseball legend had not been a happy one. Her former drama coach, Natasha Lytess, corroborated this when she revealed that, during Marilyn's time with DiMaggio, the actress would phone her day and night, often in tears, complaining about the way he was mistreating her. Conclusive proof of this can be found in the revealing deposition which Monroe delivered during their brief, 15-minute divorce hearing in Santa Monica on Wednesday 27 October 1954. It read:

> My husband would get into moods where he wouldn't speak to me for days at a time, sometimes longer, maybe ten days. If I tried to coax him to talk to me, he wouldn't answer at all, or he would say, 'Leave me alone.' He refused to permit visitors to our home. On one occasion, when he did allow someone to come to our home to see me when I was ill, it was a terrible strain. I don't believe I asked anyone to our home more than three times during the nine months we were married. I offered to give up my work in hopes that would solve our problem. But it didn't change his attitude at all. I had hoped to have love, warmth, affection and understanding out of marriage. But instead, he gave me coolness and indifference.

As quotes in two of her most recent interviews made clear, her sentiments towards him had not changed by 1962. To *Redbook* magazine's Allan Levy in May she tellingly declared, 'Believe me, there is *no spark* to be ignited. I just like being with him. We have a better understanding than we've ever had.' And to photographer George Barris in July, she remarked, 'Things just didn't work out as far as marriage is concerned.' With regard to her marrying again, she insisted, 'It *hasn't* entered my mind since the last one.'

According to several noted biographers, they were set to tie the knot again on or around Wednesday 8 August. Rumours of this were actually borne out of two short, incomplete notes that were apparently found in her room at the time of her death, and which read, 'Dear Joe, if I can only succeed in making you happy. I will have succeeded in the biggest (*sic*) and most difficult thing there is, that is to make one person completely happy.

Your happiness means my happiness and . . . ' (She corrected the mistake and removed the last six words in her second attempt at it.) Educated conjecture, however, makes me believe the notes pertained to only one thing: Joe's recent proposal of marriage.

Such is the confusion about Marilyn's final months that even those who agreed the marriage idea was a non-starter were wrong with their reasoning. Due to the fact that, in their eyes, she was, apparently, still romantically linked to José Bolaños, they asked, 'Why would she remarry the baseball legend if she was still amorously connected to the Mexican?' But as we have seen, she wasn't. To reiterate, her last personal encounter with Bolaños had taken place on the morning of Thursday 28 June and their last telephone exchange, as he admitted himself in August 1962, took place in early July, a full month before Marilyn's death. In fact she had no desire to remarry DiMaggio because, put simply, she no longer loved him. She saw him now only as a close, platonic friend.

DiMaggio was devastated. Genuinely believing she would accept his proposal and imagining he would spend the entire day (and the rest of his life) with the actress, he had even cancelled his appearance at that evening's Fifth Annual Boys' Invitational Baseball Tournament at Shepherd Stadium in Colonial Heights. His no-show naturally took everyone by surprise. It was something the ever-reliable Joe *never* did. With Marilyn's rejection still ringing in his ears, he dejectedly left her home, heading out to San Francisco to meet up with his brothers and prepare for an old-timers' baseball game which was due to take place at Candlestick Park on Saturday.

On Thursday 2 August, two phone calls kick-started Marilyn's day. The first, early in the morning, was from the London-born Broadway composer Jule Styne, who was ringing from New York to offer her a starring role in the musical *A Tree Grows In Brooklyn*, which was set to open next season. As a sweetener for his dealings with the actress, he had purchased from Spanish-born Catalan portrait painter Alejo Vidal-Quadras an exclusive drawing of her. The work, which depicted Marilyn in a transparent light blue dress, had originated from the artist's time on the set of *Let's Make Love* two years earlier, and Styne intended to present it to the actress when they met. Their conversation was brief and ended with Marilyn promising to drop in on him during her visit to the Big Apple the following week.

The second call, which came shortly afterwards, was from *New York Journal-American* newspaper journalist Dorothy Kilgallen. The arrival on her desk of the salacious note and risqué picture taken of Marilyn at the Cal-Neva just four days earlier had sent the columnist into a spin, and she was desperate to find out more. A day earlier, immediately after the small packet had arrived, Kilgallen had called Bobby Kennedy at the White House to obtain his side of this alleged romance story. Unsurprisingly, he was reluctant to provide any clues. (In truth, there was nothing to say.) So, on the morning of the 2nd, she rang Marilyn. A columnist who had made her living from showbiz tittle-tattle such as this, she was unsurprisingly a captive listener when the actress decided to speak unreservedly during the call.

Kilgallen was stunned when Monroe, now awake and riding high on a tidal wave of emotion, once more spoke about holding a press conference and talked seamlessly about her break from the Kennedys, complaining about the way she was being ignored by them and making references to 'bases' in Cuba, the President's plan to kill Fidel Castro and the contents of her 'diary of secrets'. She told Kilgallen she knew exactly what the newspapers could do with such disclosures, and boasted to the columnist how she was once again attending parties hosted by the 'inner circle' of Hollywood's elite (a reference to her visit to the Cal-Neva) and was becoming the talk of the town again. It was an optimistic phone call completely free of inhibitions.

As the phone call progressed, however, Monroe suddenly and strangely changed tack and began expressing fears for her life. For two months now, sensing that the phones in her Brentwood home were 'tapped' and perceiving that her private moments were being shared by unknown individuals, Marilyn had taken to making calls at the phone booth in the park near her home. As we know, her home was indeed being bugged. However, the declaration that most startled Kilgallen was the disclosure that President Kennedy (probably during their night together at Bing Crosby's home) had privately divulged to her details about a UFO crash in New Mexico and how he had visited a secret air base for the purpose of inspecting dead alien bodies from outer space. Marilyn's story referred to the July 1947 Roswell UFO crash and the subsequent retrieval of debris and alien cadavers.

Despite receiving extensive coverage in the press at the time, the story was not to reach notoriety until 1978 when Major Jesse Marcell, the intelligence officer of the 'Roswell 509 Bomb Group', went public about the UFO crash during an appearance on the American TV programme *Eyewitness News*. Coincidentally, Kilgallen was already familiar with the subject. In a report published in America on Sunday 22 May 1955, she had written about British scientists and airmen's long-standing convictions about 'flying saucers originating from another planet'. Following her article, Kilgallen was placed under CIA scrutiny and surveillance, which, quite conveniently, prevented her from pursuing further UFO-related stories.

Kilgallen knew that if Monroe's allegations about the President of the United States were true, the announcement of such details to the American press could both frighten the public and cause immense embarrassment to Kennedy and his ambitious plans to have NASA put men on the moon by the end of the decade. As her conversation with Monroe unfolded, she soon became aware that the actress's declarations were not just personal; they dealt with highly sensitive matters of national security. Moments after concluding the conversation, Kilgallen rang her close friend Howard Rothberg to tell him about the actress's intentions. Unfortunately, unbeknown to Kilgallen, her phones too were being tapped and every startling utterance to Rothberg that day was being recorded by the CIA.

A day later, on Friday 3 August, in a one-page report entitled 'Moon Dust Project', details of Kilgallen's conversation with Rothberg found their way into a hastily prepared CIA document, which revealed that some high government officials were in a state of 'extreme anxiety' over the fact that the Kennedy brothers had, once again, been foolishly imparting highly sensitive information to Marilyn, and that she was writing a lot of it down in her little 'diary of secrets'.

'Project Moon Dust', as it was usually called, had been in existence since 1953. Its purpose was the recovery of UFO crashes and debris from fallen space vehicles. Over the years, much scorn has been poured on the Monroe/Kilgallen file. However, close examination of it reveals that the document has a reference, MJ-12; one that associates it with the whole question of government secrecy about unidentified flying objects. Dr Steven Greer, director of the CSETI (Center for the Study of Extraterrestrial Intelligence) Disclosure Project group, remarked in his book *Extraterrestrial Contact: The Evidence And Implications* that Marilyn's file had come to his attention in 1994 by way of a 'contact with access to NSA officials'. With regard to the document's legitimacy he added that 'It has been authenticated by the best document researcher in the world.' An FBI agent even told Greer that he 'could be locked up indefinitely' for publishing the file. (He does so anyway to this day.)

In fact, the file materialised two years prior to Greer's notice of it. In the spring of 1992, it found its way into the hands of the independent researcher and private investigator Timothy S. Cooper, who claimed he received it from a former CIA worker; in all probability an archivist or somebody with access to little-known classified, historical documents. In August 1994, the file was featured on the Fox Television show *Encounters*. However, doubts about its true origins remained until the noted American writer and researcher Donald R. Burleson got onto the case.

'The fact that the details of its original release have always been a little less than clear is what spurred me on to want to authenticate it as a CIA document,' he recalled, 'which is why I essentially manoeuvred the CIA into validating it themselves . . . I put in a FOIA [Freedom Of Information Act] request for CIA records of wiretaps on Marilyn's phones, and for her diary, which they are thought to possess, and when they denied having any of this stuff, I filed an appeal based on the famous memo; they *accepted* the appeal and sent it on upstairs to their Agency Release Panel. They don't do that if, one, there's nothing that could conceivably be released and, two, if the appeal is based on documentation that they don't recognize as authentic, i.e. if the pertinent documents are thought, by them, to have been spuriously produced outside the Agency. Thus, by their own policies, in accepting the appeal, even though they ultimately didn't release anything to me, they *authenticated* the document.'

Two important names attached to the file give further credence to its validity. The document was signed by James Jesus Angleton, the most shadowy and enigmatic figure in the Central Intelligence Agency's history; and, behind the 'Top Secret' stamp at the top of the file, the name 'Schulgen' can be faintly seen. This was Brigadier General George Schulgen, Chief of the Air Intelligence Requirements Division of Army Air Corps Intelligence, and the man in charge of investigating UFOs. Due to a fear of being pilloried and ridiculed by the media, reports about the Monroe file have been continually suppressed. Interestingly, in 1991 the CIA published a document which clearly stated that the Agency had contacts or resources at every major media outlet to kill, spin or stop such stories.

Today, in a world awash with computer technology, it is very easy to scoff at stories about how in 1962 the CIA was in a high state of panic over Marilyn's plans to disclose to the public details about JFK's 'flying saucer from another planet'. But the world was a vastly different place back then; not so many years earlier, after all, the young Orson Welles' Mercury Theatre company had created a state of high panic across a naïve, late-1930s America when on Sunday 30 October 1938 they performed their radio adaptation of the H.G. Wells science-fiction story, *The War Of The Worlds*. So effective was the broadcast that thousands of people believed they were genuinely under attack from aliens with metal hands in silver-coloured spaceships. From that point on, and for many years thereafter, the US Government was keen to avert any further alien-related alarms. And such was the case with Marilyn's disclosures to Kilgallen.

On the same day, and less than 24 hours after Monroe's phone revelations, Kilgallen courageously and unceremoniously became the very first journalist to write publicly, albeit cryptically, about a Kennedy brother's relationship with Monroe. Once a private matter, only known by those in the know, it had now become public. In her *New York Journal-American* article, Kilgallen did not, however, make clear to which Kennedy she was referring. (This confusion would forever taint and dominate the actress's story in the eyes of the public, but Kilgallen would later come clean and tell friends she was in fact referring to Bobby.) But she felt she had left just enough clues for readers to make up their own minds. No doubt remembering Marilyn's breathless performance at his 45th birthday gala in May, many readers attempting to decipher Dorothy's cryptic piece incorrectly thought she was referring to the President.

In an exercise of damage limitation, JFK once more enlisted the services of former New York reporter William Haddard to put a stop to any further talk. As he had when the Kennedy/Monroe stories first began to circulate a few months ago, he paid a visit to every major newspaper editor and told them firmly, 'If you hear these rumours, they are just *not* true!'

Kennedy's honeymoon period with the American public was well and truly over by now. The overthrow in Congress, on Wednesday 18 July, of his proposed Medicare bill, which was set to aid the medical care of millions of hard-up senior citizens, came as a climax to a series of crushing developments for him. On Thursday 26 July, it was announced that America's stockpile of gold had worryingly dipped a further $90 million. At the close of business on that day, it totalled just $16,208 million, the lowest since Monday 31 July 1939. His concerns magnified when it was announced that the available supply would not be enough to finance the great movements of trade, prompting many of his detractors to point out that, under his leadership, the United States had just taken its most backward step since the conclusion of the Second World War. It was a dire time indeed for the world's most powerful man.

So, when he was handed a copy of the CIA 'Moon Dust Project' file and informed about Marilyn's intentions to hold a tell-all press conference about him and his brother, he was naturally mortified. However, the fact that most disturbed him was her intention to reveal US plans to assassinate the Cuban leader, Fidel Castro, a man who still had the actress's famous 1952 nude calendar hanging on one of the walls in his home.

Approved by the President in November 1961, 'Operation Mongoose' was a covert plan aimed at stimulating a rebellion in Cuba which the United States could support. Placed in charge of the operation was his brother, Bobby. As Alexander Haig, Kennedy's aide to the administration's task force on Cuba revealed, by late 1963 the Attorney General had orchestrated at least *eight* separate attempts to assassinate the Cuban leader.

Unbeknown to Marilyn, at exactly same time she was sounding off to a reporter, 'Project Mongoose', as it was also known, had reached a critical stage. On Wednesday 1 August, as confidential CIA documents reveal, the operation had just reached Phase III, whereby the government were ready to 'have a final look at the situation and at the means in place before giving the signal to initiate actions leading to full-scale revolt'. Scheduled to take place in October, this was just two months away. Besides the fact that Marilyn's announcement would blow apart their clandestine plans, he knew that it would also entirely ruin the hopes and political aspirations of both brothers. The fall-out from her conference, if she had progressed with it, would have been devastating. Would Marilyn's scandalous revelations have forced JFK and not Richard Nixon to become the first President of the United States to resign from office in shame?

'I'm inclined to think that if it *had* fully come out that JFK (via Bobby) had leaked classified information to Marilyn, especially in a tense international situation, he might very well have been not only impeached but possibly indicted for treason,' Donald Burleson admitted. 'And, of course, since his brother was Attorney General, he would have had to prosecute the case, step aside and appoint a special prosecutor, etc. etc. It all would have gotten very nasty.' The Kennedys could not risk this political disaster. Considering Bobby was in charge of the CIA programme to eliminate Castro, and was also the individual responsible for imparting to the actress a great deal more top secret information, it was no surprise when he was ordered by his brother to go and see Monroe personally and demand her silence.

On Thursday 2 August, following her calls from Styne and Kilgallen, Marilyn travelled over to Dr Greenson's office for another session. Afterwards, she returned home to phone Marlon Brando and invite him over for dinner. He was unable to attend, but promised to call the following week to set another date. 'Fine,' she replied.

'She didn't seem depressed,' the actor remarked in 1994. 'It's been speculated that she had a secret rendezvous with Bobby Kennedy that week . . . I don't think that. If she *was* sleeping with him at the time, she wouldn't have invited me over for dinner.' In another interview, this time from 1968, he recalled further details of that call. 'I'm pretty good at reading people's minds, and with Marilyn I didn't sense any depression or clue of impending self-destruction at all. If someone is terminally depressed, no matter how clever they are, or how expertly they try to conceal it, they will always give themselves away. I've always had an unquenchable curiosity about people and I believe I would have sensed something was wrong if thoughts of suicide were anywhere near the surface of her mind that day.'

Marilyn's make-up man Allan 'Whitey' Snyder and hairdresser Agnes M. Flanagan were visitors to her home that afternoon. 'She was as happy as we've ever seen her,' Snyder observed. With an assortment of nibbles, cocktails and glasses of Dom Perignon champagne, the trio celebrated the actress's potential new deal with the studio. Shortly after saying goodbye to her friends, Marilyn faced up to the inevitability that, in order to obtain that new agreement, she had to sever her professional ties to Paula Strasberg. In a phone call that afternoon, the actress politely told her drama coach she would no longer be requiring her and Lee's services. Their discussion became heated. Before concluding the conversation, however, and keen to remain friends, Paula asked Marilyn to drop in on her and Lee during her visit east the following week. The actress said she would.

Distressed by what had transpired, Marilyn called Dr Greenson late that afternoon and asked him to come over, which he immediately did. To help clear her mind, he suggested she should go for a drive. She agreed. Shortly afterwards, since Murray's car was in the garage being repaired, she climbed into a hurriedly summoned limousine and was driven to Holiday House, the Malibu getaway home belonging to her friend, former Tinseltown director Dudley Murphy, and his fourth wife, Virginia. The exclusive venue, which overlooked the ocean, was favoured by the show business elite. However, her time there was brief. According to Hollywood reporter Sheilah Graham, just before she departed, Marilyn consented to sign the Murphys' special celebrity guest book. Under the column 'Residence', she portentously scribbled *'nowhere'*.

Despite the actress's valiant attempts to keep her visit a secret, as she attempted to leave the building and walk back to her car, she was faced by a small, local television news crew. Gossip that the seemingly reclusive actress was out in public had spread and reporters were desperate to cover it. They were glad they did, because once again she took the opportunity to foolishly declare her ill-conceived intentions of holding a tell-all press conference.

Surprisingly, hardly any of the channels chose to run the report and, as a result, very few people now remember it. However, one who does is Judy Simms, who recalled watching the footage at her home in Greenbrook, New Jersey when it was screened as a part of that evening's news bulletin. 'I was just a teenager when I saw it,' she said. 'Marilyn was on the sidewalk, flanked by the media . . . She stated that she had a little book, and said she was going to reveal what was in it. Naturally, my ears perked up when I heard this because I was curious about what could be in that book. I remember thinking, "This could be trouble." She seemed very direct and determined. I can still see her with the mikes pushed at her. I don't recall anything else they asked her and it was brief. I have never met anyone that remembers that interview.' This is entirely predictable, since the piece was never repeated, and, at the time of writing, is still missing from the television archives.

That evening, before she travelled back home, Marilyn was escorted to Peter Lawford's beachside home where another party was under way. A friend of the actor Dick Livingstone recalled that the actress looked pallid and suggested she should get some sun.

After another restless night, and painfully aware that the tablets Dr Engelberg had prescribed for her were not working, during the morning of Friday 3 August Marilyn called him at his office at 9730 Wilshire Boulevard and asked him to drive over. At a cost of $10, using a short, small-gauge needle, he administered, to her buttocks, an injection of liver and B12 vitamins. He also billed her $25 for the house call. At the end of their brief session, he wrote out a prescription for 25, 1.525-grain Nembutal tablets, the strongest available in capsule form, with the instruction that she should take one each night to aid with her sleep. He also scribbled a prescription for two other medicines: one for 25, 25mg anti-allergy Phenergan tablets; the other for 32 of the pink-in-colour, long-acting barbiturates known as 'Pink Ladies' (which came minus a label). Using a hastily summoned taxi, Eunice Murray collected them immediately from the Vicente Pharmacy on San Vicente Boulevard and returned to Marilyn's home straight afterwards.

The hours of that afternoon were occupied by mundane, household matters. With the actress intending to leave for New York next week and Murray set to begin a six-week tour of Europe, Marilyn's Fifth Helena property was about to be shut. So, in an attempt to wrap up all the outstanding financial manners involving the house, she and Murray sat down at the table and began calculating what bills had yet to be paid. These included $28 to the Sherman Oaks Veterinary Clinic, $111.45 to the Thompson Electric Company and a total of $1,480.18 (in two separate cheques) to cover Arthur Jacobs' forthcoming publicity work for her during the month of August. One City National Bank of Beverly Hills cheque, for the sum of $124.10, to cover Murray's out-of-pocket household expenditures, was also approved by the actress. (Another, for $200, to cover her weekly wage, was authorised a day later, on Saturday 4 August.) A cheque for $52.59 to the municipal utility agency, the Department of Water and Power, was also prepared but, because Marilyn disputed the amount they claimed she owed, she refused to sign it.

Once the number-crunching had been concluded, the actress called her friend Norman Rosten in New York, chiefly to discuss her just-published *Life* magazine article. 'It was great,' he said. 'We liked the spirit.' Their 32-minute conversation soon turned to other subjects: her future and their meeting in a month. 'I'm invited to a benefit performance of a new musical [*Mr. President*] at the end of September,' Marilyn informed Rosten. 'We'll go together. Box seats, the works. We'll have a great time. We have to start living, right?' Optimism continued to flow. Marilyn excitedly spoke about her burgeoning Mexican-style garden, telling him it was going to be 'beautiful'.

Their conversation was interrupted by a long-distance call on her other line. It was film director J. Lee Thompson ringing from Yucatan, Mexico, where he was undertaking pre-production work on United Artists' forthcoming adventure movie *The Mound Builders*, starring Yul Brynner, which was set to roll in the autumn. (It would later be retitled *Kings of the Sun*.) Before dashing to the phone, Marilyn hurriedly concluded her conversation with Rosten by insisting, 'I'll speak to you on Monday.' Thompson was ringing to confirm their meeting the following afternoon. She told him it was still on and announced she was looking forward to it enormously. Then, at precisely 4pm, with the aid of another rented car, Marilyn was driven to Dr Greenson's house for their obligatory end-of-day session. After collecting her $6.05 pills from her regular dispenser, the Vicente Pharmacy, she returned home to find a guest waiting for her, attired in a bathing suit, sitting by her pool.

'I arrived at the house on Friday night after work,' Pat Newcomb recalled in an interview for *The Los Angeles Herald Examiner*. 'I was fighting a bad case of bronchitis and had decided to enter a hospital for a complete rest. But Marilyn called me and said, "Why don't you come out here? You'll have all the privacy you want. You can sun in the back [garden] and have all the rest you want and you won't have to go to a hospital." It was typical of Marilyn, this concern for friends. So I accepted her invitation. I found her in wonderful spirits. Some furnishings for her house had just arrived from Mexico. She was in a very good mood; a very happy mood.'

Another visitor to the actress's home was her attorney, Milton Rudin. His early evening visit was brief. He came to discuss the restarting of *Something's Got To Give* and the new Fox contract, which was still sitting on his desk. (It would in fact sit there for weeks and would ultimately remain unsigned. Apparently, he resisted validating it due to fears that his client would once again fall short of her contractual obligations. Since *Something's Got To Give* was not set to resume shooting until December or in the first week of 1963 at the very earliest, he felt that it would be best for all concerned if he delayed signing the contract until nearer that time – by when, he believed, Marilyn would have had enough time to recuperate and be ready for the demands of filming.) With the matter needing to be resolved, they arranged to meet at his office first thing on Monday morning. 'She seemed cheerful and anxious to get the picture started again. She was in good enough spirits,' he remarked. At precisely 7pm, with the house once more bereft of food, an assortment of fine wine, spirits and pre-cooked exotic foods, intended for both Marilyn and Newcomb, was delivered by the Briggs Delicatessen. (The bill amounted to $49.07.)

Once some of the food had been digested, at 9.30pm, Monroe climbed into her publicist's car and was driven to her favourite Italian restaurant, La Scala on the Sunset Strip. Corroborating popular myths, Peter Lawford, as well as his manager, Milton Ebbins, joined them there. The actor had an ulterior motive for doing so: to enquire about her plans for the following day.

Those who encountered the actress that night would recall she was devoid of make-up, rather edgy and, at the end of the evening, exceptionally tipsy, failing to acknowledge leading costume designer Billy Travilla when he walked over to say hello. Travilla had designed the actress's clothes in eight of her movies (*Monkey Business* in 1952 was their first, *Bus Stop* in 1956 their last) and was responsible for the most famous dress in Hollywood history: the white crepe halter-top dress and sunburst-pleated skirt the actress wore for the classic subway-wind scene in *The Seven Year Itch*. She had even signed a nude calendar for him with the words, 'Billy Dear, please dress me forever. I love you, Marilyn.' But tonight, she failed to recognise him. He apparently meant nothing to her. Seeing no recognition at all in her face when he leant forward to give her a peck on the cheek., Travilla left her table naturally hurt.

Having finished their drinks, and after saying their farewells to Lawford and his manager, Marilyn and Newcomb returned to Fifth Helena. I can reveal a fact overlooked for almost 50 years, even by the chief medical examiner and coroner, Dr Theodore J. Curphey, during his lengthy examination of the circumstances surrounding the actress's death: just as she had at the Cal-Neva, during the early hours of Saturday 4 August, in a desperate attempt to sleep, Marilyn inadvertently came close to exceeding her tolerance level. The Nembutal tablets she had promised Dr Engelberg she would take in small, regular doses were clearly not working and so, in order to reach the desired level, she consumed more. As Dorothy Kilgallen recalled, 'Shortly after midnight, she was found unconscious by the "housekeeper" Mrs. Eunice Murray (*sic* Pat Newcomb) but she was revived and she got through Saturday. Perhaps that experience accounted for her depression on Saturday . . . '

Oblivious to the can of political worms she had unleashed and the troubles about to unfold, Marilyn awoke at approximately 8.45am on the morning of Saturday 4 August. Murray was there to greet her. She had been at the property since 8am. As her car was still being repaired, her mechanic, Henry D'Antonio, had driven her there.

Pressed wearily against the kitchen wall in her white wraparound terry-cloth bath robe, Monroe sipped a glass of grapefruit juice and became agitated at her press secretary, who was still resting in bed. 'To sleep twelve hours in her house was like feasting in front of a starving person,' Murray admitted. 'I had been able to sleep and Marilyn hadn't,' recalled Newcomb. 'When I came out [at 12 midday] looking refreshed, it made her *furious*.' Her memory of that morning continued. 'Marilyn had had some calls that morning and, by the time I saw her, she was in a rage.'

It has become part of Monroe folklore that the calls in question had originated from Peter Lawford and Bobby Kennedy respectively. Rumours persist that they had followed other, far more disturbing calls, which had come during the night, the last taken by Marilyn at precisely 5.30am. During this last call, a female voice was apparently heard to scream, 'Leave Bobby alone! If you don't, you're going to be in *deep* trouble!' The vitriolic rants concluded with the actress supposedly being described as a 'tramp'. The calls, which naturally upset the actress, were believed to come from San Francisco.

In fact they didn't. The instigator of this long-believed, often-repeated story was Jeanne Carmen, the queen of low-budget B-movies and Marilyn's apparent 'best friend'. (Following Marilyn's death, Carmen carved a niche for herself by appearing in practically every Monroe television report, documentary and expose, managing to turn her fleeting encounters with the actress into a fully fledged career.) Carmen's assertion that she had once been Monroe's neighbour was quite true. She had met the actress for the first time in September 1961, when Marilyn moved back into her flat at 882 North Doheny Drive, West Hollywood, a block in which Carmen also resided. Nevertheless, their time together there was brief and, once Monroe had moved into her new home in Brentwood in February 1962, they would never see or speak to each other again.

In fact, the call which had angered Marilyn so that morning had originated from her publicist, Arthur Jacobs, who, as he revealed in interviews at the time, had rung to inform her that director J. Lee Thompson's flight to Los Angeles had been delayed and that subsequently he would be unable to attend their meeting that afternoon. (A new time of Monday at 5pm was pencilled in.) Marilyn had been looking forward to meeting Thompson immensely. Her annoyance arose from the prospect that, at the tail end of the day, she would once more be at a loose end with nothing to do and no one to see.

Further assertions have been made about the actress's final day. One was that her spirits had been rocked by the unexpected arrival in the post of a package containing two cuddly stuffed toys, a tiger and a lamb. Supposedly she was unsure of the sender's identity and put the surprise present down to an unknown admirer. However, this was another invention. Marilyn did not receive such a parcel. She'd had the toys she was apparently sent that morning for months, as testified by a posed August 1961 picture with Maf. Another toy tiger, the one pictured lying on the grass of Marilyn's back garden on the morning of Sunday 5 August, had in fact been purchased by the actress herself, from the Vicente Pharmacy, for the grand sum of $2.08, on Monday 2 April 1962.

Marilyn also apparently made a request from Murray for oxygen during the day, a fact some Monroe biographers have tried to imply was unusual or sinister. Yet as we know, Pat Newcomb suffered from bronchitis. Such a request, if she did indeed make it, would have been made merely to assist with her publicist's breathing. Additionally, one respected Marilyn biographer has led us to believe that Monroe paid another visit to Jean Harlow's mother that Saturday. This is clearly untrue, for the reasons laid out in Chapter 8. With these rumours and untruths out of the way, however, I can now reveal precisely how the remainder of Marilyn's final day panned out.

In the region of 9am, Isidore Miller called from New York, but was told by Murray, 'Marilyn is dressing. She'll call you back.' She didn't. The housekeeper evidently forgot to pass the message on. 'If she had,' as Miller remarked to *Good Housekeeping* magazine in 1963, 'she would have talked to me. She even always interrupted a business conference to talk to me. I waited and waited. Marilyn did not call.'

As I can reveal here for the first time, the actress was unable to speak to him anyway. At that precise time, for 75 straight minutes, she was lying flat out on her brown, faux-leather, 70-inch foldaway massage table, receiving her obligatory Saturday rubbing from Ralph Roberts. 'I gave her a massage that last day, in the morning from 9 to 10.15,' he confirmed. Contrary to the aforementioned myths, according to which Marilyn began the day rattled by malicious phone calls and the arrival of a strange parcel, Roberts himself recalled to reporter Joe Hymas in September 1962 that 'she was in wonderful shape and *not* tense.' His visit was the real reason why the actress chose to get up so early that morning. Before he left, he promised to ring her back that afternoon to discuss the quantity of steaks and potatoes he should purchase for the following day's barbecue.

It was at approximately 10.25am that she learnt, via the call from Jacobs, that Thompson was not coming. So, with no one special to prepare for, Marilyn decided to remain in her bath robe and stay unglamorous. In the words of *Life* magazine columnist Ezra Goodman, 'She takes hours to get her hairdo and make-up just right for public appearances, but privately she likes to scamper about without any make-up at all and with her hair dishevelled.'

At approximately 10.30am, while Murray was tending to the plants in the actress's garden, and the housekeeper's son-in-law, Norman Jeffries, having recently arrived, was attending to the house's renovations, Marilyn welcomed photographer Lawrence Schiller to her property. He had stopped by to see if the actress had signed a contract with *Playboy* magazine. Following her high-profile shoots for *Paris Match* and *Life* and the yet-to-be-published sets for *Cosmopolitan* and *Vogue*, Hugh Hefner's world-famous publication had expressed a novel idea of featuring Marilyn's face on the front cover of one of its magazines and her bottom, as you will guess, on its rear. Through a telephone conversation with Newcomb just days earlier, Schiller knew that the actress was having doubts about the piece. Not wishing to be perpetually perceived as merely a sex object, Marilyn was sceptical and therefore noncommittal about the pictorial. 'I'm tired of being known as the girl with the shape,' she had recently lamented. 'I don't want to play sex roles anymore.'

With the contract therefore still unsigned and the actress clearly uninterested in discussing the topic further for the moment, Schiller's visit was brief and he was soon on his way to Palm Springs for the weekend. But before he left, Marilyn insisted on giving him a tour of her house. 'Mind the doggy smell,' she warned. After wishing him goodbye, the actress walked back inside the property and began sifting through the set of nude swimming shots, taken on the set of *Something's Got To Give*, which he had left behind. Considering most focused on her rear side, she scribbled on the back of some of them, 'These should go to *Playboy*.' After which, she wandered back into the garden and joined Murray in the task of replacing its flowers. At midday, Pat Newcomb climbed out of her bed and, after consuming one of the housekeeper's freshly prepared herb omelettes, joined them in the allotment. Almost immediately, Marilyn imparted to her details about Thompson and made it clear she was unhappy about it. It was for this reason that Newcomb made her aforementioned remark, 'by the time I saw her, she was in a rage.'

As the afternoon rolled on, Marilyn's home received four more calls, two each from Ralph Roberts and Joe DiMaggio Jr. (The latter's first was timed at 2pm, the second at 4.30pm.) With the house's occupants busy either in the garden or in another part of the property, none were answered. Deciding where to position her recently acquired furniture was the actress's main concern. Some items had recently arrived from Mexico, while the chest of drawers purchased from the Pilgrim's Furniture Store on Wednesday had been delivered that afternoon. Marilyn paid the

$228.80 owing for the latter by way of a hurriedly scribbled cheque, which Murray handed with a smile to Earl Shero, the store's van driver.

When exhaustion from moving the furniture started to set in, the actress and Newcomb collapsed into chairs and spent some time lounging by the side of the pool and chatting. At 4pm, the items purchased from the Franks Nurseries & Flowers store three days earlier were delivered. Then, at approximately 4.15pm, allowing time for the van to be clear of the area, and giving them time to leave before J. Lee Thompson was due to arrive (they were unaware he had cancelled), two further individuals were seen entering the actress's home. According to Marilyn's card-playing neighbours, and chiefly as recalled by Mrs Elizabeth Pollard, one matched the description of Peter Lawford, the other that of Bobby Kennedy. But, unlike those before them, they were *not* expected.

A great deal of mystery still surrounds the Attorney General's precise movements that weekend. What we do know for certain was that, on Friday 3 August, Bobby, along with his wife Ethel and four of his children, had arrived in San Francisco, where he was due to record an interview for KGO-TV's popular daytime variety programme, *The Tennessee Ernie Ford Show*, and, on the following Monday, in front of 7,000 lawyers and 5,000 family and friends, address the 85th American Bar Association Convention. As the *San Francisco Chronicle* noted, he was 'with most of his family, but without his usual flashing smile'. As Kennedy walked through the airport, Major Yu of Korea held up a camera to take his picture, but unwittingly left its lens cap on. Noticing the mistake, Bobby shouted, 'Take it again. You didn't get anything.' Was he was desperate to make sure every part of his visit to San Francisco was recorded?

Immediately after their arrival, the Kennedys checked into room 4221 at the St Francis Hotel. Following this, it was believed that the Attorney General spent the next few days at a ranch belonging to his respected attorney friend John Bates, and located in Gilroy, 85 miles south of San Francisco, high in the Santa Cruz mountains. He was *not*, it was claimed, in Los Angeles or, for that matter, anywhere near Marilyn's home in Brentwood. 'Kennedy couldn't have slipped down to Los Angeles,' Bates insisted to the BBC in 1985. 'We all hiked up to the top of the ranch and had a big touch-football game, which was a typical family game of the Kennedys. Eleven of us played . . . we returned to the compound for a swim. The children showered and dressed for dinner. Bobby sat with them as they ate. It was a full, active day.'

Despite his finest attempts to protect his friend, it was fairly easy to find flaws in Bates's recollections. Several people reported seeing Bobby at Los Angeles's Beverly Hills Hotel during the evening of Saturday 4 August, while many others, including Los Angeles' Mayor, Sam Yorty, US Senator George Smathers, Los Angeles Police Chief William H. Parker (who kept Kennedy under surveillance during the visit), future LAPD Police Chief Thomas Reddin, LAPD Chief of Detectives Thad F. Brown, LAPD homicide detective Dan Stewart (who was told when he visited Marilyn's home on the morning of her death), the Chief of Homicide at the Sheriff's Department, Hugh McDonald (who was informed by Brown), former District Attorney John Dickey, Fox publicist Frank Neill (who witnessed Bobby's helicopter landing at the studio) and the meticulous, news-hungry gossip columnists Florabel Muir and Louella Parsons (who spent several weeks researching it), corroborated the fact that the Attorney General *was* indeed in the vicinity that day. The smokescreen surrounding his trip was so intense that all visual references to it were eradicated. Radio host John C. Dvorak, a former employee of the *San Francisco Examiner*, announced on his show, *Dvorak Uncensored*, that all photos taken of the Attorney General in Los Angeles on Saturday 4 August 1962 suspiciously disappeared from the newspaper's archives.

But two men were by far the best first-hand witnesses to the Attorney General's visit. The first was Peter Lawford himself, who clandestinely confirmed Kennedy's presence to his final wife, Patricia Seaton, during work on his (ultimately unfinished) memoirs. The second was LAPD employee Daryl F. Gates, who received news of Kennedy's visit courtesy of the FBI and wrote about it in his 1992 book, *Chief: My Life In The LAPD*. 'We knew Robert Kennedy was in town on August 4,' he revealed. 'We always knew when he was there. He was the Attorney General, so we were interested in him, the same way we were when other important figures came to Los Angeles.'

There was a third witness: Marilyn's house-spy, Eunice Murray, who, after 23 years of denying it, finally came clean in 1985 during interviews for the ABC and BBC television stations. She admitted that Kennedy was in the city that day and *had* in fact paid a visit to the actress's home that Saturday. 'Yes, oh sure [he was a visitor]. Oh sure,' she remarked. Then, in a statement referring to Kennedy guardians such as John Bates, Murray correctly observed, 'It became too sticky that the protectors of Robert Kennedy had to step in to protect him.'

Her ABC TV confession was scheduled to be aired for the first time on Thursday 26 September, during a 26-minute 'Marilyn And The Kennedys' segment on the station's popular 20/20 news magazine show, but it was cancelled at the eleventh hour without any explanation. A severely truncated, 13-minute version, due to be transmitted on the programme a week later, Thursday 3 October, went the same way. The show's chief reporter, the attorney, journalist and writer Geraldo Rivera, a man who had almost single-handedly helped save the station due to his ground-breaking, highly popular style of reporting, was aghast at the axing and immediately quit his post in protest. 'I'm appalled,' he blasted at the time. 'I think that story was a solid piece of TV reporting. They are not going to get away with this.' Joining him in his actions were two of the show's other presenters, television legends Barbara Walters and Hugh Downs.

The man responsible for killing the ambitious report was Roone Arledge, then president of ABC Sports and chairman of the channel. He maintained that the segment contained little substantive evidence and dismissed it as 'sleazy' and 'gossip column stuff'. To which the veteran reporter Downs was quick to remark, 'I do not associate myself with sleazy reporting . . . This so-called "sleazy" piece was more carefully documented than anything *any* network did during Watergate.'

Could the axing of the slot, however, be ascribed to other reasons, such as Mr Arledge's then ongoing friendship with Bobby Kennedy's widow, Ethel? Or possibly to Arledge's assistant, Jeffrey Ruhe, who just happened to be married to Mary Courtney Kennedy, Bobby and Ethel's fifth child? Or even to a top executive at ABC News, David Burke, who once happened to be Edward Kennedy's top aide? I'm sure it did. So did Geraldo Rivera, who publicly chastised Arledge, saying his boss was acting out of 'friendship' rather than 'sound journalistic judgment', and being quoted as saying, in another outburst, 'The decision smacks of cronyism, though I can't prove that.' Aside from ABC executives, a few scant acquaintances and Messrs Rivera, Walters and Downs, virtually no one has viewed the segment and the very few unbiased individuals who have are united in the belief that the report is something which everyone should know about. Unfortunately, 25 years on, a first screening of the feature still looks highly unlikely.

Research shows that, in all probability, during the morning of Saturday 4 August, after spending just one day in San Francisco, the Attorney General left Bates' ranch by car, boarded a plane at the Salina Municipal Airport in Saline County, Kansas, 23 miles south of Gilroy, alighted at Santa Monica Airport (which was still operating at irregular hours) and then climbed aboard Lawford's chartered helicopter, which landed at the heliport near Stage 12 of the deserted 20th Century-Fox back lot (where he was spotted by the aforementioned Frank Neill). He could not descend on his regular spot, the sand adjacent to Lawford's seafront home. On this hot Saturday afternoon, several thousand sun-worshippers were frolicking on the beach which encircled it. After disembarking, Bobby climbed into his brother-in-law's waiting Mercedes and was whisked with alacrity to Marilyn's home, reaching it, completely unexpected, in the region of 4pm.

Expecting to find the actress alone, they were taken aback to see the delivery van and both Murray and Newcomb. Also in shock was Marilyn. Still attired in her terry-cloth bath robe, she was mortified that they could just drop in on her without any kind of warning. Most alarmingly for the actress, a woman famed for her immaculate, breathtaking beauty, they had caught sight of her completely devoid of make-up and beautification. (Proof of this would come in the medical authorities' report, which unflatteringly described her body, at the time of death, as 'unkempt' and 'in need of a manicure and pedicure' – nail polish was flaking from her toes – and noted that she hadn't shaved her legs or dyed the roots of her hair. As *The Los Angeles Times* reported at the time, this indicated 'a lack of interest in maintaining her usually glamorous appearance'. If Marilyn was indeed planning to see Kennedy on that fateful day, as many historians have insisted, why would she have allowed him to see her in such an ill-prepared condition? Of course, she would not have, which leads me to the conclusion that his arrival at her house that afternoon was entirely unexpected.)

After entering the property, knowing that the house was bugged, Kennedy asked the actress if they could go somewhere quiet to chat. Still traumatised, she agreed. Speaking in 1985, Eunice Murray recalled, 'They went out on the terrace in the rear of the garden.' In an October 1985 interview with *The New York Post*'s Jack Schermerhorn, she went one stage further by revealing, 'Marilyn and Bobby were *arguing* [emphasis added] in the rear of the garden . . . ' With her threats about holding a tell-all press conference still hanging over the Kennedys, Bobby urgently needed to talk some sense into her. While they chatted, Lawford went inside the house to speak to the other two women. Sensing she was in the way, and with her car now back from the garage, at precisely 4.35pm Murray climbed into her vehicle and drove to the local market.

Despite starting in a friendly tone, Marilyn's conversation with the Attorney General soon became heated and, once inside the property, he forthrightly informed her once again that her loose talk to journalists *had* to stop. Then, against a backdrop of Frank Sinatra discs, their argument became aggressive. Giving credence to the belief that he was desperate to find the actress's little red 'diary of secrets', Kennedy allegedly began to scream, 'Where is it? Where the *fuck* is it?' He became even more agitated when she refused to tell him. Walking from one room to another, he was now a very angry individual indeed.

The fact that there was such a dichotomy in Bobby's personality was certainly not new to those who knew him. In 1968, New York comic-strip cartoonist Jules Feiffer highlighted the fact in a drawing entitled 'Good Bobby and Bad Bobby'. The good side of him was shown to be a saint, a family man and an ardent civil libertarian; the bad side was depicted as a fervent wiretapper, ill at ease with grown-ups and liberals, an extremely callous man, who would forcibly run over anyone who dared get in his or his brother's way. Unfortunately, Marilyn encountered the latter side that day.

Legend has it that, while he and Lawford frantically searched the cupboards and feverishly rummaged through her drawers, Marilyn became hysterical; unsurprising since, in front of her eyes, they were savagely ransacking her prized new home. She then ordered them to leave. They did not. Now extremely agitated herself, she supposedly screamed at Bobby, telling him she felt 'used and passed around like a piece of meat' and announcing she didn't want to be treated that way any more. 'They argued back and forth for, maybe ten minutes,' Lawford remarked in a previously undocumented 1984 interview. 'Marilyn became more and more hysterical.' As the actor recalled, she goaded Bobby further by announcing that her press conference would take place first thing on Monday.

In fact, her itinerary for that Monday confirms that Marilyn had planned nothing of the kind. In the morning, she had arranged to see Milton Rudin and in the afternoon dress-fitter Elizabeth Courtney, while a rearranged 5pm meeting with film director Lee J. Thompson at the office of her publicist, Arthur Jacobs, was set to conclude her day. (With the CIA's file detailing Marilyn's plan to hold a conference not seeing the light of day until 1992, we have to ask just how this rumour gained such notoriety before then. The answer is Robert Slatzer's 1974 publication, *The Life and Curious Death of Marilyn Monroe*. Obviously remembering the actress's outburst on the television news on Thursday 2 August, he had decided to make much more of it than it really was.)

Nevertheless, Bobby was now livid. In no uncertain terms, he told Marilyn she would have to leave both him and his brother alone. They did not want to hear from her any more. At this point, after further heated altercations, Marilyn screamed and flew into a hysterical rage. After screaming several obscenities, she supposedly flailed wildly at him with her fists and then, in her fury (according to unconfirmed reports), pounced at him with a small kitchen knife. Lawford immediately intercepted, lunging forward to grab her arm, knocking her to the floor and wrestling the knife away. The actress then lay motionless on the ground, sobbing uncontrollably.

While Marilyn's poodle Maf barked away loudly, the two men quickly departed from the property, climbed into Lawford's car and drove to the actor's beach house. Unknown to the two men, the recording equipment strategically placed throughout Marilyn's home had allowed Sam Giancana's men to eavesdrop and record every detail of what had just transpired. (Bobby would be forced into making one further visit to the house before the day was over.) The Attorney General fled the scene an anxious man. In a 1985 interview for *The Times*, private eye Fred Otash recalled that Kennedy went over to Lawford's beachside home and worryingly remarked, 'She's ranting and raving. I'm concerned about her and what may come out of this.' Naturally, they were desperate to speak to her again.

Testimony that the Attorney General travelled to Lawford's house came from two dependable sources. The first was a neighbour of Lawford's, Ward Wood, innocently observing life from his Santa Monica window, who saw Bobby climb out of the car and enter the premises. The second was the actor's mother, Lady May Somerville Lawford, who in her posthumously published 1986 autobiography, *Bitch*, announced she had called her son at this time to inform him that her home had been burgled. 'The telephone lines were very busy,' she recalled, 'but I finally got through. "I've been robbed," I exclaimed to Peter, who could not have cared less about my dwindling jewel and silver collection.' (Verification of this theft was found in bona fide LAPD records, which revealed that, during the evening of Friday 3 August, two items were stolen from her apartment at 1392 Kelton Avenue, West Los Angeles, namely two cut-glass inkwells and a silver tray inscribed 'George IV'.) In the background, during her brief, spiritless exchange with her offspring, she claimed she could hear, as she described it, the 'awful Boston accent of *Bobby Kennedy* [emphasis added]'.

Lawford was clearly uninterested in his mother's latest burglary, her third in recent weeks. 'Later,' he said before abruptly hanging up. He was more concerned about reaching Marilyn, who by now was trying to ring the President in Hyannis Port. It was a fruitless attempt. So, at approximately 5pm, Marilyn called Dr Greenson who agreed to drop by at once. He arrived 15 minutes later to find her still emotionally distraught and immediately administered a sedative: a shot of pentobarbital diluted in a glass of water. 'I came over and remained about two hours (*sic*),' Greenson informed the Los Angeles Police Department. 'She was quite upset. She was also somewhat disorientated. It was clear she had taken some sleeping pills during the day.' (She had and would continue to do so, intermittently, for the next three hours. In an attempt to calm herself, between the hours of 5 and 7pm, Marilyn consumed approximately 12 more Nembutal tablets. To speed up their effects, and to make them enter her bloodstream much faster, she employed the trick shown to her by her co-star Montgomery Clift on the set of *The Misfits*, pricking the top of each capsule with a pin and pouring its contents directly into a glass of water.)

Curious as to what had brought about her distressed state and caused the mess strewn around the place, Greenson naturally probed further. In his statement to the LAPD after Marilyn's death, he declared that Marilyn replied by telling him 'she'd had an irrational argument with Pat Newcomb' and that she 'resented the fact that Newcomb had taken some pills the night before and slept 12 hours and Marilyn had also taken pills and slept only six hours'. (Newcomb would become incensed by part of this remark. On Wednesday 19 September 1973, she rightly denied she had consumed Marilyn's medicine. 'It's outrageous,' she stormed to an *Independent* (AM) reporter. 'I'm stunned! I didn't take *any* of her pills. I slept *without* pills. I further think his remarks about a patient are unethical.') Greenson went on to inform the department, 'Marilyn was talking in a confused way. At this time, I didn't know she had been given [by Dr Engelberg] a Nembutal prescription she had filled the day before.' This part of his statement was true; much of the rest was entirely false.

As their conversation unfurled, the actress went on to divulge to Greenson all that had happened between her and the Kennedys and revealed that she had almost overdosed the previous evening. He found the revelations both surprising and startling and resolved that his latest, decisive consultation with Marilyn should be completely free of interference. Since Murray was, as we know, an invaluable spy for the doctor, she was asked, on her return to the house, to stay for the evening, something she ordinarily did only rarely. But Pat Newcomb was told to leave. Greenson implied that her presence was upsetting Marilyn. He explained, 'I said that, instead of Pat staying overnight, Pat should go home and Mrs Murray remain the night. I didn't want Marilyn to be alone.'

At 5.30pm, just as Newcomb was leaving, Marilyn peered out from the hallway and, as if to plead for her forgiveness, shouted, 'I will phone you in the morning.' Unbeknown to the actress, fearing a repeat of the previous night's scenario, Newcomb had confiscated one of Marilyn's Nembutal bottles. Before returning to her apartment, the publicist drove over to *Playboy*'s offices to return Monroe's unsigned contract and hand in the actress's annotated naked swimming shots.

A phone call interrupted Greenson's further discussions with the actress. At approximately 6pm, Ralph Roberts rang for the third time and once more, failed to reach her. 'She's not here,' Greenson told him sternly before slamming the phone down. (Eunice Murray, who usually answered the telephone, had not at that time returned to the house, having decided to drop by her apartment and collect some clothes which needed washing, ready for her trip to Europe.) Roberts dismissed the curt reply and immediately set off to Beverly Hills to buy steaks and potatoes for the following evening's barbecue.

Our tale now takes an extraordinary twist. It is at this point in my attempt to accurately piece together the events leading up to and after Marilyn's death that I become fully aware of the lies and twisted accounts emanating from practically all of the key players involved in the tragedy, and the faulty memories of the rest. One by one, it seemed that almost every one of them would chop and change their account of events on Saturday and Sunday, 4 and 5 August 1962.

We begin with her not-so-loyal housekeeper cum spy, Eunice Murray. In *Marilyn: The Final Months*, she announced that, 'Sometime between 2pm and 4pm' her friend Henry D'Antonio and his wife paid a visit to Marilyn's home. A motor mechanic by trade, D'Antonio was returning Eunice's car, which she had left with him earlier that morning on her way to Marilyn's home. The couple's request to meet the actress was thwarted when Murray informed them she was resting in her bedroom. In truth, it was shortly before 4.30pm when the couple visited; the time when Marilyn was engaged in a heated discussion with Kennedy. As you will guess, this was the *real* reason why she couldn't meet Murray's friends. The excuse that Marilyn was 'resting in her bedroom', made by Eunice both that day to her friends, and subsequently to newspaper reporters – on Monday 6 August, when asked by reporters how the actress spent her final day, Murray incredibly replied, Marilyn 'spent most of Saturday in *bed* resting . . . She wasn't ill. She was just resting' – was made for no other reason that to conceal that the actress had been speaking with the Attorney General.

Then we come to her doctor, Ralph Greenson, who informed Detective Sergeant R.E. Bryon that the reason for his visit to Marilyn's home that afternoon was because she was 'having trouble sleeping'. If we are to believe this story, it would have meant that he was trying to help Monroe rest at around 5.15 in the afternoon while her house-guest, Pat Newcomb, was still present. Greenson's justification for visiting the actress is completely blown out of the water when we read Newcomb's account of her last moments with Marilyn. 'I left at 6.30pm,' she insisted (although it was actually a full hour earlier). 'When I last saw her, *nothing* about her mood had changed. She said to me, "I'll see you tomorrow. Toodle-oo." She was in good mood, a happy mood.' Newcomb never once mentioned Monroe's tired demeanour or how Greenson was there just to get the actress rested.

Confusion was to reign further when the doctor, albeit briefly, insisted that he never even visited Marilyn that day. However, proof that he did was close at hand. On Monday 15 July 1963, he deposited an invoice for the sum of $1,400 for his services to Marilyn Monroe's estate and, according to that bill, in clear black and white, the date given as his final session with the actress was Saturday 4 August 1962.

As per his demand, Greenson's visits to Marilyn's home never exceeded the 90 minutes/two hours mark. So, at 7pm on that Saturday night, having earned his fee, he was preparing to head home. Before he left, he handed to Murray, who had just returned from her errands, a small scrap of paper bearing the telephone number where he could be reached that evening. After waving the doctor goodbye, Marilyn walked back into her home and ushered Maf into the back garden where, for a few short minutes, the two played a game of fetch-ball – the actress threw the poodle's two small toy animals, the aforementioned tiger and a lamb, into the air and he ran to retrieve them from where they had landed. The gathering dusk curtailed their game. The actress then walked back inside her home and told Murray to put Maf to bed. It was 7.05pm. (The toys were not collected, remaining motionless on the grass at the exact spot where they had landed. Hence the unusual United Press International (UPI) picture, taken on the morning of Marilyn's death, of two abandoned baubles strewn across the lawn in the actress's back garden.)

Just as Marilyn was entering her living room, her telephone rang. It was Peter Lawford. *New York Post* columnist Earl Wilson quoted the actor as saying, 'She picked up the phone herself on the second ring, which leads me to believe that she was fine.' According to Lawford, the call was to invite Marilyn to a small dinner party at his home. 'I asked her to have dinner with me, with Pat Newcomb and [Hollywood agent] "Bullets" Durgom,' he recalled, 'but Marilyn decided not to come . . . and I wound up with "Bullets".' In another interview, he remarked, 'Thinking she was lonely, I asked her to have dinner with me and some friends. But she decided not to come along. She said she was going to bed.'

In another piece, he recalled that, during their conversation, Marilyn requested the Hyannis Port number of his wife, Pat. (It was a ruse. The actress actually requested the number not for Pat but to speak to the President. The number she had been using was clearly incorrect. Staff at the White House, which Monroe had originally called, were responsible for telling the actress where the President was staying that weekend.) Lawford also admitted that Marilyn 'sounded sleepy', blithely adding, 'I've talked to her a hundred times before and she sounded no different.'

While I have no doubt that Lawford *did* call Marilyn at the time he claimed, 7.05pm, I do not believe he called to invite her to dinner that evening (which, in fact, was just a delivery of Chinese food, intended to be eaten straight out of the cardboard cartons in which it came). Why would any host invite such an important guest as Monroe to a get-together with just minutes to spare before the other, less important invited guests were due to start arriving? In any case, with his wife Pat still away at the Kennedys' compound in Hyannis Port, the small gathering at Peter's beachside home that night was, in all probability, just another of his regular, thinly veiled sex parties, attended by a few close pals and two high-class prostitutes. Since she was still traumatised by the sexually tinged events that had occurred at Sinatra's Cal-Neva Lodge the previous weekend, surely he knew that Marilyn would want no part in this kind of event.

In all likelihood, Lawford instead rang for two reasons. First, he was desperate to see how Marilyn was, following her arduous ordeal just a couple of hours earlier; second, with Bobby Kennedy still sitting by his side, the actor was desperately trying to quieten and reason with her. Only then was the appeasing, eleventh-hour offer to join them at his beach house presented. According to Fred Otash, 'She [Marilyn] said, "No, I'm tired. There is nothing more for me to respond to. Just do me a favour. Tell the President I tried to get him. Tell him goodbye for me. I think my purpose has been served." Marilyn then hung up the phone.'

Around 20 minutes later, at precisely 7.35, after imparting details of their conversation to Bobby, Lawford tried ringing the actress back. He rang several times but each time the line was engaged. (He would not be able to reach her again for 45 minutes.) Otash recalled, 'Bobby got panicky and said, "What's going on?" He [Lawford] said, "Nothing. That's the way she is."' He was used to Marilyn's occasionally busy telephone lines.

Exasperated by what had happened, realising the place was bugged and desperate to be away from the property before the guests started to arrive, Bobby got up and, using the actor's car, drove to the Beverly Hilton Hotel (which, by chance, was across the street where, several years earlier, his father Joseph had lived for a time with actress Gloria Swanson). As normal, Bobby's hotel suite had been charged to Lawford. (He would, however, fail to pay for it, as well as for all of the Kennedys' subsequent stays there, and was still shirking his financial obligations to the establishment some 15 months later, in November 1963. On Monday 4 May 1964, the Hilton Hotel Corps., the owner of the Beverly Hilton Hotel, was forced to issue a writ against him and his production firm for the sum of $9,011, to cover all outstanding lodgings, services and costs. Lawford should have settled the demand earlier. Prior to the court order, his unpaid bill stood at just $6,762.)

Interestingly, Eunice Murray, a woman infamous for perpetually changing her account of the night Marilyn died, would even briefly insist that the actress never even spoke to Lawford on the night of her death. Although her contradictions began straight after the actress's death, in time, possibly thanks to the onset of old age, it was obvious that Murray became confused as to what she could and could not say and whose story she should corroborate.

At the conclusion of Lawford's call, at approximately 7.15pm, Marilyn carried her phone out of her bedroom and placed it in a small guest room across the hall which was currently being used as a temporary storage space. As usual, to soften the sound of any possible calls, she enclosed the phone with the pillows from her bed. Afterwards, she strolled back to her bedroom, took a further handful of Nembutals and lay down on her bed. At approximately 7.31pm, just as she was on the point of falling asleep and Murray was about to watch, on CBS-affiliated station KFMB, a repeat screening of the two-year-old *Perry Mason* courtroom drama 'The Case of the Irate Inventor', the phone rang again. Murray answered it. It was Joe DiMaggio's 21-year-old son, US Marine private first class Joseph P., ringing from a public call box at his base at Camp Pendleton, 38 miles north of downtown San Diego. It was his third call of the day.

According to Eunice, she then walked across to the actress's room, knocked on its door, entered and discovered Marilyn already drowsy, spread out across the mattress. The sedatives she had taken were beginning to work. In an interview for *The New York Post*, Murray partly corroborated this when she said, 'Marilyn was already in bed when young DiMaggio called. She had already taken some sedation.' Ominously, she had lost track of how much.

The housekeeper gently awoke Marilyn, passed on the news that Joe Jr was on the phone and asked if she wanted to talk to him. She confirmed that she did. Marilyn had left orders that she should always be summoned, unless she was busy, when he or any other of her former stepchildren called. Marilyn quickly woke herself up, arose from her bed, walked to the phone in the guest room and sat down on the floor. 'She was in a very gay [happy], delighted mood when she spoke with him,' Murray remembered. 'I didn't hear the words. But I heard her laughing.' (The housekeeper delivered this account in 1974, several years before she changed her account of that night, claiming inaccurately that Marilyn picked up the phone and completed the conversation in her *bedroom*.)

Marilyn loved talking to DiMaggio. In fact, she relished speaking to all of her ex-stepchildren. As she had revealed to *Redbook*'s Alan Levy earlier in the year, she loved them more than she 'loved anyone', adding, 'I didn't want to be their mother, or stepmother, I wanted to be their *friend*.' She enjoyed her conversations with Joe Jr so much that she didn't even resent the fact that she always had to pay for them. His infrequent calls to the actress usually came reverse-charge, the last being two from San Diego on Friday 6 July. She was his sounding board for advice about his relationships, and such was the case that night when he called to announce that his 15-month engagement to 21-year-old Pamela Ries, an employee of a Kansas City trading stamp firm, had ended.

However, by the time Marilyn received this news, it was already old. They had actually split three weeks earlier, on or around Tuesday 10 July. The only paper the actress read was *The New York Times*, so she had missed the reports of it in several other dailies (*The Oakland Tribune* on Tuesday 31 July, *The Tucson Daily Citizen* and *The Bridgeport Telegram*, to name but two, one day later). Sadly, it seemed that, with regard to his return to bachelorhood, Marilyn was one of the last to know; we have to question here just how close DiMaggio Jr really was to her.

During their exchange, despite being sympathetic, she told him she was pleased the relationship had finished, as she believed the pair were unsuited. In contrast to Lawford's account that the actress 'sounded sleepy' at that time, DiMaggio recalled Marilyn as being 'Great. She was in fine form and if anything was amiss, I wasn't aware of it.' Since he was in the middle of watching a live telecast of the Baltimore Orioles/Los Angeles Angels baseball game, which was being played that night in Baltimore at the Memorial Stadium, his conversation with Marilyn was brief: just five minutes and not longer, as many have insisted. (It is worth noting that his call was the very last to be billed to that line during the actress's lifetime.)

When her conversation with Joe Jr had concluded, Marilyn returned the phone to the guest room, but instead of covering it with pillows, which she habitually did, she merely lifted the receiver up and away from its cradle. She then walked back into the living room and elatedly passed on to Murray DiMaggio's information. 'She seemed very pleased about it,' the housekeeper recalled, 'and said she was going to call somebody to tell them the news.' By way of the phone in her bedroom, that person was Dr Greenson, who at precisely 7.41pm was at home preparing for a dinner date at the home of his friends, Mr and Mrs Arnold Albert.

'While I was shaving, Marilyn rang,' he recalled in 1973. '"I have some good news," she said. "I've just had a talk with Joe Junior and he's broken up with the girl I never did like and I feel real good."' Greenson listened intently before replying, 'That's great.' He then enquired what she intended doing that evening. Unsure at first, she then said she wanted to take a walk on the beach. He dissuaded her from doing so. 'People will recognise you,' he told her. Instead, he suggested she should drink a large glass of Coke to clear her head and once more join Murray on a drive up the coast highway. The actress enjoyed driving at night. 'Sometimes we would drive for an hour,' Murray recalled in 1973, 'Zuma Beach, Point Mugu, Oxnard . . . It had a nice effect on her.'

Noticing then that one of her medicine bottles was missing, as a letter he wrote to Dr Marianne Kris testified, the actress next asked Greenson, 'Did you take my Nembutals?' He replied that he did not. He concluded the exchange by informing her, 'If you need me, you know where I'm going to be. Mrs Murray has my number. If anything happens, you know where to get in touch with me.' After replacing the receiver, the actress walked back into the living room, stopped and, under the archway, announced to Murray, who was still watching *Perry Mason*, 'I think we'd better not go for a ride,' adding, 'Goodnight, Mrs Murray. I think I'll turn in now.' She then turned and walked the four short steps back to her bedroom. Before closing its door, as an afterthought, she said, 'Goodnight, honey.' Within a few short minutes, the sound of Frank Sinatra recordings was once more heard emanating from the small, portable record player, which rested on the floor of the actress's room.

At this point, shortly before 7.55pm on the evening of Saturday 4 August 1962, things get exceptionally sketchy about the final hours and minutes in the life of Marilyn Monroe. But, after five years of exhaustive research, and after examining every surviving scrap of evidence, scrutinising each piece of medical data, listening to every relevant interview, reading all applicable transcripts, devouring each newspaper report, watching every single significant television show, listening to each consequential radio programme, and after distinguishing the fact from the fiction, the truth from the lies, I firmly believe I can finally answer the five-decade-old mystery about how Marilyn Monroe, the world's greatest film star and sex symbol, tragically died . . .

Chapter Ten

7.55pm, Saturday
4 August 1962–9.04am,
Sunday 5 August 1962

At approximately 7.55pm, Marilyn walked into her bedroom, closed the door behind her, knelt down on the floor and started playing some Sinatra albums on her small white record player. Selected others were then collected and heaped on to the deck's spindle. After this, in the region of 8pm, she began preparing for bed, which usually meant popping a small handful of Nembutals. But tonight, as she had just announced to Greenson, she could not find any. She had seemingly exhausted her supply. With this difficulty added to the disconcerting incident with Kennedy and Lawford, which was still swirling round her mind, she became restless. In an attempt to rectify this, she reached over to her bedside table and prepared, then swigged a liquid dose of the hypnotic sedative chloral hydrate.

Her bout of anxiety had caused her adrenal glands to release into her body atypical amounts of the corticosteroid hormone cortisol and adrenaline, which in turn had sparked an increase in her heart rate, blood pressure and respiration. With her physique now in such an advanced state of animation, she knew instinctively that resting that night was going to be nigh-on impossible. Her first attempt proved this. So, in a another attempt to alleviate the problem, at approximately 8.05pm, Marilyn clambered up from her bed, switched on her small table light and, assuming it would help her, lunged for several more mouthfuls of the chemical reagent.

Following many years of insomnia, she had developed a good under-standing of medication and knew instinctively to switch drugs when her body had built up tolerance to one. But now there was a difference. Unbeknown to the actress, chloral hydrate, a drug she had been taking regularly for just nine days, interacts adversely with Nembutal, large quantities of which were still swirling around her system. When it began to harm her again that night, unlike the two previous incidents at the Cal-Neva the previous weekend and in her bedroom just 20 hours earlier, the rescue tragically did not come.

Now, as she lay on her bed, the chloral hydrate she had consumed first disrupted the electrical and chemical signals between her brain and her heart and lungs, causing them to slow down artificially, misleading her body into falling asleep. Absorbed through the lining of her stomach, the drug flooded into the actress's bloodstream. Travelling to her brain, the substance then engulfed her respiratory centre, completely smothering it. Without the electrical signals from her brain, her breathing became irregular, shallow and less frequent. No doubt as a reaction to the chloral hydrate, her lungs then became congested.

Arising from her bed, she started to gasp, became drowsy and sluggish. Then, after losing her sense of judgement, and following a futile attempt to open her bedroom door, she collapsed to the floor, landing on her back. A toxic dose of drugs was now beginning to ravage her body. Frail, otiose screams were made to attract Murray's attention. But the housekeeper did not hear them. She was still glued to the television set, watching Perry Mason preside over another case. Her hearing was poor, so the volume on the apparatus was set to high. Marilyn's despairing cries for help were also drowned out by the discs, which were still spinning on her record player.

Shortly after 8.20pm, the phone on Marilyn's floor rang again. She lunged at it. It was Lawford. His 45 minutes of sporadic perseverance had paid off. Considering their previous exchange had ended so abruptly, he was desperate to speak to the actress again. According to Joe DiMaggio's close friend Walter Winchell, immediately after she answered the call, a weak, almost incoherent cry rang out. 'Get a doctor, quick,' she ominously declared. 'I think I took too many pills.' Her heart was now pumping less and less blood around her body.

Thinking it was another cry for attention, Lawford did nothing. Instead, knowing that his wife Pat was away for the weekend, he unsympathetically retorted, 'I'm a married man. I can't get involved.' As Fred Otash revealed in 1985, the actor, thinking that she was once again being overdramatic, then jokingly instructed Marilyn in an act of bravado in front of his house guests 'not to leave any note behind'. After several seconds of silence, the line went dead.

266 | The Final Years of Marilyn Monroe

With Lawford proving to be utterly useless, and with the phone still just about clasped in her hand, shortly before 8.25pm Marilyn mustered enough energy to call one other friend: Ralph Roberts. Unfortunately he was still out, collecting food for their barbecue the following day. Consequently, she was only able to reach his answering service. Her message was garbled. He would recall that the voice sounded 'fuzzy and troubled'. Those words would be her last. She slipped into unconsciousness, and then a coma, soon afterwards. The flow of blood around her body had by now turned into a trickle. With each passing minute, Marilyn's life systems began to close down, muscle by muscle, organ by organ, until eventually there was *nothing*. In medical terminology, her body had suffered from respiratory depression and a cardiovascular collapse. According to Dr George P. Varkey MB, FRCP of London, Ontario, death would have come within 25 to 35 minutes of her taking her last, lethal dose of medicine. And in Marilyn's case, it did.

Confusion over her precise time of death was to reign. Mortician Guy Hockett estimated that the actress must have died somewhere between 9.30 and 11.30pm and the coroner's office noted the time of death as 3.40am. The police, clearly confounded as to what precisely had happened, wildly estimated the time of death as 'sometime between 8pm and 3.35am'.

Although not precise in its times, the highly reliable *San Francisco Chronicle* was more accurate in its original reporting. 'Marilyn died shortly after she retired for the night at 8pm,' the paper announced. The American journalists Stan Hays and John Edwards were also pretty near the mark when, in a syndicated report filed on Sunday 5 August, they wrote, 'Doctors think she died sometime between 8pm and 9pm.' In fact, Marilyn Monroe, one of Hollywood's finest actresses, tragically passed away at approximately 8.40pm.

To begin with, Peter Lawford was not alarmed. After all, Marilyn had sounded fine during their last conversation just 65 minutes earlier and he was all too familiar with her occasional previous, melodramatic pill-popping scenes. He knew from her friends that she was apparently inclined to sometimes fake a suicide attempt in order to arouse sympathy. Anyway, he firmly believed that the tablets she consumed were not harmful; certainly not injurious enough to assist in any suicide attempt. But he was wrong. Like Marilyn, he was a pill addict and routinely believed he was never in danger with the drugs he was consuming. Worryingly, he too had no idea about an addict's tolerance before fatality. (His death at 61, on Monday 24 December 1984, from cirrhosis of the liver and heart and kidney failure, was actually precipitated by his excessive drug-taking and chronic abuse of alcohol.)

Immediately after finishing the call, Lawford replaced the receiver and, with his house guests listening on intently, made light of the situation. But within minutes, he was having misgivings. Was her condition more serious than he thought, he wondered. He tried ringing her back. The phone was now busy. Bemused, he called the operator and asked her to check Marilyn's lines. He was informed one phone was off its hook, the other was engaged in a call. To set his mind at rest, he then said he would drive out to her house and check on her personally. (It was a hollow suggestion. With Bobby Kennedy still in possession of his Lincoln Continental, he knew he couldn't do this without raising suspicion.)

George Durgom dissuaded him from doing so, saying that, if something *was* indeed wrong with the actress, it would not look good if he was seen at the property. He was after all the President's brother-in-law. After further cajoling from his house guests, the actor decided to ring the actress again. But with Marilyn now lying practically comatose on her bedroom floor, desperately trying to call Roberts, the phone was engaged, and with her other still off its hook, his call was naturally not answered. Eunice Murray would not have heard it anyway. *Perry Mason* still had three more minutes to run.

Producer Joseph Naar, another guest of Lawford's that night and a long-time friend of Marilyn's, then offered to go and see her. Lawford declined the proposal, impishly insisting that *he* was the one who should do so. Needing assurance that this was indeed the correct thing to do, the actor then called his manager, Milton Ebbins, but he too was against the idea. 'Wait a minute,' he said, 'I understand your apprehension and I think you're absolutely right but, for heaven's sake, you're the President's brother-in-law. You can't go over there on your own. If you had to call the hospital or whatever, you're going to have your picture on the front page and Jack [Kennedy]'s and everybody else's. You'd better let this be handled by people who know what they're doing and *not* you.' After finishing his call, Ebbins rang the home of Marilyn's lawyer, Milton Rudin. The time was now shortly after 8.28pm.

However, Rudin was out for the evening, socialising at a cocktail party at the home of Mildred Allenberg, the widow of Bert, Frank Sinatra's agent at the William Morris Agency. At approximately 8.30pm, following the information left on Rudin's answering service, Ebbins called the party and passed on a request for Rudin to ring him, which the lawyer did 15 minutes (and a couple of cocktails) later, in the region of 8.45. Ebbins then conveyed the story of how Lawford had called Marilyn at her home, explaining how, during their conversation, her voice seemed to fade away and when he attempted to phone her back, her line was busy. 'I'll check it out,' Rudin replied. 'I'm sure it's okay. She does this all the time. She talks to people; she takes a couple of pills and then she falls asleep with the phone hanging down.' He was not overly concerned.

In a desperate show of empathy, Ebbins also instructed Rudin to contact Ralph Greenson who, from the home of his friends the Alberts, deceitfully informed him that he had seen her earlier that day and she was fine. When this news was passed back to Lawford, knowing straight away that it was incorrect, he told Rudin to call Marilyn's residence, which he did in the region of 9.30pm – no less than 70 minutes after the actress's first desperate plea for help. Lawford's feeble indecisiveness, and that of his sluggish cronies, had cost Marilyn big-time. Her life, as we know, had sadly ebbed away.

Over at Fifth Helena, meanwhile, once *Perry Mason* had finished for another week, at precisely 8.28pm Murray switched off the television set and set about doing her chores. With the house about to be closed for six weeks and a trip to Europe to prepare for, there was a lot of tidying and washing to be done. Noticing the telephone in the guest room was still off its hook, she swiftly replaced it. She was in the garage, in the middle of doing her laundry with the help of Marilyn's washing machine, when this phone rang. It was Rudin, who immediately informed her of the actress's conversation with Lawford earlier that evening. Murray listened intently before telling him, 'Why, of course she's all right . . . the light is on and the radio (*sic*) is playing,' but promised she would check on the actress anyway. While Rudin was reporting this update back to Lawford, Murray replaced the handset and walked to her employer's bedroom. Sinatra albums could still be heard playing on the record player within.

Her gentle taps on the door were met with a deafening silence. 'Marilyn, Marilyn,' Murray whispered. There was no answer. As she confirmed in a 1982 interview with the American researcher Justin Clayton, she noticed the door was half closed. Her initial attempts to open it further proved futile. The heavy, solid wood door was inexplicably jammed more tightly than usual. Sensing something was amiss, she walked out of the house into the cold, dark August evening and round to the windows of the actress's bedroom. In *Marilyn: The Last Months*, Murray recalled, 'Behind the iron grille, I could see that the casement window was slightly ajar. The deeply recessed Spanish sill prevented me from reaching inside.'

So she rushed back inside, grabbed a poker from the fireplace and returned outside to the glazing. With the aid of the implement, she was now able to pull back the drapes and peer inside Marilyn's room. She was greeted with the sight of the actress's body, lying face up, motionless across the floor. The upper part of her torso was pressed against the lowest section of the door. Her phone was near her right hand. (The fact that Murray had discovered Marilyn's body in that position was actually uncovered in 1967 by Fred Lawrence Guiles during research on his book *Norma Jean*. He wrote at the time, 'After Mrs. Murray became worried about Marilyn, she went outside and peered into Marilyn's bedroom. The blinds were drawn, but she could make out Marilyn's body lying on the *floor* [emphasis added].' But strangely, by the time his manuscript was published two years later, in 1969, his reference to how the actress had been discovered had inexplicably been cut from the text. One wonders why.)

Now gripped by panic, Murray ran back inside the building and raced to Marilyn's room where, once more, she desperately tried to gain entrance. With the actress's inert body lying against the opening, it was a demanding task. Pressing her shoulder hard against the door, Murray managed to prise it open a tad further, just enough for her to squeeze herself in, drag the phone towards her and call Greenson to inform him of the situation. (Proof that Eunice used *this* line and not the one in the guest room came via Marilyn's phone records, which revealed that, after DiMaggio Jr's reverse-charge call at approximately 7.30pm, there were no further calls made on that line for the remainder of the night. Investigating officer Sergeant Byron of the Los Angeles Police Department would confirm this in his report of the incident, which stated with regard to the phone, GR476-1890, that 'no calls had been made during the hours of the occurrence [the actress's death]'. In fact, the phone in the guest room would not be used for another seven hours.)

Within ten minutes, Greenson was at the property. Following Murray's lead, he grabbed a poker from the fireplace, rushed back outside, smashed a pane in her other window (the one not protected by decorative, wrought-iron bars), unhooked the catch and climbed in. He dashed over to the actress's body and immediately began examining it. Less than a minute after he began doing so, he realised he was too late. Marilyn Monroe was dead. Speaking in 1973, he recalled, 'I took her pulse. No pulse, no breathing, no nothing.'

'We've lost her,' Greenson sadly announced to Murray. The doctor had hauled Marilyn's body away from the door to allow her to enter. It was now just after 10.10pm.

However, instead of ringing the local authorities to inform them of the accident, he rang first the publicity department at 20th Century-Fox and then Milton Rudin, who in turn immediately called Arthur P. Jacobs at home. But Jacobs wasn't there. He was with his fiancée, actress Natalie Trundy, at the Hollywood Bowl, watching, from 8.30pm, the 41st Annual 'Pops' show, which tonight featured the award-winning composer, arranger and conductor Henry Mancini and the American piano duo, (Arthur) Ferrante and (Louis) Teicher.

In a 1985 interview for the BBC, Trundy recalled, 'About three-quarters of the way through the concert, someone came to our [private] box and said, "Arthur, come quickly. Marilyn is dead . . . "' After being told discreetly about the situation, almost certainly by a uniformed Bowl employee, Jacobs drove his companion home to her apartment at 122 Canyon Drive, next door to where, at no. 120, Pat Newcomb lived and was currently resting in bed.

At once, he headed over to Marilyn's Brentwood home, arriving there in the region of 11pm to find those present in a state of high panic. Considering his role as the actress's publicist, his first task was to sweep the property for anything that might be classed as incriminating towards her or the studio. Cupboards were rifled through, drawers were ransacked and her two private filing cabinets were broken into. A small selection of photos, letters and incriminating telephone notepad scribbles, made by the actress during her recurrent nights of insomnia, were among the items seized. He also snatched her red pocket diary, which, in all probability, he found concealed under the mattress on the actress's bed. (Reports which said that, at this point of the evening, the entire contents of Marilyn's cabinets were seized and destroyed are false. The multitude of surviving items – letters, receipts, pictures, legal documents, mementos, etc. – which the actress had secreted away were featured and illustrated in an October 2008 *Vanity Fair* magazine piece entitled 'The Things She Left Behind'.)

It was not unusual for a film studio to cover up the death scene of one of its employees. The death of Hollywood director and producer Paul Bern is possibly one of the best examples. On Monday 5 September 1932, just four months after his marriage to Jean Harlow, Bern's naked, lifeless body was discovered in his home, lying on the floor of his bathroom. MGM's Louis B. Mayer announced that Bern had committed suicide 'because of his impotency' and inability to sexually satisfy Harlow. However, the truth was quite different: Bern had been murdered by his former wife, Dorothy Millette. Mayer knew he had to protect his prize asset, Harlow, at any cost and knew he could not release details of a mysterious woman visiting Bern that fatal night. The thought that Harlow might then be accused of murdering her husband was incomprehensible; as a convenient way out of getting them all out of this most awkward predicament, the suicide scenario was conceived.

Using the telephone in Marilyn's bedroom, Jacobs then called one of his employees, Michael Selsman, and informed him of the actress's death. He also warned him to be ready to handle a barrage of questions about it from the media and instructed him not to mention any names, in particular those of the Kennedys, in any of his statements. Jacobs had arrived at Monroe's home within minutes of Milton Rudin. (It has been impossible to prove or disprove claims that Fox publicity executives John Campbell and Frank Neill were also present in the house that night.) Just moments after they did so, a clearly agitated Greenson began shifting the blame away from himself by telling the attorney, 'God damn it. He [Dr Hyman Engelberg] gave her a prescription I didn't know about.' This was true. Greenson was completely oblivious to his colleague's actions. Furthermore, he knew full well that, if checks were made, the authorities would indeed find out that Marilyn had been given a fresh prescription for 25 Nembutals by Engelberg just a day before she died.

Discussions in Marilyn's bedroom were interrupted by another phone call. It was Lawford. Word had quickly spread that Marilyn was in a bad way. Following an order from Bobby Kennedy and an earlier tip-off by phone, he was ringing to enquire about the actress's welfare. 'Is she dead?' he asked. Murray took the call and confirmed she was. (According to recently released FBI reports, originally dated Monday 19 October 1964, Kennedy called Lawford from his San Francisco hotel room that night to enquire of Marilyn's well-being. But once again, this was inaccurate on two points. First, he did not say, 'Is she dead *yet?*' and second, he was not in San Francisco. He was still in his room at the Beverly Hilton Hotel and would not return to Frisco until later, as we will see.)

Greenson's plan to inform the authorities of Marilyn's death was halted when Lawford forcibly announced he had to delay doing so until any potentially incriminating evidence, particularly pertaining to the Kennedys, had been excised from the building. With no alternative, the doctor reluctantly agreed. Thus Hollywood's greatest-ever conspiracy was set in motion.

Following a call from Lawford, and after his party guests had departed for the night, the Attorney General drove back to the actor's property, collected him and set off in the direction of the actress's home. Once there, the two men immediately set about an all-encompassing sweep of the place. Finding and securing any incriminating evidence against the Kennedys, in particular Monroe's small red diary, was of huge importance. In all probability, Jacobs handed the diary over to the Attorney General during his visit.

After an hour of extensive searching through the cupboards, drawers and cabinets, conducted in silence, Kennedy and Lawford climbed back into the actor's car and hastily departed for the Beverly Hills Hotel. Unfortunately for the two men, their breakneck journey managed to catch the attention of a Beverly Hills police officer named Lynn Franklin. At approximately 12.40am, just 40 minutes after starting his regular midnight shift, Franklin saw a dark-coloured Lincoln Continental speed east on Olympic Boulevard in Beverly Hills. Guessing that the vehicle was going in excess of 80 miles per hour in a 35 mph zone, he switched on his red light and pursued.

Pulling the car over and going to question the driver inside, he immediately recognised Lawford behind the wheel. 'Peter, what are you doing, driving so crazily?' Franklin asked. Flashing his torch to see the other occupant of the vehicle, he noticed Kennedy sitting in the back seat. (Accusations that Dr Greenson was in the car too are logistically unfeasible.) Lawford allegedly told him they were rushing to get Kennedy back to his hotel room, checked out and on to a flight to San Francisco. The police officer ordered Lawford to slow down and then allowed the car to proceed. (When Franklin spoke to the hotel the following day, he gathered that Kennedy had checked out approximately 20 minutes after he had encountered the pair in the street.)

After picking up his belongings, the Attorney General was driven back to the actor's beachside house. (I estimate the time was now shortly after 1.25am.) Waiting for him there was a helicopter, chartered by Lawford from the Los Angeles Air Taxi Services Inc., based at the nearby Santa Monica Airport in Clover Field. In the cockpit that night was Hal Connors. Despite attempts to prove otherwise, Connors' connection to the actor was cemented on Sunday 5 June 1966, when, in an interview with the local newspapers, he innocently disclosed he had recently flown Lawford to a meeting with Jacqueline Kennedy and his then former wife, Pat.

The actor failed dismally in his attempts to keep the aircraft a secret. 'When I was talking to Peter about Marilyn's death,' Lady Lawford recalled in her book *Bitch*, 'I did not mention to him that I knew his bright yellow helicopter was not parked by the beach house. Instead a dark coloured helicopter, like the Kennedy boys used to rent, had been parked at Peter's house.' Her memory was almost perfect. The colour of the helicopter the Attorney General was believed to have used that night was blue. Moreover the photographer William Woodfield, during his research into Monroe's passing for *The New York Herald Tribune*, witnessed a log verifying that a helicopter had indeed been dispatched to Lawford's home in the early hours of Sunday morning to collect Bobby and whisk him to Los Angeles International Airport.

Amid his nervousness, the actor had also clearly overlooked the fact that the noise of the craft would awaken his sleeping neighbours. Besides their ire at having their slumber interfered with, their rage was magnified when, according to reporter Joe Hyams, the helicopter's rotating blades started to blow huge gusts of sand on to their buildings and into their swimming pools. Their anger was no doubt intensified further by the knowledge that, if they dared to complain about it to the local authorities, their grievances would have fallen on unresponsive ears. As the Santa Monica Municipal Judge, Blair W. Gibbens, inadvertently let slip to the press on Monday 1 August 1966, 'All the time Peter was married to the sister of President Kennedy, the police gave *permission* [emphasis added] to Connors to land at the Lawfords and transport them wherever they wanted to go. They, in effect, looked the other way.'

As Lawford declared to the Hollywood columnist Bob Thomas in October 1964, 'It's the *only* way to commute.' The actor adored this mode of transport so much that he used it at almost every possible opportunity, the beach at the rear of his house being his favoured pick-up and drop-off point. For example, in January 1962, during a break in the filming of *The Longest Day*, the actor made special arrangements for a helicopter to collect him there and whiz him to the nearest airport, simply to allow him to spend a few extra minutes fawning at the feet of the passing-through President. Two years later, in 1964, during work on the Carroll Baker drama *Sylvia*, he arranged for a copter to collect him every day from the beach and alight, 11½ miles to the east, in a clearing made especially for his arrival, on the back lot at Paramount where the film was being produced. (Connors admitted that, by his reckoning, between 1963 and 1966, he had landed on the beach no fewer than 27 times.)

With Bobby Kennedy safely inside, and with Santa Monica airport still closed at this time of day, the helicopter began its journey of approximately six statute miles to Los Angeles International Airport where he was booked on a 339-mile Western Airlines flight lasting approximately one hour (in all probability, plane number 720-047B N93145) back to San Francisco International Airport. A car ready to whisk him back to the Bates' family ranch was waiting for him there. (At 9.30am, Bobby joined his family for Sunday mass at the nearby St Mary's Catholic Church.)

The night was now over for Kennedy. But not for Lawford. In a 1985 interview for *The Times*, speaking by telephone from his home in Cannes, France, Fred Otash recalled that, shortly after midnight (*sic*), the actor called to say something traumatic had happened. Knowing Otash operated a round-the-clock service, Lawford arranged to meet the private investigator immediately at his office at 1342 North Laurel Avenue, West Hollywood. According to Otash, the actor arrived at (approximately) 2am, looking 'completely disorientated and in a state of shock'. He informed Otash he had just left Monroe's home, that she was dead and that Bobby Kennedy had been there earlier. He also informed him they had got Kennedy out of the city and back to Northern California.

Clearly engulfed with paranoia, Lawford asked Otash to go out to Marilyn's house to look for things he had missed and dismantle the sophisticated bugging equipment within. Having been the one who had helped secrete it in there back in February, Otash was obviously the right man to carry out such a task. After settling on a fee, he agreed to execute the request. Accompanying Otash to the actress's home that night was, in all probability, his employee, John Danoff. In less than an hour, surveillance equipment was ripped out and hard-to-budge wires were hidden away in nearby crevices. 'I took what I could find and I destroyed it; period,' Otash admitted. With the aid of dusters, the two men worked diligently to cover their tracks. The actress's place was now completely clean and, most importantly, tidy. Their sanitising was so competent that precious few fingerprints now remained in the property; not even one of Marilyn's.

However, their first task after arriving at the building (at approximately 2.25am) was to haul Marilyn's lifeless body off the floor, remove her terry-cloth bath robe and lay her down on her bed. They placed her downwards, the right side of her face against the mattress, in the direction of the bedroom door. Due to the unrelieved weight of an inert, heavy mass, Greenson and Murray found it impossible to carry out such a task on their own. The actress had been left, completely abandoned on the floor, on her back, pretty much in the position in which she perished, for well over five hours. It seemed that, even in death, as screen actress Kim Novak once remarked, Marilyn was being treated like 'a piece of meat'. No wonder she had despised Los Angeles so much.

Evidence that Marilyn's body was moved in this way and at that time is provided by the picture taken just prior to her autopsy, which was published in Anthony Summers' 1985 book *Goddess*. As this verified, the lividity – the settling and pooling of blood in direct response to gravity, which can be changed, by moving the body, only in the first six hours after death – had become 'fixed' on the right side of her face, meaning that she was in this position by the time it had become permanent – in this case, at around 2.40am. Subsequently, when the blood vessels within the body begin to break down, the lividity becomes 'fixed'. As her autopsy observed, this form of lividity was 'noted in the face, neck, chest, upper portions of arms and the right side of the abdomen'.

However, proof that she was moved into that position – in this instance, from the floor to her bed – came with the discovery, during her post-mortem, of 'faint lividity' found in her 'back and posterior aspect of the arms and legs', but which disappeared 'upon pressure'. These markings demonstrate that, in the time prior to the lividity becoming fixed, she was in a different position entirely – in this case, on the floor, lying on her rear.

In layman's terms, she died on her back and was transferred to her bed, where she was placed face down, head facing left; there, at the six-hour mark, the lividity in her body became permanent. But – as the official LAPD pictures prove – after it had become fixed and rigor mortis had set in, her head was inexplicably moved *again*, in the opposite direction, to her right, to face the wall. Her autopsy corroborated this, insinuating that her body, most prominently in her 'head and neck regions', had been moved at least twice after she died. This fact was verified by another, highly important source: the investigators in the 1982 reinvestigation into the actress's death. Their probe discovered that lividity had indeed appeared on different parts of Marilyn's body at different times.

Immediately after arriving back at his office, Otash called Lawford to inform him he had successfully completed his task. The message had to be relayed to Lawford, though. With anxiety getting the better of him, he had hit the bottle after returning home, consuming a mix of Scotch and Bloody Marys, and, by 3am, had passed out on a chair.

Meanwhile, back at Fifth Helena, the next phase of the Marilyn whitewash was ready to begin. At approximately 3.10am, just moments after Otash and his colleague had absconded from the property, Dr Greenson called Dr Hyman Engelberg, who was asleep at his home at 9730 Wilshire Boulevard. In truth, Greenson had no reason whatsoever to summon Engelberg; a fully trained doctor himself, he was perfectly capable of ascertaining Marilyn had passed away. It is therefore safe to assume that he called his colleague for one simple reason: he wanted the man responsible for prescribing the pills which had been partly responsible for killing the actress present at the scene and face-to-face with the police. Greenson evidently had no desire to face the music alone.

Engelberg arrived within minutes. 'She was sprawled over the bed, and she was dead,' he remarked in 1982 in an audio-taped interview for the Los Angeles District Attorney's office. 'I took out my stethoscope to make sure her heart wasn't beating; checked her pupils because that's one of the sensitive ways to tell if a person is dead or not. I said she was dead, which, of course, Dr Greenson knew anyway, but I had to go through the motions.' Original reports insist he pronounced her dead at precisely 3.35am. Fifty minutes later, at approximately 4.25, he decided to call the Los Angeles Police headquarters. 'Marilyn Monroe has died,' he solemnly announced. 'She's committed suicide. I'm Dr Hyman Engelberg, Marilyn Monroe's physician. I'm at her residence. She's committed suicide.'

Later, when asked by the Department why he had taken so long to make this call, he replied, 'We were stunned. We were talking over what happened. What she had said.' In another interview, Engelberg explained the procrastination this way. 'The reason there was a delay in calling the police is that normally you don't call the police, you call the mortuary to remove the body. Dr Greenson and I discussed this back and forth.' He added, 'I strongly insisted that, because of whom she was and that it might be a suicide, we should call the police.'

Engelberg's call was then passed on to the West Los Angeles Police Division. On the other end of the line was the station's weekend watch commander, Sergeant Jack Clemmons. The doctor reiterated the fact that Marilyn Monroe had committed suicide. Immediately after ending the call, Clemmons made a note of the time, assigned another officer to take his place, climbed into his police car and drove along Sunset Boulevard in the direction of the actress's home. During the journey of approximately three miles, he radioed for a squad car to meet him there. Knowing that scoop-hungry reporters regularly eavesdropped the police airwaves, he feared that, once news of the actress's demise had filtered out, an army of hacks, curious bystanders and news and television reporters would descend on the property, and he wanted some assistance, in particular a sergeant to take charge of the scene and another to protect the area.

For one fleeting, incredulous moment, the thought crossed his mind that this whole thing might be a hoax. 'It seemed incredible,' he recalled in 1966. 'I didn't want somebody playing a big joke on the Police Department so I decided I would go to the scene.' The notion of it being a prank, however, evaporated the moment he pulled up on the driveway of the property and met the people inside.

At approximately 4.35am, after hearing the washing machine and dryer hard at work in the garage, he was met at the front door by Eunice Murray. Following confirmation from her that Marilyn had indeed passed away, he was led into the bedroom where he caught sight of the actress's two doctors seated on chairs, next to her body, which was lying outstretched diagonally across her bed. A sheet was high over her head and a champagne-coloured blanket was tucked up around her shoulders. The sergeant recalled she was lying in what he described as the 'soldier's position'. Her face was on a pillow, her arms were by her side, her right arm was slightly bent and her legs were stretched out perfectly straight. Clemmons instinctively knew that she had been placed that way. (As we learnt earlier, Greenson, Otash and Danoff had strategically laid her in that position just over two hours earlier.) Her head was at the top left of the bed, her feet at the bottom right. As the surviving LAPD photo shows, the left side of her face was now resting on the pillow, the complete opposite of the way she was when the lividity on her body became fixed. This would prove to be the first of several major blunders in the conspiracy. Importantly, in complete contradiction to the long-believed folklore, there was no telephone in Marilyn's hand.

Moreover, despite the widely publicised stories which said that the only thing she wore in bed each night was the perfume Chanel No.5, the truth was actually quite different. Believing it essential to help keep her shape, as everyone who knew the actress would testify, she wore a bra to bed every night of her mature life. But this night, she was *not* wearing one.

In an interview with the biographer George Carpozi Jr, the exceedingly forthright Clemmons remarked that the scene 'looked to me as though a murder had been committed. The body had been moved. The room had been straightened out. I saw all the classic elements of an attempt to cover up a homicide to make it seem like a suicide.'

In 1982, during the Los Angeles District Attorney's reinvestigation of the case, the man in charge of the probe, Mike Carroll, poured scorn on Clemmons' claims. 'His opinion was not based on any kind of professional training or experience,' he remarked in 2006 during CBS Television's *48 Hours Mystery* show on the investigation. 'He was not a detective; he was not an experienced detective and certainly *not* a homicide detective.' During Clemmons' many years of policing, however, he had witnessed a vast number of suicide victims and, in his opinion, an overdose of sleeping tablets usually caused victims to suffer spasms, vomiting and foaming of the mouth before they died in a distorted position. But there was nothing like that here. (Nor should he have expected it. Expelling doesn't always occur in situations like these, as any pathologist will testify. The victim simply goes to sleep.)

Furthermore, the room was in impeccable order. The actress's few sparse belongings had seemingly been arranged neatly around the room; her clothes had been neatly folded and stacked; purses and handbags had been lined up in a straight line against the wall; correspondence was stacked under her bedside table in tidy piles. It was the first time in his long career that Clemmons had been called out to an overdose case and found the room in which the victim had apparently died in such perfect condition. Although there had in fact been no murder, but with regard to a cover-up he was quite correct.

'Who else is here?' Clemmons enquired. 'Two doctors,' Murray replied before making introductions. He would recall Engelberg as being 'remorseful' and Murray as 'scared' and 'very, very quiet', adding that she spoke in 'hushed tones'. Amazingly, at no time during his visit did he confront Milton Rudin, who was still at the property, concealed in the guest room. During Clemmons' eventful 40 minutes at the property, he watched Murray flit nervously from one room to another, executing chores such as loading medium-sized cardboard boxes into her car and emptying (and then dumping into the trash can) the contents of Marilyn's refrigerator.

Her use of the house's Hotpoint washing machine and dryer, stored in the garage, was, in his opinion, her strangest action. He correctly guessed she had been doing this for several hours and was currently on her third load. When pressed on the matter, she replied truthfully that, since the house was about to be sealed off, and with so many people about to descend on it, she was just meticulously carrying out her duties as a housekeeper by making sure that the property was clean, tidy and presentable.

The seemingly outlandish behaviour at Marilyn's home that night did not end there. Clemmons would recall Greenson as being 'sarcastic' and 'unnatural'. When Clemmons first entered the actress's bedroom, the psychiatrist had his head buried in his hands. But after a few moments he raised it. 'He had a strange, unusual *smirk* on his face,' Clemmons recalled. 'He had a sort of leer, which was out of place.'

The sergeant was then shown a table alongside the bed which, besides a copy of the gardening magazine, *Horticulture*, contained a total of 15 empty prescription pill bottles. Some had labels; some did not. (The officer drafted in to replace Clemmons, Sergeant Robert E. Byron, would also recall seeing the same number. However, according to Dr Thomas Noguchi's autopsy report, only eight containers were found beside Marilyn's bed. I can clear up this discrepancy: the seven other bottles were, according to mortician Guy Hockett, non-prescription and therefore not required for the actress's autopsy. The eight in question were 2 x Librium (dated 7 June and 10 July 1962), 1 x sulfathalidine (25 July 1962), 2 x chloral hydrate (25 July 1962 and 31 July 1962), 1 x Nembutal (3 August 1962) and 1 x Pink Ladies (also from 3 August but devoid of a label). Strangely, there was also one for nodular (cystic) acne, now empty but dated some nine months earlier, on Saturday 4 November 1961.)

Engelberg was naturally aghast at this huge amount, only one of which, Nembutal, had been authorised by him. He was also shocked to see the containers for chloral hydrate. It was a drug he never used or prescribed. In an interview with the LAPD, he insisted, 'I knew *nothing* about chloral hydrate. I *never* gave her chloral hydrate.' Since it was a country in which you could purchase any drug you chose, he firmly believed that Marilyn had purchased them in Tijuana during her trip to Mexico in February, rather than, as was in fact the case, receiving them via Greenson.

One of the other bottles on the actress's night stand, Clemmons was told, had once contained Nembutal tablets. It was lying upside down; its top was just an inch or two away. In an attempt to shift the blame away from himself and on to his colleague, Greenson then remarked, 'She must have taken all of these.' 'That's a lot of pills,' Clemmons replied. Engelberg recalled later, 'At the bedside, I remember clearly the empty bottle of Nembutal, which I had given her. I remember having the impulse of saying [to myself], "Oh God, I'm gonna get involved in this.

Maybe I'll hide the bottle." I then said [to myself], "Oh, to hell with it. I didn't do anything wrong . . . '" When asked by Clemmons, Engelberg confirmed that he had indeed approved a 25-tablet, prescription refill of the drug (no. 20858) just two days previously. The general consensus, much to Greenson's relief, was that Marilyn must have expired after consuming that entire bottle and *not* by swallowing the chloral hydrates. He knew that, if it was deemed that his actions had accidentally caused her death, he could face an involuntary manslaughter charge which, under Californian law, carries a maximum sentence of four years in prison.

With that fact in mind, Clemmons became suspicious when he noted that there was no drinking glass in the room. Without this, he wondered, how could she have possibly swallowed the amount of pills which she was credited with taking? His suspicions intensified when he was informed that the bathroom in her room had been shut off due to remodelling and, as Murray remarked, that Marilyn had not ventured out of her room again after she retired for the night shortly before 7.55pm. (His scepticism increased when, just a few days later, back at the station, he glanced at the photos of the death scene taken for the coroner and noticed that a drinking receptacle had now miraculously materialised in the images. It was obvious that it had been placed in that position at approximately 5.15am when Clemmons departed from the scene and headed back to the police station. This was *another* almighty oversight in Greenson and Murray's attempts to suppress what had happened.)

As the sergeant began scrutinising the bedroom he kept bumping into the other individuals present. 'It looked like a convention,' he recalled. Clemmons took another glance at the body and then asked Murray if he could use the telephone. He was told he could and was led by the housekeeper into the kitchen, where the apparatus was now being stored. (Rudin had moved it there. With him using the guest room as a hideout, he did not wish to be discovered.) Clemmons' call back to the Police Department served two purposes: first, to put out another request for policemen at the scene (his first appeal was strangely unheeded); second, to enable him to pass the bad news on to a colleague.

'Hello, Jim,' he said. 'I'm at Marilyn's house . . . Yeah, that's right. She's dead. It looks like an OD [overdose]. I knew you'd want to know.' He was speaking to James E. Dougherty, Marilyn's first husband, who was sitting in his squad car in North Hollywood, just 10 miles from the actress's home (and not lying in bed with his wife, as some previous Monroe biographers have claimed), when he received the call on his police radio. Exercising immense decorum, at no time during the conversation did the sergeant remark to Dougherty he felt that there was a conspiracy going on at the home.

Clemmons placed the phone back into its cradle and walked back to the actress's bedroom where he began collecting statements. Right from the start they were riddled with discrepancies. Murray started by telling him she had discovered Marilyn's body at approximately 12 midnight and called Dr Greenson shortly after. In a 1966 interview, Clemmons remarked, 'According to what they were telling me, all of this occurred shortly after midnight. I told them, "No one is going to go along with four hours sitting around with a corpse on your hands, when you know very well that you have to call the police." They didn't want to answer but I pressed.' He asked again, why had they taken so long to contact the police? Greenson immediately interjected, insisting that they could not do so until they had received permission from 20th Century-Fox's publicity department. This was of course nonsense. Clemmons knew then he was not hearing the truth. 'That's not an answer,' he retorted.

He dropped the matter, content in the knowledge that Detective Sergeant Robert Byron, the next officer summoned to the scene, would get it all sorted when he officially started the investigation. (Despite seeing first-hand the many abnormalities at the scene, as a law enforcement officer Clemmons' job was simply to determine the facts and log the information in a police report. The onus would be on others in his department, in this case Byron, to question and pursue any oddities in the case.) 'Since I had made an issue of the fact that it had taken them four hours to call the police,' Clemmons recalled to the American press in 1972, 'they decided, by the time I left and before Byron arrived, that no one was ever going to buy this four-hour business so they had better change their story.' Which was exactly what they did.

When Byron arrived and started asking questions, Murray at once began insisting that she had found the actress's body 'shortly after 3am'. (Strangely, no one at the LAPD ever thought to question this discrepancy.) This time was the one picked by most of the national newspapers. According to one report, compiled by the *New York Herald*'s Joe Hyams, the housekeeper 'awoke suddenly from a sound sleep with the ominous feeling that something was not right'. In another, she was awakened by an uneasy dread she couldn't explain and, through the gap under the actress's bedroom door, found Miss Monroe's light still burning, her door locked and no answer to her knock. 'Somehow, it didn't seem right,' she was quoted as saying. 'It seemed strange and unusual.' So she went outside and looked in the bedroom window. 'I saw Miss Monroe lying on the bed. That's when I called Dr Greenson.' Official reports of the actress's death say Murray phoned the doctor at precisely 3.35am.

Murray's recollection of a light shining from underneath Marilyn's bedroom door on the night she died has been a major topic of debate for many years. According to folklore, a new extremely thick, shag-pile, white woollen carpet produced in India had just been laid in the room and the chance of seeing any kind of light emanating from under the door was minimal. Legend has it that the covering was so deep that, until a suitable amount of wear and tear had taken place, it was impossible to even shut the door.

On both counts, this was untrue. As Linda Nunez, the daughter of the family who, in 1963, moved into the actress's home recalled, the carpet in the room *was* indeed thick, but certainly not enough to prevent the door from being closed. Going by this testimony, it is therefore extremely likely that Murray's recollection of seeing a light emanating from under her employer's door on the night she died was true. Furthermore, regardless of what we have previously been told, haunted by the happenings at the Payne-Whitney Clinic just 18 months before her death, Marilyn *never* locked the entrance of the room in which she slept.

Her friend Dorothy Kilgallen queried the 'locked-door' ruse at the time. In her column published on Sunday 19 August 1962, she asked, 'Why was Marilyn's door locked that night when she *didn't* usually lock it?' Another individual to corroborate this was Ralph Roberts. Due to his regular, late-night visits to her bedroom, he knew first-hand that Marilyn *never* locked the door of her room. As we learnt in a previous chapter, her secretary Cherie Redmond remarked she could not find a lock in the property that worked. (This was, in fact, attributable to one simple reason: the safety of the previous occupants' children.)

In another interview (carried out during the afternoon of Monday 6 August), Murray remembered she 'went to bed at midnight and noticed that the light was still on in Marilyn's bedroom but didn't think that was unusual'. Then, with confusion clearly setting in, in another interview carried out on the exactly the same day, she contradictorily claimed that she 'walked out into the hallway and saw the telephone cord under Marilyn's door. That's all I needed as a clue. I knew immediately that something was terribly wrong, because after midnight, with the telephone in her room and she hadn't put it to bed, well I knew something had to be wrong.'

This was another anomaly. Greenson, her personal make-up artist, Allan 'Whitey' Snyder and many other friends all recalled receiving regular late-night calls from the actress. The *Daily Mirror* journalist Donald Zec even penned a piece honouring her nocturnal actions. Published on Monday 25 January 1960, it was entitled 'Marilyn's On The Line – At Half Past Three In The Morning'. Greenson even corroborated the fact, remarking to George Carpozi Jr that the actress called him at 'two in the morning, three, four, five in the morning, countless, countless times'.

Among the many others who would recall sharing late-night conversations with Marilyn was the actress and singer Eartha Kitt. In a 1989 interview, she revealed that the actress used to call her because 'she was fighting the same feelings as me. Both of us were orphans. Both of us suffered from that terrible nameless fear that haunts you when normal people are sleeping. Like me, she knew success. She knew what it was like to be an idol. But what does that mean when, deep down, you know that you were not important enough for your own mother to want you?'

So, if Murray was indeed lying, as it seemed, what was she covering up? The fact that she had failed so miserably in her duty to watch over the actress, was guilty of tampering with the scene and that she had actually discovered Marilyn's body five and a half hours prior to the time she officially declared to the authorities, were the most likely answers. Her intent not to incriminate herself was prevalent in her second police interview about the incident, which took place at her Ocean Avenue home at 8.30 on the morning of Friday 10 August. In his report of their discussion, Lieutenant Armstrong, Commander of the West Los Angeles Police Division, was forced to conclude, 'Mrs Murray was vague and possibly evasive in answering questions pertaining to the activities of Miss Monroe . . . ' He summed up by saying, 'It is not known whether this is, or is not, intentional.'

Greenson naturally did his utmost to substantiate Murray's tales. According to his later statement to Sergeant Robert Byron, he received a phone call from Murray shortly after 3.05am. Immediately after ending it, he rushed by car to the actress's house, took a poker from the fireplace, smashed a window to gain access to her bedroom, reached in, unlocked the latch, climbed in and discovered the actress dead, face down on her bed, phone receiver in her right hand. In an interview with Maurice Zolotow, he disclosed more about the night, saying, 'Her finger was still in the dial,' while Murray recalled to the same writer that the phone was 'under her body'.

Marilyn had indeed been discovered in her bedroom, phone receiver near her right hand, by Murray shortly after 9.30pm. But Clemmons did not see the receiver in her hand at 4.35am, as both he and the LAPD's pictures would confirm. As any pathologist will testify, a person dying as a result of a barbiturate overdose would be likely to relax upon death and let go of any item they might be holding, such as a telephone, before they slid into a life-threatening coma. The scenario whereby Marilyn had committed suicide and was found in her bed with her phone clasped in her hand had, in all probability, emanated from Arthur Jacobs. A top-level spin-doctor, his yarn was accepted by every major press bureau across the globe.

Marilyn's chauffeur, Rudy Karensky, and Murray's son-in-law, Norm (summoned to repair the window in the bedroom), were soon at Fifth Helena; so too was the actress's friend, reporter James Bacon, who raced to the property immediately following a tip-off from the Associated Press news agency. He was admitted to the premises after misleadingly telling a policeman at the scene he had been sent from the coroner's office. Inez Melson, the legal guardian of the actress's mother, appeared shortly after. At once, she requested to see the actress's body and the room in which she died. 'There were pill bottles everywhere,' she recounted to biographer Fred Lawrence Guiles in 1968, 'some empty, some full on the night stand and dresser. I walked into the bathroom and saw the cabinet's shelves crowded with Marilyn's allergy pills, tranquillizers and sleeping tablets. I had an impulse to run through these two rooms, snatching up the bottles and hiding them in my bag, but I knew that was impossible.'

At approximately 5.05am, Detective Sergeant Byron and his colleague, Sergeant Marvin Iannone, as well as officers Coberley, McGuire, Curran and Gillis, arrived to relieve Clemmons of his duties. Moments after Iannone's arrival, he began a walking tour of the actress's home and, as he recalled, found 'nothing unusual or amiss'. However, his feeling soon changed when he walked into the actress's bedroom and took a more prolonged look at Marilyn's body. In his original report, he made it quite clear that, in his opinion, 'rigor mortis had set in by the time police arrived'. His already interesting statement became even more thought-provoking when he remarked, 'While I was there, Dr Greenson was so visibly shaken that he would not return to the bedroom where Miss Monroe's body lay.' (This original, 1962 remark clearly casts doubt on Byron's later comment that Greenson had gone by the time he arrived at Monroe's house.)

Though he obviously never disclosed his true feelings to the police, the doctor clearly felt certain that the Attorney General's highly traumatic, completely unexpected visit to Marilyn's home the previous afternoon had played a key part in her death. Evidence of this can be found in a surviving audio-taped interview between him and William Woodfield, the photographer and independent Marilyn investigator. Several months after her demise, when pressed about the incident, an evidently troubled Greenson was heard to reply, 'I can't explain myself or defend myself without revealing things I don't want to reveal. You can't draw a line and say, "I'll tell you this but I couldn't tell you this." It's a terrible position to be in to have to say I can't talk about it because I can't tell you the whole story. Listen . . . *talk* to Bobby Kennedy.'

Wiretapper and electronics expert Bernard Spindel even went on record as saying Kennedy was *present* at the time Marilyn died. In a heavily censored FBI document dated Monday 13 March 1967 – but not released until Tuesday 13 June 1972 – he said proof was attainable by 'listening to the various recordings'. The validity of his claim was elevated on Thursday 15 December 1966, when, in a nine-hour operation, the Manhattan District Attorney's office raided Spindel's home on charges of illegal eavesdropping. In a report in *The New York Times* published six days later, on Wednesday 21 December, it was revealed that some of the seized material contained 'tapes and evidence concerning circumstances surrounding and causes of death of Marilyn Monroe, which strongly suggests that the officially reported circumstances of her demise are erroneous'.

Doubts were cast on their authenticity when, in his report of the incident, the Manhattan Assistant District Attorney, Ronald Carroll, wrote, 'Spindel's asserted desire to have the tapes made public appears to have been a ploy . . . The tapes were, in fact, heard by staff investigators and *none* of the tapes contained anything relating to Marilyn Monroe.' Unsurprisingly, however, Spindel was unrepentant, insisting in a separate interview that 'The tapes and files *did* concern the actress's death, and contained facts and data in which the names of Bobby Kennedy and Peter Lawford *were* mentioned.' The equipment and recordings evidently meant a lot to Spindel and later, in a motion before the New York Supreme Court Judge, Owen McGivern, he unsuccessfully sought to retrieve them.

After initially going missing, the audios apparently resurfaced in 1968. A price of $50,000 was supposedly placed on them, and a deal with a former policeman was seemingly struck. As the right-wing journalist Ralph de Toledano, a key figure in the United States' Conservative movement, remarked to the BBC in 1985, 'Just prior to the sale, Bobby was assassinated. Had Bobby not been shot, I am convinced that those tapes would have been duplicated and sent across the country to various newspapers and would have had tremendous impact [in discrediting him] in the coming [Presidential] campaign.' According to Fred Otash, they are probably 'the most exciting tapes ever made, with the exception of Watergate'. However, as of 2010 the recordings have still not materialised and, in all probability, are never likely to do so.

Moments after his arrival, and since there was no logical reason for anyone still to be on the property, Sergeant Iannone began asking everyone to leave. His request came at a time when the number of people gathered outside had started to swell significantly. News of Marilyn's death had, unsurprisingly, spread rapidly on the news wires and the area was now overrun with a vast number of television and newspaper reporters and nightwear-wearing bystanders, many of whom attempted to either drive past the house or walk by and gawp ghoulishly through the gates. For some inexplicable reason, a fire engine even descended on the property.

Working on orders from the police administrator, Baldo M. Kristovich, the area had to be cordoned off. A seal was placed on the entrance to the house and the notice, 'Any person breaking into or entering these premises will be prosecuted to the fullest extent of the law', was posted on the building's front door and gates.

Despite doing this, the officers called to the scene that day still failed in some of their other duties. Clemmons neglected to declare the property a crime scene, a forensic investigation team was not summoned and the police failed to carry out a full inventory of everything contained in the house. The police also failed to effectively secure the scene. Yellow tape should have sealed off the entire property, not just the front gates, while everyone inside – friends of the actress, reporters and innocent bystanders, who were allowed to roam around freely – should have been asked to leave much earlier. As one police offer sarcastically observed, 'It was like Grand Central Station that morning.' As a consequence of their lingering, vital evidence could have been either contaminated or destroyed. The property was not completely sealed until 8.30am, approximately four hours after Sergeant Jack Clemmons had appeared at the scene and 45 minutes after Marilyn's body had been taken to the morgue.

Inspector Ed Walker of the Los Angeles Police Department arrived, siren silent, at the same time as Pat Newcomb. The latter had left her apartment immediately after receiving a 5am call from the actress's attorney, who was still camped out at Marilyn's house. 'Something's happened to Marilyn,' Rudin solemnly announced. 'She's dead.' (Aside from speaking to Newcomb, 75 minutes earlier, in the region of 3.45am, the attorney had also made a progress-report call to Lawford's business manager, Milton Ebbins. Attempts to speak to the actor personally had proved futile. He was still inebriated in a chair.)

Immediately after receiving the news, a shell-shocked Newcomb clambered out of bed, threw a raincoat over her nightclothes, grabbed her sunglasses to protect her weary eyes and climbed into a car driven by her next-door neighbour, Natalie Trundy. She arrived at Marilyn's home 15 minutes later but was barred from entering. The large gates of the house had been shut tight and were remaining so. When the hacks caught sight of Marilyn's press secretary, clad in pyjamas and wearing shades, desperately trying to gain access to the property, they immediately descended upon her and, amid an orgy of flashbulbs, wasted no time in trying to obtain a quote.

'How do you feel about Marilyn's death?' one forcibly asked. The question caught Newcomb off guard and she snapped back, 'When your best friend kills herself, how do you feel? What do you do?' Accusations that she also screamed, 'Murderers! You murderers! Are you satisfied now that she's dead?' were denied by the publicist. But allegations that she shouted 'Keep shooting, vultures' at the photographers were *not*. She was hysterical with grief and police had to move in to restrain her. Her outbursts could be heard all the way down Fifth Helena.

She soon calmed down, however. 'This must have been an accident,' Newcomb dejectedly remarked to another reporter. 'Marilyn was in perfect condition and was feeling great. We had made plans for today. We were going to the pictures this afternoon.' At that moment, the gates of the property suddenly swung open and she was seemingly permitted to enter. In fact it was a mistake and within moments of her arrival, police were asking her to *leave*. But she was not listening and made it clear that she had no desire to move. She walked in an almost hypnotic state through the property and managed to stagger into the bedroom in which she had stayed on Friday night. Patrolmen at the scene did their best to comfort her.

Newcomb's departure from the bungalow two hours later, at approximately 7.45am, coincided with that of the wagon carrying Marilyn's body to the mortuary. Even then, the police had to forcibly evict her, allowing her to make one call – to her psychiatrist, whom she agreed to meet at once – before they did so. Contrary to previous reports, at no time during her visit to Fifth Helena did Newcomb see the actress's body.

It was during this point of the morning that, while Marilyn lay dead on her bed, her emerald and diamond earrings, given to her by Frank Sinatra in September 1961 and worn for the only time at the Golden Globes event in March 1962, were plundered from her bedroom wardrobe. Always believing they would one day be stolen, she had secreted them in the tip of one of her shoes, a fact known only by her close associates.

An ambulance dispatched by Schaefer Ambulance Services of 4627 Beverly Boulevard, the largest private ambulance company in the city, had arrived at the scene just moments after Newcomb. In the vehicle were attendants Ken Hunter and Rick Stone, who recalled pulling up at the house and seeing her 'standing outside screaming'. The two men then entered the bungalow and strode into Marilyn's bedroom. In December 1982, during the reinvestigation into her death by the Los Angeles County District Attorney's Office, Hunter recalled that Marilyn was lying on her side, head facing right, and was 'pretty cold . . . she was blue . . . like she had settled, like she had been laying there a while . . . I could look across the room and tell that she was dead.' He didn't touch the actress's body but his colleague, Stone, briefly did. In Hunter's words, he 'checked her just to see if [she was] dead or not'. After being informed the body would be removed by a mortician, they immediately left.

Regardless of the tale told by some previous Monroe biographers, this was the *only* Schaefer ambulance summoned to the actress's home that weekend. Legend has it that, in the region of 10.10pm, during the evening of Saturday 4 August, Eunice Murray made an emergency call to the local Schaefer Ambulance Services. Company employees James Hall and Murray Liebowitz arrived at Marilyn's property within minutes of receiving a private emergency, Code 3 – lights and sirens – call and discovered the actress in a comatose state, slumped on her bed, on her back, her head hanging over its edge. In a 1982 interview for a British tabloid newspaper, Hall claimed that his original attempts to save Marilyn's life had been successful. 'The colour started coming back into her cheeks,' he recalled. Within minutes, Dr Greenson arrived at the scene. Shocked to discover the actress was still conscious, he ordered Hall to remove the resuscitator from her mouth and began massaging her heart. He did this for a few minutes before reaching into his bag, pulling out a syringe with a long needle filled with a brownish fluid and injecting it straight into Monroe's heart, chipping one of the actress's ribs in the process. In Hall's words, 'he was trying to find her heart. He had to count down her ribs to locate it, just like a novice. A few minutes later, he pronounced her dead.'

The tale continued with Monroe being strapped to a gurney, wheeled out to the ambulance, driven by Messrs Hall and Liebowitz to the nearby Santa Monica General Hospital and left in the ER (emergency room). However, for some inexplicable reason, the two ambulance men then decided to turn round and return Marilyn's body to her home. The vehicle arrived back at the property at approximately 10.25pm and within minutes of its arrival, her body was being wheeled back into the house and laid out neatly across the bed in her room. With no first-hand knowledge of the situation, the company's owner, Walt Schaefer, even inadvertently added to the ruse by telling the BBC in 1985, 'She was alive when she was picked up,' before admitting Marilyn 'succumbed at the hospital'.

However, this entire tale was pure fabrication, as can be discerned from five irrefutable facts. One, Marilyn's post-mortem clearly showed that there were 'no needle marks' on her body and it is inconceivable that two respected Los Angeles coroners, Thomas T. Noguchi and John Miner, could overlook the damage to her rib-cage and the fatal puncture marks to her heart. Second, for strict hygiene and safety reasons, doctors are not permitted to carry syringes of this size, with the needles attached, in their bags.

Third, it is abundantly clear that the lividity on her body became fixed while she was lying on her bed, the right-hand side of her face nearest to the mattress. Besides, if the actress's body *had* indeed been carried from her house, loaded into the ambulance, driven to the hospital, left in the emergency room, escorted to her property and then transferred back into her bedroom, the marks of faint lividity on her body would have changed in an obvious and un-fakeable manner and would not have appeared in the way they did during her autopsy.

Fourth, when the diligent Marilyn researcher Milo Speriglio put James Hall under a lie-detector test in the early 1980s, as he recalled in his 1986 book, *The Marilyn Conspiracy*, he saw the needle 'almost jump off the scale'. Hall apparently made good money from his tale. Besides appearances in a couple of Marilyn documentaries, he also sold his story to *The Globe* newspaper for $40,000, appearing in the edition published on Tuesday 23 November 1982. When Speriglio protested about the piece, the paper's editor shrugged off the complaint, saying Hall's story 'sells papers'. It was obvious that certain parts of the media were less concerned about spreading lies about the last night of Marilyn's life than with making sales.

And fifth, in 1982, when the Los Angeles District Attorney's office reinvestigated the case, the leader of the inquiry, Mike Carroll, contacted the two men whom he believed were in charge of the Schaefer ambulance sent to Marilyn's house on the morning after she passed away. However, he did *not* get in touch with Hall and Liebowitz. Instead, he contacted Ken Hunter and Rick Stone and, according to the latter, it was he and not Hall who saw Dr Greenson pull a large hypodermic syringe out of his medical bag and place it in the actress's heart. The matter became farcical when Liebowitz denied that he was ever at the house that morning. Hunter summed up the scenario perfectly when, in response to Carroll's question about the incident, he replied, 'That's *bullshit!*')

Now back behind his desk at the West Los Angeles Police Division, at 5.25am Sergeant Clemmons began filling out his investigations report. Despite his many misgivings about the case, he still wrote 'Barbs – overdose' as the cause of Marilyn's death. He had evidently taken both Greenson and Engelberg at their word. It was a clear rush to judgement, since at that moment there was no way of knowing whether this was the case or not. Immediately after completing his account, and before he drove back to Fifth Helena, he called the coroner's office. In turn, a deputy at the bureau called the Westwood Village Mortuary in Westwood Memorial Park. Mrs Guy R. Hockett, the wife of the managing director, took the call. 'This is the coroner's office,' Deputy Coroner Howard Cronkite announced. 'I have a hearse call for you. Marilyn Monroe is dead.' Mrs Hockett was immediately stunned but, thinking it was another hoax call, responded by saying, 'You're kidding,' before hanging up.

She told her husband about the call. 'We get all kinds of calls like that,' Guy later remarked. However he decided to ring back just to check. He was horrified to discover that this was no crank call. Accompanied by his son, Don Hockett immediately jumped into his battered light-blue 1950 Ford panel truck and arrived at Marilyn's house in Brentwood shortly after 6.30am.

Moments after entering her bedroom, Hockett ordered everyone out. He and his son had work to do. Glancing down at the actress's lifeless body, he observed that her face was bereft of make-up and her uncombed hair was in a shocking state, a result of the painful treatments she had received from colourist Pearl Porterfield. Noticing the deep purple colouring of her body, he asked Sergeant Byron how long the actress had been dead. When he was told three hours, he gave his son an under-standing glance. His many years of experience told him she had been dead for a lot longer than that. Immediately after examining the actress's body, Hockett echoed the sergeant's earlier sentiments by announcing that 'rigor mortis was advanced.' In order for it to be strapped to the trolley, it took him in the region of five minutes just to straighten the body out. Only a corpse in such an advanced state of rigor mortis would require such an action. (While rigor mortis has been known to set in as little as three hours after death, taking into consideration the time of year and temperature of the room, in Marilyn's case it was likely to occur in a minimum of five to six hours.)

Working with his son, Hockett then wrapped the actress's body from head to toe in a shroud made of a cheap, pale blue woollen blanket, obtained from her bed, and strapped it, hands across stomach, onto a narrow tubular stretcher. At 7.45am, the undisputed Queen of Hollywood was unceremoniously wheeled out of her bedroom, through the front door, past the handful of reporters and the curious and 50 feet down the driveway, where she was trundled into the cargo space of a station wagon and transported to the Westwood Village Mortuary. There, for approxi-mately one hour, she was discarded in a storeroom strewn with coats, drafting tables and dust brushes. Lights were turned off and the door locked. To all intents and purposes, Marilyn's body had been left alone, in the dark in a shed. There was no certainly no dignity in her death.

At 9am, her cadaver was picked up by employee Clarence Pierce and, following a request by Milton Rudin, brought to the County Morgue in the Los Angeles Hall of Justice where she was weighed (117 pounds), measured (height 65½ inches), photographed (hair blonde, eyes blue) and fingerprinted. In preparation for her post-mortem, she was then placed in Crypt 33 and assigned a coroner's case number, hers being 81128. Her next-of-kin was listed as 'Gladys Baker – address unknown'. At 10.15am, coroner's assistant Eddie Day wheeled Marilyn's body out, laid it onto stainless-steel table number 1 and prepared it for its autopsy.

Back at Fifth Helena, in order to obtain suitable material for the day's television news bulletins and the following morning's newspapers, a handful of reporters had been allowed on to the bungalow's forecourt. While some happily took shots of the outside of the building and images of Monroe's living quarters through her windows, others overstepped the mark. Desperate to get a glimpse of the room in which the actress had died, film crews began poking their cameras obtrusively through the window Dr Greenson had smashed in order to reach the actress approximately nine hours earlier. Their shots were interrupted when an officer, catching sight of their actions, rushed over to the glazing and pulled across the white-coloured drapes which were hanging directly in front. Once the photographers and film crews had obtained their images and been ushered off the premises, the police began covering the windows with large, heavy, evidence-preserving cloth.

One respected Monroe biographer suggested that the actress *always* slept with her windows covered that way. However, close examination of the photos and newsreel footage taken on the morning of the actress's death, before the sealing took place, clearly shows that, as Eunice Murray recalled, curtains were *all* that hung across the windows in Marilyn's bedroom. Considering that the glazing adjacent to her bed faced the dark backyard, there was simply no need for such thick curtains. The same author also suggested that, each night, before bedtime, the actress would staple these heavy curtains to the frames. 'She *never* stapled the drapes,' Murray confirmed to Maurice Zolotow in 1973.

With such a high press presence, making a discreet exit from Marilyn's was hard for everyone. Murray's path to her green Dodge car had to be taken via the kitchen, up the side courtyard and by the guest apartment. When she reached her vehicle, she was helped into it by her son-in-law, Norman. Newcomb and Marilyn's dog Maf were close behind. With Murray at the wheel, the car was driven out of the property and on to the corner of Carmelina and Sunset where Newcomb had arranged to meet her doctor. Afterwards, the publicist was dropped off at home.

Her telephone was, unsurprisingly, ringing when she opened her apartment door. For 48 hours, she remained by the apparatus, fielding calls from all over the world. It was estimated that the tally reached over 250. Journalists from as far away as England, Paris and Tokyo were desperate to know what precisely had happened to the world's most famous screen actress. All she could do was reiterate, as she believed, that 'Marilyn's death just had to be an accident' and 'things were going too well for her for it to have been anything else.' When fatigue began to set in, she varied her response by saying, 'She has been in a marvellous mood lately and the studio had assured her she would be allowed to finish *Something's Got To Give.*'

Murray too headed home. One day later, amid accusations from Marilyn's friends that she had sold her 'exclusive' version of the tragedy to a national magazine, she was driven out to Chatsworth, a district in the San Fernando Valley, to visit her daughter Marilyn LaClair and her family. She returned to her home at 933 Ocean Avenue, Santa Monica the following morning, Monday 6 August, to find reporters camped outside. Her landlord advised her to give them what they wanted, a quote or even a short interview. She reluctantly agreed on the latter, allowing two or three reporters into her apartment at a time. Sitting on a couch in her living room, Murray did her best to answer their questions.

Unsurprisingly, when her replies were published in the following day's papers, she was misquoted, her answers twisted, particularly with regard to Marilyn's mysterious last call. When asked about the call by the Los Angeles Police Department, she had replied, 'I don't remember the call, the time the call came in and I don't know who it was from.' Evasive though it sounded, she was telling the truth on all three counts. Now she told a United Press International journalist, 'Miss Monroe seemed *disturbed* after the phone call.' But there was no way that she could have known this. People wondered whether she had been tipped off about Lawford's fumbling and was ready to unite with Marilyn's friends against him. It was more likely that, for Murray, no doubt in a state of exhaustion, confusion was already setting in.

On Tuesday 7 August, Murray reluctantly returned to 12305 Fifth Helena Drive. She had been asked to help choose the clothes for the actress's funeral the following day. Despite it being the task of Marilyn's half-sister, Berniece Miracle, and Inez Melson, they had requested Murray's help due to her obvious first-hand knowledge of the actress's garments. (Murray and Melson returned to the house five days later, on Sunday 12 August, to tearfully pack up Marilyn's belongings for storage.)

While Murray was performing her motherly duties, fielding questions from the press and making preparations for her former employer's burial, Monroe's friends continued to vent their anger over the actress's death, in particular towards her so-called housekeeper. Once more, Dorothy Kilgallen was used as their mouthpiece. One close associate of Marilyn blasted to her, 'The reporters out in California missed a bet in accepting the identification of Eunice Murray as a "housekeeper". If she's just a plain ordinary housekeeper, I'm a circus acrobat.'

The unnamed friend's tirade raged on:

Why didn't the press ask her where she'd kept house before and for whom? I think they would find out she was a personal friend, an interior decorator and that she had moved in at the request of one of

Marilyn's doctors to stick close and not let the actress out of her sight. Marilyn was too miserable to be allowed to lock herself in a room with a lethal dose of Nembutal.

You can wager a small sum that she has sold her exclusive version of the tragedy to a national newspaper. She certainly didn't tell much to the reporters. For instance, she told them, 'Marilyn seemed disturbed after the last telephone call. When she went to her bedroom she really was depressed.' But Mrs. Murray never explained what Marilyn did or said to convey the impression that she was disturbed and depressed and if Marilyn *was* very disturbed and depressed at 8pm why did Mrs. Murray wait until 3am before checking her? If she was just a housekeeper, why would she be checking on her employer at all, prowling around at three o'clock in the morning looking for a light under the floor? She should have kept to her own quarters, not gone snooping and speculating. Of course, if she was an unofficial bodyguard to Marilyn, it was something else again.

In a piece for *The Oneonta Star*, Kilgallen wrote:

So poor Marilyn's death is liable to remain a mystery, quite unnecessarily because Hollywood pulled another of its hush-hush jobs. If this same sad thing happened in Cincinnati the facts would have been given out and it would have been all over in a few days. But this is California and nobody has stopped talking about it because it wasn't handled in a clear-cut manner. In the land of Perry Mason, Marilyn's death has become 'The Case of the Prowling Housekeeper'.

Just days after Marilyn's funeral, Murray checked out of her apartment at 933 Ocean Avenue, Santa Monica, leaving no forwarding address. Her neighbours in the block claimed that, shortly after the actress's demise, she had suddenly come into money and, according to many, embarked on an extended six-month trip to Europe. In fact this excursion lasted just six weeks, the same period that Marilyn was due to be away for, in New York, Washington and Mexico. 'The trip was planned for a long time,' Murray remarked to Maurice Zolotow in 1973. 'Marilyn had made arrangements to have somebody come to the house while I was away. I flew to Montreal and then to Paris and then to Geneva where I met my sister and her husband . . . we rented a car and drove through Switzerland, France, Holland and Germany. I never made any efforts to conceal my whereabouts . . . I've never run away in my life. When I'm travelling, I always leave my number with my daughter.'

As for Pat Newcomb, shortly after Marilyn's funeral on Wednesday 8 August 1962, she parted company with the Arthur Jacobs Press Agency. Her efforts to prevent photographers from taking images of her and reporters from obtaining stories about her had caused immense damage with the press, so much so that her employer had no choice but to fire her. Immediately after her sacking, she checked out of her Santa Monica apartment and then, as a guest of Peter and Pat Lawford, she flew to the Kennedy compound in Hyannis Port, Massachusetts and took up residence in their summer cottage in Marchant Avenue. She soon became a member of the Kennedys' staff.

On Sunday 12 August, she was pictured with, among others, JFK and the Lawfords aboard Kennedy's yacht, the *Manitou*, on a 12.35pm cruise around Johns Island, Maine. One week later, on Sunday 19 August, she was seen in the President's company again, this time at Lawford's home. At the end of the month she travelled to Europe. When she returned to America in February 1963, thanks to Bobby Kennedy, she was placed on the government payroll as a motion picture specialist for the US Information Agency in Washington DC.

On Friday 22 November 1963, the day that President Kennedy was tragically shot in Dallas, Texas, Newcomb helped take care of Bobby's children. By December that year, she had resumed her work in Hollywood as a publicist and was handling the affairs of movie actress Arlene Dahl; by October 1964, she was assisting Kennedy with his New York senatorial campaign. She returned to Tinseltown in 1966 to manage the career of actress Natalie Wood. Following Bobby Kennedy's death in June 1968, Newcomb returned to 20th Century-Fox, resurrecting her role as a publicist, when, during production of the musical *Hello Dolly*, she began running the affairs of the singer and actress Barbra Streisand. Impressed by her continued silence over Monroe, the singer apparently chose Newcomb personally for the job.

In August 1970, Newcomb arrived back in Washington to work for R. Sargent Shriver's recently formed Congressional Leadership for the Future, campaigning on behalf of Democratic candidates throughout the country for November's Congressional races and travelling extensively throughout the United States, assisting with speeches, luncheons and dinners, participating in community events and gaining support for candidates. In later years, she became a vice-president at MGM.

Unsurprisingly, throughout her career, her loyalty to Monroe was unending and as far as the actress was concerned, she was always reluctant to speak. For weeks after Monroe's death, she received several offers, most notably from the *New York Journal-American* newspaper, requesting her to tell her side of Marilyn's story. She spurned them all. 'Marilyn paid me my salary during her lifetime,' she remarked to the Hollywood columnist Mike Connolly, 'and I'm not going to write any post-mortems about my best friend.' She touchingly kept her word, and does so to this day.

Peter Lawford was never able to truthfully put pen to paper about the incident. He was aware that, if he did, he would have to confirm to the world that he had utterly failed the actress in her time of need. Regardless of the original, highly publicised reports that Joe DiMaggio Jr was the actress's last caller that night, there is no doubt that Lawford was the very last person to speak to Monroe, by way of that 8.20pm telephone call. Moreover, we can totally disregard the accounts of Marilyn's short-lived boyfriend, José Bolaños, garment millionaire Henry Rosenfeld and hairdresser Sydney Guilaroff, and of Marilyn's self-proclaimed best friend, Jeannie Carmen, who all claimed to have spoken to the actress on the night she died – Rosenfeld at 9pm, Guillaroff at 9.20, Bolaños (from a bar in Santa Monica) at 9.30 and Carmen at 10. Since Marilyn had passed away by 8.40pm, it was impossible for them to do so.

Fearing recriminations, Lawford would, to begin with, deny making that last call to Marilyn. However, close friends of the actress knew he had done so and proceeded to make it public, telling Dorothy Kilgallen who decided to announce it publicly in her syndicated column just three days after Monroe's death. She brazenly wrote, 'They [the friends] also have it figured out that Peter talked to her over the telephone after Joe DiMaggio Jr, not before, as Peter indicated when he blithely told the investigators that she sounded sleepy but otherwise perfectly fine.'

Gossip of Lawford's shortcomings spread throughout Tinseltown within days of her death, and most of the Broadway/Hollywood crowd began maliciously referring to him as 'The man who failed Marilyn Monroe the most.' His name was mud at every bar, grill, dinner party and film set. In March 1966, reporters discovered that Lawford had been furtively visiting the actress's crypt and depositing three fresh, yellow daisies, one of the actress's favourite flowers. He would harbour guilt about her death for the remainder of his life.

Lawford was nevertheless responsible for originating one of the most persistent myths concerning Marilyn's last hours – that of her immortal, final words, 'Say goodbye to Pat [his wife], say goodbye to the President and say goodbye to yourself because you're a nice guy.'

His con actually began the day after her death. On Sunday 5 August, during a heated discussion with Lady Lawford about Marilyn's death (she forthrightly told him he could have done more to help her), the actor, in a determined attempt to mollify his mother, suddenly announced that the actress had actually ended their conversation with a special message.

However, it wasn't the famous line we all know. Tailored to be more flattering towards Lawford himself, it began life as, 'Say goodbye to Pat, say goodbye to Jack [JFK] and say goodbye to yourself, because you're a nice guy, Charlie.' (Charlie was the nickname given to Lawford by his fellow Rat Pack members because of his cigarette cough, which reminded them of the character Charlie the Seal in the 1942 Abbott and Costello film comedy, *Pardon My Sarong*.)

And thus the legend of Marilyn's last words was born. Missing completely from his interviews with the *San Francisco Chronicle* of Thursday 8 August 1962 and the *Los Angeles Herald-Examiner* of August 1962 (in which he insinuated that it was he and not José Bolaños who was the last person to speak to the actress), as well as from pre-1970s biographies of the actress, it would actually take Lawford nine years to release full details of the actress's supposed final line.

In 1971, at a time when his career was heading for the doldrums and high-profile acting jobs were almost non-existent (bit-parts in television shows such as *Bewitched*, *The Virginian* and *The Doris Day Show* were among the highlights), he began basking in his glorious past, particularly in the fact that he had been the very last person to speak to Marilyn Monroe. Seeing it as a way of resurrecting his failing career, he wasted no time in resurrecting his 'final phone call' ruse to anyone who would listen. Having once gone to great lengths to deny it, he was now revelling in the fact.

In October of that year, he recounted his highly exaggerated story to the veteran author Earl Wilson, who published it for the very first time in his Hollywood expose, *The Show Business Nobody Knows*. The tale gained extra impetus a little over two years later when the writer reiterated it in his January 1974 publication, *Show Business Laid Bare*. Now, almost four decades on, the fictitious farewell speech has successfully managed to worm its way into the public consciousness, Monroe folklore and practically every book, magazine and television programme ever produced about the actress. But the truth is, she never said it. The goodbye speech was a figment of Lawford's guilt-riddled imagination, produced to appease his mother's fury.

At 5pm on Thursday 16 October 1975, following the publication in *Oui* magazine of an article titled 'Who Killed Marilyn Monroe?' by the investigative reporter Anthony Scaduto, in which the Los Angeles Police Department was severely criticised for its original handling of the case, the division was finally spurred into interviewing Lawford for the very first time. The setting was his then home at 1006 Cory Avenue, Los Angeles. But the information he provided was essentially worthless. No longer a part of the Kennedy clan, but with a close friendship with JFK's widow

Jacqueline to consider, he vehemently denied that Bobby Kennedy had been in Los Angeles during the weekend of 4 and 5 August 1962 and misleadingly claimed to have called Marilyn on that Saturday evening just to ascertain why she hadn't yet arrived at his home.

Moreover, at that time, according to his former manager, Milton Ebbins, he was already losing touch with reality and almost always 'out-of-it' on alcohol, cocaine and other mind-bending drugs, a totally unreliable eyewitness to almost everything that had transpired in his volatile past. Evidence of his inability to recall the night of Marilyn's death had come in 1974 during an interview with the reporter Ken Hood, in which Lawford disclosed that his wife was away 'in New York' and that Marilyn had been invited to his home that night to 'play a game of poker'.

His next recollection has a ring of truth about it – 'Her manner of speech was slurred . . . Her voice became less and less audible' – but what followed did not. He then claimed that he began yelling at her in an attempt to revive her, describing it as a 'verbal slap in her face'. The report quoted Lawford as correctly saying he had a 'gut feeling that something was wrong' and revealed that he still blamed himself for not going over to her home.

The fact that Lawford told the police that, on the night of Marilyn's death, he had 'tried to convince her to forget about her problems and join him and his wife, Pat for dinner' further corroborates Ebbins' accusation. The actor had evidently forgotten that Pat was away that weekend with her brother, John, and various other members of the Kennedy family in Hyannis Port.

Also made to suffer for the loss was Dr Greenson. Hate mail began arriving at his home and office immediately after Marilyn's passing, calling him a 'criminal', 'a communist quack' or a 'Hollywood murderer'. He took her death badly. Evidence of this came on Sunday 15 August 1962, when, in a letter to the actress's close friend Norman Rosten, he typed, 'It is so hard to write about because writing makes it all so real and all so final and one keeps hoping it isn't true or permanently true. I think I can accept the fact that Marilyn died, but it is so hard to believe that we will never see her again or hear her . . . '

The lives of Murray, Newcomb and the Kennedys, as well as, albeit under an intolerable weight of guilt, those of Lawford and Greenson, were indeed continuing. Meanwhile, on the morning of Sunday 5 August 1962, Marilyn Monroe's body lay flat out on a stainless steel mortuary table. All that awaited her was her autopsy and burial. Her body was still warm when Kay Gable became the first friend and celebrity to pay tribute to the fallen star. 'I heard the [news] flash over the air at 7am [Pacific

Daylight Time],' she solemnly declared. 'I went to mass this morning and prayed for her.'

Tributes were naturally relentless for the rest of the day. Director George Cukor was the next to comment. 'I just can't think. It's infinitely sad. Very tragic. There had been some talk of resuming production on the picture [*Something's Got To Give*] but nothing was definite. I don't think the actual disappointment of the film led her into this. I think she had these problems all her life which she tried to conquer. The great pity is, was I as helpful as I could have been? This is what one thinks when something like this happens.'

Columnist Dorothy Kilgallen spoke as a friend when she remarked, 'When I first heard Marilyn was dead, I said, "Oh no, it can't be," which is what almost everyone else said. But, as the voice on the telephone filled in the details, I found myself thinking, "Of course, of course. This is the way it would have to be, nude, the pill bottles, the record player, all alone . . . "' Immediately after hearing of the actress's demise, the British actor, singer and *Let's Make Love* co-star, Frankie Vaughan furiously declared, 'Hollywood has got to carry the can for this.' His accusation was naturally shot down by those in Tinseltown. In another comment, Cukor blasted, 'It is an awful lot of nonsense the charge that Hollywood claimed her life . . . Hollywood, in a sense *created* her.' His opinion was shared by John Huston, director of *The Misfits*. 'The girl was an addict of sleeping pills and she was made so by the God-damn doctors,' he proclaimed. 'It had nothing to do with the Hollywood set-up.' A columnist for the Hearst Corporation concurred. 'Man, those head-shrinkers, pro and amateur, sure did a great job on that poor dame, didn't they?'

Possibly the most revealing remarks about the actress came from her former acting coaches, Lee and Paula Strasberg. In a statement prepared that morning, they correctly hypothesised, 'She did *not* commit suicide. We have no doubt that what happened was an unfortunate accident. She did have trouble sleeping but the pills didn't help her a great deal.' Tellingly, they added, 'She had not taken any for a long time and she must have taken an overdose by accident. If it had been suicide, it would have happened in a quite different way. For one thing, she couldn't have done it without leaving a note. There are other reasons, which we cannot discuss, which make us certain she did not intend to take her life.' (The latter was an obvious reference to Marilyn's firing of the Strasbergs on Thursday 2 August.)

This belief was corroborated by Inez Melson, who remarked, 'Marilyn didn't have the temperament to commit suicide,' and by Dean Martin, who declared, 'I refuse to believe she took her life intentionally. I'm sure it was an accident. She was at my home a few days ago and she was very happy.' Her former husband, Arthur Miller, was in complete agreement. 'I am sure Marilyn's death was not deliberate,' he remarked. 'She did not kill herself. I am convinced it was a terrible accident.'

Photographer George Barris concurred. Referring to his recent photo shoot with the actress, he commented, 'The girl spent five hours on a windy beach posing for pictures. The girl would never throw in the towel. She would not have worked so hard with me on the story of her life had she intended to take it. She had a lot to live for, and I know she felt that way too.' Publicist Rupert Allan was equally accurate when he remarked, 'Marilyn could *not* have intended to kill herself that night because she was too vain to have allowed herself to lie in a coffin with a dark patch in that blonde hair.'

Naturally, there was confusion too. When informed of her death, a stunned Gene Kelly was quoted as saying, 'I am deeply shocked by this whole thing. I really don't know what to say. I was going to see her this afternoon. We had a project on file for next year. She was in excellent spirits, very happy and very excited about her future projects. I just don't understand it.' Equally in shock was Marilyn's great screen rival Jayne Mansfield, who remarked, 'I just can't believe it. I'm so sorry. I'm really so sorry.' When asked for a quote, Jacqueline Kennedy offered only, 'She will go on eternally.' While in Italy, actress Sophia Loren, when told of Monroe's passing, was unable to comment. She simply broke down and cried.

It wasn't just political figures or movie stars who were affected. Millions of ordinary people across the world were grief-stricken by Marilyn's death. America reported a rash of suicides. In New York, one such victim left a note saying, 'If the most wonderful, beautiful thing in the world has nothing to live for, then neither must I.' There were others in Mexico. Suicides by three teenage girls were attributed to the actress's death. Police said photographs of Monroe were found in the rooms of each girl. Two of the deceased took sleeping pills; the third drank a bottle of rum, smashed it and used a piece of it to slash her wrists.

News of the actress's passing naturally featured in every newspaper around the world, with the film industry taking the brunt of the blame. Moscow's *Izvestia* led the charge when it dramatically wrote, 'Marilyn Monroe was a victim of Hollywood. It gave birth to her and it killed her.' Stockholm's *Dagena Nyheter* agreed, saying 'She is the victim of the glaring lights, the too severe demands, the cracking whips, the cheers and the juggling in the big circus tent of movies.'

However, Rome's *Il Tempo* took an alternate perspective when, in a reference to the heavy demands modern movie stars are forced to endure for their art, it sensationally declared that she was murdered by *us*. 'Who killed her?' it asked. 'If we look ourselves in the face, we are forced to answer, "*We did*!"' Meanwhile, other papers in Europe had an altogether different take on the matter. Germany's *Frankfurter Abendpost* spoke for many when it lugubriously remarked, 'The world took her completely to her heart and now the world seems a heartbeat poorer.' But it was in Marilyn's homeland of America where, quite possibly, the best tribute to the star was written in *The New York Post*: 'The impact of Marilyn Monroe's death was international. Her fame was greater than her contributions as an actress,' was perhaps the finest at summing up this highly emotive situation.

Her passing, naturally, featured prominently on every television news bulletin. Special, full-length tribute programmes about her were also speedily prepared. America's leading psychologist, Dr Joyce Brothers, even devoted one of her NBC shows to the actress, and asked, 'If it was suicide, why?' As part of its *Special Report* series, the company also hastily produced a one-hour radio presentation about Marilyn. Entitled 'Fame Is Fickle', it featured swiftly recorded tributes from people who had been closely associated with her, such as George Cukor, Richard Meryman and Milton Greene. However, some of those featured were not so close – psychiatrist Dr Cornelia B. Wilbur for one, who cropped up to discuss Marilyn's mental condition at the time of her death, although the actress had not even been her patient.

Aside from the tidal wave of tributes, accusations and wild speculations, at 6.04am precisely Los Angeles-West Coast time (9.04am East Coast time) on the morning of Sunday 5 August, a call deriving from GLobe 1-1900 in Santa Monica was made to President John F. Kennedy at the White House. Since Kennedy was away for the weekend at the family's compound in Hyannis Port, the operator there had to convey the call. Telephone logs reveal that the exchange lasted little more than 20 minutes. The caller was his recently roused, clearly disorientated, half-intoxicated brother-in-law, Peter Lawford. There was but one reason for his call: to pass on the news of the death of Hollywood's most famous star.

Chapter Eleven

The Fallout

Sunday 5 August 1962–Monday 28 October 1985

At 7am on Sunday 5 August, Dr Thomas T. Noguchi, the 35-year-old Deputy Medical Examiner of Los Angeles County, arrived at his office at the Hall of Justice on Temple Street. He was given to working on Sundays. They were was the busiest for a Los Angeles coroner. For some reason, Sunday just happened to deliver more unexplained deaths and suspicious fatalities than any other day. Routinely, he removed his coat, sat down behind his desk and glanced down at the list of persons who had passed away in suspicious circumstances during the previous 24 hours. This day, however, would stand apart from the others. Among the inventory of 18 that morning was the name 'Marilyn Monroe'. Thinking it was a bizarre coincidence for two women to share such a world-famous moniker, he at once dismissed it. The thought that the woman on the list could be the renowned movie star whom he had idolised for so many years was simply incomprehensible.

At this juncture, his phone rang. It was his boss, Dr Theodore Curphey, calling to inform him that the person in question was indeed the well-loved actress. Once a legend of the silver screen, she was now coroner case no. 81128. Curphey instructed a shell-shocked Noguchi to perform her post-mortem personally and not to entrust it to any assistant.

Beginning at 10.30am, on stainless-steel table no. 1, Monroe's autopsy took five hours, during which Noguchi took samples of her blood, liver, stomach, urine, kidney and intestines. He also sent for testing eight drug bottles found on her bedside table. Recalling his examination of her body, he said, 'There was no evidence of an injection. I looked for needle marks. This is a standard part of any autopsy. There were no needle marks on the surface of her body, which might indicate the use of any drugs administered . . . The examination I made [also] included the contents of her vaginal passage, which were made on a smear and studied under a microscope. There was no indication of sexual intercourse.'

John Miner, an employee of the District Attorney's office, was in attendance when Dr Noguchi carried out his autopsy and concurred as to how the two of them examined the cadaver, looking intently for any needle marks and finding none.

In addition, it was noted in the 'Anatomical Summary' of the autopsy that, besides the lividity on her face, there was also 'slight ecchymosis of the left-side of the back and left hip'. Ecchymosis – also known as a bruise or a contusion – is an injury to biological tissue in which the capillaries are damaged, allowing blood to seep into the surrounding tissue. Marked by a purple discolouration of the skin, it is usually caused by blunt impact. In Marilyn's case, in all probability it occurred was when she was either haphazardly bundled up off the floor and placed on the bed or when she was moving furniture around with Newcomb the previous afternoon.

Later, when he scrutinised his colleague's autopsy report, Miner admitted there was one thing about it that bothered him: a reference to 'congestion and purplish discoloration of the colon'. As many conspiracy theorists have insisted, this would be consistent with the administering of an enema and thereby of poison. During research on this project, I discussed this notion with a noted pathologist, who remarked, 'What you're doing with the enema is you're giving a high dosage level of drug. You have a rapid absorption into the body.' Interestingly, he concluded by saying, 'If the poison had been administered this way, it *wouldn't* have got as far as the stomach. It would *only* have gone into the intestine.' In a multitude of cases, this would be so. However, with regard to Marilyn, it was *not*. According to her New York internist, Dr Richard Cottrell, in the summer of 1961, as a result of her emotional stresses, she was diagnosed as suffering from colitis, a form of inflammatory bowel disease, and this ailment alone accounted for her, seemingly bruised and discoloured, 'purplish' colon. Furthermore, as many coroners will agree, when people die, this part of the body begins to discolour anyway.

The autopsy showed that Marilyn's blood contained the equivalent of 8mg of chloral hydrate and 4.5mg of Nembutal per 100mg. This meant that in the five-minute period immediately prior to her death, she had dissolved and swallowed approximately 17, 500mg capsules of choral hydrate, double her regular daily intake and (in a period up to 7pm) a dosage totalling approximately 2,400mg of Nembutal – in other words, the concentration contained in 24 pills, just one shy of Friday's prescription. The 13 per cent of it found in her liver proved she had been slowly absorbing the drug for a prolonged period of time before she died. As we know, Marilyn started consuming Nembutal at around 5pm, approximately 3 hours 40 minutes before she passed away.

Furthermore, thanks to the cross-tolerance of chloral hydrate with Nembutal, Marilyn already had a high tolerance to both drugs, even though she had been prescribed the former for only a short time. Moreover, thanks to the phenomenon called tachyphylaxis, a medical term describing a swift decrease in the response to a drug after repeated doses over a short period of time, she needed larger and larger doses to have an effect.

Two details noted by Noguchi are often put forward by conspiracy theorists as an indication that Marilyn died by means other than an overdose of barbiturates. First, there was an absence of 'refractile crystals', the residue left by the drugs, which would have been expected to be present in the actress's stomach at the time of death. As the autopsy report stated, 'The stomach is almost completely empty . . . No residue of the pills is noted. A smear made from the gastric contents examined under the polarized microscope shows no refractile crystals . . . The contents of the duodenum are also examined under the polarized microscope and show no refractile crystals.'

This fact was actually of little significance. As Marilyn was a barbiturate addict, her stomach would become as familiar to drugs systematically ingested as it was to food regularly eaten. The drugs would have been so swiftly digested and passed into the intestines that a habitual drug user such as herself might die with no trace of the pills whatsoever in their stomach.

It has also been suggested that the absence of any traces of yellow dye from the Nembutal capsules in her stomach is significant. However, considering Marilyn died several hours before she was found and over 12 hours before her autopsy, there was no reason why any such dye should·be present. As coroners agree, the acid in a stomach quickly absorbs and destroys the gelatine capsules, since that was what they are designed to do. Besides, Nembutal itself does not possess a colouring agent and hence does not leave a trail. Instead, the so-called yellow colouring originates from the capsule, which means that, if she had broken open the pills and, prior to swallowing, mixed the contents with a glass of water – which she frequently did – there would be no stains in her stomach.

It is also worth remembering that the absorption time decreases when a subject uses the medicine on a regular basis, which Marilyn was known to do. In truth, the 24 Nembutal capsules would have dissolved in her body within just 20 minutes, as they were designed to do. The fact that she could consume such a vast quantity in such a short period of time was not new to those who knew her. Director John Huston remarked that, during the shooting of *The Misfits* in 1960, he once saw her devour 20 or more tablets in just one day, as well as drinking copious amounts of alcohol.

As Noguchi's autopsy report shows, he specifically requested that the intestines, the stomach and their contents were tested and saved for further study, which might have identified further drug residues and enabled a more certain assessment of the cause of death to be made. Yet, when the report from the toxicological laboratory arrived, he noticed that the lab technicians had not tested the other organs he had sent them. They had examined only the blood and liver and not the stomach and the intestine. So why the failure? As Noguchi admitted, 'The evidence found in the analysis of the blood and the liver, together with the empty bottle of Nembutal, and the partly empty bottle of choral hydrate, pointed so overwhelmingly to suicide that the head toxicologist, Raymond J. Abernathy, apparently felt that there was no need to test any further . . . But I should have insisted. I didn't follow it through as I should have done. As a junior member of the staff, I didn't feel I could challenge the departmental heads on procedures.' Just a few weeks later, in late August 1962, Noguchi thought better of it and asked Dr Abernathy if he had kept the stomach and intestine that he had sent him. But he was shockingly informed that, since the case was now closed, they had been disposed of too.

As in all cases of what are known as 'equivocal suicides', where it was undetermined whether the death was by accident or suicide, Dr Curphey assigned a team of behavioural scientists to examine fully Marilyn's lifestyle. Working from two battered desks, shoe-horned into a poky 12 by 10 foot office situated in the basement of the Los Angeles Veterans Administration mental ward, the team was headed by the aforementioned Dr Robert Lipman, a psychiatrist and professor at the UCLA, Dr Norman Tabachnick, a medical doctor, and Dr Norman L. Farberou, PhD, head of the Suicide Prevention Center.

On Monday 6 August, the unit set about their psychological autopsy by interviewing those familiar with the actress's daily routines. They contacted first the people who knew her best, both personally and socially, and then her psychiatrists in both New York and Los Angeles. Dr Ralph Greenson told the investigators, 'Marilyn had certain deep emotional problems but was responding well to treatment.' The medical staff at New York's Payne-Whitney clinic, where she had been hospitalised in February the previous year, were also interviewed. In addition, the suicide team made contact with everyone in and around Hollywood who was known to have spoken to the actress in the last few months, including her lawyers, and concluded their examination by attempting to make an informed exploration of Marilyn's final day, with special emphasis on her concluding minutes. To do this, they naturally paid a visit to the actress's home in Brentwood. The results of their findings were then passed on to Curphey.

Ever since Marilyn's death, reporters tipped off about her last phone call had been referring to it as the 'mysterious phone call in the night'. Original newspaper accounts even suggested that the caller was Marilyn's erstwhile Mexican friend, José Bolaños, and speculated the actress had killed herself because of his unrequited love. On Tuesday 7 August, while Peter Lawford watched on silently, rigidly refusing to come forward with the information they required, officers from the Los Angeles Police Department began their search to track Bolaños down. Their trawl covered Los Angeles and naturally his native land. When they did manage to find him at his home in Mexico, , he defensively clarified – speaking through an interpreter, since his English was poor – that he had not made the call, was not responsible for Marilyn's (apparent) sudden depression, had not seen her since the end of June and had not spoken to her since the first week of July.

But for the aspiring actor and screenwriter, this slice of reflected glory only managed to reignite his unquenchable taste for further fame and admiration. On Monday, 13 August, after seeing what newspapers would do (and pay) for any kind of Marilyn exclusive, he came out of hiding to fly to Los Angeles's Westwood Memorial Cemetery, where he was seen mournfully placing flowers at the actress's crypt. Posing solemnly as he did so for both the *New York Daily News* and the *Philadelphia Daily News*, he then revealed that he had been under sedation for four days following Marilyn's death, verbally attacked Joe DiMaggio for banning him from her funeral and criticised the baseball legend for the way the actress had been buried. 'It was a terrible thing to take this girl who was show business herself and put her away in a drawer in an abandoned cemetery,' Bolaños exclaimed. 'If this girl had died in Mexico, she would have had a state funeral.'

To cap it all, he then sensationally insinuated that he did after all, speak to the actress on the night she died and was told 'something shocking, something that will one day shock the world.' Well, the world waited . . . and waited . . . and waited but the story never came. Biographer, Anthony Summers even pressed him on the matter during research for his highly exhaustive, 1985 Monroe book, *Goddess*. But Bolaños still wasn't talking. Why? Because simply he had no tale to tell. In the end, he wound up taking whatever he had in mind, which amounted to nothing, to his grave.

As a footnote to this tale, on Sunday 14 July, 1963, he wed the 33-year-old, Mexican-born, film actress, Elsa Aquirre. They divorced soon after. His voracious appetite for success in the film industry was unabated and in December 1966, in yet another desperate attempt to be seen on the arm of some other famous female, he began dating the Italian-born screen star, Gina Lollobrigida. But, as with Marilyn, the relationship was nothing but a short-lived, rather nebulous one. Remembered now as 'Marilyn Monroe's lover', opportunist Bolaños died in his homeland on Saturday 11 June, 1994.

News of the actress's financial shortfalls became public on Tuesday 7 August, when reporter Joe Hyams of the *Herald Tribune* news service announced, 'Marilyn Monroe died [on] Sunday (*sic*) with less than $100 in her savings account and only $4,700 in her personal checking account.' When pressed on the matter, Milton Rudin explained away the deficit by insisting she had a lot of bills and was involved in litigation over past debts, including a tax case pending in New York. He then lent weight to Hyams' accusation by coming clean and admitting Marilyn's estate could 'ill afford the $100-a-day guards that are now posted in front of the actress's home in Brentwood'. In fact, in her five bank accounts and in cash at her two homes, the actress died with just $6,813.17 to her name.

Her already depleted estate would be drained further by the salvo of invoices which began landing on executor Aaron F. Frosch's desk at 120 East 69th Street, New York within weeks of the actress's death. Some were from companies or individuals that the actress had some unfinished business with, such as the Department of Water and Power (who sub-mitted a bill for $203.31), the Southern Counties Gas Company (who requested a payment for $185.62), the General Telephone phone company (for $274.61), the New York Telephone Company ($40.36), the Magnetic Springs Water Company ($3.60), the Reese Period Furniture company ($313.92), the Rand-Fields Incorporated Airline Company ($205.59), United Airlines Incorporated ($411.18), the Saks clothing company ($388.32), photo agency Globe Photos ($5,000), cleaner B.J. Denihan ($1,241.60), gardener Sam Tateishi ($939.55), and secretary Cherie Redmond ($689.30).

Others, however, originated from many of the actress's so-called close friends and associates, including Milton Rudin of the law firm Gang, Tyre, Rudin & Brown who submitted a $10,000 bill for 'legal services', Dr Ralph Greenson, for 'professional services' ($1,400), Dr Hyman Engelberg, likewise ($478), make-up man Allan 'Whitey' Snyder, strangely for 'photographic' reasons ($1,800), Agnes M. Flanagan for 'hairstyling' ($840), publicist Arthur. P. Jacobs, for 'reimbursement of expenses' ($797.85), masseur Ralph Roberts ($470), and friend Norman Rosten's wife, Hedda, for an unknown reason ($882.01).

Unpaid taxes took a substantial share. The IRS (Inland Revenue Service) moved quickly to assess and make claims for the current year, which included the California Franchise Tax ($2,614.24) and the 1962 Federal Income Tax bill ($21,724.72). But, after re-examining her files, the IRS discovered that Monroe was actually liable for tax for the previous *four* years. In order to reduce her tax bill, Marilyn had essentially deferred her salary contracts. After her death, she could make no more business deductions and hence, her previous 'deferred incomes' were now answerable for tax.

An invoice for 1958 (to the tune of $22,665.49) was swiftly calculated and submitted to the estate. Then, in an attempt to bring her file up to date, invoices for 1959, 1960 and 1961 were considered and a bill to the tune of $70,000 was soon dispatched. An additional demand (for $10,000), to cover the income tax assessment for the estimated years between 1958 and 1962, was also presented by the New York Income Tax Bureau. With such a major problem to be sorted, it was no surprise that Monroe's accountant, Jack M. Ostrow, was forced to submit a hefty bill for $2,500 for his services to the estate.

The avalanche of claims did not end there. Eunice Murray's son-in-law, the so-called 'handyman' Norman Jeffries, was next when he submitted a bill for two weeks' wages ($360). Murray herself was close behind. With jaw-dropping gall, instead of presenting one invoice, she tendered *two*. The first, for the sum of $400, was for 'housekeeping' after Marilyn's death, despite the fact she was, in her own words, out of the country on a six-week 'tour of Europe'. The second, for a staggering $1,000, was to pay for her 'services in remodelling and decorating decedent's home' in California, despite the fact that she had done neither. The audacity of it all increased another echelon when drama coach Paula Strasberg, from her home in New York, handed in a bill for a whopping $32,269.37 to cover 'services rendered and expenses in connection therewith'. (After several negotiations, she felt compelled to reduce her bill by just $10,000.) Cash-strapped, heartless 20th Century-Fox were next in the queue, promptly submitting a $500,000 'breach of contract' suit against Marilyn's estate. In essence, they were suing her over her failure to finish *Something's Got To Give*. (The suit was unsurprisingly contested and rightly dismissed.)

The estate's executor, Aaron Frosch, did nicely out of this too. His law firm, Weissberger & Frosch, presented a $15,000 bill for 'legal and accounting services'. However, quite possibly the most poignant bills received were for the sum of $5,000, a personal loan from Joe DiMaggio to help with the purchase of Marilyn's 12305 Fifth Helena Drive home, and for $58.57 still owing to the Vicente Pharmacy on San Vicente

Boulevard. The latter meant that, sadly, the actress had died still in arrears for the drugs that had killed her.

On Thursday 9 August, the day that Inez C. Melson, Marilyn's former business manager and now guardian of her mother, was appointed by Frosch to serve as a 'special administratrix' of the actress's estate in California, the attorney prematurely made public details of Monroe's woefully outdated will, made on Saturday 14 January 1961. A spokesperson for his firm announced, 'It is a simple will and may surprise some people who are left out. I understand that Joe DiMaggio knew the will's contents and was guided by them in deciding who to invite to the funeral.' In the antiquated wish-list, admitted to probate and officially published on Friday 10 August, it was revealed that Marilyn had (via her cash, life insurance, personal effects and shares in Marilyn Monroe Productions Inc.) left in excess of $1 million and had provided her institutionalised mother, Gladys Baker, with an income of $3,500 a year. The sum of $10,000 was left to her half-sister, Berniece Miracle.

However, mouths dropped when it was announced that a lifetime revenue of $2,500 per annum had also been bequeathed to the widow of Marilyn's one-time drama coach, Michael Chekhov, and a 25 per cent slice of any remaining residues from the estate had been bestowed to two people the actress had actually excised from her life, namely her New York psychiatrist, Dr Marianne Kris, and her acting coach, Lee Strasberg, the latter of whom in addition was left a large slice of the actress's personal clothing and effects.

There were disagreements over the will from the start. In October, Melson disputed the document, claiming it had been written out while Marilyn was under the undue influence of both main beneficiaries. Her claim was dismissed and the will was admitted into probate. Almost three years later, on Monday 21 June 1965, it was announced that Marilyn's estimated $1 million estate had indeed been almost entirely consumed by taxes, in this case, the highest federal rate of 70 per cent. Despite the fact that the estate had, at that juncture, collected a sum in the region of $800,000 through deferred salaries and sales of film rights to television, there were no allowable exemptions or expenses. Furthermore, the IRS also reassessed the actress's estate as $118,000 for disqualified deductions between the years 1958 and 1962. By now, in total, Federal income tax had claimed $452,000, state tax $64,850 and inheritance tax $150,000. With $173,288 still owing to various preferred creditors, the executors of Monroe's estate were forced to formally notify the family and friends mentioned in the will there would be, for the foreseeable future anyway, 'no significant amount for any beneficiary'.

There wasn't even enough spare money to pay for the care of Marilyn's mother, Gladys. Her bill at the Rockland Sanitarium in Glendale now stood at $4,133. Special means to pay for it were urgently discussed with the executors of the estate, but with no help coming from that direction, an appeal for donations was immediately put out. In response, a hand-addressed envelope arrived, containing an unsigned note which read, 'Put this on Marilyn's mother's bill.' The gift consisted of . . . two $1 bills. It was the *only* contribution. 'Not a soul in Hollywood has come forward since it was disclosed that there may not be enough money in Miss Monroe's estate to pay for the care of her mother,' Melson dejectedly remarked at the time. The wrangling over the actress's money would roll on for another eight years.

In the interim, in the first week of August 1962, the official investigation into Marilyn's death was still continuing. The actress had (officially) passed away five days earlier and the American media was beginning to ask why it was taking so long for Los Angeles's highly trained medical team to reach its conclusion. In most cases of suicide, the coroner's office would take just 24 hours to disclose to the public the pathological assessment as to the contents of the deceased's stomach and the nature of any drugs that might have caused their death. When quizzed by reporters about his team's apparent unhurried demeanour, Theodore Curphey snapped back, 'My investigation is being routinely conducted.'

On Friday 10 August, in a hastily arranged press conference to appease the fast-emerging cluster of inquisitors, Dr Curphey announced vaguely that 'more than one drug' may have caused the actress's death, adding that he 'may still order an inquest' but would not decide until he had received a final report from poison experts the following week. He announced that his experts had taken away for testing the contents of at least 12 prescription bottles found on her bedside table. Curphey also admitted that, to begin with, he had even looked into the possibility that Marilyn might have swallowed a fast-acting poison such as cyanide in addition to the overdose of sleeping pills.

His ambiguity ended when Curphey startlingly, and quite suddenly, announced the first findings of Raymond J. Abernathy, the principal toxicologist on the case. 'Marilyn died from a massive overdose of drugs nearly *twice* [emphasis added] that needed to kill her.' (The toxicologist's actual statement to Curphey was 'Her [Marilyn's] blood stream contained nearly twice as much barbiturate as necessary to kill a person.') This dramatic admission was reproduced in practically every major newspaper around the world (including the British tabloid, the *Daily Mirror*, on Saturday 11 August), but hardly anyone was inquisitive enough to query further Curphey's announcement. One American-based reporter, though, was.

Moved by this extraordinary statement and the inexplicable delays on the case, he was propelled to investigate further. His article, published on the front page of the *San Francisco Chronicle* on Sunday 10 August 1962, became one of my most remarkable discoveries during my research. There, in clear, bold black and white, was the headline: 'Strange Pressures On Marilyn Probe'. The report, which emanated from *The New York Times*, read as follows:

'Strange pressures' are being put on Los Angeles police investigating the death of Marilyn Monroe, sources close to the probers said last night. 'This is why,' the sources said, 'Coroner Theodore J. Curphey has failed thus far to make public just what poison was found by toxicologists in the stomach of the 36-year-old actress. That is also why police investigators have refused to make public the record of phone calls made from Miss Monroe's home last Saturday evening, hours before she took an overdose of sleeping pills. The police have impounded the phone company's taped record of outgoing calls. The purported pressures are mysterious. They are apparently coming from persons who had been closely in touch with Marilyn in the last few weeks . . . Normally in suicide probes, the record of such phone calls would have been made available to the public within a few days.

Without any shadow of a doubt, in the knowledge that Marilyn had attempted to contact President Kennedy and had seen his brother Bobby just hours before she died, the US Government had taken a keen interest in the case and was determined to oversee the proceedings. (Curphey had bowed to similar pressure three years earlier, when on Tuesday 23 June 1959, at a press conference in Los Angeles, he declared that the *Superman* television actor George Reeves had committed suicide with a self-inflicted gun shot, despite the fact that many, including his mother, firmly believed that he had actually been murdered.)

One week later, on Friday 17 August, after almost two weeks of probing, the verdict was finally reached in the Monroe inquiry. In a small, scruffy room, into which 30 newsmen had packed, Los Angeles coroner Theodore Curphey began by announcing that Marilyn 'had suffered from psychiatric disturbances for a long time' and had 'experienced severe fears and frequent depressions'. His report continued with the declaration that her 'mood changes were abrupt and unpredictable. Amongst symptoms of disorganisation, sleep disturbance was prominent, for which she had been taking sedative drugs for years and was familiar with and experienced in the use of sedative drugs and was well aware of the drugs. [In July, with Greenson] Miss Monroe had been taking psychiatric treatments, resulting in an effort to reduce her consumption of the drugs and it was partly successful during the last two months.'

With Dr Norman Farberou sitting dependably by his side, he went on to confirm that Monroe had died from 'acute barbiturate poisoning . . . remnants of the drug pentobarbital [Nembutal] sleeping pills were found in her liver and chloral hydrate was found in her blood . . . [and] there was no distinguishable physical evidence of foul play . . . Miss Monroe had unwittingly and unfortunately played the greatest role of her career. The method of her death may accomplish some good by bringing to the attention of the public the work being done in Los Angeles County to help those who are contemplating self-destruction.'

His team of suicide investigators, he explained, had said that Marilyn may not have intended to die when she took the overdose; their findings showed, he said, that she had 'more than once tried to kill herself when she was disappointed or depressed'.

His announcement complied with reports released the previous week, which stated that Monroe had previously tried to commit suicide four times, twice before she was 19. The psychologists said that, after each of the earlier attempts, Marilyn had called for help and had been saved. They added that the pattern of events leading up to the actress's passing on the evening of Saturday 4 August was the same except for the fact that this time she was not rescued. 'We have learned that Miss Monroe had often expressed wishes to give up, to withdraw and even to die.' (In a 1982 interview with the investigators carrying out a fresh probe into the actress's death, Dr Hyman Engelberg flatly rejected this allegation. 'I'm not aware of any deliberate suicide attempt,' he insisted. 'I was only aware of the one time when she currently had too much to drink and had taken possibly slightly more than she should have [a reference to the July 1962 weekend at the Cal-Neva]. But that was *not* a suicide attempt.')

Basically corroborating Dr Thomas Noguchi's findings, Curphey then announced that 'Marilyn's death was caused by an overdose of the sedative Nembutal. She received a prescription for about 40 or 50 tablets only three days before her death. The bottle was found empty in her room . . . Now that the final toxicological report and that of the psychiatrist consultants have been received and considered,' he concluded, 'it is my conclusion that the death of Marilyn Monroe was caused by a self-administered overdose of sedative drugs and the mode of death is probable suicide.' The adjective 'probable' was used because Marilyn left no suicide note. The policy of the coroner's office was to qualify the word 'suicide' unless the victim had left a note.

Asked by a member of the press whether the actress was 'quite disturbed' when she died on Sunday 5 August (*sic*), Farberou replied indirectly by saying, 'I can tell you this. I think it would be safe to speculate on the fact.' He also admitted that his team's investigation had uncovered certain 'conflicts' in Marilyn's personality. 'I am not at liberty to tell you what is in the report,' he admitted, 'but we did investigate fantasies and thoughts of death and dying.'

When Dr Curphey announced to the world's media that Marilyn's death was down to a 'probable suicide', however, Noguchi flipped. He immediately rushed to Dr Robert Lipman, the chairman of the suicide prevention team assigned to the actress's case, and demanded to know how he could possibly say that Marilyn's death was a 'probable suicide' when there was no medical evidence of her ever having taken orally any sedative drugs. Lipman replied, 'That was not really my department. I canvassed the views among Marilyn's psychiatrists and doctors as to what they thought and studied their documentation.' As Noguchi dejectedly remarked, 'The actress could have swallowed the Nembutals herself and the residues of the capsules could have gone straight through and down into the large intestine. But it was *never* tested. So no one can *ever* know for sure.'

Nevertheless, the actress's death certificate was altered according to the verdict announced by Curphey. Under 'Mode of Death' Noguchi had circled 'Suicide' but at a later date had added the word 'probable' in pencil. In an August 1973 interview with the Monroe biographer Maurice Zolotow, Noguchi explained how he reached this decision. 'On the basis of my examination, plus my toxicologist report plus the report of the behavioural scientists, I arrived at the verdict of probable suicide, based on acute barbiturate poisoning, specifically an overdose of Nembutal and chloral hydrate. Either of these would have been enough to kill Miss Monroe.

'While it is true that persons habituated to Seconal, Nembutal, Sodium Amytal, Tuinal and other varieties of heavy barbiturates sometimes lose count and accidentally kill themselves, in my experience this kind of accident, brought about by what the profession calls "automatism", where the victim automatically consumes more pills than he/she can handle, only applies if you take three or more pills and you lose count and you may unwittingly take say, 10 pills resulting in a 1.5 per cent milligram concentration which is enough to kill you. But when there are 40 or 50 capsules involved, it indicates a deliberate intent to commit suicide.'

When asked why there were no residues of Nembutal in her stomach, Noguchi replied, 'This is not uncommon. A person addicted to barbiturates develops what we call a "dumping syndrome", which is to say that the stomach dumps the drugs more quickly than usual into the intestines, as the stomach is conditioned to so much Nembutal . . . It was also common to find the stomach empty when the victim has not had any food during the time previous to the overdose.' (True. Marilyn did not eat a thing on her final day alive.) Summing up, he correctly declared Monroe's death a 'clear case of barbiturate poisoning', confirming that is was 'self-induced as I have seen in all my years as a forensic pathologist and I would estimate that I have performed and supervised over 1,000 post-mortems.' (Due to his subsequent autopsies on world-famous personalities such as Bobby Kennedy and the actresses Sharon Tate and Natalie Wood, Noguchi would go on to become sardonically known as the 'coroner to the stars'.)

On Wednesday 12 August 1970, chiefly due to the reselling of television rights to her – at that time, rarely seen – 1957 movie, *The Prince and the Showgirl*, the actress finally managed to do in death what she had failed to do in life: get out of debt. On that day Aaron Frosch proudly announced to the press, 'We've *finally* managed to pay off everything,' with creditors set to receive '100 cents on the dollar'. With a value of $1,250,000, he went on to estimate that, from that moment on, a sum of $20,000 a year or more would roll into the estate.

However, his joy would prove premature. Just over five years later, on Tuesday 16 December 1975, Marilyn's estate once more fell foul of the IRS when it was announced that it now owed more than $90,000 in back taxes and interest. According to the California Franchise Tax Board, in a suit filed that day in the superior court, a sum of $51,243 in taxes, between the years 1963 and 1970, was sought, in addition to $12,080 in penalties and, significantly, $27,604 interest from Aaron Frosch. It was the first time that those close to the estate had become aware of the attorney's suspect ways. Their fears were confirmed in March 1981 when, in a suit initiated by Marianne Kris, he was sued for $200,000 for illegally plundering Marilyn's estate. The doctor claimed that Frosch had illegally paid himself wages from the estate. (The suit was settled out of court for an undisclosed sum.)

In 2010, thanks to royalties and the proceeds of her movies and image rights, the actress is still in the black, generating – via CMG (Curtis Management Group) Worldwide, the licensing agent for MMLLC (Marilyn Monroe Licensing Co.) – on average more than $8 million annually. Most of it goes to Anna Strasberg, Lee's widow, whom he met at the Actors Studio in 1967 and married three months later. Lee Strasberg died in February 1982, at which point the Monroe inheritance passed onto his wife. Almost immediately, she began launching her own Marilyn Monroe licensing business, hiring the astute Los Angeles lawyer Roger Richman to secure lucrative publicity rights. It worked. In that year alone, the Monroe estate earned $71,253. (Six years later, in 1988, it had risen to $1.1 million.)

Between 1983 and 1995, Richman struck many money-making licensing deals, among them a 'Marilyn Monroe Boutique' at Bloomingdale's department store in New York, print and television adverts for Absolut vodka and cosmetics company Revlon Inc., plus an assortment of dolls, T-shirts and coffee mugs. In 2000, Strasberg created Marilyn Monroe LLC, which, in her opinion, owned Monroe's publicity rights. She has a controlling interest in that entity; the Anna Freud Centre, a London psychiatric institute that inherited Dr Marianne Kris's stake after her death in November 1980, owns the rest. Jeffrey Lotman, chief executive of the Los Angeles licensing firm Global Icons, announced recently that after Elvis Presley, Marilyn Monroe and actor James Dean are the most valuable dead-celebrity brands. (At the time of writing, I have no doubt that Michael Jackson will soon feature among these.)

However, there was a severe setback for MMLLC in their multi-million dollar operations when, on Monday 17 March 2008, Judge Margaret M. Morrow, of the United States District Court, Central District of California ruled that CMG and MMLLC did *not* in fact own the 'right of publicity' for Marilyn Monroe, insisting that they had been playing 'fast and loose with the courts' simply to benefit from a recently passed California law, which granted rights of publicity to a celebrity's estate.

Commenting on the decision, Surjit Soni of the Pasadena-based Soni Law Firm, counsel for the parties representing photographers Tom Kelley and Milton H. Greene, said, 'This ruling reconfirms that MMLLC and CMG's stranglehold on the Marilyn Monroe licensing business is *broken*. Licensees who have, according to *Forbes* magazine, paid approximately $7 million in royalties to CMG in 2007, which represents over $50 million in wholesale revenues, are now free to license Marilyn Monroe photographs directly from the copyright owners at a *lower* total cost and a *higher* profit potential.' The decision paved the way for licensees to work directly with the respective owners of some of the actress's iconic images, many of which soon gathered together under the 'Marilyn Monroe Licensing Group' banner at Legends Licensing LLC. The right to exploit Marilyn's images this way was upheld by the United States District Court of New York on Tuesday 2 September 2008.

Meanwhile, the certainty of Dr Thomas Noguchi in 1973 about how exactly the screen legend died had failed to dampen the ardour of Monroe conspiracy theorists. Thanks in part to the numerous biographies and highly embellished, tell-all articles about the star which appeared at regular intervals throughout the 1970s and early 1980s, it came as no surprise when, on Wednesday 11 August 1982, following a recent exposé in *The New York Post* newspaper and amid outcries that there had been a cover-up in the original probe, the Los Angeles County Board of Supervisors unanimously called for a new investigation into Marilyn's death.

At the request of one of their supervisors, Mike Antonovich, the Board ordered John Van Der Kemp, Los Angeles's District Attorney, to investigate charges made by Lionel Grandison, a former coroner investigator, that there were irregularities in the original inquiry and that he may have been 'pressurised' into signing the actress's death certificate. He had also been quoted as saying the original 1962 investigation was incomplete and that a red diary, which detailed Marilyn's relationship and conversations with the late Attorney General, Bobby Kennedy and her knowledge of CIA activities, had disappeared while at the coroner's office.

In response to the growing speculation, Antonovich remarked that the allegations were serious enough for the District Attorney's office to look into them. The board unanimously concurred that if any of the charges were substantiated the case would be referred to the Grand Jury. The District Attorney's office meanwhile moved quickly to say that no investigation into the actress's death was under way other than a review of statements made in a seven-part series which had appeared in *The New York Post* and which chronicled the strange circumstances surrounding Marilyn's passing. At the behest of the county board of supervisors, Assistant Deputy District Attorney Mike Carroll was placed in charge of the investigation.

Interestingly, Theodore Curphey, the coroner in charge of the original 1962 inquiry, chose not to be a part of this new probe and even refused to co-operate with the investigators. 'I'll be goddamned if I'll get involved,' he told a DA investigator. Yet the District Attorney did not even serve him with a subpoena. Why? Was it because he knew far more about Monroe's death than he had revealed back in 1962? Furthermore, why didn't the investigators pursue him and insist that he participate? Regrettably, we'll never know. Curphey passed away in November 1986.

The inadequacies of this new investigation did not end there. The County Board of Supervisors did not even bother to interview homicide detective Sergeant Robert Byron, the officer who had taken over from Sergeant Jack Clemmons on the morning after Marilyn's death and the man responsible for filing the police report that evening. But individuals such as Dr Hyman Engelberg and the ambulance drivers that night, Rick Stone and Ken Hunter *were* questioned. Ralph Greenson regrettably was not. He had died of heart failure three years earlier in November 1979.

The investigating team began by asking themselves, 'Was there a murder that night?' Dr Noguchi's original autopsy report was re-examined and the few surviving police photos taken that evening were scrutinised. The probe accumulated a total of 309 documents and over five hours' worth of audio-taped interviews. But after just three and a half months, the fresh inquiry into Marilyn's death was closed down. In December that year, Mike Carroll issued a statement which said that there was 'no credible evidence supporting a murder theory'. The report added, 'There was a possibility that the death had been accidental, but suicide was more likely.' When asked by the CBS *60 Minutes* show in 2006 if there had been a cover-up surrounding Marilyn's death, Carroll replied, 'As there was no murder, there was nothing to cover up, other than embarrassing information or connections.' Regrettably, that was an area the team failed to examine.

Summing up, the reinvestigation uncovered no evidence of foul play, but concluded that the original probe into Marilyn's death had not been conducted properly. It was determined that the officers who arrived at the actress's home in Fifth Helena that night had failed to secure the scene; people freely came and went, possibly contaminating or destroying evidence. The reinvestigation also revealed that (as Dr Thomas Noguchi revealed) all lab work, tissue samples, and test results from the autopsy had disappeared from the county coroner's office immediately after the official ruling had been made public. (Noguchi claimed that misplacement of samples had *never* happened in another case, before or since.) The report also confirmed, as I detailed in a previous chapter, that Monroe's body may well have been moved after her death, as lividity (settling of blood) had appeared in different parts of her body at different times. But in truth, the new investigation was hampered from the start. Practically all the original police files pertaining to Marilyn's death had been destroyed in compliance with departmental procedures.

Other documents relevant to the case were also missing, notoriously Marilyn's telephone records. Due to where the actress lived, at the base of the Santa Monica Mountains, every call she made from her home in Brentwood was classed as long-distance and therefore logged. Following the announcement that she had been found dead in her bed clutching a phone, reporter Joe Hyams, working on another piece for *The New York Herald Tribune*, was determined to see her records and discover to whom she was talking just before she perished. So too was Florabel Muir, a crime correspondent employed by the huge, New York-based media conglomerate, the Hearst Corporation. However, their endeavours would prove to be fruitless. Someone had beaten them to it. As an employee at the General Telephone Company in Brentwood announced to Hyams at the time, 'All hell's broken loose down here. You're not the only one interested in Marilyn's calls.'

It appears that, immediately after her death, and with extreme discretion, Marilyn's direct-distance dialling records were impounded by Secret Service men, described as wearing 'dark suits' and 'well-shined shoes'. Her demise had now become a 'highly secretive, intelligence division operation'. As Hyams would remark, to his knowledge, it was the first time that someone's phone records had been seized so fast to protect someone or something. The key to this benevolent cover-up was surely the protection of Bobby Kennedy.

Acting on the orders of J. Edgar Hoover and LAPD Chief William H. Parker, records of her final calls were confiscated by Captain James Hamilton who, as noted by the Kennedy Library, was a very close friend of the Attorney General. Four months after Marilyn's death, Parker supposedly took a 723-page file about the actress's death, which included details of her phone records, and showed it to 'someone' in Washington. Curiously, according to correspondence held in the aforementioned library, on Wednesday 12 December 1962 Parker met with Bobby Kennedy at the College Park Motel in College Park, Maryland for what was described as a 'mutual matter of interest'. The cover-up over Marilyn's death was well and truly underway at this point and, naturally, Parker was the chief organiser.

Endeavours by reporters to see this file took an unfortunate twist on Saturday 16 July 1966, when, at a convention of the Second Marine Division Association in the Pacific Ballroom of Dallas' Statler Hilton Hotel, in front of more than 1,000 Marine veterans, and just moments after he had received a plaque citing him as one of the nation's foremost police chiefs, Parker collapsed to the floor and started to gasp. He was rushed to the Central Receiving Hospital but was pronounced dead 35 minutes later at precisely 11.10pm. He was 64. Immediately after his demise, journalists believing his death would now lift the veil of secrecy surrounding Marilyn's last phone calls, descended on Parker's office only to find them missing once again; an unnamed, recently resigned intelligence man from the FBI had beaten them to it, broken in and made off with the file in which they were contained.

The file mysteriously reappeared 16 years later when, in 1982, the investigators at the Los Angeles District Attorney's office were handed a copy by the Los Angeles Police Department. By this time, however, its original 723 pages had been whittled down to just 54. (It is highly likely that the first case file had been destroyed some 20 years earlier. Fresh searches for it, on both hard copy and microfilm, were undertaken by the LAPD on Tuesday 27 August 1974 and Wednesday 22 October 1975. Their trawls, however, would prove to be fruitless.)

Interestingly, the remaining pages from the original 1962 investigation did not derive from the police department, but from the home of former Chief of Detectives Thad Brown, Chief Parker's successor. Brown had passed away 12 years earlier in October 1970 and had apparently once remarked to Virgil Crabtree, the US Treasury's assistant chief of intelligence in Los Angeles, that a White House number, scribbled on a piece of crumpled paper, had been found among Marilyn's bed sheets on the night she died. Therefore he firmly believed (incorrectly as it would turn out) that she had tried calling President John Kennedy in the moments before she died and was desperate to keep the fact a secret. As we know, the actress did indeed attempt to speak to Kennedy that day, but it was hours, not minutes before she passed away.

Announced as being found among Brown's own 'private archives', the details of Marilyn's final phone calls were actually found in a file stored among other possessions in his garage at his home. Through the dogged determination of many recent Monroe biographers, most notably Milo Speriglio and Anthony Summers, details of the actress's last phone calls are now much clearer. However, a great many pages of the original 1962 file are still missing.

Moreover, on Thursday 19 August 1982, just eight days after the new investigation had started, actor Ted Jordan, a star of television's classic, long-running western series Gunsmoke, came forward to claim he had the actress's red diary. 'I hesitated to say anything [about it] for many, many years,' he announced to the press, 'because I was afraid.' However, serious doubts were cast on his claims when, following Jordan's revelation, Chris Harris, a spokesman for the Beverly Hills antique dealer Doug Villiers, announced that he had upped his $100,000 offer to $150,000 for the item and even arranged an appointment with the actor to discuss it. But Jordan did not show up. Mike Carroll even went public, declaring he would like to discuss the diary with Jordan. His calls were, curiously, not returned.

A further attempt to reopen Marilyn's case came on Monday 28 October 1985, when, at a news conference held shortly after he resigned as foreman of the Los Angeles County Grand Jury, Sam Cordova called for a new investigation, saying that two rulings of suicide had left unresolved questions. The Board of Supervisors asked the jury to consider such an inquiry. However, the District Attorney, Ira Reiner, was uninterested, contending that there was no need for a new probe, and remarked that Cordova was making the plea for a special prosecutor so as to gain personal publicity. It was, as Reiner asserted, 'the swan song by a man hungry for popular attention'.

Their opinion has not changed 15 years on, in 2010. In the eyes of the Los Angeles County Board of Supervisors, on the night of Saturday 4

August 1962 (or on the morning of Sunday 5 August), Marilyn Monroe committed suicide because, quite simply, she was depressed. Los Angeles police officials concur with this, insisting they have no reason whatsoever to doubt it. Despite numerous requests by historians and fans alike to exhume her body for a fresh, modern-day, all-answering DNA test (examination of her fingernails or a few strands of hair would be able to determine whether poisons or paralysing drugs were present in her body at the time of her death, resolving the matter once and for all), the Board's decision is final and the chances of them changing their opinion is now extremely remote.

Chapter Twelve

Goodbye, Marilyn

Sunday 5 August 1962–Wednesday 8 August 1962

Early on the morning of Monday 6 August, police in New York cordoned off Marilyn's 444 East 57th Street apartment, seized the assets within and placed them in the police department's property clerk's office, pending any court action of her will. (They would remain there for five years, until the third week of November 1967.) The sealing, a normal procedure in out-of-town deaths, was ordered by the actress's New York attorney, Aaron R. Frosch. The police's inventory noted 41 items, including four fur coats (one of which was a white ermine), seven stoles, a number of fur hats and several articles of jewellery, namely diamond pins, earrings, rings and gold charms, one of which evinced the inscription, 'Don't be bitter – Glitter'.

Assessors would place a value of $1,423 on the fur and jewellery, and of $11,057 on her personal effects, clothing and furniture. Cash totalling just $3.50 was also found. It was no better at Marilyn's other home at Fifth Helena, where clothing and personal effects totalling just $1,550 and furniture and fittings amounting to just $2,486 were found.

In Los Angeles, one day earlier, the coroner's office had received a telegram from Gainesville, Florida. It was from Berniece Miracle, Marilyn's elder half-sister and, due to her mother's illness, the actress's next-of-kin. It announced that Joe DiMaggio would be taking care of the actress's body.

The search for Marilyn's immediate family members was being handled by mortuary employee Lionel Grandison. He had located her mother, Gladys, in nearby La Crescenta but was told by the director of the Californian sanatorium where she was institutionalised that she was incompetent. The suggestion to contact Miracle came from Mrs Inez

Melson, Monroe's former business manager and now conservator of Gladys' estate. However, when Grandison contacted Miracle, a telegram came back authorising the release of Marilyn's body to either Melson or Joe DiMaggio. She had neither the resources of strength to handle such matters. And so, with Melson too declining responsibility, it was down to good old, ever-dependable Joe to take charge of this emotive matter.

DiMaggio was in San Francisco with his brothers Dominic and Vince for a baseball Old-Timers Show at Candlestick Park when he learnt the tragic news. His sister, Marie, had informed him after hearing the summary in a radio bulletin. DiMaggio had just finished eating breakfast when the phone call came through. Moments later, there was another. It was Grandison, asking him if he would be prepared to come to Los Angeles to 'identify Marilyn's body'. He agreed. 'He just walked out without a word,' Dominic remembered. DiMaggio went back to his room and called Miracle. She asked him if he would begin making arrangements for the funeral. 'Yes,' he replied,' and she announced she would 'arrive [in Los Angeles] as soon as possible'.

Later that Sunday evening, DiMaggio dejectedly boarded his United Airlines plane for California. Throughout the journey, he sat sorrowful and declined to speak to anyone. Visibly grief-stricken, lines·were etched in his face when he alighted at Los Angeles International Airport at 10.37am on Monday 6 August. Refusing to make any statements to waiting newspaper reporters, he immediately went into seclusion in suite 1035 at Santa Monica's Fairmont Miramar Hotel at 101 Wilshire Boulevard. Incessant sounds of sobbing were heard emanating from his room.

However, he did not remain there for long. He had the unenviable chore of identifying his former wife's corpse. When he reached the county morgue, situated in the coroner's office in the Hall of Justice, 211 West Temple Street, he was visibly shaking. An attendant greeted him at the entrance and led him down a long, silent corridor which ended with a room lit by a cold fluorescent lamp. DiMaggio found himself in a room containing 50 death compartments. Crypt number 33 was pulled out. The white sheet covering the body within was pulled back and, as he antici-pated, it was that of the actress. Attached to her left big toe was a tag, which identified her as being case number 81128.

Noticing the welt of red blotches along the right side of her face, Joe nodded numbly to the questions the attendant asked and confirmed that this was indeed the body of Marilyn Monroe. His breath came in short bursts as the attendant draped the sheet back over the actress's body. He took one more look at the woman he loved so deeply and walked out. By the time he had completed this arduous task, Marilyn's body had been lying, unclaimed, on the cold mortuary slab for almost 21 hours.

DiMaggio, however, was not the first non-mortuary employee to see the actress's cadaver in this post-autopsy state. It was *Life* magazine's Leigh A. Weiner who, just nine hours after its examination, ghoulishly photographed Monroe's body as it lay in the crypt. In the early hours of Sunday 5 August, Weiner and his colleague, columnist Thomas (Tommy) Thompson, were sent on an assignment to cover the actress's death. While Thompson was preparing the text, Weiner drove across town to Marilyn's home in Brentwood. He arrived to be greeted by the sight of a handful of policemen and approximately 15 other photographers.

Soon, the front door of the property swung open and Marilyn's lifeless body was wheeled out and loaded into the back of the coroner's black van. Weiner's camera captured the moment, but it certainly was not the 'exclusive' shot his editor had requested. 'It wasn't much of a picture at all,' he lamented to *The Los Angeles Times*. Using a nearby call box, he then hastily called his boss to deliver the bad news and was promptly instructed to 'try and get a picture of the body in the morgue' – but only on the provisos that the images be tasteful, that he should not break any laws and that he should do his utmost not to tarnish the magazine's excellent reputation. Weiner rushed back to his car and tailed the van all the way to the morgue.

Having waited for almost 18 hours, he climbed out of his vehicle shortly before midnight on that Sunday evening, walked to the building and strode up its long corridor. In his bag, aside from his camera, was a brown paper bag containing two bottles of whisky. He asked the three on-duty guards if they knew a friend of his who used to work there, pulling the drink from his rucksack and asking them whether they would like some. Two accepted; one declined. Small talk soon gave way to the day's big talking point: the death of screen legend Marilyn Monroe.

In an attempt to entice them further into his scheme, Weiner then suggested that, since she had died in nearby Brentwood, her body must have been brought here. At once, the teetotal member of the night crew announced that this *was* the case, adding that her body was 'Right here, in Crypt 33,' before asking, 'Do you want to see it?' But before Weiner could reply, one of the other men interjected by saying, 'Wait a minute. Ever seen a dead body before?' When the photographer announced he had, the men relaxed and the short walk to the actress's body was taken. He reached the crypt just as an assistant was preparing to fasten the aforementioned tag to Marilyn's big toe. The man opened the door of the crypt and slid the drawer out. A thin white sheet concealed the actress's body. Just as the employee was attaching the label, Weiner asked the man if he could take a photo of it. There were no objections.

Weiner lifted his camera from his bag and began snapping away. Overcome by emotion, he was unable to restrain himself. The photo of the toe led to another' then another, then another, each one becoming progressively more explicit and sinister. Besides the image of the toe tag, he also managed to capture, in every conceivable angle, images of the actress's unclad body sprawled on a marble slab, with and without the sheet. 'Before long I had taken five rolls of film,' he recalled for *The Los Angeles Times*. After an hour in the room, at approximately 1am, Weiner left and drove to the airport to send his undeveloped images to his magazine. DiMaggio, the next visitor to Marilyn's crypt, would not arrive for another 13 hours.

Unsurprisingly, *Life* chose not to use any of Weiner's images. On Sunday 22 August 1982, on the 20th anniversary of Marilyn's death, Weiner was interviewed in the 'Cal' section of *The Los Angeles Times*. During the piece (from which the preceding quotes were taken), he was asked, 'Have you ever taken a picture that bothered you?' Without hesitation, he cited the shots he had taken of Marilyn Monroe in the crypt shortly after her death.

At approximately 2.30pm on Monday 6 August, before leaving the morgue to begin arrangements for the funeral, DiMaggio instructed that his former wife's cadaver that be transferred to the Westwood Village Mortuary in West Los Angeles where, at 11am on Tuesday 7 August, Allan Snyder desolately arrived to administer the actress's make-up for the very last time. Armed with a flask of gin, he adhered to a promise he had made to the star in jest in 1953 just after she had finished shooting *Gentlemen Prefer Blondes*.

During a brief stay in hospital, and in response to a request for a photograph, Marilyn had summoned Snyder to her bedside to make her up. As he was doing so, she said to him, 'Promise me something, Whitey. If anything happens to me, if I ever die, nobody must touch my face except you. Promise me you will make me up.' He smiled and replied, 'Just bring the body back while it's still warm.' The request that her personal make-up man should prepare her for her funeral replicated the scenario at the death of Monroe's great idol, Jean Harlow, back in June 1937. Many years later, the actress reminded him of his pledge with a short engraving on a gold money clip, which read, 'Whitey Dear, while I'm still warm, Marilyn.'

In a phone call during the afternoon of Sunday 5 August, DiMaggio rang Snyder to enquire, 'You will do it, won't you? You promised.' DiMaggio had one further request. 'Can you make her look as gorgeous as she did in the pictures?' 'Oh yes,' Snyder replied. 'I sure can, Joe.'

'I had never made-up a dead person before,' Snyder remarked to the *Chicago Tribune* in 1973. He arrived to find the actress spread out on a steel table. He went over and touched her on the forehead. If he didn't, he knew fear would overcome him and he would turn and run out. 'As soon as I started working,' he recalled, 'I got so intent on doing it right, that it didn't bother me. It was just like she was asleep.' He put a special, rouge-coloured foundation on her face, known as the '20th Century-Fox' base, and followed it with eye shadow and lipstick. 'She looked beautiful,' Snyder recalled in 1963. 'She looked the way you wanted to remember her.' In another interview, he remarked, 'It was the hardest and best job I have ever done. I'm only sorry the general public didn't see her.'

He completed his task in the anteroom at precisely 3pm. Just as he was leaving, he ran into DiMaggio. 'Okay, Joe,' Snyder affirmed. The baseball legend shook his hand and thanked him for coming. The make-up man then watched the baseball legend walk over and sit down beside Marilyn's coffin. 'He was alone with her many times,' remarked a mortuary source. 'He was a man obviously bereaved, a man still very much in love with her.' The next morning, the day of the funeral, Snyder returned to the mortuary early to find the baseball legend still sitting in the same position. His eyes were red, watery and inflamed. Although DiMaggio had in fact returned to his hotel room late on Tuesday night and returned to the Westwood mortuary just a few hours later, at 7.30 on Wednesday morning, Snyder believed that the baseball legend had remained by his former wife's coffin all night.

Funeral director Allan Abbott spent two days at the Westwood Village Mortuary assisting in the preparations for Marilyn's funeral. On the morning of the service, the embalmer decided to use a surgical procedure to reduce the swelling which, through the post-mortem, had developed in the back of her neck. So he cut away some hair, made an incision and sutured it up tight. Naturally, because of this damage to Marilyn's already thin tresses, studio hairdresser Sydney Guilaroff was summoned. 'When she was dead, they rang me and asked me to dress her hair,' he recalled in 1966 for *Films and Filming* magazine. 'I couldn't do it. But I told them I had one of her wigs left from *The Misfits*, which I could re-style the way she wore it at the end.' Guilaroff immediately set about cutting and shaping one of the wigs and sent it over.

Eunice Murray decided the actress would want to be buried in her chartreuse, pale green Pucci dress and matching green chiffon scarf. She instinctively knew that the outfit was a favourite of Marilyn's and fondly recalled seeing her in it at her press conference in Mexico City just six months ago. Berniece thought otherwise and suggested something in either blue or white, but Eunice stood firm. The actress should be dressed in *that* pale green outfit.

Monroe's funeral took place at 1pm Pacific Daylight Time (4pm Eastern Daylight Time) on Wednesday 8 August, at the Westwood Village Mortuary chapel in the grounds of the Westwood Memorial Park Cemetery, at 1218 Glendon Avenue in West Los Angeles. It was only the second such event to be held in the park's new oratory. It was said that DiMaggio chose this location as the actress's final resting place because of its obscurity. Due to its location, within a block of houses, parking garages and high rises just off Wilshire Boulevard, the cemetery was originally almost impossible to locate and was once one of the best-kept secrets in Los Angeles. Poignantly, it stood just a mile away from 20th Century-Fox's studios.

Marilyn's body arrived in a new 1962 Cadillac Eureka hearse. Allan Abbott, Sydney Guilaroff, Allan 'Whitey' Snyder and mortuary employees Ronald Hast, Leonard Krisminsky and Clarence Pierce were the pallbearers. Before entering the chapel, Joe DiMaggio gazed up towards the sky as if to say, 'At least the sun has chosen to shine for her this day.'

Among the many floral tributes, four dozen red roses and the text of an Elizabeth Barrett Browning love sonnet had been dispatched to the cemetery by a mysterious stranger. The flowers had been ordered by a man described as a 'theatrical gentleman in his early 30s' from florist George Reppert at his House Of Flowers store based in New Brunswick, New Jersey. 'The man parked a large white sports car outside (my shop), walked in and ordered the flowers,' Reppert recalled at the time. '"I want $50 worth of red roses, only the best, sent to the funeral of Marilyn Monroe," he said. He told me to sign the card, "In loving memory." He also ordered the complete text of "How Do I Love Thee" by Miss Browning to accompany the roses.' Regrettably, we shall never know the identity of this enigmatic individual.

The private and sombre service began with the strains of Tchaikovsky's Sixth Symphony and featured, at Marilyn's request, Judy Garland's classic 1939 recording, 'Over the Rainbow'. The service was conducted by Reverend A.J. Soldan, a Lutheran minister from the Village Church of Westwood, who read a non-denominational service including Psalm 23, chapter 14 of the Book of John, and excerpts from Psalms 46 and 139. The Reverend's service was based on the quotation, 'How fearfully and wonderfully she was made by the Creator.' Later, at the entombment, he intoned, 'For as much as it pleased almighty God to take the soul of Marilyn Monroe, we therefore commit her body, earth to earth, ashes to ashes, dust to dust, sure and certain of hopes for eternal life.' The Lord's Prayer was also read.

DiMaggio's original choice to read a tribute at the service was Marilyn's close friend, the poet-author Carl Sandburg. Due to his poor health, he was unable to attend, but he kept his promise of writing a eulogy to the actress, which he wired from his home in North Carolina. It was delivered at the service by a tearful Lee Strasberg. In full it read:

Marilyn Monroe was a legend. In her own lifetime she created a myth of what a poor girl from a deprived background could attain. For the entire world she became a symbol of the eternal feminine. But I have no words to describe the myth and the legend. I did not know this Marilyn Monroe.

We, gathered here today, knew only Marilyn, a warm human being, impulsive and shy, sensitive and in fear of rejection, yet ever avid for life and reaching out for fulfilment. I will not insult the privacy of your memory of her, privacy she sought and treasured, by trying to describe her whom you knew to you who knew her. In our memories of her, she remains alive not only a shadow on the screen or a glamorous personality. For us Marilyn was a devoted and loyal friend, a colleague constantly reaching for perfection. We shared her pain and difficulties and some of her joys. She was a member of our family. It is difficult to accept the fact that her zest for life has been ended by this dreadful accident.

Despite the heights and brilliance she attained on the screen, she was planning for the future. She was looking forward to participating in the many exciting things which she planned. In her eyes and in mine her career was just beginning. The dream of her talent, which she had nurtured as a child, was not a mirage. When she first came to me I was amazed at the startling sensitivity which she possessed and which had remained fresh and undimmed, struggling to express itself despite the life to which she had been subjected. Others were as physically beautiful as she was, but there was obviously something more in her, something that people saw and recognized in her performances and with which they identified. She had a luminous quality, a combination of wistfulness, radiance, yearning to set her apart and yet make everyone wish to be a part of it, to share in the childish naiveté which was so shy and yet so vibrant.

This quality was even more evident when she was in the stage. I am truly sorry that the public who loved her did not have the opportunity to see her as we did, in many of the roles that foreshadowed what she would have become. Without a doubt she would have been one of the really great actresses of the stage.

Now it is at an end. I hope her death will stir sympathy and understanding for a sensitive artist and a woman who brought joy and pleasure to the world. I cannot say goodbye. Marilyn never liked goodbyes, but in the peculiar way she had of turning things around so that they faced reality, I will say au revoir. For the country to which she has gone, we must all some day visit.

Throughout the subdued 23-minute service, Marilyn's body lay in a partially opened, bronze-carved, $800 casket lined with champagne-coloured satin. In her hands was a posy of baby pink tea-cup roses, a gift from DiMaggio, who sat with his son Joe Jr near the front of the chapel.

'I have never seen Marilyn look more beautiful, like a small child,' remarked Don Prince, an operative at 20th Century-Fox, who had been employed to help with the arrangements. 'At the funeral, I was heartbroken,' Sydney Guilaroff admitted. 'Her sister came up to me and said, "Don't cry, she's better off where she is." I looked up and thought, "That's true." Marilyn *was* at last at peace.'

In total, there were 23 invited guests, although 31 were in the chapel during the service. In addition to the aforementioned DiMaggio, Miracle, Melson, Guilaroff, Snyder and Lee Strasberg, the others present included Pat Newcomb, Eunice Murray, Dr Ralph Greenson, his wife Hildi and two children, Dan and Joan, Lee's wife Paula, Inez's husband Pat, Joe's son Joe Jr and close friend George Solotaire, and Snyder's wife, Beverly and daughter, Sherry.

Friends from Marilyn's near and distant past included Aaron Frosch and Milton Rudin, personal secretary May Reis, acting coach Lotte Goslar, former foster parents Enid and Sam Kindelcamps, friends Anne and Mary Karger, chauffeur Rudy Kadensky, hair stylists Agnes Flanagan and Pearl Porterfield, long-time friend, confidant and masseur Ralph Roberts, personal maid Florence Thomas and a neighbour of hers from New York, Richard Diebald. Walter Winchell, a close pal of DiMaggio, was the only newspaper reporter permitted into the chapel. For the most part, it was a day rich in respect. As author George Miller remarked, 'It was a lesson in dignity Hollywood had needed for many years.'

At Joe's request, Allan Abbott was positioned at the chantry's door to check names against the list of invitees and to hand out the special memorial programme. Controversially, following DiMaggio's strictest instructions, not one of Monroe's Hollywood friends was on this inventory, even though many flew in to Los Angeles especially. Dean Martin was one. Marilyn's co-star on *Something's Got To Give* was on holiday with his family at the Alisal Dude Ranch in the Santa Ynez Valley, near Santa Barbara, when he heard that the actress had died. Upon hearing the news, he immediately cut short the vacation and drove the 150 miles back to Los Angeles just to attend her funeral. But his plans were in vain. He was not permitted to come.

Another such individual was Pat Lawford. She was 'shocked' to discover that she had been barred from attending, as was her husband Peter. At his Santa Monica beach house that day, Lawford told newsmen, 'Pat flew in on Monday night from Hyannis Port where she had been vacationing with the kids, just to attend Marilyn's funeral. But we were not invited. I don't know who's responsible. But the whole thing is badly handled.' He concluded, 'Marilyn had lots of good friends here in town that will miss her terribly and would love to have attended her final rites.'

On the day of the service, Sergeant Robert Byron of the Los Angeles Police Department attempted to contact the actor, but was told by his secretary that he was 'not available for an interview' and had 'taken an airplane' to an unknown destination. Lawford's aide added that she did not 'expect to hear from him' and would put out a request for him to 'request the department at his earliest convenience.' In fact, at 1pm, shortly after speaking to the reporters, he had caught a flight to join the rest of the Kennedys at their compound in Hyannis Port. He would manage to evade speaking to the authorities about Marilyn's death for a further 13 years. Frank Sinatra was naturally aghast at the rejection. Through his office, he issued the following brief statement, although his name did not appear on it: 'Some of the people who are at the funeral *barely knew* [emphasis added] Marilyn. Her half-sister, who apparently is in charge of inviting or barring guests, only met Marilyn *once* in her whole lifetime last summer.' The actress's long-standing publicist, Arthur Jacobs, was quick to side with the singer. In a short statement released on the day of the burial, he remarked, 'About half the people in there [the service], wouldn't even be there if Marilyn had anything to do with the invitations. A lot more of her friends *would* be there.'

DiMaggio ran the funeral with an iron fist. Among the other celebrities excluded were Sammy Davis Jr, Gene Kelly and the Mirisch brothers (the producers of *Some Like It Hot*). The repercussions spread far and wide. A day before the funeral, *The New York Post* quoted Milton Rudin as telling DiMaggio, 'You are keeping out Marilyn's close friends.' To which he apparently replied, 'If it hadn't been for some of her friends, she wouldn't be where she is.' Even a request by Lawford for those barred from the service to attend a special midnight organ tribute for Marilyn was rejected. DiMaggio's close friend, reporter Walter Winchell, was asked why the baseball legend had barred Tinseltown from the simple service. 'Would you invite your wife's murderer to her funeral?' he retorted.

Furthermore, DiMaggio was determined to avoid the Hollywood flamboyance which had ruined many film-star funerals in the past. Just prior to the service, a spokesman forlornly explained, 'I think it's a shame that Marilyn's friends could not be there to pay their final respects. If we allow the Lawfords in, then we'd have to allow half of the big stars in Hollywood. Then the whole thing would turn into a circus.' As Donald Stewart, a columnist for *Uncensored* magazine, wrote, 'The cause [of Marilyn's death] was listed as an overdose of sleeping pills, but the real killer was Hollywood. Joe DiMaggio knew this. That was why he refused to turn the funeral into a circus. Not a single movie star or executive was allowed to attend the last rites for America's Golden Girl.'

Meanwhile, in a joint statement issued on the day of the funeral, DiMaggio, Miracle and Melson announced, 'We could not in conscience ask one personality to attend without perhaps offending many, many others and for this reason alone, we have kept the number of persons to a minimum. Please, all of you remember the gay [happy], sweet Marilyn and say a prayer of farewell within the confines of your home or your church.'

Guy R. Hockett, the managing director of the Westwood Village Memorial Park, was quick to point out that their decision to keep the number count low was actually down to the 'space limitations'. But in truth, despite the forceful protestations from Marilyn's Milton Rudin, DiMaggio did not want Marilyn's Hollywood acquaintances there. He had blamed them for her death and he was not ready to forgive. As the actress's New York publicist John Springer revealed, the names of Lawford, Sinatra and Dean Martin had been included in the original inventory of invitees, but when DiMaggio saw it, he became angry and began furiously crossing them off, one by one. Speaking in 1998, Springer said, 'He looked at the list and said, "No, no, no, no, no, they're the people that killed her." I have *never* seen a man so grief-stricken.'

Neither of Marilyn's other husbands were present. Arthur Miller was perhaps the more surprising absentee. When a reporter called asking whether he would be attending, he immediately snapped back, 'She won't be there,' and hung up the phone. He admitted he had answered without thinking. But in truth, he was never going to go. As Miller remarked in his 1987 autobiography, *Timebends*, 'The very idea of a funeral was outlandish . . . to join what I knew would be a circus of cameras and shouts and luridness was beyond my strength . . . and to me it was meaningless to stand for photographs at a stone.'

After the service, and just at the point when they were preparing to escort Marilyn's body to her crypt, DiMaggio had a sudden desire to see his former wife just one more time. As they opened her coffin, a gust of wind blew some of Marilyn's wig hair out of the casket. People watching nearby gasped in shock. It appeared as though she was rising up out of the coffin. Just before the casket was closed for the very last time, DiMaggio leant over, kissed his former wife on the forehead and whispered, 'I love you, I love you, I love you.' It was out of character for such a reticent man, but perhaps that made it all the more sincere. Her casket was then hermetically sealed. DiMaggio strode out of the chapel and with grief continuing to engulf him, was seen with his head in his hands, furtively wiping tears from his eyes.

Dutifully followed by DiMaggio, his son, who was dressed in his Marine Corps uniform, and the other mourners, the hearse was driven 125 yards and, once a blanket of carnations had been removed, the coffin was slid into a crypt in a pink marble hall at Westwood's 'Corridor of Memories'. Marilyn's final resting place was near the grave of Grace Goddard, formerly McKee, the woman who had befriended her early in her life. Touchingly, Marilyn had taken care of Grace's burial arrangements nine years earlier. In front of the actress's crypt was a plain marble slab, which simply read: 'Marilyn Monroe 1926–1962'. The actress was finally at peace.

Following orders from Chief Bill Parker, more than 50 Los Angeles police officers were in attendance to watch over the proceedings and keep out the uninvited. Forty security guards, hired especially by 20th Century-Fox, assisted them. The funeral director, Allan Abbott, ordered six more. At a cost of $578.25, charged to Marilyn's estate, they were hired from the privately run guard and detective organisation, the Pinkerton National Detective Agency. Their directive from DiMaggio was simple: stop anyone not invited by him or Berniece Miracle from entering the cemetery at any time during the service.

Barriers were set up outside the north wall of the cemetery to accommodate the 100 members of the press, while snappers not allowed to enter positioned themselves high above, atop the nearby Kirkeby Building. *Life* magazine's Leigh Weiner and the world-renowned freelance snapper Gene Anthony were the only two photographers permitted to stroll freely during the proceedings that day, although film-maker David L. Wolper was present to capture a celluloid record of the event. (Short clips would appear in his 1964 movie, *Legend Of Marilyn Monroe*.) Going through the large number of photos taken by Weiner, it's interesting to note that Joe's apparent niece, June DiMaggio, was nowhere to be seen among the mourners. She has claimed on numerous occasions, most notably in *Playboy* magazine, that she was at the Westwood ceremony that day.

In death as in life, Marilyn managed to attract a huge throng of curious fans. By the time of the service, approximately a thousand of her worshippers had gathered on the streets and clambered on to walls surrounding Westwood Memorial Park; around one hundred, in order to get the best vantage point, had been clustered in position since midnight. (Originally, there had been more. The crowd thinned when they were informed by the police that there would be no public viewing of Marilyn's body.)

Unfortunately, many of the remaining rubbernecks had clearly not dressed for such a sombre occasion. To accommodate the scorching 93-degree heat, many had arrived sporting abbreviated swim suits and two-piece bikinis. The women in colourful Capris and brightly coloured sun dresses and men in summery sport shirts and swimming trunks stood in stark contrast to the cemetery's decidedly solemn surroundings. Thankfully, to begin with, they were orderly, dignified and sentimental and observed the unfolding events in a respectful silence.

The service drew to a close and the mourners dutifully began to depart. Just as Eunice Murray was exiting the cemetery, a man called out to her. It was Bill Alexander, the owner of the Brentwood Country Mart store. When the actress was perusing the contents of his shop just seven days before, he had strolled up to her and heart-warmingly requested her hand in marriage. 'Do you realise,' Alexander told Murray, 'that's it's just a week ago to the hour that you and Miss Monroe were in my shop.' Murray was shocked. As she remarked in *Marilyn: The Last Months*, 'It was difficult to believe. The whole world had changed meanwhile.'

Regrettably, the bystanders' discretion at the service did not last. Just minutes after the mausoleum housing Monroe's body had been sealed and the mourners had slowly and silently departed, approximately 200 observers began streaming up the paths leading to the actress's final resting place. Their harmonious walk soon turned into a discordant run. Their mission was clear. They wanted to snatch a souvenir from Marilyn's crypt.

Once they reached it, they began pushing and shoving each other. Flowers were disrespectfully trampled as they ruthlessly fought over buds, ribbons and sprays sent by movie-industry people and close friends such as Arthur Miller, Frank Sinatra, Clinton Webb, Shelley Winters, Billy Wilder and Jack Benny. The damage did not end there. The cross of flowers purchased by Berniece Miracle and the huge heart of red roses, white carnations and orchids sent by Joe DiMaggio were also sent flying.

Due to the superb work of two burly security guards, the unruly individuals were prevented from getting near Marilyn's vault. But pandemonium still raged. When one reserved, highly respectful onlooker vented her disgust at the theft of the actress's flowers, a woman clutching a handful of blossoms snapped back, 'Why shouldn't I? It's silly just to leave them here. They'd just die.' 'Of course they would,' a second woman concurred, twirling a single red rose. It was a truly sad finale to a genuinely emotional day.

On the day of the funeral, three eminent Hollywood actresses – Lisa Kirk, Rosalind Russell and Carroll Baker – arrived in New York en route from Southampton, England aboard the *Queen Mary*. When waiting photographers requested them to pose, they linked arms, flashed their widest smiles and broke into a spontaneous, high-kicking dance routine. The Associated Press distributed this picture with a caption saying how 'shocked and saddened' by Monroe's death the actresses were. It was a typical Hollywood reaction: business as usual, beneath a thin coating of crocodile tears. The world was indeed carrying on and getting back to normal. Within days of the funeral, a bill for $4,352 from the Westwood Village Mortuary was dispatched to the executors of Marilyn's estate.

At 5pm, several hours after the actress's entombment, Los Angeles County district attorney John Miner, who had been present at Marilyn's autopsy, paid a visit to the Beverly Hills home of Ralph Greenson. During the call, after giving his word he would not divulge its contents, Greenson apparently played to Miner a 40-minute audio-tape recording of the actress supposedly talking about, among other subjects, her father-in-law Isidore Miller, actress Mae West, fan Robert Slatzer, Attorney General Bobby Kennedy and President John Kennedy. Miner would recall that Marilyn sounded 'anything but suicidal'. 'She had very specific plans for her future,' he would announce years later. 'She knew exactly what she wanted to do.' (Dr Greenson's widow, Hildegard, would later tell *The Times* she did not know whether the tapes existed and had never heard her husband discuss them.)

At 5.30pm, DiMaggio returned to the Westwood Memorial Park Cemetery in an automobile driven by a friend. The car stopped but he did not get out. He simply sat and stared at the mausoleum for many minutes in meditation. He wanted to say one final, private farewell to the one woman he truly loved. DiMaggio never stopped thinking about her; nor did he ever consider forgiving those responsible for her death.

Days after the funeral, DiMaggio apparently remarked to Walter Winchell, 'If one of those Kennedys had showed up . . . I would have taken a baseball bat and bashed in their faces. All of those sons-of-bitches killed Marilyn.' His anger towards them ran deep. Three years later, on Saturday 18 September 1965, at New York's Yankee Stadium, he stood in a line-up honouring the 2,000th major league game played by the Yankees' Mickey Mantle. Bobby Kennedy was in attendance, smiling and shaking the hands of everyone in the queue – everyone bar Joe, who decided to take one step back and avoid him altogether.

Joe DiMaggio's devotion to Marilyn was evident for the next two decades. Every week until the first week of August 1982, exactly 20 years after her death, he had a standing order with the Parisian Florist store in Beverly Hills to place, three times a week, six red roses in the black metal vase at Marilyn's grave, just as he had promised her when she told him of actor William Powell's vow to the dying Jean Harlow. DiMaggio always paid the $500-a-year bill for Monroe's flowers in advance.

Unlike Marilyn's two other husbands, or the other men who knew her (or *claimed* to have known her), Joe refused to write a tell-all book or talk about her publicly. He even declined a $50,000 offer to discuss his former wife in the popular monthly women's magazine *McCall's*. People knew it was taboo to even ask him about her. If anyone dared to do so, he would forcibly say, '*Stop* right there.' The words would fall like a curtain in front of him.

Never remarrying, the baseball legend passed away on Monday 8 March 1999, aged 84, following complications from lung cancer. According to his lawyer and confidant, Morris Engelberg, his very last words were, 'I'll *finally* get to see Marilyn.'

So there we have it. In conclusion: throughout my exhaustive examination, it became copiously clear to me that, by and large, history was dutifully respectful to the legacies of the late President Kennedy, his wife Jacqueline and brother Bobby, to name but a few. Yet, aside from the multitude of devoted Marilyn worshippers around the globe, hardly ever did I come across evidence which expressed concern about how the multitude of malicious, unfounded and fabricated allegations about the actress, concocted either to protect the guilty or to line the pockets of money-hungry glory seekers, might actually tarnish *her* legacy. I found this abhorrent.

Moreover, the long-believed assertion that the actress had deliberately taken her life was, in my opinion, a slur on her extremely warm, generous and exceedingly affectionate character. In closing, I seriously hope that, some day, the charge of 'probable suicide' on her death certificate be changed to simply, 'accident'. She deserves this. She has not earned the stigma which suicide brings. Now, with the results of my meticulous, five-year investigation being made public for the first time, I genuinely hope that it will go a long way towards rectifying this. Then, and only then, will you, Marilyn, be able to finally rest in peace.

I sincerely hope that, one day, you do . . .

Index